Jihad and Genocide

Studies in Genocide: Religion, History, and Human Rights

Series Editor: Alan L. Berger, Raddock Family Eminent Scholar Chair of Holocaust Studies, Florida Atlantic University

Genocide is a recurring scourge and a crime against humanity, the effects of which are felt globally. Books in this series are original and sophisticated analyses describing, interpreting, and articulating lessons from historical as well as current genocides. Written from a range of scholarly perspectives, the works in this series articulate patterns of genocide and offer suggestions about early warning signs that may help prevent the crime.

Jihad and Genocide, by Richard Rubenstein, President Emeritus and Distinguished Professor of Religion at the University of Bridgeport

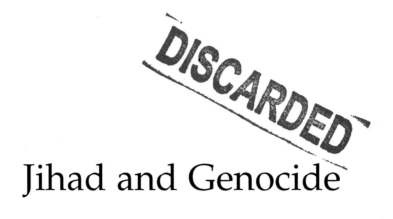

Jihad and Genocide

Richard L. Rubenstein

ROWMAN & LITTLEFIELD PUBLISHERS, INC.
Lanham • Boulder • New York • Toronto • Plymouth, UK

Published by Rowman & Littlefield Publishers, Inc.
A wholly owned subsidiary of The Rowman & Littlefield Publishing Group, Inc.
4501 Forbes Boulevard, Suite 200, Lanham, Maryland 20706
http://www.rowmanlittlefield.com

Estover Road, Plymouth PL6 7PY, United Kingdom

British Library Cataloguing in Publication Information Available

Library of Congress Cataloging-in-Publication Data

Rubenstein, Richard L.
  Jihad and genocide / Richard L. Rubenstein.
    p. cm. — (Studies in genocide: religion, history, and human rights)
  Includes index.
  ISBN 978-0-7425-6202-8 (cloth : alk. paper) — ISBN 978-1-4422-0198-9
(electronic)
  1. Jihad. 2. Islamic fundamentalism. 3. Islam and world politics. 4. Arab-
Israeli conflict. I. Title.
  BP182.R83 2010
  297.7'209—dc22   2009032040

∞ ™ The paper used in this publication meets the minimum requirements of
American National Standard for Information Sciences—Permanence of Paper
for Printed Library Materials, ANSI/NISO Z39.48-1992.

Printed in the United States of America

Contents

Preface

This book is the fruit of my attempt to comprehend the meaning of a term concerning which I had heard little before the beginning of the twenty-first century, *jihad*. As a matter of fact, I attended an international conference of Jewish and Muslim scholars in Cordoba, Spain, in August 1999 but I do not recall *jihad* being discussed during the three-day gathering, in spite of the fact that Osama bin Laden and Islamist leaders from Egypt, Pakistan, and Bangladesh had proclaimed a "Declaration of the World Islamic Front for Jihad against the Jews and the Crusaders" on February 23, 1998. Since that time, *jihad* has come to influence the lives of millions on almost every continent. Thousands of Jews, Christians, and Muslims have perished as random victims of indiscriminate *jihad*. To protect themselves, millions more have submitted to security checks and the indignities they sometimes entail every time they travel by air or enter a public building. Whether in the form of a petty annoyance or the threat of injury and death, *jihad* has willy-nilly become a part of all of our lives.

Nevertheless, this book is not a comprehensive study of *jihad*. It is an inquiry into the genocidal potentialities of *jihad*. That focus has been made necessary because, explicitly or by indirection, major religious and political leaders within the world of Islam have threatened genocide as the means by which they intend to secure victory against some of their adversaries, especially my coreligionists. Having been a young adult living in safety in the country of my birth during the years in which the extermination of Europe's Jews took place, I know that such threats are deadly serious and can neither be dismissed nor ignored.

I could not have pursued this effort alone and I wish to express my gratitude to those who have actively assisted or encouraged me in this endeavor. First and foremost I am singularly grateful for the encouragement, advice, and forbearance of my wife Dr. Betty Rogers Rubenstein. If anyone has made a very real sacrifice so that this work could be brought to fruition, it is she. I wish also to thank Professor Alan L. Berger of Florida Atlantic University, the editor of this series, for inviting me to consider doing a book in this series as well as for his encouragement, support, and patience during the time that I have been working on the project. I also wish to thank Sarah Stanton, Rowman & Littlefield's editor of this project, for her support. I am grateful to President Neil Albert Salonen of the University of Bridgeport for granting me a semester during which I could devote my efforts solely to research on this book. I also wish to thank Arielle Caron of the University of Bridgeport for her editorial work on this book, and Dr. Thomas Ward, dean of the university's International College, for making Arielle Caron's services available to me.

Bat Ye'or, Dr. Andrew Bostom of Brown University, Mr. Jerome Gordon, Professor John Kelsay of Florida State University, Professor John K. Roth of Claremont McKenna College, and Professor Danny L. Balfour of Grand Valley State University have given me invaluable insights into one or more of the issues dealt with in this work. I am grateful to each and every one of them for their support and counsel.

Finally, I am especially indebted to the online data services of the Florida State University Library without which it would have been difficult, if not impossible, to complete this project. In the course of research for this work I have also availed myself of the services of the libraries of the University of Bridgeport, the Jewish Theological Seminary, the New York Public Library, Yale University, and the online services of the Asher Library of the Spertus Institute of Judaica. I am most thankful for the invaluable assistance these institutions have given me.

Fairfield, Connecticut
15 June 2009

Introduction

Why I Have Written This Book

On the morning of September 11, 2001, I sat at my desk happily putting the finishing touches on the manuscript of the second edition of *Approaches to Auschwitz*, which I coauthored with Professor John K. Roth of California's Claremont-McKenna College.[1] I began that morning with an enormous sense of satisfaction that I was finally completing my share of a very arduous task. At the time, I had devoted the better part of a career of half a century to research, writing, and lecturing on the Holocaust and the terrible phenomenon of genocide.

At about 8:45 A.M., I turned on the TV for the morning news and learned that American Airlines Flight 11 had just crashed into the 110-story North Tower of New York's World Trade Center (WTC). I understood immediately that the crash was no accident. On February 26, 1993, Ramzi Yousef, an Islamic terrorist, had detonated a car bomb under the same tower with the intention of toppling it into the South Tower, collapsing both towers and hoping to kill the 250,000 people at work in the structures. Yousef and his accomplices meant to commit mass murder in the heart of New York. They failed to bring down the towers, but six people were killed and 1,042 injured in the attempt.[2] As I watched in horror, I knew that Islamic extremists, whom I shall henceforth identify as Islamists, had finally succeeded. My horror was intensified, if that were possible, when I watched United Airlines Flight 175 crash into the twin South Tower. Minutes later, I learned that yet another plane had crashed into the Pentagon, and that United Airlines Flight 93 crashed into a field in Somerset County, Pennsylvania, failing to reach its target, which was apparently either the White House or the U.S. Capitol.

Within the space of little more than an hour, the United States had experienced the most devastating attack on its homeland in its entire history. The iconic structures of American financial and military power had been successfully assaulted and only the selfless bravery of the doomed passengers on United Airlines Flight 93 prevented a similar strike on the center of American political power.

Apart from sheer horror, my immediate reaction was to ask myself whether our book on the Holocaust had instantly become an exercise in futility. Without delay, I sent John Roth an e-mail message saying that, as important as was the Holocaust, it happened sixty years ago and we were facing a very real present danger. I told him that henceforth my efforts were less likely to be focused on the Holocaust than on the threat of radical Islam. John was supportive in his reply, but insisted that both were equally important.[3] He was, of course, correct. As is evident from much of the material in this book, there is more than a little affinity between National Socialism and Islamic extremism. As partners in World War II, both sought the utter destruction of the Jewish people, a project Islamists have never abandoned. As is evident from a multitude of hateful sermons, media propaganda, and street demonstrations (all too many of which are available on the Internet), today's Islamists have recycled some of National Socialism's most vicious anti-Semitic propaganda while peddling the obscene canard that the Israelis are latter-day Nazis.

In 1952, my senior year as a student at the Jewish Theological Seminary of America, I was accepted for admission to Harvard Divinity School. The Holocaust had cast a very long shadow over my decision to continue graduate studies at an historically Protestant institution. The Holocaust had taken place in Christian Europe and was not without the support of important segments of European Christendom. I wanted to understand the history and the present status of the complicated and ambivalent relationship between Judaism and Christianity and Harvard Divinity School seemed like a good place to start.

The focus of my studies there was overwhelmingly Eurocentric. My most memorable experience was Paul Johannes Tillich's course on classical German philosophy.[4] The son of a Lutheran pastor with a doctorate from the University of Breslau (now Wroclaw, Poland), Tillich served as a chaplain in the German army during the First World War. In the years immediately before Adolf Hitler's coming to power, Tillich, then a professor at the University of Frankfurt, expressed his strong opposition to National Socialism in speeches and lectures. As soon as the Nazis took over, they dismissed him and he joined the faculty of New York's Union Theological Seminary. Tillich's course did more to enlarge my understanding of European Christian culture than any other course I took at Harvard.

One of the requirements of my degree program was to take a year's work in a religious tradition other than Judaism or Christianity. In the academic year 1953–1954, I took a course on Islamic origins followed by a course on the history of Muslim faith. At the time, Islam seemed to be a remote curiosity that I was required to study. I certainly did not carry away from those courses the idea that any version of Islam could constitute a deadly threat to my people, my country, and my civilization. That would come later.

Unfortunately, neither I nor the overwhelming majority of Harvard students of the period had the slightest inkling of the writings of such Islamist thinkers as Hassan al-Banna (1906–1949), Sayyid Qutb (1906–1966), and Syed Abu a'la Mawdudi (1903–1979). Uncompromising enemies of Western civilization, their quest for universal Muslim domination shaped the worldview of the perpetrators of 9/11 and may affect the lives and destiny of every man, woman, and child in the twenty-first century.

Ten days after 9/11, President George W. Bush addressed a joint session of the U.S. Congress, in which he sought to make a distinction between the perpetrators of 9/11 and the peace-loving Islamic mainstream. The president declared:

> I also want to speak tonight directly to Muslims throughout the world. We respect your faith. … Its teachings are good and peaceful. And those who commit evil in the name of Allah blaspheme the name of Allah. The terrorists are traitors to their own faith, trying in effect to hijack Islam itself.[5]

Undoubtedly, in a moment of unprecedented national crisis, the president's first responsibility was to calm a potentially explosive inter-religious situation. Nevertheless, in retrospect one can ask whether his statements or the somewhat similar sentiments expressed by President Barack Obama in Cairo on June 4, 2009, were accurate. In reality, Islamist enmity toward the infidel West, such as was manifest on 9/11, is not a consequence of a small, unrepresentative group "hijacking" a religion whose "teachings are good and peaceful." On the contrary, the kind of Islamist hostility that drove Islamist terrorists to act on 9/11 and all too many other occasions is deeply rooted in centuries of Islamic tradition. As Professor Mary Habeck has observed concerning Qutb, al-Banna, and Mawdudi, the spiritual mentors of contemporary radical Islam: "None of these theorists could have had any impact in the Islamic world if their arguments had not found some sort of resonance in the religion of Islam."[6]

My first hint that a version of Islam might constitute an irreconcilable menace came in the aftermath of the Six-Day War of 1967. As that war approached, my wife Betty and I feared that the Arabs would be able to make good on their promise to drive the Jews into the sea. Ahmed Shukairy, the Palestine Liberation Organization's first leader, predicted Israel's "complete destruction" in the coming war while Hafaz al-Asad of Syria promised to "destroy the Zionist presence in the Arab homeland."[7]

Within a week Israeli forces had swept to the Suez Canal, occupied all of the West Bank, and had taken Quneitra on the Golan Heights, about forty miles from Damascus. Betty and I were determined to visit Israel as soon as possible. We arrived close to *Tisha b'Ab*, the midsummer fast day that commemorates the destruction of the Jerusalem Temple by the Babylonians in 586 B.C.E. and the Romans in 70 C.E. For the first time since the Bar Kokhba revolt of 132–136 C.E., the Temple precincts were in sovereign Jewish hands. When we arrived in Jerusalem, all the hotels in Jewish West Jerusalem were fully booked. Jews from all over Israel had come up to Jerusalem and were turning the traditional day of mourning into a day of rejoicing. We were advised to stay at the National Palace Hotel in Arab East Jerusalem. The hotel management was clearly in a state of shock. We were apparently their first Jewish guests. While they treated us courteously, they were understandably not happy about the circumstances that had brought us to them.

The morning after our arrival we decided to explore the Old City of Jerusalem which had been barred to Jews from 1947 to 1967. As we entered by the Damascus Gate, a thin, physically fit Arab in his early twenties offered his services as a guide. It was quickly apparent that he thought we were Christian. We had entered the Old City from the Arab side and, with her blue eyes and reddish-blonde hair, Betty had often been taken to be Christian. Betty and I silently came to the same conclusion: We were eager to hear his opinions, not our own. For an hour and a half we listened to a hateful tirade against Jews and Israel. He made no secret about his determination to do anything he could to reverse the Arab defeat.

When the tour was over, I paid him and said, "I want you to know that we are Jewish."

He was surprised but then said, "You people have long memories. What makes you think that ours are any shorter?"

"We don't."

He was young, energetic, obviously intelligent. His English was excellent. It was all too obvious that he would never agree to peace with Israel under any circumstance. I had no doubt that there were very many more like him. Israel had won a battle, but with young men like that as enemies, it had not won the war. Moreover, I could see no material advantage peace with Israel might bring that would persuade him to work toward it.

Even after that encounter, I still believed that the Arab-Israeli conflict was primarily a dispute over territory that might with time, patience, and compromise be amenable to a viable solution both sides could live with.

That appears to be the position of those who favor the so-called "two state solution" of two peoples "living side-by-side in peace and security" but who ignore the "Roadmap," a step-by-step blueprint adopted in 2003 by Israel, the Palestinian Authority, and the "Quartet" (the United States, the European Union, the UN, and Russia).[8] Among the obligations the Palestinian Authority agreed to, but never implemented, as indispensable conditions for statehood were "an unequivocal end to violence, terrorism, and incitement" against Israel.[9] The fatal flaw of those who seek a two-state solution while downplaying the Roadmap lies in the fact that a *critical mass* of Muslims define the struggle against Israel as a *defensive jihad* "against the infidels who raid the abode of Islam."[10] Put differently, such Muslims believe they are under an unconditional religious obligation to expel the Jews who, they believe, have forcibly taken possession of a portion of the abode of Islam.

Over the years, I met and came to know a number of Muslim religious leaders regarded as "moderate" who were willing to enter into dialogue with Jews and Christians at interreligious conferences.[11] In no case did I ever meet one who did not look forward to the eventual demise of the State of Israel and the reincorporation of its territory into *dar-al-Islam*, the abode of Islam. I am especially mindful of my encounters with two distinguished Muslim authorities, Professor Ismail al-Faruqi (1921–1986) and Sheikh M. A. Zaki Badawi (1922–2006). Professor al-Faruqi taught for many years at Temple University and made the claim that "Islam offers a perfect solution to the Jewish problem which has beset the Jews and the West for two millennia." Elaborating on that "solution," he described the conditions under which Jews would be permitted to live as an "*ummah* community," that is, a religio-national community, under Muslim domination:

> [Islam] requires the Jews to set up their own rabbinic courts and put its whole executive power at its disposal. The *shariah* (sic), the law of Islam, demands of all Jews to submit themselves to the precepts of Jewish law as interpreted by the rabbinic courts, and treats defiance or contempt of the rabbinic court as rebellion against the Islamic state itself, on a par with like action on the part of a Muslim vis-à-vis the Islamic court.[12]

What al-Faruqi failed to specify was that under such a regime Jews would be *dhimmis*, a humiliated subject people. Moreover, such a community would have no place for Reform, Conservative, or secular Jews. Any rejection of Orthodox Jewish authority would make a person liable to the same punishment as a Muslim in rebellion against *shari'a*. Put differently, the penalty for noncompliance with rabbinic courts under the conditions of dhimmitude offered by al-Faruqi as a "solution" would be death inflicted not by Jewish but by Muslim authorities. As we shall see, al-Faruqi's proposal is both moderate and humane in comparison with the "solutions" offered by more radical Muslim leaders.

Sheikh M. A. Zaki Badawi was a graduate of al-Azhar University in Cairo with a doctorate in Modern Muslim Thought from the University of London. He served as the principal of London's Muslim College. In its obituary, the *Guardian* newspaper called him "Britain's most influential Muslim."[13] He was also an Honorary Knight Commander of the Order of the British Empire. For a number of years, mostly in the 1990s, Betty and I attended international conferences at which he was also present. We were impressed with his urbanity, sophistication, and broad knowledge of world affairs. Normally, we sat with him and his wife at dinner, as we often did with Professor al-Faruqi. One evening, Zaki Badawi interrupted our train of conversation by unexpectedly bringing up the subject of Israel. "They'll really have to go, you know," he informed me. His wife, an English convert to Islam, added, "Like the Crusades." There was no point in arguing with him. Other Muslim scholars had told me the same thing, but none had his standing or authority.

Occasionally, I would ask my Muslim colleagues in dialogue, "Where would the Israelis go?" Inevitably, I would receive a formulaic response: "Back where they came from." While some Western countries might accept a few especially talented Jews, if they survived a Muslim onslaught, the vast majority would find no haven anywhere. Moreover, because of the incessant demonization of Israel in left-wing, pro-Arab propaganda, whatever fate befell the Israelis would be reckoned as no more than what they deserve as colonialists and imperialists, if not latter-day Nazis. We discuss that defamation and its genocidal potentiality in the following chapters.

Zaki Badawi and the Muslim scholars who wanted to send the Jews back where they came from were not entirely forthcoming. They were highly intelligent, well-informed men who could as easily draw the lines between the dots as could I. They knew that a defeat of Israel's Jews would result in their extermination, but they had no intention of spelling it out, at least in a Western language if not in Arabic. This was especially true of Zaki Badawi because of his position in Great Britain. In his time, on those ceremonial occasions at which Britain's leading figures in religion appeared together, Zaki Badawi was the Muslim representative who appeared with the Archbishop of Canterbury Rowan Williams and the Chief Rabbi Sir Jonathan Sachs. Zaki Badawi was too skilled a diplomat publicly to advocate a position on the Middle East with long-term genocidal consequences.[14] By the time I came to know him, I had no doubt that the Arab-Israeli conflict was as much a religious as a political conflict with a genocidal outcome should the Muslims prove victorious.

Moreover, there have always been influential opinion makers and government leaders in the United States and Europe for whom the establishment of the State of Israel was an historic mistake and who would welcome Israel's demise as the *real* solution to the problems of peace and stability in the Middle East.

Evidently, when he served as prime minister, Ariel Sharon saw this as a potential danger. On October 11, 2001, one month after 9/11, he warned that the United States risked appeasing Arab nations the way European democracies appeased Hitler on the eve of World War II and with the same result. When Sharon introduced the memory of Neville Chamberlain and the Munich agreement of 1938 into the peace process, there were very few Western officials who openly advocated an end to the State of Israel. Nevertheless, he was apprehensive that some high officials were advocating a "solution" that would ultimately have the same result.

Diplomats and political leaders usually express their views with a measure of finesse, but not always. For example, speaking to an audience in Alexandria, Egypt, in May 2004, Michel Rocard, France's Socialist prime minister from 1988 to 1991, called the establishment of Israel "an historic mistake" and described that nation as a "unique and abnormal ... entity that continues to pose a threat to its neighbors until today."[15]

Similarly, shortly after 9/11 the late Daniel Bernard, ambassador of France to the United Kingdom, declared at a private London gathering, that the current troubles in the world were all because of "that shitty little country Israel."[16] The ambassador asked, "Why should the world be in danger of World War Three because of those people?"

What is seldom discussed publicly by the Western elites who see Israel's demise as the solution to the problems of the Middle East is the likely fate of Israel's Jews were the Muslims ever to achieve that objective. One reason for the reticence may be a pervasive amnesia concerning why so many Jews came to Israel in the first place. Starting in the 1880s, there was a direct correlation between the rise of European anti-Semitism and the decision of so many Jews to uproot themselves and migrate to Palestine.

When the war ended in May 1945, all of Europe had become a charnel house for the Jewish survivors. Unwelcome in the countries of their birth, an estimated 250,000 found shelter under miserable conditions in displaced persons camps in Germany, Austria, and Italy. Their number was augmented by Eastern European survivors who, when they attempted to return to their homes, often found that they were returning to deadly pogroms.[17] Apart from all national and religious sentiments, the Yishuv, the Jewish settlement in Palestine, was the only community that unconditionally welcomed the majority of both the survivors of the Holocaust and the Jews from Arab lands who were forcibly expelled by government action and mob violence in the post–World War II years.[18]

For many Jews, the Holocaust, the expulsion of approximately nine hundred thousand Jews from Arab lands, and the return of the Holocaust survivors to Palestine exemplified a fundamental theme in Jewish religious experience, exile (*galut*) and return. Certainly, the *Shoah* demonstrated the most extreme perils of *galut*; return to the Land of Israel represented fulfillment of the dream of the end to exile. Unfortunately, return from exile could only be achieved by a war that involved a new exile, the flight of hundreds of thousands of Arabs from the land in which some, but by no means all, of their ancestors had been domiciled for centuries. Not without reason, the Arabs called their defeat in 1948 *al-Naqba*, the catastrophe.

Regrettably, I am enough of a student of history to know that civilizations often have their beginnings in military combat. In the era of St. Augustine (354–430 C.E.) and St. Ambrose (340–397 C.E.), for example, North Africa, Rome, and Milan were part of one unified, Roman-Christian world known as Romania.[19] With the Umayyad conquest of North Africa in the seventh century, that world was split apart by the success of Islamic arms. Similarly, without the *reconquista* Christian civilization would never have been reconstituted in Spain.

Undeniably, Palestine's defeated Arabs had real grievances, but all too many of their leaders offered the Jews who had settled in the Land of Israel only the choice of expulsion or extermination. We see this in the Covenant of the Islamic Resistance Movement, known by its acronym Hamas, a document all too often ignored by political leaders who contend that the inclusion of Hamas in the so-called peace process is indispensable.[20] As we read in the chapter on "The Fruits of Rage" in this work, the covenant clearly and unambiguously states that Hamas's long-term objective, *the destruction of the State of Israel and the extermination of its people, is grounded in an unconditional religious imperative regarded as binding on all Muslims.* Unfortunately, there are high-ranking proponents of the so-called peace process within the governments of the European Union and the United States who argue that with the proper inducements Hamas can either be persuaded to change its position on peace with Israel or can join a Palestinian government led by Mahmoud Abbas, president of the Palestine Authority. Such a government, they claim, could credibly forswear terrorism and provide the basis of "two nations living side-by-side in peace and security."

I have never forgotten the following scene in Eli Wiesel's memoir *Night*:

My neighbor, the faceless one, said:
"Don't let yourself be fooled with illusions. Hitler has made it very clear that he will annihilate all the Jews before the clock strikes twelve, before they can hear the last stroke."
I burst out:
"What does it matter to you? Do we have to regard Hitler as a prophet?"
"I've got more faith in Hitler than in anyone else. He's the only one who's kept his promises, all of his promises, to the Jewish people."[21]

Hitler kept his promise until the total collapse of the Third Reich. Today, there are leaders throughout the Islamic world who are once again making the same promise. There are also those in the West who ignore the renewed expression of those promises and are urging Israel to come to terms with the very people who pledge publicly and unconditionally to destroy them. For Israel to follow such counsel would be suicidal. If the Holocaust has any meaning for Jews it is that they must believe those who promise to destroy them especially when they actively seek, as does Iran, the weapons with which to do so. They at least are telling the truth and intend to keep their promise if they can.

The Gaza war of 2009 gave Israel yet another taste of what to expect from the United Nations and the so-called international community if it agrees, as many are urging them, to a two-state solution without the safeguards spelled out in the Roadmap. Without those safeguards, sooner or later Israel would find that its people are subjected to rocket attacks and other forms of aggression coming from groups within the newly independent Palestinian state. In divided Jerusalem rockets could be launched from Arab neighborhoods a few blocks from their Jewish counterparts. Palestinian authorities would, of course, deny that they are responsible, but the rockets would continue sometimes sporadically, sometimes rapidly. If Gaza is the model, the Israeli government would try to refrain from retaliation until its own population had enough and demanded action. When the effort to put an end to the attacks finally comes, the provocations would once again be ignored by the so-called international community and Israel would be subject again to virulent demonization not only from angry Muslims but from the media and left-wing academic circles throughout much of the Western world. As we note in this book, during the Gaza war of 2009 there were calls for another Holocaust and the restarting of the gas chambers in the street demonstrations in many of the cities of the Western world, as well as in sermons, cartoons, and other propaganda especially in the Arab media. Ironically, a dishonest peace would be worse than honest recognition that the conflict cannot be resolved under present circumstances.

Having spent most of my career writing and teaching about the Holocaust, I now find myself once again confronted by sworn enemies of the United States and Israel who have promised to exterminate my people. With knowledge gained over many decades, I feel I have no option but to take these people at their word.

That is why I have written this book.

1

The Domain of Islam
and the Domain of War

No Islamic concept deserves more scrutiny than that of *jihad* for, as formulated by Muslim jurists on the basis of the Qur'an and the *hadiths*,[1] the concept is fundamental to the relationship between Muslims and non-Muslims. Insofar as *jihad* is fundamental to that relationship, it is our purpose to explore its possible connection with genocide.

The basic meaning of *jihad* is "to exert oneself."[2] That concept rests in turn upon a religiously legitimated worldview in which the world is divided into two irreconcilable realms, *dar-al-Islam* (literally, "the house of submission," i.e., submission to God), the realm of Muslim dominance where theoretically justice and peace are said to prevail, and *dar-al-Harb* ("the house of war"), the rest of the world, which is characterized by heedlessness, disorder, internal strife, and unbelief.

According to Bassam Tibi, an internationally recognized authority on Islam, it is not possible to reconstruct a single Islamic ethic of war and peace from the Qur'an. Nevertheless, Tibi maintains that the dichotomous division of *dar-al-Islam* and *dar-al-Harb* is the basis for all Islamic concepts of war and peace.[3] For strict Muslims, there can be no neutral domain that is neither *dar-al-Islam* nor *dar-al-Harb*.[4] Since *dar-al-Harb* constitutes *ipso facto* a challenge, if not a threat, to Islam understood as the only true religion, Muslims are under an unconditional obligation to undertake *jihad* against its inhabitants.[5]

Nevertheless, *jihad* does not necessarily involve military effort. It may take the form of nonmilitary activity. One of the most frequently cited traditions ascribes such a nonviolent meaning to *jihad:*

> A number of fighters came to the Messenger of Allah [Muhammad] and he said: "You have done well in coming from the 'lesser *jihad*' to the 'greater *jihad*.'"
>
>   They said. "What is the 'greater *jihad*'"? He said, "For the servant [of God] to fight his passions."[6]

The argument that self-mastery is the "greater *jihad*" has often been used for apologetic purposes. One of the most spectacular may have been an address, originally titled "My American Jihad," that was delivered at Harvard's 2002 commencement by Zayed Yasin, past president of the Harvard Islamic Society and a member of the senior class.[7] When queried by CNN concerning his choice of topic, Yasin responded that he wanted "to talk about *jihad* . . . as a moral and a personal struggle to do the right thing."[8] In so characterizing *jihad*, Yasin was not saying anything with which some very well-known Western scholars such as John Esposito would take issue.[9] By contrast, in 2003 the Islamic Affairs Department of the Royal Embassy of Saudi Arabia, in Washington, issued the following exhortation on *jihad* on its website:

> Muslims are required to raise the banner of *jihad* in order to make the Word of Allah supreme in this world, to remove all forms of injustice and oppression, and to defend the Muslims. If Muslims do not take up the sword, the evil tyrants of this earth will be able to continue oppressing the weak and [the] helpless.[10]

The authoritative *Encyclopedia of Islam*, new edition, also stresses the military aspect of *jihad*: "In law, according to general doctrine and in historical tradition, the *jihad* consists of military action with the object of the expansion of Islam and, if need be, its defense."[11] In his book-length study *of jihad*, David Cook of Rice University concurs with these views and dismisses the apologetic interpretation of *jihad* typified by Esposito as "bathetic and laughable." According to Cook,

> In all the literature concerning jihad—whether militant or internal jihad—the fundamental idea is to disconnect oneself from the world, to die to the world, whether bodily (as in battle) or spiritually (as in the internal jihad) . . . aggressive conquest-came first, and then additional meanings became attached to the term.[12]

That *jihad* need not necessarily entail overt military action is also evident in the fact that there is another Qur'anic term, *qital*, used to signify military action to compel nonbelievers to convert to Islam or "come under its sway as a protected people."[13] From the perspective of classical Islam, *jihad* does not necessarily connote sanctified military action but rather an essentially peaceful undertaking for the sake of God-fearing humanity. Before military action can be undertaken, it must be preceded by *da'wa*, that is, the calling of the unbeliever to accept the relationship with God signified by submission to *dar al-Islam*.[14] As a last resort, when nonbelievers resist that call, as do believing Christians and Jews, *jihad* can take the form of *qital*, and is then regarded as a righteous action against infidels who hinder the spread of Islam. Moreover, however perceived by non-Muslims faithful to their own traditions, Muslims never regard *jihad* as gratuitous aggression but as an effort to spread the one true religion through the expansion of *dar al-Islam* which is identical with *dar-al-Salam*, the abode of peace. (As a practical matter, Muslims are hardly likely to use force when the power equation weighs against them.)[15]

In spite of the obligation to expand the domain of Islam by whatever means necessary, some Muslims and sympathetic non-Muslims today claim that Islam is fundamentally a "religion of peace," a view expressed by former president George W. Bush on the occasion of his visit to the Washington Islamic Center shortly after September 11, 2001, and on other occasions since.[16] As implausible as this may appear to most non-Muslims, it is consistent with the way Islam has been traditionally understood, but, as Bassam Tibi observes, at least among Islamic radicals, "peace" can have a very distinct meaning:

> Islamist totalitarianism promotes Islam in a self-congratulatory manner as a religion for peace, but this is a model for peace that is dependent on the extension of *Hakimiyyat Allah* [Allah's rule] over the whole of humanity. *The clear implication of this view is that there can be no world peace without the global domination of Islam* (emphasis added).[17]

A similar view is expressed by Majid Khadduri (1909–2007), formerly of Johns Hopkins University: "Thus jihad may be regarded as Islam's instrument for carrying out its ultimate objective by turning all peoples into believers."[18]

As we shall see, there is much reason to take seriously Tibi's comments about Islamic totalitarianism's aspirations to global dominance. Since Muslims believe that enduring peace and civic harmony can only be achieved by unconditional obedience to Allah, the project of spreading knowledge of Islam and calling upon non-Muslims to submit to conversion *(da'wa)* is seen as an invitation to join in the creation of a universal order of peace, justice, and harmony under Allah. When, however, nonbelievers decline that call, they are not regarded as being faithful to their own traditions but rejecting the sovereignty of Allah and his God-centered world order.

Hence, at least theoretically, Muslims are obliged to wage war until the unbelievers either become Muslim or acknowledge Islam's supremacy and accept "protected" status within the Islamic world as a religious minority, or *dhimmis*. In the final analysis, however, as Majid Khadduri has stated, Muslims believe that universal world peace under Allah requires the conversion or submission of all of humanity to Islam.[19]

Until that felicitous condition is achieved, Muslims are, at least theoretically, always in a state of war—some would call it conflict or tension—of varying degrees of intensity with non-Muslims who remain true to their own traditions and reject the call to Islam. Faced with a more powerful adversary, Muslims may negotiate a *hudna* (truce) of limited duration but not a permanent cessation of the effort to spread Islam. Moreover, traditional Muslims hold that non-Muslims have only themselves to blame if they refuse the call to Islam and Muslims are compelled forcibly to bring about their submission. Such measures are not considered *harb* or war but *fatuha* or the "opening" of unbelievers to the world of Islam.[20]

Given that framework, it is possible for Muslims to regard *any* war waged for the expansion of Islam as morally justified whereas wars waged against Muslims are by their very nature unjust. In fairness, it must be stated that non-radical Muslims moderate that view, often citing the verse, "You shall not kill—for that is forbidden—except for a just cause." (Qur'an, 6.151) The problem arises in defining "a just cause." As we have seen, *qital* against *anyone* who resists the call to Islam is considered both justified and mandatory.

Insofar as war has moral constraints in Islam, it is *in the way war is conducted*. According to Tibi, "Any war against unbelievers, whatever its immediate ground, is morally justified." Nevertheless, Tibi adds that this condition can be interpreted to mean "war as a permanent condition between Muslims and non-believers" does not necessarily involve active aggression.[21] For example, theoretically women, children, and the elderly cannot be targeted in war unless they themselves are seen as actively resisting the call to Islam. Certainly, all Israelis and arguably most, if not all, diaspora Jews would, by their support of the State of Israel, fall under that category. In extreme situations, *shari'a*, the corpus of Islamic jurisprudence, stipulates that "necessity overrides the forbidden" and the definition of what constitutes "necessity" is conveniently vague.[22] Additionally, while Muslim tradition excludes the targeting of women, children, and the elderly, it does not exclude their sale as slaves, nor does it exclude the slaughter of male members of a hostile or resisting community. More often than not, such slaughter has the effect of destroying the defeated community since enslaved women and children, bereft of male protectors, are at the mercy of their Muslim conquerors and slave masters.[23] As the empire of Islam expanded, the slaughter of the men and the enslavement of women and children of a defeated tribe or city became a common practice.[24] When practiced wholesale, the result could be considered a form of ethnic cleansing or cultural genocide.

In the slaughter of the men of the Jewish tribe of Banu Qurayzah, the principal Jewish tribe in Medina, and the enslavement of the tribe's women and children at Medina in 627 C.E., Muhammad himself became Islam's paradigmatic role model for the permissible practice of wholesale murder and enslavement of those who actively oppose the spread of Islam.[25] During the unsuccessful siege of Medina by the pagan Meccans, the Banu Qurayzah schemed with Muhammad's Meccan opponents. Although the negotiations came to naught, Muhammad seems to have regarded the Banu Qurayzah as having violated their treaty with him. After an armed conflict, the tribe surrendered unconditionally. Its fate was decided upon by Sa'd ibn Mu'ādh, a judge handpicked by Muhammad, who decreed that all the men should be put to death and the women and children sold as slaves. The next day the Prophet ordered between six hundred and nine hundred men led to the Market of Medina.[26] Trenches were dug and the men decapitated in the Prophet's presence. Muhammad chose one of the better-looking Qurayzah women for himself. Not surprisingly, she saw the light and converted to Islam. The ownerless property was divided as spoils of war among Muhammad's followers.

According to the Scottish scholar W. Montgomery Watt (1909–2006), apart from conspiring with the enemy, there were "deep underlying reasons" for the executions: Jewish "verbal criticisms of Qur'anic revelation" were seen as attempts "to undermine the foundation of the whole Islamic community."[27] Watt comments on the event:

> It has to be remembered that . . . in the Arabia of that day when tribes were at war with one another or simply had no agreement, they had no obligations towards one another, not even of what we would call common decency. *The enemy and the complete stranger had no rights whatsoever.* When men refrained from killing and being cruel, it was not from any sense of duty towards a fellow-man but out of fear of retaliation by the next-of-kin (emphasis added).[28]

Implicit in Watt's "explanation" is the judgment that such practices no longer have any currency among Muslims. At least among contemporary Islamists, that is by no means the case. Sayyid Qutb (1906–1966) and radical Islamists such as Osama bin Laden, Ayman al-Zawahiri, and their followers take the behavior of Muhammad and his Rightly Guided Companions as the paradigmatic role models for the vanguard that is to overcome *jāhiliyya*, defined by Qutb as the "state of ignorance of the guidance of God," and restore the sovereignty of Allah to humanity.[29] Far from being ancient history, the massacre of the Banu Qurayzah helps to define the permissible in *jihad* for contemporary radical Islamists.

The Muslims who participated in the slaughter of the Banu Qurayzah demonstrated that their allegiance to Islam "came before all other alliances and attachments." Insofar as radical monotheism entails a rejection of ancestral Gods, *ipso facto* it creates a new community and new values.[30] Islam was such a new community, arguably the most revolutionary in all of human history. The rapid spread and durability of Islam over more than thirteen centuries among so great a variety of peoples and cultures led to reflections on and authoritative interpretations of what God required of both the individual and the community. The multiplicity of situations in which Muslims have confronted non-Muslims is one of the reasons why Bassam Tibi claims that it is not possible to reconstruct a single Islamic ethic of war and peace from the Qur'an. And, while certain elements of that ethic have remained constant, such as the distinction of *dar-al-Islam* and *dar-al-Harb*, depending on time, place, circumstance, and interpreter, a fairly wide variety of interpretations have developed over time.[31]

THE INFLUENCE OF SAYYID QUTB

In view of the fundamental concern of this book, the genocidal potentialities of *jihad*, we would do well to examine, however briefly, the interpretation of the ethic of war and peace of Sayyid Qutb, one of the twentieth century's most influential Muslim thinkers. [32] Qutb was born and received his early education in a village of the Asyūt District (*Markat Asyūt*), some 235 miles by rail south of Cairo, Egypt. [33] In spite of the fact that his parents sent him to a modern primary school rather than a traditional Qur'anic school, he memorized the entire Qur'an at an early age. At thirteen, he was sent to his maternal uncle in Cairo to continue his education. He was a student at Dar al-Ulam College from 1929 to 1933 where he was exposed to modern Egyptian and Western intellectual trends and literature.[34] Upon graduation, he was appointed an inspector of the Ministry of Public Instruction.[35]

Initially impressed with Western secular culture, Qutb came to reject it as corrupt, barbaric, and hopelessly immoral. He first achieved a reputation as a poet, and then became prominent as a literary critic.[36] In 1949 the Ministry of Public Information gave him a two-year scholarship to study American educational administration during which time he spent several months at Colorado State Teachers College in Greeley, Colorado, now the University of Northern Colorado. Greeley was a conservative town, but there was little, if anything, about it or America that Qutb did not hold in contempt.[37] Predominantly white Protestant, Greeley was not the sort of town in which a sensitive, well-educated, dark-skinned Egyptian could feel at home in the immediate post–World War II years. He especially resented what he took to be American support of the new State of Israel in 1948. His American experience reinforced his conviction that anthropocentric, cultural modernity had been the spiritual destroyer of the West and threatened to destroy the world of Islam as well.

Returning to Egypt in the summer of 1951, he joined the Islamist Muslim Brotherhood and quickly assumed a leadership role. When in July 1952 a group of army officers, known as the Free Officers Movement, forced King Farouk to abdicate and took power, Qutb and the Brotherhood supported the new regime. Relations soon broke down when it became clear that the new government had no intention of establishing an Islamic state. The officers were Pan-Arab, secular nationalists and modernizers. As Emmanuel Sivan, professor of Islamic history at the Hebrew University in Jerusalem, has pointed out:

> as long as most proponents of secular Arabism remained sufficiently vague in their formulations, and as long as the overriding goal was to chase out the British and French colonial rulers, the [Islamist] MB [Muslim Brotherhood] fitted well into the nationalist fold, its alliance with less religiously oriented nationalists cemented on the battlefields of Palestine and the Suez Canal.[38]

For Islamists such as Qutb, the *ummah* consisted solely of the worldwide community of truly believing Muslims. Neither in Muhammad's time nor today could there be any place for Christians within the world of Islam, save as *dhimmis*. Nevertheless, it is hardly surprising that many well-educated, Arabic-speaking Christians took leadership positions in the Arab nationalist movement:[39] If being an Arab speaker native to the Arab Middle East constituted one's primary identity and Christianity a secondary identity, then their second-class, *dhimmi* status would finally be overcome. In addition to sharing a common hatred of Jews and a genuine desire to expel the Israelis from Palestine, one must ask whether an important element in Christian Arab nationalism might have been the desire to overcome their inferior *dhimmi* status within the Muslim world. One is reminded of the attraction Bolshevism had for nonreligious Jews with its seductive, but ultimately deceptive, promise that proletarian membership rather that Jewish religion or ethnicity would determine their primary identity and permit them to escape from pariah status into the world of left-wing socialism.

Although Arab Christians were partners with Muslims in the struggle against Israel, Islamists like Qutb considered their presence in the Arab nationalist movement "reason for alarm."[40] Unlike secular Arab nationalists, the Islamists sought to create an Islamic community governed by *shari'a*. In such a community, Arab Christians were *dhimmis* and no *dhimmi* could have a position of leadership or authority, save within their own subordinate minority communities.

There were other reasons for Islamist disenchantment with the secular, Free Officers' movement. On October 1, 1954, President Gamal Abdul Nasser renewed a treaty with Britain permitting British troops to return to Egypt if Turkey or any Arab state were attacked.[41] On October 26, 1954, Abd al-Latif, a Muslim Brother, attempted unsuccessfully to assassinate Nasser. As a leader of the Muslim Brotherhood, Qutb was suspected of complicity in the plot, arrested, brutally tortured, and sentenced to twenty-five years at hard labor, later reduced to fifteen because of his poor health.[42]

The colonels who seized power did not hesitate to use extreme measures against their opponents.[43] Horrified by the assassinations and the torture to which prisoners were subjected, Qutb became convinced that the guards and the torturers were not true Muslims nor could Nasser's state be considered a Muslim state in anything but name.[44]

Qutb used his ten prison years to write. His most influential book *Milestones* (*Maalim fil-Tariq*), also known as *Signposts,* was published in 1964 after having been circulated in the form of private letters to his brothers and sisters. The book was condemned as a heretical abomination by the *ulema* of Cairo's al-Azhar University, Egypt's senior religious establishment. Moreover, the more traditional members of the Muslim Brotherhood "considered it a simultaneously fascinating and repellent text." Gilles Kepel, a French authority on radical Islam, rightly characterized the work as "the royal road to the Islamicist movement of the seventies."[45] Although banned by Egyptian authorities, the book became an international best seller and the most influential Islamist document of the twentieth century.

Through the intervention of President Abd al-Salaam Arif of Iraq, Qutb was released from prison toward the end of 1964 but not for long. On August 30, 1965, Nasser announced that a "new Muslim Brotherhood conspiracy" had been uncovered. Considered the ringleader, Qutb was once again arrested, tortured, tried with two other Muslim Brothers, and hanged on August 29, 1966.[46]

According to Mahfouz Azzam, Qutb's lawyer at the trial, when sentence was pronounced, Qutb declared, "Thank God, I performed *jihad* for fifteen years until I earned this martyrdom."[47] As the date of his execution approached, Nasser realized that Qutb was more dangerous dead than alive. He dispatched Anwar Sadat to the prison to promise Qutb that if he appealed his sentence, Nasser would show mercy and would even offer him the post of minister of education, a post he had already been offered and turned down at the beginning of the regime. His sister, also a prisoner, pleaded with him to save himself for the sake of "the Islamic movement." Qutb responded, "Write the words. My words will be stronger if they kill me."[48]

Like the English word "martyr," which is of Greek derivation, the Arabic word *"shaheed"* means "witness" in the sense of bearing witness to one's beliefs even at the cost of one's life. Sayyid Qutb understood that there could be no stronger evidence of his religious and moral seriousness than his willingness to sacrifice his life for his beliefs. Whatever one may think of Sayyid Qutb's views, there can be no doubt concerning the sincerity with which he held them or his personal incorruptibility. Qutb understood that his *jihad* consisted in setting forth his vision in his writings and leadership in the Muslim Brotherhood. His refusal to be bought off by Nasser and Sadat left no doubt of his uncompromising seriousness. It should also have left no doubt concerning how dangerous his ideas and his personal example could be.

Qutb's fully developed thought rests upon his doctrine of *jāhiliyya*, which he defines as the "state of ignorance of the guidance of God."[49] Gilles Kepel, William Shepard, an Australian scholar, and others see Qutb's understanding of *jāhiliyya* as decisively influenced by his viciously brutal prison experience.[50] The term itself occurs only four times in the Qur'an where it referred to the society of unbelief, ignorance, and barbarism that prevailed in the Arab world before the advent of and in opposition to Muhammad.[51]

According to Qutb, *jāhiliyya* did not disappear with the coming of Islam. On the contrary, he insists that *jāhiliyya* is the fundamental characteristic of contemporary society and that it continues to prevail wherever and whenever Islam is either rejected or ignored.[52] *Jāhiliyya* is the polar opposite of Islam which proclaims the absolute sovereignty of God. By contrast, *jāhiliyya* represents the pretensions to sovereignty of fallible human beings. Qutb holds that when men claim they can govern themselves unaided by divine guidance, they make gods of themselves and arrogate to themselves prerogatives that properly belong to God alone. For Qutb, democratic self-government is nothing other than *jāhiliyya* and constitutes a most profound rebellion against God's rule.[53] Moreover, contemporary *jāhiliyya* is far more sophisticated and duplicitous than older expressions of the attitude because it is capable of using science and technology to foster its objectives.[54]

Qutb does not restrict his ascription of *jāhiliyya* to the non-Muslim world. His prison experience taught him that the states of the contemporary Islamic world are ensnared in *jāhiliyya* and hence are only nominally Muslim. For Qutb, such states are humanly created political entities and *ipso facto* in rebellion against God. He rejected as illegitimate not only Nasser's Egypt but most, if not all, of the states of the Muslim world of his time. Only insofar as a political leader carries out the will of Allah, as expressed in the *shari'a*, can he claim genuine legitimacy. By thus defining political legitimacy, Qutb rejects all claims to legitimacy of the entire civilization of secular, democratic modernity.

Nor did Qutb confine himself to abstract analysis. He was engaged in a multidimensional *jihad* to overcome *jāhiliyya* that called for practical and, sooner or later, violent action. He sought the restoration of the ideal Islamic community which, he argued, required a "vanguard of the *umma*" that would take as its model the original Qur'anic generation, "sweep away the influence of *jāhiliyya* from our souls" and withdraw from the larger, godless world as a first step in replicating the achievements of Muhammad and the "rightly guided caliphs," his four successors.[55] Qutb held that they were the proper model for the vanguard that would overcome *jāhiliyya* and restore God's original covenant. He insisted that compromise is impossible between the world of *jāhiliyya* and the world of Islam:[56]

> Islam, then, is the *only Divine way of life* which brings out the noblest human belief characteristics, developing and using them for a human society. Islam has remained unique in this respect to this day. *Those who deviate from this system . . . are truly enemies of mankind* (emphasis added).[57]

Note that all who "deviate" from Islam, defined by Qutb and his followers as the entire non-Muslim world, are without exception "enemies of mankind." Moreover, true Muslims have therefore no choice but to take up *jihad* against the modern culture of *jāhiliyya*, as Muhammad did successfully in his time. As noted, the power of *jāhiliyya* has been strengthened in the modern world. The Enlightenment intensified the conflict between Islam and *jāhiliyya* by replacing the sovereignty of God with that of man. In the nineteenth century, "Karl Marx, a Jew, developed the philosophy of materialism, while in the political area an unholy alliance between Christian imperialism and Zionism was forged."[58] In "our modern time" this *jahili* alliance has become an aggressive force aiming at nothing less than the destruction of Islam altogether.[59]

Qutb's radically dichotomous division of the world into Islam and *jahiliyya* prevented him and those whom he influenced from having a realistic understanding of secularization, which has been defined as "the process by which sectors of society and culture are removed from the domination of religious institutions and symbols."[60] This is a far cry from Qutb's belief that an active assault is being perpetrated against Islam or any other religion. Ideally, secularization fosters freedom of choice in matters religious. Such freedom is not absolute. Secular governments have placed limits on the public practice of some religious traditions. In September 2004, France, for example, banned the wearing of the *hijab*, the Islamic veil for females, and the display of other religious symbols in state schools. Free choice of religion is often constrained by familial, communal, and social bonds, but in a truly secular society the state can never act as the constraining agent.

How different is Qutb's view. For him, a truly Muslim state will actively determine Muslim moral and religious behavior with the severest penalties for deviance. Such a state will also determine the degree of toleration granted to *dhimmis* or "protected" non-Muslims. According to Qutb, the purpose of *jihad* is to establish "God's authority" which secures "complete freedom for every man . . . by releasing him from servitude to other human beings so that he may serve his God."[61] True freedom for Qutb can exist only in a polity governed by *shari'a*. Qutb acknowledges the Prophet's dictum that "There is no compulsion in religion" (Qur'an 2:256). He claims that after victory, "Islam gives the conquered people "complete freedom to accept or not to accept its beliefs."[62] We have noted elsewhere what Qutb's "complete freedom" would mean for non-Orthodox Jews. There would be comparable constraints on Christian *dhimmi* communities.

Given the viciousness of the military regimes that governed Egypt and Syria in Qutb's time, one can understand how Qutb could imagine an Islamist regime as liberating, at least for believing Muslims. Nevertheless, those who read Bat Ye'or's *The Dhimmi* or Andrew Bostom's *The Legacy of Jihad* will get a starkly contrasting and more accurate picture of the "freedom" *dhimmis* would receive after submission to such an Islamic regime.[63] The conditions endured by *dhimmis* ranged from the merely humiliating to outright rape, slavery, and murder, none of which carried any penalty for the Muslim perpetrators.

Qutb's description of the *dhimmis'* "freedom" under Islam also ignores the role of forced conversions in bringing non-Muslims into the fold in spite of the assurance that there is "no compulsion in religion." The fear induced by the conquering Muslim armies was often enough to persuade non-Muslims of the "truth" of Islam, especially when enemy men were slaughtered and women and children enslaved, as in the case of the Banu Qurayzah and in the twentieth century during the Armenian genocide.

According to Qutb, *jahiliyya* will only be defeated by *jihad* which he understands in fundamentally religious rather than territorial terms. Rejecting the idea of the "defense of the homeland of Islam" as a valid basis for *jihad*, he wrote: "The soil of the homeland has in itself no value or weight, from the Islamic point of view." The homeland is worthy of defense only when "on that soil God's authority is established and God's guidance is followed."[64] Territorial wars, such as those fought by European powers between 1815 and 1914, were limited in objective. As Qutb understands, in principle *jihad* can have no limits. He tells us that God "made Islam a universal message, ordained it as the religion for the whole of mankind . . . and made it to be a guide for all the inhabitants of this planet in all their affairs to the end of time."[65]

Hence, Qutb warns against the "naïve" assumption that "preaching and exposition" (*da'wa*) alone would suffice to persuade "the whole of humankind throughout the earth" to heed Islam's call to "freedom."[66] While not denying that "preaching and exposition" have a role to play, he argues that the *jahili* world will place obstacles in the way and that committed Muslims will be compelled to remove them "by force."[67]

Qutb argues that just as the Muslim vanguard in Muhammad's time took up arms against what they took to be *jahili* aggression, the contemporary Muslim "vanguard" must use force against modern *jāhiliyya*. According to William Shepard, Qutb's idea of *jihad* is consistent with the following comment of [Abu 'Ali] Mawdudi (1903–1979), one of the intellectual fathers of modern radical Islam:

> Islam is not the name of a mere "Religion", nor is Muslim the title of a "Nation". *The truth is that Islam is a revolutionary ideology which seeks to alter the social order of the entire world and rebuild it in conformity with its own tenets and ideals.* "Muslims" is the title of that "International Revolutionary Party" organized by Islam to carry out its revolutionary programme. "*Jihad*" refers to that revolutionary struggle and utmost exertion which the Islamic Nation/Party brings into play in order to achieve this objective (emphasis added).[68]

Qutb also rejects the idea, current in some Muslim circles, that *jihad* is purely defensive, arguing that had not Islam employed aggressive force in the time Muhammad, Abu Bakr, 'Omar, and 'Uthman, it would never have achieved the widespread dominion that it did.[69] As we shall see, this is a theme echoed by Osama bin Laden.

There is some debate concerning whether Qutb was calling for outright revolutionary violence. Shepard reminds us that Qubt envisioned his revolution as falling in two stages, the first resembling the nonviolent Meccan stage of the Prophet's mission, in which the power equation weighed against the new and fragile faith, and the second akin to the later Medinan stage, in which the reverse was true. In the modern version of the Medinan stage, Qutb would probably have advocated violent action. Shepard argues that Qutb saw the nonviolent, "Meccan" stage as relevant "in his time," but not the later, violent Medinan stage. Qutb believed that the West's technological and scientific advantage would last for several centuries. While Qutb considered resort to violence "premature," Shepard believes that Qutb would resort to it "when the time came."[70]

When the opportunity arose, Qutb was convinced that the physical destruction of *jāhiliyya* would be the only solution.[71] Moreover, he argued that total destruction would be "ethically justifiable" because *jāhiliyya's* evil is *ipso facto* rebellion against God and aggression against those striving to create a world wholly obedient to His Will. Since *jahili* unbelievers seek to destroy Islam, such a destructive *jihad* is regarded by Qutb and other radical Islamists as purely defensive and entirely justifiable.

Moreover, Qutb argues that only true Muslim believers partake of full humanity while unbelievers are in some sense subhuman.[72] Hence, the destruction of infidels violates no ethical or moral principle. On the contrary, killing unbelievers, however implemented, is a positive gain for the restoration of the world to conformity with the Creator's original intent. As Hansen and Kainz point out, in Qutb's theological universe, the idea that there is something wrong with killing unbelievers rests upon the mistaken conviction that mortal life is to be positively valued. In reality, respect for life and fear of death are expressions of materialism and, as such, *jāhiliyya*. Hansen and Kainz conclude: "In sum, *Qutb's interpretation of the world contains all elements necessary to justify any kind of mass murder in the name of 'faith'* (emphasis added)."[73] Moreover, Qutb's ascription of a paranthropoid identity to nonbelievers exactly parallels National Socialism's characterization of those targeted for destruction as *Untermenschen* (subhumans). Denial of full humanity to such a group is a major step on the road to their guilt-free extermination.[74]

In sum, Qutb's fundamental view of the world is expressed in the following statement:

> There are two parties in all the world: the Party of Allah and the Party of Satan—the Party of Allah, which stands under the banner of Allah and bears his insignia, and the *Party of Satan, which includes every community, group, race and individual that does not stand under the banner of Allah* (emphasis added).[75]

AYMAN AL-ZAWAHIRI

Ayman al-Zawahiri (b. 1951) was one of the founders of Egyptian Islamic Jihad and became second in command to Osama bin Laden when that group merged into al Qaeda in 2001. At fourteen, al-Zawahiri was already a member of the Muslim Brotherhood. At fifteen, he learned of the execution of Sayyid Qutb. During his high school years, he read Sayyid Qutb and Abu a'la Mawdudi.[76] In his book, *Knights under the Prophet's Banner*, al-Zawahiri acknowledged the movement's indebtedness to Qutb. It was Qutb, al-Zawahiri claimed, whose call for faith in the oneness of God and submission to his absolute sovereignty (*hakimiyya*) "fanned the fire of Islamic revolution against the enemies of Islam at home and abroad."[77]

Al-Zawahiri responded to news of Qutb's execution by helping to form a clandestine group dedicated to putting the thinker's ideas into action.[78]

He was much affected by the stories his favorite uncle Mahfouz Azzam had told him about the torture Qutb endured while in prison and the purity of Qutb's character. Azzam and Qutb had maintained a lifelong relationship. Qutb was Azzam's third-grade Arabic teacher. In Qutb's later years, Azzam was Qutb's personal attorney, executor of his estate, and one of the last people to see him before his execution.[79]

President Anwar Sadat was assassinated on October 6, 1981, by Lieutenant Khaled Istambouli, a committed Islamist. Seventeen days later al-Zawahiri was arrested and accused of attempting to overthrow the regime. He was absolved for lack of evidence but was sentenced to three years in prison for gun possession.[80] Like Sayyid Qutb, he was brutally tortured while in prison and like Qutb he was radicalized by the experience which he described in the following passage:

> After Sadat's assassination the torture started again, to write a new bloody chapter of the history of the Islamic movement in Egypt. The torture was brutal this time. Bones were broken, skin was removed, bodies were electrocuted and souls were killed. . . . They used to arrest women, make sexual assaults, call men with women's names, withhold food and water and ban visits. And still this wheel is still turning until today . . . The Egyptian army turned its back toward Israel and directed its weapon against its people.[81]

Al-Zawahiri's account is consistent with what we learn from other sources including Qutb himself. Al-Zawahiri broke under torture and betrayed the hiding place of Essam al-Qamari, a military officer on active duty and one of al-Zawahiri's closest friends.[82] Lawrence Wright has commented aptly on the prison conditions described by al-Zawahiri:

> Human rights advocates in Cairo argue that torture created an appetite for revenge, first in Sayyid Qutb and later in his acolytes, including Ayman al-Zawahiri . . . Egypt's prisons became a factory for producing militants whose need for retribution—they called it justice—was all consuming.[83]

Qutb's book *Milestones* served as the program of radical Islam in the last quarter of the twentieth century. Shortly after its 1964 publication, the scope and shock of Israel's victory in the Six-Day War of 1967 contributed to the radicalization of the Arab world that tended to view historically significant events through the prism of religious interpretation. Coming less than a generation after *al-Naqba*, the "catastrophe" of the creation of the State of Israel, the speed and thoroughness of Israel's 1967 military triumph constituted a major communal trauma. However, a small group of Islamists, led by Sheikh 'Ali Abduh Isma'il, saw no difference between Israel and Nasser's Egypt. They considered both to be infidel powers fighting each other out of materialist motives.[84]

The letters of some Muslim Brotherhood prison inmates reflect this view. With Israel in mind, one inmate writes to his mother: "Can He [Allah] bestow his victory upon people who have been fighting Him, His religion, and His true believers . . .?" Between 1962 and 1967, Nasser had strong Soviet support in socialist Egypt's war against traditionalist Yemen. His forces had the distinction of being the first Arab army to unleash a poison gas attack on fellow Muslims.[85] Referring to that war, another inmate asks in a letter, "Can those who massacred Muslims in Yemen by napalm bombs and poison gas . . . and allied themselves with infidel Russia . . . have the upper hand?"[86] Qutb's writings thus appeared at a propitious moment. Egypt's defeat by Israel in 1967 lent credibility to Qutb's view that Arab states, such as Egypt, were in reality corrupt *jahili* entities, apostate states no better than the infidel states of the West.

Initially, al-Zawahiri responded by working to defeat the "near enemy," his own country, on the assumption that once the near enemy was overcome, the *umma* would rally and defeat "the far enemy," the United States.[87] Two years after his release from prison in 1984, al-Zawahiri, who was trained as a physician, made a third trip to Peshawar, then known as "global capital of radical Islamism" where he met Osama bin Laden (1957–) for the first time.[88]

OSAMA BIN LADEN

Like al-Zawahiri, Bin Laden was also strongly influenced by Qutb. Bin Laden joined the Muslim Brotherhood while a high school student in Jedda, Saudi Arabia.[89] At the school, a young Syrian physical education teacher assembled an Islamic study group consisting of a few exceptional boys and slowly indoctrinated them in some of the ideas of violent *jihad*.[90] *New Yorker* staff writer Steve Coll reports an interview some thirty years later with a member of the study group who prefers to remain anonymous for reasons of personal safety. Bin Laden's former schoolmate told Coll that the Syrian would tell stories to the fourteen-year-old boys that were "mesmerizing." He recalled one in particular that was about "a boy who had found God" and wanted to please Him. The father was not pleased and tried to hinder him by "pulling the [prayer] rug out from under him when he went to pray." The Syrian explained that the father had a gun and described the steps the boy, whom he called "righteous" and "brave," took to shoot his father. The Syrian concluded his story by telling the boys, "Lord be praised—Islam was released in that home!"[91]

Although the teacher did not use Sayyid Qutb's language, his logic was the same: No ties of familial obligation can impede the imperative of absolute obedience to what the Islamists held to be Allah's will. From an Islamist perspective, by preventing his son from fulfilling his religious duty, the father had become an enemy of God and deserved death. Given the Islamist version of the doctrine of absolute divine sovereignty, a youthful parricide had been transformed into a saintly defender of the faith. The teacher was imparting to a group of impressionable fourteen-year-olds from elite Saudi families the idea that no human claim of loyalty, obligation, or mercy possesses any validity if it could be established that Allah's sovereignty was in any way compromised. For example, as Lieutenant Khaled Istambouli, the radical Islamist who assassinated President Anwar Sadat, emptied his assault rifle into his victim's body, he shouted "I have killed Pharaoh." Although his decision to assassinate Sadat was partly a response to what he considered the unjust arrest of his brother Muhammad, Islambouli's choice of words was apt. Pharaoh was considered an incarnation of the god Horus and at times Ra. As such, he represented the worst aspects of *jāhiliyya*, the substitution of the sovereignty of man for that of God. In effect, *jihad* as understood by radical Islamists was *a license to kill* any person the Islamists considered a *jahili*. We return to that issue below.

In 1976 Osama bin Laden entered King Abdul Aziz University in Jeddah, Saudi Arabia. At the time, its faculty included many of Egypt's most influential radical Islamists. After the 1954 attempt on Nasser's life, there was an exodus of Egyptian educators to Saudi Arabia, many of whom were affiliated with the Muslim Brotherhood. However, by welcoming Nasser's Islamist opponents, the kingdom helped to propagate Sayyid Qutb's views at Saudi institutions.

While Osama bin Laden was a student at the university, the school's Egyptian personnel included Muhammad Qutb, Sayyid's younger brother and disciple, and Abdullah Yusuf Azzam (1941–1989), called the "Lenin of international *jihad*."[92] Azzam is credited with having been a principal mentor of Osama bin Laden and having recruited between sixteen thousand and twenty thousand *mujahideen* (persons involved in *jihad*) from twenty countries for the war against the Soviet Union in Afghanistan before his assassination in 1989. He received his Ph.D. in 1973 from al-Azhar University in *fiqh* (Islamic Jurisprudence). This gave him the authority most other active *jihadists* could not match. While in Cairo, Azzam became a friend of Sayyid Qutb's family and became acquainted with Ayman al-Zawahiri and other followers of Sayyid Qutb, as well as Sheikh Omar Abdul Rahman, the blind sheikh currently serving a life sentence in a maximum security federal prison for his role in planning the first bombing of the World Trade Center on February 2, 1993.

A Palestinian, Azzam is considered a central figure in the worldwide development of the twentieth-century militant Islamist movement. He is credited with having transformed the movement both ideologically and militarily from a collection of distinct national movements into a globalized, pan-Islamic movement that recognizes no borders.[93] His ideas were derived from Sayyid Qutb's description of *jāhiliyya* as a threat to Islamic life everywhere: He wrote:

> *Jihad* must not be abandoned until Allah alone is worshipped. *Jihad* continues until Allah's Word is raised high. *Jihad* until all the oppressed peoples are freed. *Jihad* to protect our dignity and restore our occupied lands. *Jihad* is the way of everlasting glory.[94]

Azzam had little use for the claim that "the greater jihad" is the struggle for self-mastery. On the contrary, Azzam argued that the *hadith* on which that interpretation was based was a fabrication and that *jihad*'s primary meaning is *physical combat* against "injustice," the existence of Israel being one of many examples. A representative example of his views on *jihad* as physical combat was delivered in a sermon videotaped at Brooklyn's al-Farook Mosque in 1988: "Whenever *jihad* is mentioned in the holy book, it means the obligation to fight. It does not mean fight with the pen or to write books or articles in the press or to hold lectures."[95]

He also issued an important *fatwa* (an opinion on Islamic law issued by a recognized Islamic scholar) in which he held that *jihad* is obligatory on every Muslim individually and on the entire *umma* collectively. While not denying the central importance of Palestine, he argued that "we should begin with Afghanistan before Palestine."[96] In Afghanistan, the war that aimed to establish an Islamic state could properly be understood as a *jihad* whereas Yassir Arafat's secular alliance of socialists, nationalists, Muslims, and Christians working to create a secular Palestinian state could hardly qualify.[97]

After the Soviet invasion of Afghanistan in December 1979, Azzam left Saudi Arabia to participate in the Afghan *jihad*. Settling first in Islamabad, he then moved to Peshawar where his family joined him in 1982. Together with Osama bin Laden, he established the *Maktab al-Khidamat,* also known as the Afghan Services Bureau, in Peshawar. Although the *Maktab al-Khidamat* claimed to be a travel agency for young people seeking to travel to Pakistan and central Asia, it was in reality a conduit for the vast sums the Saudis were making available to the Afghan resistance as well as a recruitment center for the worldwide inflow of young Muslims eager to fight in Afghanistan as *mujahideen,* or "holy warriors." As the enterprise developed, it provided basic military training and medical care for the *mujahideen*. The organization was also the source out of which al Qaeda sprung.[98]

As the Soviets began their withdrawal from Afghanistan, it was clear that Azzam disagreed with Osama bin Laden and Ayman al-Zawahiri on a number of critical issues. These included the future of *jihad* and *tafkir* (excommunication), i.e., who could legitimately be declared a heretic and by whom. Given Qutb's argument that *jāhiliyya* and Islam cannot coexist and that nominally Muslim states are apostate, it followed that in such states both those who lead and those who follow are heretics. They recognize only human sovereignty. Hence, their lives are forfeit, at least in principle.

Azzam rejected that position. In his book *The Defense of Muslim Lands*, he asks rhetorically whether a loyal Muslim can "fight alongside Muslims that are below acceptable levels of Islamic education" or with Afghanis, some of whom are dishonest, some "even wear talismans," and where such forbidden practices as smoking are widespread. Azzam responded: "We must choose from two evils: which is the greater evil: that Russia takes Afghanistan, turns it into a *Kaffir* [infidel] country and forbids *Qur'an* and Islam for it. Or, one fights *jihad* [together] with a nation with sins and errors?"[99] There was no choice for Azzam. He insisted that intentional killing of civilians, especially women and children, was forbidden.

As the Russians withdrew, Azzam saw Palestine as the next field for *jihad*. Unable to work with Yassir Arafat, he helped to create Hamas, an offshoot of the Egyptian Muslim Brotherhood, as a counterweight to Arafat's secular Palestine Liberation Organization (PLO).[100] Nevertheless, although Azzam wanted to start with Palestine, he accepted Qutb's idea of an Islamist vanguard to serve as the nucleus out of which the future Islamic, global empire would be created. As a prelude to the inevitable war between the world of Islam and world of nonbelievers, he regarded violent, aggressive *jihad* as indispensable for the reconquest of the Iberian peninsula, Bosnia, the Philippines, Kashmir, Somalia and Eritrea, and the Muslim states of the Soviet Union.[101]

We have noted that Muhammad Qutb, Sayyid's younger brother, was one of the Islamist luminaries present at King Abdul Azziz University when Osama bin Laden was a student. The younger Qutb had been arrested in Egypt on July 29, 1965, a month before his older brother, on charges of having conspired to kill Nasser and overthrow the government, the very same offense for which Sayyid Qutb was executed.[102] Released from prison in 1972, he settled in Saudi Arabia where he taught at King Abdul Azziz University and succeeded in spreading his brother's ideas.[103] Although Osama bin Laden did not take formal classes with Muhammad Qutb, he is reported to have attended his public lectures. Years later Jamal Khalifa, a friend and fellow student of Osama bin Laden at the university, told Lawrence Wright, "We read Sayyid Qutb. He was the one who affected our generation."[104]

In Jeddah, Muhammad Qutb was admired both as Sayyid's brother and for having endured Nasser's prisons. He sought to defend his brother's theological legacy which was under attack by moderate Islamists, the most important being Hasan Hudaybi, the supreme guide of the Muslim Brothers in Egypt. Like Sayyid Qutb, Hudaybi published his own prison book, *Du'ah, la Qudah* (*Preachers Not Judges*), in which he held that no Muslim could charge another Muslim with being an infidel as long as he recited with understanding and internal assent the *shahada*, the Muslim profession of faith: "There is no god but Allah and Muhammad is the prophet of Allah." (*La ilaha illa Allah wa-Muhammad rasul Allah.*) Although the more moderate Islamists were hesitant to attack Qutb by name, they did criticize his writings as according legitimacy to attacks against anyone regarded by the extreme Islamists as an infidel.[105] Muhammad Qutb had no intention of jeopardizing the haven he had found in Saudi Arabia. While he agreed with his brother that Muslims are under an unconditional imperative to war against *jāhiliyya*, he was careful to insist that Saudi Arabia was a truly Muslim rather than a *jahili* state. According to Khalifa, Osama bin Laden originally agreed with Hudaybi but changed his views and came to agree with Sayyid Qutb. By so doing, Bin Laden "opened the door to terrorism." The seeds of al Qaeda's future growth had been planted.[106]

THE LUXOR MASSACRES

The issue separating Qutb's followers from those who refused to treat nonbelievers as fair game can be seen in the events that culminated in the 1997 Luxor massacres. In July 1997 the Islamist lawyer, Montassir al-Zayyat, who was later to write a critical biography of al-Zawahiri, brokered a deal known as the nonviolence initiative between *Jamaat al-Islamiyya* (the Islamic Group) and the Egyptian government. In return for the group's pledge of nonviolence, the Egyptian government agreed to release imprisoned members of the organization. Absent such an agreement, the prisoners would in all likelihood have spent the rest of their lives in prison. The deal was approved by many of the senior members of *Jamaat al-Islamiyya* as well as the leaders of al-Zawahiri's *al-Jihad* group (Egyptian Islamic *Jihad*). Initially, the government released two thousand *jihadis*.[107]

Ensconced in his secure refuge in Afghanistan, al-Zawahiri angrily denounced the deal as a surrender to the *jahili* Egyptian government. To spoil the agreement, he planned an attack on foreign tourists visiting the temple of the female pharaoh Hatshepsut near Luxor, one of Egypt's most important tourist sites. On November 17, 1997, six members of *Jamaat* al-Islamiyya, calling themselves *Jihad Talaat al-Fatah* (*Jihad* of the Victorious Vanguard), carried out the attack. They murdered and mutilated fifty-eight unsuspecting foreign tourists who were visiting the temple, including a five-year-old British child and four Japanese couples on their honeymoons. Some tourists were decapitated. The bodies of others were mutilated with butcher knives. One elderly Japanese tourist was found eviscerated with a pamphlet stuffed in his body that declared "No to tourists in Egypt" and was signed "Omar Abdul Rahman's Squadron of Havoc and Destruction."[108]

As the trapped and terrified tourists were methodically gunned down, their murderers cried out, *"Alla hu Akhbar!"* ("God is Great!"). Nor did the attackers spare the site's Muslim guides and service employees. They were considered guilty of serving the *jahili* state. In al-Zawahiri's eyes, they fully deserved their fate.[109] This was *jihad* as understood by Qutb and al Qaeda.

Thirty-six of the fifty-nine slain tourists were Swiss. According to Swiss federal police, Osama bin Laden financed the operation although some Islamists denied this.[110] As we shall see, whether or not Bin Laden was involved, the attack was consistent with the understanding of *jihad* that he shared with Ayman al- Zawahiri, Sayyid Qutb, and other radical Islamists. Al-Zawahiri's objective was to bring down the government of Hosni Mubarrak by destroying the financial base of the allegedly apostate Egyptian tourist industry, a mainstay of Egypt's fragile economy. Instead, the assault produced shock and dismay even among some Egyptian Islamists and brought to an end the cooperation the Muslim "street" had previously been willing to extend to the extremists.[111]

Nevertheless, al-Zawahiri insisted that the slaughter of the unsuspecting tourists was a fully justified expression of *jihad*. He blamed the police and held the victims responsible for their own fate. Although the tourists had come to Egypt as a result of Egyptian efforts to attract them, al-Zawahiri characterized their very presence in the country as "aggression against Muslims and Egypt."[112] In his mind, the slaughter was permissible because of the alleged aggression. As such, the massacre qualified as "defensive *jihad*."[113] In view of Sayyid Qutb's view teaching that all non-Muslims without exception "are truly enemies of mankind," al-Zawahiri's justification is hardly surprising.[114]

In the isolation of Khandahar, Afghanistan, it did not take long for Osama bin Laden and al-Zawahiri to determine the alleged identity of the real villains. On February 23, 1998, *al Quds al-Arabi* published the full text of a "Declaration of the World Islamic Front for Jihad against the Jews and the Crusaders." The document was signed by Bin Laden, al-Zawahiri, and an Islamist leader from Egypt, Pakistan, and Bangladesh respectively.[115]

The document was new, but its grievances had been troubling Bin Laden and other radicals for quite some time.

After citing some of the more militant verses of the Qur'an, the declaration lists three major grievances against the United States. They were:

- The United States has been "occupying" and "plundering" the lands of Islam "in the holiest of its territories, [Saudi] Arabia," using its bases "as a spearhead to fight against the neighboring Islamic peoples."
- Not content with the protracted blockade [the Crusader-Jewish alliance] has imposed, they "come to annihilate what is left of this people and to humiliate their Muslim neighbors."
- If the Americans' aims behind these wars are religious and economic, the aim is also to serve the Jews' petty state and divert attention from its occupation of Jerusalem and murder of Muslims there.

According to Stephen Jen, chief currency analyst at Morgan Stanley, as of July 2008, the revenues of oil-exporting countries were running at about $7 billion a day, or $2.5 trillion annually. As a result, oil-consuming nations, such as the United States, were experiencing a monumental transfer of wealth to oil-producing nations such as Saudi Arabia.[116] It is difficult to reconcile such figures with Bin Laden's claim that the United States was "plundering" the wealth of Saudi Arabia or with his other wild accusations against the United States, such as: "You brought . . . AIDS as a satanic American invention."[117]

Moreover, the American presence in Saudi Arabia was never an "occupation." When Saddam Hussein's forces invaded Kuwait, Saudi leaders *asked* the United States to deploy troops in the kingdom. American forces remained there until September 2003.[118] Over time, their presence became a source of irritation for both countries. When the last American troops departed, one American diplomat commented that "the alliance had become a little bit of poison, and both sides were glad to see it end."[119]

Even one American in Saudi Arabia was too much for Bin Laden. Like all believing Muslims, Bin Laden regards Arabia as the Muslim Holy Land par excellence where God bestowed his revelation on Muhammad. On his deathbed, Muhammad is reputed to have said: "Let not there be two religions in Arabia." Whether he did or not, in 641 C.E. the caliph Umar, the second Sunni caliph, decreed that Jews and Christians should be removed from Arabia in fulfillment of the Prophet's injunction. When the first Gulf War started, Osama bin Laden offered his services to defend the kingdom, claiming that the Saudi army together with his forces, hardened by their experience in Afghanistan, would suffice to defend the country. Instead of relying on Bin Laden's holy warriors, the Saudis turned to President George H. W. Bush and his infidel forces for help.[120]

Having stated his grievances, Bin Laden concluded his 1998 Declaration of War by defining the true character of the American offense: "All these crimes and sins committed by the Americans are a clear declaration of war on Allah, his messenger, and Muslims."

This is not the kind of war that Carl von Clausewitz, the Prussian military theorist, envisaged when he defined war as "a continuation of politics by other means." According to Bin Laden, in its "war" against God, America seeks the destruction of God's religion, Islam. As noted, Sayyid Qutb held that there are only two parties in the world, the party of God and the party of Satan. And, for Bin Laden, the United States is the undisputed leader of the party of Satan. Such accusations may seem preposterous. Nevertheless, Bin Laden and other *jihadis* have used them to galvanize support for their global terror campaign against the United States and its allies. For Bin Laden, there could be only one response to America's "war against God." He called upon faithful Muslims everywhere:

> To kill Americans and their allies, both civil and military, is an *individual duty of every Muslim who is able, in any country where this is possible*, until the Aqsa Mosque [in Jerusalem] and the Haram Mosque [in Mecca] are freed from their grip and until their armies, shattered and broken-winged, depart from all the lands of Islam, incapable of threatening any Muslim (emphasis added).

Further verses from the Qur'an follow and then the declaration continues:

> By God's leave, we call on every Muslim who believes in God and hopes for reward to obey God's command to kill the Americans and plunder their possessions wherever he finds them and whenever he can. Likewise we call on the Muslim *ulema* and leaders and youth and soldiers to launch attacks against the armies of the American devils and against those who are allied with them from among the helpers of Satan.

Bernard Lewis has aptly described Bin Laden's declaration as a "license to kill."[121] He has also pointed to the significance of Bin Laden's claim that *jihad* against America is an *individual* obligation. When a Muslim community is compelled to defend itself, *jihad* becomes the individual obligation for every Muslim and Bin Laden's catalogue of grievances carried the message that the *umma* itself was under attack. By contrast, when the community embarks on an offensive war, volunteers and professionals may suffice to discharge the obligation of *jihad*.[122]

A LETTER FROM AMERICA

After the 9/11 attack on the World Trade Center and the Pentagon, there was considerable reflection in the United States on what had taken place and why. On February 12, 2002, sixty distinguished American thinkers, assembled by the Institute for American Values, drafted a letter titled "What We Are Fighting For: A Letter from America" which was posted on the institute's website.[123] The letter stated that Americans were fighting to defend themselves and these universal principles:

1. All human beings are born free and equal in dignity and rights.
2. The basic subject of society is the human person, and the legitimate role of government is to protect and help to foster the conditions for human flourishing.
3. Human beings naturally desire to seek the truth about life's purpose and ultimate ends.
4. Freedom of conscience and religious freedom are inviolable rights of the human person.
5. Killing in the name of God is contrary to faith in God and is the greatest betrayal of the universality of religious faith.

Three Muslim responses, one purportedly from Osama bin Laden, were posted on the website: (a) Bin Laden's "Letter to America," (b) a response from the London-based Movement for Islamic Reform in Asia (MIRA) which was bitterly critical of past American policies,[124] and (c) a response signed by 153 leading Saudi scholars, titled "How We Can Coexist."[125] The Saudi letter elicited a vehement denunciation written or authorized by Bin Laden, "Al Qaeda's Declaration in Response to the Saudi Ulema: It's Best That You Prostrate Yourselves in Secret."[126]

In reality, there is little, if any, evidence that the Saudi scholars prostrated themselves before their Western counterparts. They declared that "the human being is inherently a sacred creation" and that "it is forbidden to kill a human soul unjustly." The Saudi scholars took issue with the MIRA response that asserted that the perpetrators of 9/11 were "justified in striking civilian targets," although the scholars insist that there is a "causative relationship" between "American policy and what happened." Like all of the Muslim responses, the scholars see American policy in the Middle East, especially its alleged support of "the Jewish state of Israel on Palestinian land," as impelling the 9/11 terrorists to action. They also reject the American affirmation of the separation of church and state as contrary to their understanding of the ultimate unity of the religious and political orders. They claim that they are "committed to fighting against terrorism," but object to focusing on Muslim terrorists alone and insist that the State of Israel commits the "most loathsome kind of terrorism possible" against the Palestinian people, including "mass murder," an allegation that cannot stand impartial scrutiny. The scholars conclude by commenting that "the use of military force . . . provides no real guarantee for the future." As an alternative, they call for "more avenues for dialogue and the exchange of ideas."

In his letter, "Moderate Islam Is a Prostration to the West," Bin Laden heaped contempt on the Saudi scholars. He also wrote a response to the American thinkers, but Raymond Ibrahim, the knowledgeable editor of *The Al Qaeda Reader*, considers Bin Laden's answer to the Saudis to be "extremely important" because of the "doctrinal arguments" it employs to refute the Saudi scholars.[127] Bin Laden begins by commenting that the very name of the Saudi letter, "How We Can Coexist," is proof of its defeatism because it adopts the false premise that one of the foundations of Islam ". . . is how to coexist with infidels!"[128] He complains that the Saudi scholars, whom he characterizes contemptuously as "advocates of inter-religious dialogue," fail to deal with the doctrine of *wala'* and *bara'*, the Arabic words for "loyalty" and "enmity" respectively. *Wala'* conveys the idea of friendship, loyalty, and devotion; *bara'* expresses disavowal and repudiation. In an Islamic context, the terms express loyalty toward fellow Muslims and enmity toward nonbelievers.[129]

BIN LADEN: THE QUR'AN'S ABRAHAM AS AN ISLAMIC MODEL

Bin Laden cites the behavior of Abraham as depicted in the Qur'an as defining the fundamental relationship between Muslims and non-Muslims: "You have a good example in Abraham and those who followed him, for they said to their people, 'We disown you and the idols that you worship besides Allah. *We renounce you: enmity and hate shall reign between us until you believe in Allah alone.*'" (Qur'an 60:4)[130] Bin Laden comments on the verse:

> So there is an enmity [between Muslims and infidels], evidenced by fierce hostility, and an internal hate from the heart. And this fierce hostility—that is, battle,—ceases only if the infidel submits to the authority of Islam . . . But *if the hate at any time extinguishes from the hearts [of the Muslims], this is the great apostasy; the one who does this [extinguishes the hate from his heart] will stand excuseless before Allah.* Allah's Almighty Word to His Prophet recounts in summation the true relationship: "O Prophet! Wage war against the infidels and hypocrites and be ruthless. Their abode is hell—an evil fate (emphasis added)." (Qur'an 9:73)[131]

Raymond Ibrahim comments that "if every Muslim followed this doctrine, a clash between the Muslim world and the non-Muslim world would inevitably occur—which is precisely what al Qaeda seeks."[132]

Bin Laden takes special offense at the Saudi statement that "History has taught us that guarantees of safety are not ensured by power." Such statements, he argues, could only be true if "*jihad*—especially offensive *jihad*" is rejected. For Bin Laden, this is impossible since offensive *jihad* is "an established and basic tenet of [Islam]" whose "Divine foundations" are "built upon hating the infidels, repudiating them with tongue and teeth till they embrace Islam or pay the *jizya* with willing submission and humility." He adds that the "defense of Muslims is [ensured] through *jihad* —not [through] dialogue and coexistence. . . . It is our *only* option for glory, as has been continuously demonstrated in the [Islamic] texts."[133]

Bin Laden is also offended by the Saudi scholars' statement that "many in the Islamic world" regard the September 11, 2001, attacks as "neither legitimate nor welcome, due to all the values, principles, and moral standards that we have learned from Islam."[134] For Bin Laden, the attacks were fully justified in Islamic law. He argues that by denying the legitimacy of the September 11 attacks, the scholars reject offensive *jihad*. By so doing, they reject the Prophet and his Rightly Guided Companions as authoritative models of Muslim behavior. Bin Laden reproves the scholars for "lying" when they claim that "many in the Islamic world did not welcome the attack of September [11]." He calls their statements "repugnant bowing to the infidels" and declares:

> This is the furthest from the truth. Indeed, happiness and joy have not entered many Muslim homes in decades as it did after what befell the Crusaders, thanks to these blessed strikes—and we implore Allah for more like them.[135]

Bin Laden also faults the Saudi scholars for "not welcoming" the attacks because they were allegedly contrary to "all the values, principles, and moral standards that we have learned from Islam." He reminds them:

> Muslims are obligated to raid the lands of the infidels, occupy them, and exchange their systems of governance for an Islamic system, barring any practice that contradicts sharia (sic) from being publicly voiced among the people, as was the case at the dawn of Islam.[136]

Rejecting peace with the world of the infidels, Bin Laden continues his defense of Islamic terrorism: "O you intellectuals! . . . Islam is spread with the sword alone, just as the Prophet was sent forth with the sword."[137] Bin Laden rejects the scholars' definition of terrorism as "unjust aggression against life and property," pointing out that Muhammad and his

Companions after him "assaulted the lives, properties, and women of the infidels, who were living in secure and settled cities."[138] Finally, he complains that the scholars "reject the clash of civilizations, and mean to ward it off its specter through justice, the preservation of rights and values. . . . " In rebuttal, he cites a saying of the Prophet, "No nation ever forsook *jihad* without becoming degraded" and reminds the scholars of the Qur'an's injunction: "You are obligated to fight, even though you may hate it."(Qur'an 2:216).

Finally, we consider Bin Laden's open letter to the American people, "Why We Are Fighting You," which was posted on the Internet in October of 2002.[139] Bin Laden begins by referring to the American declaration and the Saudi response. He finds both letters unsatisfactory and proceeds to his own response based on two questions:

1. Why are we fighting and opposing you?
2. What are we calling you to, and what do we want from you?[140]

Bin Laden answers the first question with a litany of complaints, the sum total of which are expressed in the first sentence: "Because you attacked us and continue to attack us."[141] However, as one reads the literature of radical Islam, it becomes apparent that the radicals see *any non-Muslim resistance against jihadi aggression* as an illegitimate act of aggression against Allah and his religion! Because *jihad's* objective is always the enlargement of Allah's dominion, resistance is considered rebellion against God. In colloquial English, the situation can be likened to the tossing of a coin in which the rules of the game are: "Heads, I win; tails, you lose." There is neither nuance nor ambiguity in the extremists' view of the other. Using language that Iran's president Mahmoud Ahmadinejad would soon echo when he declared "Israel must be wiped off the map."[142] Bin Laden identifies America's alleged "support" of Israel as her worst offense and calls Israel's creation "a crime that must be erased." Bin Laden further argues that the Jews have no historic right to Palestine and that Muslims are the inheritors of both "Moses and the *real Torah that has not been changed*." An important reason why Muslims reject the Jewish claim is that it is based on the Bible, a document Muslims regard as a falsified and distorted account of the only true repository of God's eternal revelation, the Qur'an.

There are irreconcilable discrepancies between accounts in the Bible and the Qur'an. Muslims account for these discrepancies by alleging that the Bible has been deliberately falsified. For example, in the Hebrew scriptures the patriarch Abraham is commanded by God to offer his son Isaac on Mt. Moriah in Jerusalem (Genesis 22:1–18). At a very early stage in Islamic tradition it was determined that Abraham was commanded to sacrifice Ishmael, not Isaac, at Mount Mina near Mecca.[143] Muslims accused Jews and Christians of *tahrif*, that is, distorting the actual biblical text or its meaning.[144] That is why Bin Laden speaks of "the real Torah that has not been changed" by which he means the Qur'an.

Bin Laden further claims that the Arab conquest of Palestine in 638 C.E. was in reality a restoration of the land to its original owners: "Palestine and Jerusalem returned to Islam, the religion of all the prophets."[145] He also repeats the allegation, often made by Muslims hostile to Israel, that "the Israelis are planning to destroy the Aqsa Mosque" under U.S. protection. As in his 1998 "Declaration Urging Jihad against Jews and Crusaders," Bin Laden again complains that Americans "steal our wealth and oil at paltry prices," actions that he characterizes as "the biggest theft ever witnessed by mankind in the history of the world."[146]

He then complains again about the presence of American armed forces in Muslim lands, whose purpose, he argues, is "to protect the security of the Jews and to ensure the continuity of your pillage of our treasure." His last major accusation is his accusation that the United States is responsible for the death of 1.5 million Muslim children in Iraq as "a result of your sanctions" for which "you amazingly did not show concern."[147] Having stated his grievances, Bin Laden then claims al Qaeda's right to take revenge for the "oppression and aggression" visited upon Muslims. Citing Islamic tradition, he asserts: "It is commanded by our religion and intellect that the oppressed have a right to return the aggression. *Do not expect anything from us except jihad, resistance, and revenge* (emphasis added)."[148]

As David Blankenhorn, the organizer of the American group that wrote "What We Are Fighting For," has observed, the purpose of Bin Laden's letter, ostensibly addressed to an American audience, is "to expand the constituency for holy war in Arab and Muslim society."[149] Blankenhorn points out that, whereas the 1998 declaration justified *jihad* as a means of compelling the United States to withdraw its troops from Saudi Arabia, lift sanctions against Iraq, and abandon support for Israel, the 2002 letter makes the call to *jihad* "total and unconditional." Moreover, Bin Laden uses the fact that the United States is a democracy to justify turning every single American, military and civilian, into a legitimate target. The American people, he tells us, "choose their government by way of their own free will [through democratic elections]—a choice that stems from their agreement with its policies." They must, therefore, pay the price for their choice.

Having answered his first question, Bin Laden proceeds to his second question: What are we calling you to, and what do we want from you? His reply is simple and direct: "We are calling you to Islam," by which he means unconditional conversion to Islam, replacing the American constitution with its separation of religion from politics with the "*sharia* of Allah," and offering Americans the traditional choice of conversion, *dhimmi* status, or death. He makes it clear that such a transformation would involve both a complete reversal of American foreign policy and a moral transformation from what he sees as "the worst civilization witnessed in the history of mankind" to one in which Allah's law reigns supreme.[150]

Bin Laden concludes with a solemn warning: "If you fail to respond to all these conditions, then prepare to fight with the Islamic *umma*" which he characterizes as "The *umma* of martyrdom—the *umma* that desires death more than you desire life." And he is utterly confident that his version of Islam will prevail: "If the Americans do not respond, then their fate will be that of the Soviets that fled from Afghanistan to deal with their military defeat, political breakup, ideological downfall, and economic bankruptcy."[151]

On the surface, Bin Laden's threats seem preposterous. Here is the leader of a group located in a wild and unreachable part of either Afghanistan or Pakistan convinced that it can bring down a nation of 300 million possessed of a continental territory and the full array of the most advanced technological weaponry. However, al Qaeda may have certain advantages that must be guarded against. It is a virtual community unhindered by national boundaries. Beyond the consent of the governed, the territorial state's ultimate source of power is its ability to deter both internal and external enemies. When Bin Laden proudly proclaims that his followers desire death more than life, he is in reality saying: *Nothing you can do will deter us.* When he and other Islamists proclaim that the *shaheed*, the martyr, is guaranteed a blissful existence in Paradise, we can translate his meaning into language less strange to us. In our nontheological language he is saying "Our true identities are not limited to our individual experience; our true identity is so completely submerged in that of the *umma* that as long as it survives and prevails, we shall survive and prevail with it."

Because *jihadi* groups constitute a globalized virtual community, they can be said to resemble the Lernaean Hydra, a monstrous serpent with many heads in Greek and Roman mythology. Until Hercules finally succeeded in killing the serpent, every time he cut off one head, two more grew. The United States, and indeed the Western world, is confronted by a protean, hydra-headed enemy, the worldwide network of informally related *jihadi* groups. The elimination of any one group is likely to lead to the establishment of others. And there is no way that the United States or any other major power can satisfy the *jihadis* save through abject surrender. Bin Laden's statement of al Qaeda's objectives, the conversion of the United States to Islam or its destruction, has been echoed repeatedly and explicitly by other Islamists.

Such ambitions may seem far-fetched, but Bin Laden is convinced that it was the *mujahideen*, the Muslims involved in *jihad*, not the United States and its allies, that defeated the Soviet Union in Afghanistan. Like most, if not all, Muslims, Bin Laden also has an historic memory of transforming predominantly Christian communities into communities governed by *shari'a* (Islamic law). By means of *jihad* within less than one hundred years after the death of Muhammad, Muslims created a world empire that extended from France to India in which previously Christian regions, such as Asia Minor, North Africa, and the Iberian Peninsula were converted to Islam.

One of the questions posed by the threat of al Qaeda is: to what extent do its views correspond to those of the Islamic mainstream? There is no easy answer. Nevertheless, *let us keep in mind that no matter how terrible the acts perpetrated by Islamic extremists, they have been without exception associated with appeals to Islam.* As John Kelsay reminds us, "Those carrying out the attacks were and are Muslims. More importantly, . . . when these people give reasons for their actions, they cite Islamic sources and speak in Islamic terms."[152] Furthermore, when Osama bin Laden states his war aims, he does not demand territory from the United States but religious conversion. Similarly, when Mahmoud Ahmadinejad wrote a letter to President George W. Bush, it was unlike any letter one head of government had ever before written to an American president in modern times. After a long list of what he considered unjust actions on the part of the United States, including its support of the allegedly unjustifiable creation of the State of Israel, and an observation that liberal Western democracy has failed to "realize the ideals of humanity," Ahmadinejad expresses his confidence that "through faith in God and the teachings of the prophets, the people will conquer their problems." By "faith in God and the teachings of the prophets," Ahmadinejad meant only Islam. As a Muslim, Ahmadinejad sees Muhammad as the "messenger of God" or the prophet of Allah par excellence. Ahmadinejad then concluded his letter with a question that was also an invitation to convert to Islam: "Do you not want to join them? Mr. President, Whether we like it or not, the world is gravitating towards faith in the Almighty and justice and the will of God will prevail over all things."[153]

A number of observers have commented on the strangeness of Ahmadinejad's letter as an expression of intergovernmental communication. They fail to understand that, like Osama bin Laden, Ahmadinejad does not formulate his correspondence in terms of conflicts of national interest but of the call to Islam. And, as Robert Spencer reminds us, there may be a sinister element in both letters. Traditionally, *jihad* must be preceded by a call to unbelievers to accept Islam and the attack can only follow the unbelievers' refusal to accept the call. Spencer cites a *hadith* in which Allah is depicted as commanding:

> Invite them to (accept) Islam; if they respond to you, accept it from them and desist from fighting against them. . . . If they refuse to accept Islam, demand from them the *jizya* [the tax on non-Muslims specified in Qur'an 9:29]. If they agree to pay, accept it from them and hold off your hands. If they refuse to pay the tax, seek Allah's help and fight them (Sahih Muslim 4294).[154]

We do not know, and perhaps can never know, what proportion of the Muslim world is willing to act upon the imperative of endless *jihad* until the entire world accepts Allah or the humiliating subordination of *dhimmi* status under Islamic domination. Those Muslim scholars who say that they seek dialogue on the basis of equality with non-Muslims are at an enormous disadvantage. As Bin Laden proudly points out, the behavior of contemporary Islamists resembles that of Muhammad and his conquering successors far more than do the behavior and values advocated by the more moderate Saudi scholars. Although the term "fundamentalist" is more appropriately applied to certain Christian movements, the Islamists have fewer problems of literal interpretation of those verses in the Qur'an that refer to *jihad* and the global ambitions of Islam than do the Saudi scholars.

The scholars are at a further disadvantage. *All too often, it is impossible to distinguish moderate from extremist Muslims.* Ayman al-Zawahiri gives us insight into the problem in his discussion of *taqiyya*, the Islamic doctrine that permits Muslims to lie or dissemble their true beliefs in their dealings with non-Muslims when convinced that such behavior is required for personal safety or to safeguard the interests of the *umma*. In his treatise on "Loyalty and Enmity" al-Zawahiri reminds his readers that friendship with nonbelievers is strictly forbidden in Islam. This is even true of infidel family members as he illustrates in the following Qur'anic text:

> Allah Most High said: 'O you who have believed! If your fathers and brothers love infidelity more than belief, then do not befriend them; and whoever of you befriends them sins. (Qur'an 9:23)[155]

Al-Zawahiri also cites a *hadith* that tells of how Abu Ubayda bin al-Jarrah, one of Muhammad's ten companions, slew his own father because of the latter's persistent praise of idols. When he heard of the slaying, Muhammad is reputed to have said: "By him who holds my soul in his hand, none of you believes unless I am dearer to him than his father, his son, and all mankind."[156] This saying is clearly consistent with the ethos of radical monotheism in which familial and tribal loyalties have always been subordinate to the God who commands, "Thou shalt have no other Gods before me. (Exodus 20:3)" Let us also recall the Syrian physical education instructor in Osama bin Laden's high school in Jeddah who praised a boy for murdering his own father when the father interfered with his saying prayers. If the *hadith* is authentic, then Muhammad himself approved the parricide.

According to al-Zawahiri, to dwell among infidels "jeopardizes one's soul." Nevertheless, there are situations in which contact with them is unavoidable. In such circumstances, al-Zawahiri insists that one may deceive an unbeliever but not befriend him. "At any time or place," a person who "fears their evil [of unbelievers] may protect himself *through outward show—not sincere conviction.*"[157] As evidence, al-Zawahiri cites a *hadith* of al-Bukhari through al-Darda: "Truly, we grin to the faces of some peoples, while our hearts curse them."

If the spokesmen of al Qaeda and other radical Islamists are to be believed when they address themselves in Arabic to their fellow Muslims, and there is no reason to doubt them, they are conducting a long-term, globalized *jihad* against the entire non-Muslim world that began almost fourteen hundred years ago and continues to this day. In this monumental struggle of long duration, the Islamists have a singularly powerful weapon in *taqiyya*. For the first time in human history, a great civilization has more or less voluntarily opened its gates on a nonreciprocal basis to members of an alien civilization in large numbers. And they have done so without any realistic attempt to discern who among the immigrants is irrevocably committed to the destruction of the host civilization or to its transformation into a dependent and subordinated extension of the civilization of Islam. Moreover, when Islamists employ *taqiyya* to assure their hosts of the benign character of their traditions despite the fact that they are committed to an unyielding policy of Islamic dominance, their hosts seldom have the knowledge to detect the deception.

The term "fundamentalist" is not inappropriate as a characterization of the beliefs, values, and norms of the Islamists. Their values are intrinsic, not extrinsic, to their civilization. Their quest for dominance is not based on a self-validating, secular will to power. They claim legitimacy for even their most destructive behavior and objectives solely on the basis of what their God has revealed to their Prophet and what, rightly or wrongly, they believe He requires of them. And, as they tell us and demonstrate repeatedly, they are willing to die for their beliefs. Whatever their civilization may be, it is not based on the kind of bourgeois possessive individualism so prevalent in the West.

If the behavior of Muhammad and his Companions has had normative status in the minds of the Prophet's followers throughout history, the non-Muslim world is not likely ever to see an end to offensive *jihad* and its ultimate objectives. On the contrary, there is always likely to be an indeterminate but significant number of Muslims who regard their archetypal model as the appropriate solution to the world's problems. Moreover, as the destruction of the World Trade Center and the damage done to the Pentagon on September 11, 2001, demonstrate, in a globalized information world, informal networks of committed Islamists do not require a state apparatus or a permanently fixed location to do horrendous damage, not excluding a nuclear, biological, or electronic attack, on a targeted society.

2

Jihad and Genocide:
The Case of the Armenians

Too little has been written about the genocidal potentiality of Islam, yet the first genocide of the twentieth century, the precursor of the Holocaust, was perpetrated by a Muslim country against its Christian population, the 1915 massacre of Turkey's Armenian minority. Moreover, that genocide was preceded by an earlier near-genocidal massacre of between one hundred thousand and two hundred thousand Armenians under Sultan Abdul Hamid II (1877–1909) in 1894–1896, and the slaughter of an additional thirty thousand in the Adna region in 1909.[1] The violence of 1894–1896 was carried out under the Sultan's traditionalist leadership in what he and his circle believed was the defense of the Ottoman Empire. The more thorough-going massacre took place during World War I. It was carried out by the modernizing Young Turks in what they believed to be the defense, not of the multinational Ottoman Empire, but of the Turkish *nation*.

The difference in regime and objective has led to a disagreement concerning the 1894–1896 massacres and the 1915 genocide. Vahakn N. Dadrian, arguably the most authoritative contemporary scholar on the Armenian genocide, holds that the earlier massacres were part of an ever-intensifying series of assaults that culminated in the 1915 genocide.[2] Ronald Grigor Suny holds that Abdul Hamid was a traditional imperial monarch who was prepared to use murderous violence to "keep his Armenian subjects in line." Nevertheless, "he did not consider the use of mass deportation to change the demographic composition of Anatolia."[3] While not denying that religion played a part in both the 1894–1896 massacres and the 1915 genocide, Suny argues that in 1915 the ideology motivating the Young Turk perpetrators was primarily ethnic and nationalistic. Moreover, he argues that, in all likelihood, the genocide would *not* have occurred had it not been for the war and the "foreign policy blows" that led to "the loss of much of European Turkey in the years immediately preceding the Great War"[4]

There are, however, sufficient areas of agreement between Dadrian and Suny to suggest that religion did play a most significant role both in the massacres of 1894–1896 and the genocide of 1915. Admittedly, the role of religion is more readily apparent in the events of 1894–1896. At the time, the Ottoman polity was, at least in theory, a sacred society ruled by the sultan-caliph who, as caliph, was widely recognized by Sunni Muslims as both the imperial sovereign and the successor to the Prophet. According to Dadrian, the fundamental common law principle governing the relations in the Ottoman Empire between the Muslim elite and non-Muslim subjects was a quasi-legal contract, the *Akdi Zimmet* (contract with the ruled nationality), in which the sovereign guaranteed the safety of "their persons, their civil and religious liberties, and, conditionally, their property in exchange for the payment of poll and land taxes, and acquiescence to a set of social and legal disabilities"[5] In essence, the *Akdi Zimmet* was in spirit and substance the *dhimma,* the Muslim pact of submission that terminated the state of war with Christians, Jews, and Zoroastrians and stipulated the conditions under which they were permitted domicile in Islamic lands as subject peoples.[6] *Strictly speaking, Islamic tradition envisages no such thing as enduring peace between faithful Muslims and infidels.* There can be a truce when combat appears unlikely to succeed. There could also be conditional toleration in a multinational, multireligious empire, based on the hierarchical gradation of status, such as the Ottoman in which the distinctions of rulers and ruled, Muslims and non-Muslim, were maintained.[7] Nevertheless, *there are no inalienable human rights for non-Muslim subject peoples.* Their rights are *contractual* and *conditional* based strictly upon fulfillment of the *dhimma.* Whenever a *dhimmi* or a *dhimmi* community failed to do so, the contract of submission and protection became *ipso facto* null and void and the state of war could be resumed.

During the nineteenth century, a crisis arose in the relations between the subject communities and the Ottoman Empire as a result of the modernizing Tanzimat (reorganization) reforms and the resulting dissonance between traditional common law and the newly formulated public law. The reforms were initiated in 1839 by Sultan Abd al Majid (1823–1861) under the prodding of the Western powers and Russia. The reforms guaranteed the honor, life, and property of all Ottoman subjects, regardless of race or religion. In 1856, a second, expanded edict of reform asserted the equality of all Ottoman subjects, Muslim and non-Muslim.[8] Given the religiously legitimated, traditional subordination of non-Muslims to

Muslims, the decree, known as the *Hatt-i Hümayun* of 1856, was bitterly resented by the overwhelming majority of Muslims, especially in view of the role foreign pressure had played in bringing about what amounted to the formal abolition of *dhimmi* status.

The reactions of both the Muslim and non-Muslim populations were recorded by Cevet Paþa, an astute observer and a high Ottoman official:

> In accordance with this *ferman* [edict] Muslim and non-Muslim subjects were to be made equal in all rights. This had a very adverse effect on the Muslims. Previously, one of the four points adopted as the basis for peace agreements had been that certain privileges were accorded to Christians on condition that these did not infringe on the sovereign authority of the government. Now the question of (specific) privileges lost its significance; in the whole range of government, the non-Muslims were forthwith to be deemed the equals of the Muslims. Many Muslims began to grumble: "Today we have lost our sacred national rights, won by the blood of our fathers and forefathers. At a time when the Islamic *millet* was the ruling *millet*, it was deprived of this sacred right. This is a day of weeping and mourning for the people of Islam."
>
> As for the non-Muslims, this day, when they left the status of *raya* [*dhimmi*] and gained equality with the ruling *millet*, was a day of rejoicing. But the patriarchs and other spiritual chiefs were displeased, because their appointments were incorporated in the *ferman*. Another point was that whereas in former times, in the Ottoman state, the communities were ranked, with the Muslims first, then the Greeks, then the Armenians, then the Jews, now all of them were put on the same level. Some Greeks objected to this, saying: "The government has put us together with the Jews. We were content with the supremacy of Islam."
>
> As a result of all this, just as the weather was overcast when the *ferman* was read in the audience chamber, so the faces of most of those present were grim. Only on the faces of a few of our Frenchified gentry dressed in the garb of Islam could expressions of joy be seen. Some notorious characters of this type were seen and heard to say: "If the non-Muslims are spread among the Muslims, neighborhoods will become mixed, the price of our properties will rise, and civilized amenities will expand." On this account they expressed satisfaction.[9]

In 1876, a liberal constitution was proposed by Midhat Pasha (1822–1883) during his brief second tenure as Grand Vizier. At first, the new sultan, Abdul Hamid II (reigning from 1876 to 1909), was inclined to accept the constitution, but quickly changed his mind and effectively terminated the period of Tanzimat reforms. The rest of his reign was a period of unremitting, conservative reaction. The likely negative consequences of reform were already understood in 1856 by an earlier grand vizier, Mustafa Reşid Pasha (1800–1858), a brilliant diplomat. In a memorandum

addressed to the sultan in the wake of the reforms of that year, Reşid fore-
saw the possibility of a "great slaughter" as a result of the efforts to establish the civic equality of all Ottoman subjects through legal enactment.[10]

Reşid's views were prescient. Muslim traditionalists regarded the
emancipation of Jews and Christians as profoundly offensive. Before
emancipation, payment of the *jizya*, the poll tax imposed upon all male
dhimmis, symbolized their subjection, inferior status, and suspension of
jihad. By voiding *dhimmi* disabilities, traditionalists believed the *dhimma*
had been rendered null and void. In their eyes, *dhimmi* emancipation did
not mean an end to civic disabilities but the *restoration of the state of war
against the dhimmis*. Under the circumstances, the traditionalists believed
that, at least in theory, the *umma*, the Muslim community, could commit
any outrage against them.[11] Moreover, these actions were regarded "not
only as justified but also as mandatory and even as praiseworthy."[12]

Peter Balakian has described one of the most agonizing disabilities imposed upon the Armenians because of their *dhimmi* status:

> Another burden solely for the Armenians was the *kishlak,* or winter-quar-
> tering obligation, which enabled Kurds and Turks to quarter themselves,
> their families, and their cattle in Armenian homes during the long winter
> months. The fact that the Kurdish way of life was nomadic and rough and
> the Armenian dwellings did not allow for much privacy made the intrusion
> unbearable, and knowing that the unarmed Armenians had neither physical
> nor legal recourse, a well-armed Kurd or Turk could not only steal his host's
> possessions but could rape or kidnap the women and girls of the household
> with impunity.[13]

In the 1880s, Armenian exiles in Europe, influenced by Western ideas
about national self-determination and the "people" as the source of political legitimacy, began to campaign for national autonomy. The Armenians did not initially seek full political independence, but nationalism
provided a powerful legitimation for separation from the multinational
Ottoman Empire. As such, it was profoundly subversive of the imperial
order. Armenian rebels in the Caucasus also organized raids into Ottoman territory. The vast majority of Armenians sought amelioration of
their situation within the empire, but, by 1890, an Armenian Revolutionary Federation was established in Tiflis (Tbilisi, the capital of Georgia)
that demanded Armenian freedom "with gun in hand."[14] In 1891, the
sultan responded by raising a force of Kurdish Muslim irregulars and
sanctioning their predatory attacks on Armenians.[15] Within a year, the
Kurds had formed cavalry units totaling fifteen thousand men. Assured
of legal immunity, the Kurds attacked and spread terror among Armenians in the capital and the hinterland. In 1893 Armenian revolutionaries posted placards in many towns and cities calling on Muslims to rise

up against the sultan's oppression. Since, as noted, the sultan was also the caliph, combining the traditional functions of political and religious leadership, the Armenian action was seen by traditionalists as a radical breach of the *dhimma*.

Another source of Turkish resentment stemmed from the fact that the Armenians were a "market dominant minority."[16] Very often, discriminated minorities, barred from service in the military or the state bureaucracy and subject to other forms of social and vocational discrimination, rely on education and training for their economic survival and well-being to a much greater extent than do indigenous majorities. Such minorities are also likely to be concentrated in urban centers and to specialize in urban trades and crafts, finance, and the professions. Their capital consisted in what was in their heads and could not be taken from them. Often subject to expulsion, they formed diaspora networks that were intrinsically advantageous in both finance and commerce. This has been the case with the European Jews before World War II, the Chinese in Southeast Asia, the Lebanese in West Africa, and the Armenians in the Ottoman Empire.

During the nineteenth century, Armenians tended to rise above the Turks economically. The more affluent sent their sons abroad to receive their education in a rapidly modernizing Europe. As Christians, they had links to Europe that were not available to the Muslim majority. Diaspora Armenians sent home remittances and brought back new machines and technology to their families in the empire. When the sale of Muslim lands to non-Muslims was permitted by the reforms of 1856, Armenians had the resources to buy up large landholdings, especially after 1870.[17] This resulted in a reversal of status in a world newly oriented toward industry and commerce. Resentment was bitter and fed upon itself so that Abdul Hamid II's efforts to undo the emancipatory reforms received widespread Muslim support.

Actual massacres first broke out in the summer of 1894 in Sasun, in southern Armenia. Turkish authorities used Armenian resistance to a system of double taxation and officially sanctioned Kurdish violence and sexual abuse of Armenian women as a pretext for indiscriminate rape and slaughter.[18] As news of the outrages quickly spread to Europe, Britain, France, and Russia demanded a commission of inquiry. These same powers also sought to persuade the Ottoman government to adopt reforms in those provinces where most of the Armenians were domiciled. The sultan made an empty show of accepting some reforms, although he had no intention of implementing them. In September 1895, Armenians demonstrated in Constantinople in order to pressure the sultan and the European powers to implement the reforms. The police and radical Muslim elements in the capital city responded with ten days of massacre and terror. About the same time, an unprovoked, premeditated massacre began in the city of Trebizond on the Black Sea (Adalian). The massacres then spread through almost every town with a significant number of Armenian inhabitants. There was nothing spontaneous about the massacres. They were in fact military operations that began and ended daily with the call of a bugle.[19]

The worst massacre occurred in the city of Urfa, known to the ancient world as Edessa, where Armenians constituted about a third of the population. In December 1895, after a two-month siege of the Armenian quarter, Armenian leaders gathered in their cathedral and requested official Turkish protection. The Turkish commander agreed but then surrounded the Cathedral of Urfa, after which Turkish troops and the mob rampaged through the Armenian quarter burning, looting, and killing all adult males. Twenty-five hundred Armenians were burned alive in the cathedral. Dadrian comments that *wherever possible the killing was done in such a way as to emphasize the religious nature of the deed*.[20] Lord Kinross describes the manner in which the slaughter was assimilated to a sacrificial ritual:

> When a large group of young Armenians were brought before a sheikh, he had them thrown down on their backs and held by their hands and feet. Then, in the words of an observer, he recited verses of the Koran and *"cut their throats after the Mecca rite of sacrificing sheep."*[21]

The mosques were places of incitement; the Christian churches served as slaughterhouses. Murderous mobs were urged on by their imams. The worst butchery often followed Friday services. Dadrian also comments on the importance of local religious authorities in the implementation of the massacres. The sultan in distant Constantinople could issue orders for the massacres, often framed in covert language, but the interpretation, planning, and implementation of such orders required the leadership of local authority figures. Because of the empire's theocratic nature, local religious leaders used their authority to assure the mob that the massacres were in accordance with the *Seriat* (*shari'a*).[22] With very few exceptions, the *muftis* (jurisconsults who dispensed formal legal opinions), *kadis* (magistrates and guardians of law and order), *ulemas* (Muslim theologians), and *mullahs* played a crucial role in conferring religious legitimacy on the slaughter.[23] In many locations, after the men were killed the mob sought to force surviving widows and children to convert. Those who refused were murdered.[24]

The massacres constituted an unprecedented level of violence on the part of the Ottoman Empire against one of its subject peoples. In spite of pressure from the Great Powers, Abdul Hamid II was clearly determined to frustrate Armenian hopes of reform. He also sought to crush any Armenian attempt to organize politically. Estimates of the number of dead range from one hundred thousand to three hundred thousand. Tens of thousands emigrated; thousands were forcibly converted to Islam. Moreover, the sultan understood that he could deal with his subjects with utter impunity because the Great Powers were more interested in good relations with his empire than the fate of a minority subject people. From his point of view, the Armenians got what they deserved. By seeking to overcome their religiously defined subordinate status and seeking the help of foreign rulers, they had broken their contract and had placed themselves in a state of war with his realm in which no violence, expropriation, or violation was out of bounds.

The massacres of 1894–1896 can be characterized as pre-genocidal. Abdul Hamid's slaughter had irretrievably marginalized and dehumanized the Armenians. The massacres thus prepared the way for the full-scale genocide and ethnic homogenization perpetrated by the modernizing twentieth-century regime of the Committee of Union and Progress, the Young Turks.

THE YOUNG TURKS

The political agenda of the Young Turks was different from that of the sultan. They were a Turkish nationalist reform party that responded to the weakness of the Ottoman Empire as manifested in Austria-Hungary's annexation of Bosnia-Herzegovina in 1908, Italy's seizure of Libya and the island of Rhodes in 1912, the independence of Albania in 1912, and the Ottoman defeat in the First Balkan War of 1912–1913 that led to the loss of much of the Ottoman Empire in Europe. Moreover, as noted, in the empire itself, Muslims had been losing ground to *dhimmi* minorities, the Greeks, Jews, and Armenians, who dominated the world of commerce and the professions. The Young Turks were modernizing, rationalizing "progressives" who understood, as did the Japanese elites at the time of the Meiji Reformation of 1866–1869, that, absent modernization, the independence and territorial integrity of their respective empires would be in peril. In 1908, the Young Turks effectively overthrew Abdul Hamid II's traditionalist regime. In their initial enthusiasm, many Armenians made an understandable but deadly miscalculation. They assumed that the overthrow of an inefficient and corrupt traditional regime by one that was less corrupt and more rational augured well for their own community. The Young Turks had given public assurances of equal treatment of the empire's non-Muslim minorities, but the logic of their nationalist, modernizing revolution made ethnic homogenization rather than diversity the almost inevitable political outcome.

The first generation of Turkish revolutionaries was divided on the issue of working with the Armenians, as was evident at the First Congress of the Ottoman Opposition that met in Paris in February 1902. Some of the more liberal Young Turks thought that an alliance with the Armenians would get a favorable response from the Europeans. Armenian activists declared that cooperation with the Turkish revolutionaries was conditional on the implementation of reforms in the six Anatolian *vilayets* (provinces) with significant Armenian populations to be guaranteed by the European powers. The conditions were acceptable to the majority attending the Congress but were vehemently rejected by the nationalist minority. The latter regarded European support as wholly at odds with their fundamental objective, the creation of a strong, independent Ottoman realm in which the traditional status hierarchy would remain more or less intact. The views of the minority ultimately carried greater weight as they represented the dominant tendency among most Young Turk organizations and newspapers.[25]

According to Suny and other scholars, in the first decade of the twentieth century there was a shift by the Young Turks from what he characterizes as an "Ottomanist orientation" that emphasized the equality of the *millets* in a multinational society to a more Turkish nationalist position that stressed the predominance of the ethnic Turks over the subordinate communities that were regarded as "the protected flock of the sultan," Armenian, Catholic, Jewish, and Orthodox.[26] Until World War I, loyalty to the empire remained part of Young Turk rhetoric, but it was increasingly supplanted by nationalist ideology. The shift placed the Armenian political leaders in a difficult position. Their community was to be found on both sides of the Ottoman-Russian border. In addition, the Armenians were split into two factions, largely along socioeconomic lines. The Dashnak, members of the Armenian Revolutionary Federation (*Hai Heghapokhakan Dashnaksutiun*), represented the Armenian petty bourgeoisie of Anatolia; the patriarchate represented the wealthy commercial class of the capital and other larger cities.[27] The Dashnak ultimately sought autonomy if not complete Armenian independence. The patriarchate and its allies sought a restoration of their traditional privileges as *dhimmis* in the *millet* system that was threatened by the centralizing tendencies of government.

When the war began, the Dashnak urged Armenians to volunteer in the Ottoman army. In Tsarist Russia, the Dashnak urged Armenians to enlist in the Tsarist army. As a result, both the Tsarist and the Ottoman governments suspected the Armenians of disloyalty. The situation was aggravated by the dangers confronting the Ottoman Empire in 1914 and 1915. In November 1914, over the objections of field commanders,

Turkish forces led by Enver Pasha, minister of war and one of the ruling Young Turk triumvirate, attempted to regain land in the Caucasus lost to the Russians in 1878. Enver's effort ended catastrophically at Sarikamis, a Turkish town in the Caucasus. In the west, Djemal Pasha led an attack in February 1915 on the Suez Canal that also ended in defeat. In March 1915, in response to a Russian request for aid, Allied naval forces under Admiral Sir John de Robeck, commander of the Aegean Squadron, made preparations to force a passage through the Dardanelles Strait. The evacuation of Constantinople began and the state archives and the empire's gold reserves were sent away. Most observers anticipated the empire's collapse. However, on March 18, 1915, as a result of an unsuspected Turkish minefield in the Strait, five Allied warships were destroyed. The Allied attempt to force the Strait ended in disaster. [28]

When the Young Turks contemplated evacuating from Constantinople to the Anatolian heartland, they could not ignore the issue of security. Anatolia's population was mixed. In addition to Turks, it was inhabited by Greeks, Armenians, and Kurds whose loyalty was suspect in Turkish eyes. Some Greek civilians were deported from the coastal areas, but those deportations were not genocidal in intent. In the first months of 1915, the Young Turks responded to the defeat at Sarikamis by blaming the Armenians, whom they accused of sympathizing with the Russians.[29] The Ottoman authorities disarmed and demobilized Armenian soldiers who were then forced into labor brigades and compelled to dig their own graves before being shot.[30]

Rumors of the slaughter spread in the Armenian villages.[31] On April 20, 1915, the Armenians of Van rose up in self-defense when Djevdet Bey, the recently appointed governor of Van and Enver Pasha's brother-in-law, demanded that the Armenian leadership hand over four thousand men for the Ottoman army's labor battalions. With no illusions concerning the fate of the men if they complied, the leadership refused, an action depicted by the Turks as a revolutionary uprising.[32] The Armenians held out in Van until May 14, 1915, when the city was captured by the Russians with the aid of some Armenian guerrillas who proclaimed Van the capital of an independent Armenian republic. When the Turks recaptured the city in July, they were infuriated by what they regarded as Armenian treason and launched a massacre, butchering the men, and robbing, raping, and leaving the women to die. Dr. Clarence B. Ussher, an American medical missionary in Van, reported that 55,000 Armenians were killed there in May.[33] On April 24, 1915, the ministry of the interior ordered the arrest of Armenian parliamentary deputies, former ministers, and some intellectuals. Thousands were arrested, including 2,345 in the capital, most of whom were subsequently executed.[34]

On May 27, 1915, a new emergency law was promulgated, the Temporary Law of Deportation. The law authorized military leaders to order the deportation of population groups on suspicion of espionage, treason, and military necessity. With this sweeping authorization and without explicitly naming the Armenians, the Turkish government arrogated to itself the genocidal deportation of its Armenian population. Shortly thereafter, Djevdet Bey, Van's governor, gave an order to "exterminate all Armenian males of 12 years and older" in that border region.[35] Actual genocide had begun in April 1915, with the rounding up and deportation of Armenian men in one population center after another. The men were usually imprisoned for several days, after which they were marched out of town and massacred. Later women, children, and older men were also deported. The women were often raped and mutilated before being killed. Thousands of the female deportees were given the choice of conversion to Islam or death. Having lost their men and completely at the mercy of hostile Turks and Kurds, many of the women converted. We return to that subject below.

In June 1915, the government began to use the railroads to expedite deportation and extermination. Freight cars were employed to transport thousands to remote areas where they were left to starve to death while being assaulted by the ravages of nature and human malice. Many were murdered outright. The Armenian deportees were among the first men and women in the twentieth century to learn that human rights are inseparable from political status. Having been deprived by the Ottoman government of all political status, save that of outlaw, there was no abuse that could not with impunity be inflicted upon them.

The extermination project was thoroughly modern in spirit and implementation from its initial planning stages to its execution.[36] Mass extermination was advocated in the planning sessions as the appropriate "scientific" response to the universal struggle of the races for survival.[37] Like other modernizing elites of the period, the largely European-trained Young Turks interpreted the relations between races and nations in Social Darwinist terms. Above all, the Young Turks had a reliable, centralized bureaucratic network. Taalat Bey, one of the ruling triumvirs and minister of the interior, did not entrust the assignment to old-fashioned provincial bureaucrats but sent Young Turk bureaucrats to act as his personal representatives and, when necessary, to punish governors and local governors who, out of compassion or greed, failed to carry out orders. There was a special organization with responsibility for organizing the massacres. At the local level, much of the actual killing was carried out by death squads who were given the name of "Butcher Battalions."[38]

Taalat Bey spelled out the objectives of his government in a telegram to the Police Office in Aleppo, Syria, dated September 15, 1915:

It has been reported that by order of the Committee [of Union and Progress] the Government has *determined completely to exterminate the Armenians living in Turkey.* Those who refuse to obey this order cannot be regarded as friends of the Government. Regardless of the women, children or invalids, and however deplorable the methods of destruction may seem, an end is to be put to their existence [i.e., the Armenians] without paying any heed to feeling or conscience (emphasis added).

Minister for the Interior,

Taalat[39]

The Young Turks characterized their aggression as "deportations," and insisted that they were acting in the interests of national security. However, it was quickly apparent that the number of victims far exceeded the nineteenth-century massacres. In 1915 deportation had acquired a new and sinister meaning. It had become an instrument of extermination in which no fewer than 1 million Armenians perished.[40]

Many volumes have been written about the Armenian genocide. One of the earliest was also one of the most comprehensive, the report assembled by Viscount James Bryce in 1916 in partnership with Arnold Toynbee and presented to Sir Edward Grey, the British foreign secretary. The authors concluded their report with an observation concerning the slaughter: "It was a deliberate, systematic attempt to eradicate the Armenian population throughout the Ottoman Empire and it has certainly met with a very large measure of success."[41]

To this day, Turkish authorities have denied that genocide ever took place, and insist that their actions were necessary defensive measures against a disloyal and rebellious minority.[42] That claim has been refuted by the vast majority of responsible scholars. Nevertheless, the Turkish government has used every threat in its diplomatic arsenal to prevent any friendly government from officially taking issue with its denial of genocide.

As noted above, there is little reason to doubt that Abdul Hamid's massacres were in large measure religiously motivated. The sultan-caliph was responsible for mass murder on an unprecedented scale, but extermination of the entire community was beyond his capacities. Not so, the Young Turks. Within months after Turkey's entrance into the Great War, the decision to exterminate the Armenians had been taken. When the deed was done, the justifications the Young Turks offered were largely political and economic.

When I first wrote about the Armenian genocide of 1915, I stressed the modernity of the enterprise and its economic, political, and military motives.[43] I did not consider the possibility that the perpetrators' motives might have included a very important religious component. Today, I would argue that religion was an indispensable component in the motivation for genocide. It was certainly an indispensable element in defining the otherness of non-Muslims in the Ottoman Empire. I would further argue that the crimes perpetrated against the Armenians were regarded by the Turks as legitimate defensive methods of dealing with *dhimmis* who had violated the conditions of the *dhimma*, and, hence, were outlaws for whom everything, including life, property, freedom, and family, was forfeit. I would also argue that the persistent Turkish genocide denial—so different from the German way of dealing with their genocide—has been due, at least in part, to the Turkish belief that they did no wrong in exterminating the Armenians, a belief that rests ultimately on the traditions of *jihad* and the *dhimma*.

In the massacres of 1894–1896, Turkish authorities were quite open about religious legitimations. In 1914 religion was once again an important component in the conduct of Turkish authorities, this time in the way the war was initiated and its purposes defined. On November 2, 1914, the Ottoman Empire declared war on the Entente powers, Britain, France, Russia, and their allies. On November 13, the Ottoman sultan, in his capacity, as caliph, issued an appeal for *jihad*. The next day Mustafa Hayri Bey, the Sheikh-ul-Islam and as such the chief Sunni religious authority in the Ottoman world, issued a formal (and inflammatory) declaration of *jihad* "against infidels and enemies of Islam." *Jihad* pamphlets in Arabic were also distributed in mosques throughout the Muslim world that offered a detailed plan of operations for the assassination and extermination of all "unbelievers" except those of German nationality, the empire's wartime ally.[44] Killing squads and their leaders were "motivated by both the ideology of *jihad* and pan-Turkism influenced by European nationalism."[45] While the practical influence of the *jihad* on the masses was limited, "it later facilitated the government's program of genocide against the Armenians."[46] It is also worth noting that although the Sheikh-ul-Islam was customarily appointed by the sultan, Hayri Bey was appointed by the Committee of Union and Progress, the Young Turks who were to instigate the genocide.

According to historian Ara Sarafian, in addition to the killings and general massacres, a large number of Armenians were "'abducted,' 'carried off,' or 'converted to Islam.'"[47] Sarafian argues that "the fate of this latter class of Armenians was part of the same genocidal calculus as those who were murdered." It is estimated that in 1915–1916 between one hundred thousand and two hundred thousand Armenians, most of whom were women and children, escaped death by converting to Islam. The absorption of these converts into the Muslim community had the same objective as outright genocide, the elimination of the Christian Armenian community as a demographic presence in the Ottoman Empire. In addition to killing a very large number of Armenians through forced marches and starvation, the deportations served to weaken and terrify women and children who had lost their male protectors before or during the deportations. According to Sarafian, "young women and children were rendered prime candidates for absorption into Muslim households after they were isolated from their families and terrorized during the forced marches and execution of their elders"[48]

Sarafian contends, with considerable justice, that the authorities were implementing a "single policy of destruction" in both the outright murder of adult males and in the absorption of Armenian women and children into the Muslim community. The same Ottoman bureaucrats who controlled the deportations were also in charge of the conversion program. In the initial stages of the assault on the Armenians, there were "voluntary" conversions. Some individuals were selected by individual Muslims for absorption into their households. In addition, government agencies distributed Armenians to Muslim families. Children in government-sponsored orphanages were converted and directly absorbed into the Muslim community.

Events in Trebizond are illustrative of how the program functioned. Between July 1 and July 18, 1915, five deportation convoys left Trebizond. Oscar Heizer, the American consul, reported that most of the deportees were killed by their guards shortly after leaving.[49] Approximately three thousand children, girls up to fifteen years old and boys no older than ten, were placed in a number of houses designated by the Turks as "orphanages." Another three hundred were housed in the American missionary school, which was turned into an orphanage. Both orphanages were subsequently closed down by an official sent from Constantinople to supervise the extermination of the Armenians. Some children were drowned by the Turks; others were distributed to Muslim households, where, according to Heizer, they were assimilated as Muslims within weeks.[50] Elsewhere, U.S. consul Leslie Davis reported on the passage of thousands of deportees through Harpoot, which was situated on a principal route to the deserts of Syria. Davis wrote that hardly any men had survived among the deportees. Subject to constant beatings, with little or no food or water, the victims were rapidly dying. The gendarmes guarding the Armenians refused to permit them to leave the convoy or to receive aid from American missionaries. They did, however, permit Turks to visit the convoys with doctors to select "the prettiest girls" for their own purposes. Davis further reported that the Turks were not only seeking to exterminate the Armenians; they were also seeking to absorb a large number as Muslims. Sarafian concludes that there was a mass transfer of Armenians into Muslim households in 1915. By destroying the Armenian social structure in the early stages of the genocide through the murder of young men, heads of families, and community leaders, the Turks were able to garner "the ideal candidates for absorption" into Muslim households and the general Muslim population.[51]

As cruel as was this program, it was fundamentally different from the Nazi Final Solution. Suny has observed that "To a considerable degree, religious differences were transmuted by both the Armenians and the Turks into racial and national differences, far more indelible and immutable than religion"[52] Nevertheless, Suny's qualifier, "to a considerable degree" is important. For the Nazis, the racial divide between the so-called Aryans and non-Aryans was absolute and unbridgeable. In the National Socialist universe, there was no room for an absorption program for non-Aryans, save for a miniscule number of "Honorary Aryans." Some Poles and others with the appropriate physical characteristics could be absorbed, but not the Jews. By contrast, even in genocide, religion made a difference in the Ottoman Empire. Conversion could and did save some Armenians even as it destroyed their community. Moreover, as noted, both the extermination and the conversion process were fully consistent with Islamic tradition in the eyes of the Turks.

Nor were the Armenians the only Christian minority eliminated by the Turks, albeit by somewhat gentler means. In January 1923, after Greece's failed invasion of Turkey's Anatolian mainland and Turkey's repudiation of the 1920 Treaty of Sèvres, at Turkey's insistence both countries agreed to an "exchange" of populations. Between 1923 and 1930, 1.25 million "Greeks" were "repatriated" from Turkey to Greece; a smaller number of "Turks" departed from Greece to Turkey. However, as Bernard Lewis points out, the exchanges did not imply acceptance of the European principle of nationality in which Greeks and Turks, "unwilling or unable to live as national minorities among aliens," elected to return to their homeland and live among their own people. In reality, the great majority of Anatolia's "Greeks" spoke little or no Greek. They spoke Turkish among themselves although they wrote in the Greek script. Similarly, many of the "Turks" in Greece and Crete spoke Greek among themselves and knew little or no Turkish. The expulsions were actually based on religion. Turkish-speaking Christians faithful to the Greek Orthodox Church were expelled to Greece, a "homeland" they had never known, while Greek-speaking Muslims were expelled to Turkey.[53] The Armenian genocide, the absorption-conversion program, and what was, in effect, the expulsion of Turkey's "Greeks" all shared a common objective, the elimination of a significant Christian demographic presence from Turkey. The methods varied, but all three can be seen as religiously motivated state-sponsored programs of population elimination.

Finally, I take note of an authoritative report based entirely on Arab sources entitled "Contemporary Islamist Ideology Authorizing Genocidal

Murder" by Yigal Carmon in which he demonstrates that today's radical Islamists regard genocide as a legitimate weapon against those whom they regard as enemies of Islam.[54] Holding that Islam is now under attack, they see unremitting *jihad* as both defensive in character and *the single most important Muslim religious obligation*. It is obligatory for Muslims without restriction or limitation. No weapons or types of warfare are to be excluded. Without exception, all infidels are to be fought and, barring conversion, are to be exterminated. I must, however, stress that these are the views of the most radical elements within contemporary Islam. We do not know the extent to which the extremists can persuade or compel the Islamic mainstream to share their views.

3

The Nazi-Muslim Connection and Hajj Amin al-Husseini, the Mufti of Jerusalem

More than any other historical actor, Hajj Amin al-Husseini (1895–1974) served as the connecting link between the world of Islam and National Socialism before, during, and after World War II.[1] Between 1917, when Lord Arthur James Balfour (1848–1930) wrote to Lord Walter Rothschild (1868–1937) informing him that "His Majesty's Government looks with favour the establishment in Palestine of a national home for the Jewish people" and the 1948 Israeli War of Independence, no Muslim leader played a more important, albeit controversial role, in the attempt to thwart the establishment of that "national home" than Hajj Amin al-Husseini. His war against the Jews was never a territorial conflict amenable to negotiation and compromise; from start to finish, it was an uncompromising *jihad* in the path of Allah. The Mufti would have considered even the slightest concession to the Jews a betrayal of and a rebellion against God Himself. His story is important not only for what it tells us about the continuing Israeli-Palestinian conflict, but for the light it sheds on the enduring conflict between the West and Radical Islam.

Amin al-Husseini, the future Mufti of Jerusalem, came from one of Jerusalem's most powerful Arab families, the Husseinis.[2] In 1912 Amin studied Islamic jurisprudence, theology, and philosophy for one year at Cairo's al-Azhar University. In 1913 he went on a pilgrimage to Mecca, earning the honorary title of "Hajj." When war broke out in 1914 Hajj Amin enlisted in the Ottoman army, serving as an artillery officer. In November 1916, he was stricken with dysentery and sent home. He never returned to his unit.

As early as his student days, Amin saw Zionism as a long-term threat to Palestine's Arabs. In 1918, he is reported to have made his views known to I. A. Abbady, a Jewish scholar and translator born in Palestine. Abbady and the future Mufti were the Hebrew and Arabic translators respectively in Reuters' Jerusalem news bureau for several months. Amin is reported to have told Abbady that he did not object to Jews born in Palestine but that "those alien invaders, the Zionists, will be massacred to the last man. We want no progress, no prosperity [from Jewish immigration]. Nothing but the sword will decide the future of this country."[3]

It is worth noting that at the time there was no hint of support for a *worldwide* program of extermination in the future Mufti's remarks. Having served in the Ottoman army, he was undoubtedly aware of the 1915 Armenian genocide, but as much as he hated Jews, a global genocide would remain beyond his reach for several decades. Moreover, until 1937 the Mufti apparently believed that he could end the Zionist project by political and diplomatic means and was willing to work with the British in the hope of getting them to revoke the Balfour Declaration. Although he played a leading role in fomenting murderous anti-Jewish riots in Palestine in 1920, 1921, 1929, and 1936–1939, his basic motive appears to have been to convince the British that the Arabs would never tolerate an autonomous Zionist community in Palestine and that it was in Britain's interest to side with the Arabs.

It was not until the Mufti's World War II sojourn in Nazi Germany, during which time he worked closely with leaders of the SS (the *Schutzstafel*) and the *Reichssicherheitshauptamt* (Reich Security Head Agency, RSHA), the organization responsible for the implementation of Hitler's "Final Solution of the Jewish Problem," that he came to understand that the Nazi Final Solution could also be the Arab Final Solution. The equation was simple: Every Jew the Nazis murdered was one less Jew who could enter Palestine.

THE MUFTI'S EARLY ACTIVISM

Hajj Amin's anti-Jewish activism began in earnest during the weeklong Nabi Musa (Prophet Moses) festivities that began April 4, 1920, when he helped to incite an angry Arab mob, both Muslim and Christian, to deadly violence against Jews.[4] Five Jews were murdered and 216 wounded, 18 critically. Two Jewish girls were raped.[5] In response, Ze'ev (Vladimir) Jabotinsky, founder of Haganah, led an armed Jewish self-defense group against the rioters. Five Arabs were killed and 21 wounded.[6] Hajj Amin fled to Transjordan, as the Kingdom of Jordan was then known, but was sentenced in absentia to ten years in prison for his role in the bloodshed.

Later that summer, Sir Herbert Samuel, the first British High Commissioner for Palestine and a member of a prominent Anglo-Jewish family, pardoned him while Jabotinsky was sentenced to fifteen years in prison. He was released within a year.

A year later, from May 1 to May 7, 1921, there was another bloody riot. Forty-five Jews were killed and 146 wounded, and 48 Arabs were killed and 73 wounded while the Arab police stood by or joined in. Unlike the Nabi Musa riots, these seem to have been unplanned, although the publication of a translation of *The Protocols of the Elders of Zion* and a stream of viciously anti-Jewish propaganda in the Arabic press contributed to an atmosphere conducive to explosive communal violence.

The Mufti's biographers differ as to his culpability, but the riots did not hurt him politically.[7] On May 8, 1921, Samuel appointed Amin Mufti of Jerusalem in spite of his weak qualifications. The Muslim electors were supposed to choose from the top three candidates. Amin ranked fourth. Having studied for only one year at Cairo's al-Azhar University, the preeminent Sunni institution for Islamic jurisprudence, he was not considered as knowledgeable as the other candidates. He did, however, have the support of the prestigious Husseini family and senior members of the British colonial administration, most of whom were hostile to Zionism and persuaded that Hajj Amin and his powerful family could maintain law and order.[8]

As Mufti, Hajj Amin was a senior government official in the colonial administration. In 1922 he was elected president (*Rais al 'Ulama*) of the Supreme Muslim Council (SMC), an institution authorized by the British to direct Muslim religious affairs. In that position, he had "unlimited rights of patronage and control over the Islamic religious hierarchy of Palestine, over Moslem (sic) schools, religious courts, and *waqf* (Muslim religious trust) funds."[9] One of the SMC's most important functions was the appointment of imams in Palestine's mosques. Given his religious authority and his control over patronage, the new Mufti quickly became Palestine's most powerful Muslim leader.

During the 1920s one of the Mufti's most important initiatives was the renovation of the *al-Aqsa* Mosque and the Mosque of Omar, also known as the Dome of the Rock. Both were situated on the Temple Mount, or the *Haram al-Sharif* as it is known to Muslims. The mosques had fallen into disrepair and with British support the Mufti organized a massive fund-raising campaign in 1923 and 1924 throughout the Muslim world. By the end of the decade the Dome of the Rock was renovated and plated with gold.[10]

The campaign for the *Haram al-Sharif* was religiously motivated. It was also an important step in the transformation of the Arab-Jewish conflict from a local political dispute to a larger religious conflict. The predominantly secular Zionists had no plans to rebuild the Jerusalem Temple, a project that would have necessitated the destruction of Islam's third holiest site, but some Zionist leaders were imprudent enough to exploit Jewish yearnings for a restored Temple for fund-raising purposes.[11] Unfortunately, the Muslims tended to believe that Jewish colonization plans ultimately involved the destruction of the site and its replacement by a restored Third Temple. Although such rumors were hardly credible, as the religious leader of Palestine's Muslims, the Mufti understood their propaganda value. Throughout his career, Hajj Amin never ceased to claim that the *Haram al-Sharif* was endangered by the alleged plans of the Yishuv, Palestine's Jewish community, for the Temple's restoration.

In addition to continuing resentment over the Balfour Declaration, Arab fears over the fate of the *Haram al-Sharif* finally exploded in 1928 and 1929 in a series of bloody incidents over the right of Jewish worship at the Western Wall, the only remaining part of the ancient Temple built by Herod and, as such, Judaism's holiest site. The structure is also the western wall of the *Haram al-Sharif* from which Muhammad is said to have begun his night journey to heaven. Arabs call the wall *al-Buraq* after the steed which Muhammad is alleged to have tethered there.[12]

The Ottoman Empire considered Jewish worship a privilege, not a right. In theory, Jews were not permitted to bring to the site an ark containing the Torah scrolls, chairs or benches for the elderly, or a screen to separate the sexes, as was customary in Orthodox synagogues.[13] Nevertheless, long-standing, informal arrangements with the Muslims living in the neighborhood usually enabled them to get around most of the restrictions. Under the British Mandate, Jews began openly to bring religious articles to the site, while Muslims saw any concession as a first step toward a Jewish takeover of the entire Temple Mount.

On September 23, 1928, the eve of Yom Kippur, Jewish worshippers set up benches and a partition between the sexes. Learning of the situation, the Supreme Muslim Council filed a complaint with British authorities who ordered the partition dismantled. The next morning, Yom Kippur day, worshippers ignored the order whereupon British officers forcibly took down the partition. The world Jewish community reacted with outrage.

Initially, the Mufti was confident that the British authorities in Palestine would back the Muslims and, at least publicly, counseled his followers to avoid violence. He was, however, less confident about Zionist influence in London and Geneva, seat of the League of Nations, which, he feared, might compel local authorities to favor the Jews. By November 1928, he adopted an activist strategy, distributing leaflets throughout the Muslim world claiming that the Jews planned to take over the *al-Aqsa* Mosque. This led to attempts to disrupt Jewish services at the wall and beating and stoning of Jews. For example, mules were driven through the area where the Jews prayed, often dropping excrement.[14]

At the same time, the Mufti convened a General Muslim Conference in Jerusalem with delegates from Palestine, Syria, Lebanon, and Trans-jordan. Resolutions were passed claiming that the wall was more sacred to Muslims than to Jews and that the rights of Jews at the wall did not "go beyond a mere favor" granted by local residents. Phillip Mattar, a sympathetic biographer of the Mufti, found the Mufti's argument weak: "The Mufti . . . ignored the legal point that after centuries of worship the Jews had established a customary right to pray at the wall."[15] Mattar also noted that the Mufti ignored the fact that there were informal arrangements between the local residents and the Jews that allowed the Jews to bring benches and other objects to the wall for worship.

The Zionists responded to the mounting tension by demanding control of the wall. A few even advocated restoration of the Temple, thereby adding credibility to the Mufti's accusations. On Wednesday, August 14, 1929, six thousand Jews demonstrated in Tel Aviv shouting "The wall is ours" while some three thousand in number gathered at the wall for prayer. The next day was Tisha B'Ab, the traditional fast day commemorating the destruction of the Temple in 586 B.C.E. and 70 C.E. Several hundred Jews demonstrated at the wall, once again shouting "the wall is ours."

Rumors spread among the Arabs, apparently by plan, that the Jews were intending to march on the Temple Mount. Activists allied with the Mufti distributed propaganda leaflets urging Arabs to "save" the allegedly endangered sanctuary. One leaflet accused the Jews of having "violated the honor of Islam and raped the children and murdered widows and babes."[16] After an inflammatory Friday sermon on August 16, 1929, demonstrators organized by the Supreme Muslim Council and chaired by the Mufti marched out of the *Haram* to the wall where they burned Jewish prayer books and other religious articles.

The following Friday, thousands of Arabs, many armed with knives, assembled on the Temple Mount. After prayers, they attacked Jews and set fire to Jewish shops throughout the city. The next day a Jew was killed in Jerusalem. With an undermanned, predominantly Arab police force, the British could do little to control the situation. At the government's request, the Mufti and several other Muslims leaders called on the Arabs to "avoid bloodshed" and resolve the issues peacefully. Nevertheless, the Jews suspected that the Mufti was clandestinely inciting the rioters.[17]

The worst carnage took place in Hebron during the week of August 23, 1929. About sixty-seven unarmed, anti-Zionist Orthodox Jews of all ages were the victims of the mob's homicidal rage. Ironically, three days earlier the Hebron Jewish community had rejected a Haganah offer to defend them, claiming that they trusted Hebron's Arab leadership to protect them.[18] Some of the victims were castrated, others tortured, decapitated, and/or burned alive. Women were raped before being murdered.[19] In at least one case, a child was beheaded by an Arab policeman in British service.[20] In one week, 133 Jews were murdered and 339 wounded.[21]

The inevitable commission of inquiry met during March 1930. The Zionists accused the Mufti of having fomented the violence. In his testimony, the Mufti accused the Jews of attacking the Arabs and referred to the infamous forgery *The Protocols of the Elders of Zion* as evidence, as he was frequently to do throughout his career.[22] While faulting the Mufti for failing to restrain his followers, the commission, headed by Sir Walter Shaw, absolved him of complicity. The commission also recommended that the issues of Jewish immigration, the wall, and the sale of Arab land to Jews be reconsidered. One member, Lord Harry Snell, disagreed with the commission's finding absolving the Mufti. In 1937, the commission's report was reexamined and Lord Snell's minority report was determined to be well-founded.[23] Nevertheless, it was once again clear to the Arabs that violence pays.

THE ARAB REBELLION: 1936–1939

The Shaw Commission's report found that the "fundamental cause" of the 1929 violence was Arab "racial animosity" stemming from Jewish immigration and "fear for their [the Arabs'] economic future."[24] From the start of British rule, most officials in the foreign and colonial offices, as well as the military, were convinced that the creation of a Jewish homeland would not only alienate the Arab population but would require the use of force against the indigenous majority on behalf of Jews of Russian origin thought to be Bolshevik. The same officials failed to distinguish between Zionism and Bolshevism.[25] Doubts were also expressed concerning Palestine's absorptive capacity, which ultimately proved far greater than the British officials anticipated.

After the riots, London set up a Royal Commission headed by Sir John Hope-Simpson to investigate the related issues of Jewish immigration, settlement, and land sales. On October 21, 1930, Simpson issued the commission's report opposing further Jewish immigration primarily on the grounds that the land was not able to support continued immigration.[26] On the same day, the colonial secretary Lord Passfield (Sydney Webb) issued a white paper based on the Shaw Report that placed stringent limits on further Jewish immigration and land purchase.[27] The Passfield White Paper did not stand for long. On February 13, 1931, Prime Minister Ramsay MacDonald wrote to Chaim Weizmann effectively reversing the

Passfield restrictions on immigration and land purchase.[28] Nevertheless, once again experience taught the Mufti that violence paid off.

As the British-appointed Mufti of Jerusalem, Hajj Amin had to play a double game. His core followers were implacable opponents of Zionism prepared to do whatever was necessary to destroy the Yishuv. Yet, he was dependent upon the Mandatory government for his position and the power that enabled him to be a leader in the struggle against the Jews. As long as he believed that pressure, diplomacy, and politics could realistically achieve his objectives, he was determined to avoid an open break with the British.

Nevertheless, his heart was elsewhere. In the early 1930s, enthusiasm for Adolf Hitler and National Socialism was very strong in much of the Arab world, save for Arab communists. Even before January 31, 1933, when Hitler came to power, the Mufti and other Arab leaders recognized their affinity with National Socialism based largely, but not entirely, on National Socialism's hostility to Jews and Judaism.[29] Like the Nazis, the Mufti also believed in the *Führerprinzip*, the principle of top-down, dictatorial leadership and unconditional obedience from below. Arab leaders also saw in the uniformed *Hitlerjugend* a model for their own youth militias, the *Futtuwa*.

Although a few Germans saw an affinity between Islam and National Socialism, most did not reciprocate Arab enthusiasm until 1936. Before then, the Nazis had a measure of racial contempt for Arabs as Semites, a contempt expressed by Hitler in *Mein Kampf*. In addition, Hitler initially hoped for an alliance with England, which he saw as an Aryan Germanic nation capable of holding back Asiatic "hordes" from the Mediterranean and from Europe.[30] By 1936 both the Arabs and the Nazis understood that they were united in a common hatred of the Jews and a shared hostility to British rule in the Middle East.

By 1938 articles began to appear in the Arab press in which Hitler was likened to the Prophet Muhammad and praised as the "*Mahdi*" who, according to Sunni and Shi'ite tradition, is expected to arise before the day of judgment, institute a global Islamic kingdom of perfect justice, and, in the last days, fight alongside the returned Islamic prophet Isa (Jesus) against *Daijal*, the Antichrist or false Messiah who is often depicted as in league with the Jews.[31] Congenial contacts were developed between Arab leaders in the Middle East and the leadership of the National Socialist Party. Arab delegations were regularly invited to National Socialist Party congresses and Arab nationalist organizations modeled their organization and structure after comparable National Socialist organizations.

Nevertheless, initially National Socialist Germany had strong economic and demographic motives for supporting German-Jewish emigration to Palestine. Nazi Germany's first Jewish policy was elimination through emigration, not extermination. In August 1933, the German economics ministry signed the *Haavara* Agreement with the Zionist Organization of Germany and the Anglo-Palestine bank. German currency restrictions had hitherto prevented Jews from taking their money out of the country. Under the new agreement, Jewish assets could be placed in special blocked bank accounts in Germany and the funds paid to German exporters for merchandise, including agricultural and industrial machinery, to be sold to both Jews and Arabs in the Middle East. The proceeds from the sales were deposited in the Anglo-Palestine Bank. When the Jewish emigrants arrived in Palestine, they received a partial reimbursement in pounds sterling from the Jewish Agency, a semiautonomous arm of the World Zionist Organization.[32]

The agreement stimulated German industry at a time of large-scale unemployment. It also fostered the very emigration the Arabs sought to prevent. Refugees did not enter Palestine penniless. They were able to leave Germany with a portion of their assets intact, an important consideration for the British. The agreement was controversial in those Jewish circles that sought to undo Hitler's anti-Semitic policies by a worldwide boycott of German goods. By contrast, the Zionists saw no future for Jews in Germany, and the agreement did enable some forty thousand Jews to escape the Holocaust.[33]

While the Mufti was unwilling to fight the British openly in the mid-1930s, other Arab leaders were entirely willing, the most important being the Syrian-born religious militant, Sheikh 'Izz al-Din al-Qassam. The sheikh became politically active after French troops occupied Damascus on July 26, 1920, and forced into exile Faisal, the Hashemite king of Iraq, who had been made king of Greater Syria (Syria and Lebanon) by the Syrian National Congress on March 7, 1920. Opposing French occupation, al-Qassam formed a guerrilla band, gave its members military training, and implanted in them "a strong sense of *jihad*."[34] Sentenced to death by the French, al-Qassam escaped and made his way to Haifa.[35] Shortly thereafter, he was appointed imam of Haifa's al-Istiqiāl Mosque. By the mid-1920s, he was sufficiently well-established to begin openly preaching *jihad*, although he was not yet ready to take up arms against either the British or the Jews.

As Jewish immigration to Palestine increased under the pressure of European anti-Semitism and the rise of Hitler, so too did Arab radicalization. As a consequence of Jewish land purchase, thousands of Arabs experienced eviction, involuntary urbanization, and downward social mobility. However, rural out-migration and its destabilizing consequences was a global phenomenon. The growth of modern anti-Semitism was partly due to the rationalization of agriculture in Eastern Europe that had transformed a goodly portion of that region's peasants into involuntary migrants, landless wage workers, and/or members of the urban under-class. Agriculture rationalization also transformed Europe's Jews from a complementary economic class in predominantly agrarian Europe into a class thrown into competition with the newly urbanized European peasants.[36] It was largely to escape the more disruptive consequences of that development that Jews had immigrated to Palestine.

As Arab radicalization intensified, it took on a religious aspect. Al-Qassam became one of the first Muslim religious leaders personally prepared to give up his life in *jihad* against Palestine's Jews.[37] In 1930 he obtained a *fatwa* from the Mufti of Damascus, Sheikh Badr al-Din al-Täj al-Hasani, authorizing *jihad* against the British and the Jews.[38] In 1930 and 1931, Qassamites launched attacks on Jewish settlements, killing a number of Jews and destroying a large number of trees and other property. One Qassamite group attacked Moshav Nahalal, the first Zionist cooperative agricultural community, on December 23, 1932. They threw a bomb into a house in the Moshav, killing a father and son. The attack was not a rogue operation. Al-Qassam himself was present when it was planned at Qassamite headquarters.[39]

The existence of the clandestine Qassamite terror network finally came to light when the killers were caught and confessed. An investigation followed in which al-Qassam was not named. Nevertheless, he decided to suspend active operations temporarily. Living in the port city of Haifa, al-Qassam witnessed the growing Jewish immigration and was determined to end it. He was reported to have sent the Mufti a message in 1933 informing the latter of his intention to start a revolt in the north and requesting Hajj Amin to do the same in the south. The Mufti is reported to have declined, declaring that he was seeking a political rather than a military solution.[40]

With the rise of Nazi Germany and Italy's successful war against Abyssinia (October 1935–May 1936), the Arabs hoped that Germany and Italy would defeat England and France in the coming global war, "liberate" Palestine, and destroy the Yishuv. In the meantime, Palestine's Arab leaders understood that Britain was willing to pay a heavy price to maintain peace in the Middle East.

When an arms shipment consisting of eight hundred rifles and four hundred thousand rounds of ammunition intended for a Jewish importer in Jaffa was accidentally discovered on October 16, 1935, al-Qassam decided to resume guerrilla operations. On the anniversary of the Balfour Declaration, November 2, 1935, the Arabs responded to the weapons discovery with mass demonstrations in Nablus and Haifa. Shortly thereafter, al-Qassam left Haifa to engage in *jihad* in the northern hill country. Before departing, he informed the Mufti of his plans and requested that the latter join him in calling for *jihad* against the British.[41] The Mufti sent an unspecified amount of money, but did not want to break with either al-Qassam or the British.

On November 7, 1935, some of al-Qassam's followers clashed with three policemen serving the mandatory government. Two were Arab, one Jewish. Sparing the Arabs, they killed the Jew. The police began a manhunt and on November 19, 1935, found al-Qassam with some followers in a cave near the Arab village of Ya'bad. A gun battle ensued in which al-Qassam refused to surrender and commanded his companions to join him in a fight to the death. The fight lasted between four and six hours. Its effects continue to reverberate to this day.

Two of his companions were killed with al-Qassam, who became a *shaheed*, a Muslim martyr serving the cause of Allah.[42] On March 2, 2002, the Izz al-Din al-Qassam Brigades, the military wing of Hamas, launched its first of many Qassam rockets from Gaza at an Israeli target that were to provoke a military response from Israel in 2009.

Wholly underestimating the significance of al-Qassam's death, the British delivered the bodies of al-Qassam and his companions to their families two days later. The next day, thousands attended his funeral. Arab Haifa went on strike and prayers were said for al-Qassam and his companions in every Palestinian town and village.[43]

Opinions differ concerning Hajj Amin's relations with al-Qassam. *Nevertheless, whatever their differences, both saw the destruction of the Yishuv as an unconditional religious imperative.* After al-Qassam's death, it was in the Mufti's interest to claim strong ties with him. For very different reasons, the Zionists had a similar interest in stressing the Mufti's ties with al-Qassam. The Zionists wanted to discredit Hajj Amin as a trustworthy negotiating partner with the British. At the time, the Mufti was not inclined actively to initiate *jihad* against the Jews. Such a move would have compromised his carefully cultivated public posture of moderation.[44] Nevertheless, Hajj Amin could hardly ignore the political impact of al-Qassam's death and began to build bridges and offer financial support to the Qassamite movement.

Some of al-Qassam's followers survived and were determined to carry on *jihad*. On April 15, 1936, Qassamites killed two Jews and wounded another in an ambush near Tulkarm. On April 19, unemployed peasants and migrant workers from Syria ran amok in Jaffa, killing nine Jews and wounding sixty. The incident was followed by Zionist acts of retaliation and further violence, whereupon the British declared a state of emergency. The same night, representatives of the main Arab factions met in Nablus and declared a four-day general strike.

Ten days later, representatives of six major Arab political groups met in Jerusalem and established the Arab Higher Committee (AHC) with Hajj Amin as chairman. The AHC assumed leadership of the Arab struggle.

Before the month was out, the committee declared that the general strike would not end unless the mandatory power put an end to Jewish immigration and land transfers. The committee also demanded a popularly elected legislature, a move that would have ensured an Arab majority and political control of Palestine. The AHC declared that if its demands were not met by May 15, Palestine's Arab community would turn to active resistance.[45] In effect, the committee issued an ultimatum. The Arab Revolt of 1936 was under way.

As noted, the revolt was encouraged by Arab perception of British weakness in dealing with Germany and Italy, and by Britain's problems in Egypt, India, and elsewhere in her far-flung empire.[46] The revolt also marked the beginning of active German and Italian support of the Mufti and the Arab cause.

Italy appears to have been the first to offer such support. Britain and Italy were at odds over Italy's invasion and annexation of Abyssinia, and the Italians saw aid to the Arabs as a step toward fulfilling Benito Mussolini's ambition of transforming the Mediterranean into *Mare Nostrum*, "our sea." If Count Galeazzo Ciano, Italy's wartime foreign minister, is to be believed, the Mufti and his movement received funds from Italy at this time.[47] Inevitably, Mussolini's neo-Roman empire would have led to the exclusion of Britain from the Middle East and blocked its maritime route to India. Germany also began to send funds and military supplies, though on a smaller scale, to the Arabs in Palestine.

As head of the Arab Higher Committee, Hajj Amin was responsible for organizing the general strike. Wearing one hat, he counseled moderation; wearing the other, he was involved in clandestine warfare against both the British and the Jews. Nevertheless, the AHC denied any connection between Hajj Amin, the rebellion, and terrorism. As one contemporary British observer commented, the Mufti appeared to be "playing a double game."[48]

Sir Arthur Wauchope, high commissioner for Palestine at the time, also had a balancing problem. He was aware of the Mufti's need to balance his roles of Arab leader and mandatory official. Wauchope also had to decide whether to use force to end the Arab revolt or rely on the Mufti's ability to hold Arab extremists in check. Initially, he relied on the Mufti, but to no avail. The AHC voted to continue the strike and called for nonpayment of taxes beginning May 15, 1936, on the principle of "no taxation without representation." This did not sit well with the British and the high commissioner drew up contingency plans for the deportation of the Mufti and the committee.[49] The Mufti continued to avoid a breach with the British, but the leaders of the normally more moderate Nashashibi clan, the Husseini family's most important Jerusalem rivals, steadily applied pressure on the Supreme Muslim Council to join the strike. As president of the council, Hajj Amin could not openly do this without losing his position as Mufti, which may have been why the Nashashibis pressured him.

In addition to violence done to people, Arabs deliberately destroyed orchards and groves, uprooting an estimated two hundred thousand "Jewish" trees.[50] Initially, British forces were overwhelmed and lost control of much of the country, but on September 7, 1936, they proclaimed martial law. Twenty thousand troops were brought in from Britain and Egypt. Several thousand auxiliary Jewish policemen were also recruited. These measures enabled the government to gain control of the urban areas, but the rural areas were largely controlled by the rebels who, aided by volunteers from Syria, Iraq, and Transjordan, conducted a campaign of increasingly competent guerrilla warfare. However, by September the rebellion had spent itself. It was over in October after the AHC employed the charade of responding to an "appeal" it had itself solicited from Arab rulers to end the strike. Nevertheless, the British did not meet the Arab demand to end Jewish immigration.

Once again, the British set up a royal commission of inquiry, this time headed by Lord William Robert Peel, to investigate the situation. The commission arrived in Palestine in November 1936. The Mufti refused to appear before the commission unless Jewish immigrations were immediately suspended, a condition the commission rejected although it did reduce the immigration quota from forty-five hundred to eighteen hundred. The Mufti finally agreed to testify in January 1937 after it became obvious that his hard-line position was counterproductive.

When the Mufti testified, the commission asked him whether "the country can assimilate and digest the 400,000 Jews now in the country?" He replied, "No." He was then asked whether the removal process would be "kindly or painful." The Mufti replied evasively: "We must leave all this to the future."

Undeceived by Hajj Amin's evasions, the commission offered the following comment:

> . . . we cannot forget what happened recently, despite treaty provisions and explicit assurances, to the Assyrian [Christian] minority in Iraq; nor can we forget that the hatred of the Arab politician for the [Jewish] National Home has never been concealed and that it has now permeated the Arab population as a whole.[51]

The committee was under no illusions concerning the likely fate of Palestine's Jews under Arab rule. Iraq had gained independence from Britain in August 1933. One year later Iraqi Muslims perpetrated a massacre of Iraq's Assyrian Christian population, a *jihad*, in which more than three thousand were murdered, with women and children raped and tortured. When British prime minister Ramsay MacDonald learned of the slaughter, he hurried to London from Scotland to deal personally with the crisis. By contrast, King Faisal of Iraq booked a flight to Switzerland "to continue his cure."[52] This royal son of the Sharif of Mecca and guardian of Islam's holiest site had no intention of letting humanitarian considerations restrain either the *jihad* or his "cure."

In its report published July 7, 1937, the Peel Commission concluded that the original mandate was unworkable and that the only viable solution would be to partition Palestine into separate Jewish and Arab states. The commission recommended that the Jews be given less than 20 percent of the territory, approximately five thousand square kilometers, primarily in the north and the coastal plain. Peel also recommended a population transfer of 225,000 Arabs out of and 1,250 Jews into the Jewish state, so that the latter would not contain almost as many Arabs as Jews.[53]

The Zionists were bitterly divided over the commission's proposal but finally accepted it at the Twentieth Zionist Congress in August 1937 by a vote of 299 to 160. Led by David Ben Gurion, the Zionists saw the real beginnings of the Jewish state in two fundamental aspects of the proposal: a miniature Jewish state and population transfer. They were also confident that the proposed state would not remain confined to its original borders.

In the early 1920s, political leaders and senior bureaucrats, including some Arabs, looked with a measure of favor upon population transfers. In spite of their human dislocations, such programs were not considered ethnic cleansing but a "humane" method of "solving" intractable minority problems and achieving national integration. For example, in accordance with the Treaty of Lausanne of 1923 that brought to an end the Greco-Turkish War of 1919–1922, Greece and Turkey agreed upon a compulsory population exchange of approximately 1.5 million "Greeks" and four hundred thousand "Turks." The transfer brought to a close the three-thousand-year-old ethnic Greek presence in Asia Minor. Nevertheless, the exchange was cited as a model to be followed by the Peel Commission when it proposed partition.[54]

In accepting the commission's recommendations, Ben-Gurion believed that the transferred Arabs would be resettled in underpopulated Transjordan. In 1922 the original League of Nations Mandate for Palestine had been divided into two distinct administrative units, the territory east of the Jordan River, designated as Transjordan, and the western territory which continued to be known as Palestine. Jewish settlement was strictly forbidden in the territory east of the Jordan.[55]

The Mufti rejected the Peel Commission's partition proposal and was prepared to prevent the establishment of a Jewish state, no matter how small its territory and by whatever means necessary. As we shall see, the means came to include a genocidal *jihad*. For their part, the British decided that the Mufti had outlived his usefulness. On July 17, 1937, they attempted unsuccessfully to arrest him. He managed to escape to his *Haram al-Sharif* sanctuary where he was effectively immune from arrest or seizure. He received supporters at his sanctuary and called a Pan-Arab congress that met in Syria September 8 to 10, 1937. Attended by four hundred delegates, the conference opposed the partition and sought to enlist Arab support for the Palestinian cause.

As Zvi Elpeleg comments, the *raison d'être* of the 1937 conference was the belief that political pressure alone would suffice to persuade the British to change course. Hence, violent action was to be directed solely against Jews and moderate Arabs.[56] The turning point for the British came on September 26, 1937, when Lewis Andrews, the acting district commissioner for Galilee, and his bodyguard were assassinated by Qassamite gunmen as they were leaving the Anglican Church in Nazareth. Two days earlier, two Arab notables, one a wealthy landowner and the other a land dealer, were slain, undoubtedly in retaliation for land sales to Jews. The *New York Times* described Andrews as "one of the closest friends of the High Commissioner and also one of the most important officials of the Palestine government."[57] Andrews was also known to have helped establish Jewish communal settlements in Galilee. As usual, the Arab Higher Committee expressed "horror and condemnation of this painful incident" and urged Arabs to refrain from violence.[58]

The Mufti's double game came to an end on October 1, 1937, when the British declared the Arab Higher Committee and all local Arab national committees responsible for "the existence of an organized campaign of terrorism."[59] The government arrested and deported the four members of the committee it could find to the Seychelles Islands in the Indian Ocean. Having taken refuge in the *Haram al-Sharif*, the Mufti was not arrested but the British removed him from the presidency of the Supreme Muslim Council and deprived him of control of an annual income of £70,000, a large sum at the time.

The British actions had the predictable effect of strengthening the Mufti's authority as the leader of the revolt. From the *Haram*, he continued to maintain contact with other revolt leaders and no longer pretended moderation. On October 13, he escaped in disguise and made his way to French-controlled Lebanon.[60] A wave of terror began the very next day. Some suspect that before his escape the Mufti assembled a group of guerrilla leaders and instructed them to launch it.[61]

Out of reach of the British and tolerated by the French, the Mufti was now in a position openly to direct Arab gang leaders in their attacks on Jews and their property and to disrupt British military and civilian installations. Widespread sabotage followed. The Arabs were in complete control in many localities. Even Jerusalem's Old City had to be retaken from the rebels. In addition to terror attacks against Jews and the British, the Mufti's targets now included rival contenders for Arab leadership, such as the Nashashibis and others who stood in the way of his absolute domination of Arab Palestine. A veritable civil war followed. Political differences often gave way to old feuds and murder as the method of settling grievances. The situation became so perilous that in September 1938 a group of Haifa intellectuals sent a representative to the Mufti in Lebanon to ask him to issue a *fatwa* declaring that the murder of an Arab by another Arab was an unpardonable offense. He refused.[62]

By the summer of 1939 the rebellion had spent itself, but it was hardly a failure. On May 17, 1939, the British government published the white paper that provided for the limitation of Jewish immigration to seventy-five thousand in the next five years after which "no further Jewish immigration will be permitted unless the Arabs of Palestine are prepared to acquiesce in it." It further stipulated that, as of the date of publication, "the High Commissioner will be given general powers to prohibit and regulate transfers of land."[63]

When France and Britain declared war on Germany on September 3, 1939, French authorities placed the Mufti under virtual house arrest and asked him to announce his support for the Allies. He had other ideas. On October 13, 1939, having bribed the French chief of police in Syria, he escaped to Baghdad.[64]

Hajj Amin's arrival in Iraq was hardly welcome news for the government of Nuri al-Sa'id, Iraq's pro-British prime minister, but the Mufti's leadership of the Arab cause in Palestine had made him a popular hero. A British Intelligence Report dated December 1, 1941, reads in part:

> As soon as he [Hajj Amin] arrived, he was generally acclaimed as an Arab national hero and parties were given in his honor by every leading personality from the Prime Minister downwards, as well as by all Nationalist Clubs and Societies. To these parties were invited other well known Syrian and Palestinian political refugees as well as Iraq's own reactionary politicians and they became a veritable demonstration of Arab nationalist feeling and unity.[65]

Nuri al-Sa'id requested that the Mufti refrain from "undesirable activities," a promise he could hardly have been expected to keep once he found his bearings. As in other Arab countries, Iraqi sentiment was strongly pro-German. Unlike Britain and France, Germany was not seen as an imperialist, colonial power. As noted, the rise of National Socialism was viewed positively in much of the Arab world that shared National Socialism's hatred of the Jews and its desire to bring down the British and French colonial empires. The latter theme was expressed in a popular verse in the local dialect that made the rounds in Damascus, Homs, and Aleppo:

No more 'monsieur'; no more 'mister'
God in heaven; on earth Hitler.[66]

On March 31, 1940, Iraq's pro-British prime minister resigned and was succeeded by the pro-Axis Rashid 'Ali al-Qailani, sometimes referred to as Gailani, a development in which the Mufti played an important part.[67] Rashid 'Ali was prime minister from Nuri's resignation to January 31, 1941. He was succeeded in turn by pro-British Tāha al-Hāshimi who served for two months until forced out of office by a pro-Axis coup that restored Rashid 'Ali to office on April 3, 1941.

Now the Mufti was free openly to pursue his pro-Axis political objectives. The British Intelligence Report cited above lists some of the principal sources of his funding:

The ex-Mufti's funds . . . were considerable. . . . He was voted ID 18,000 [Iraqi dinar=Pound Sterling] by the Iraqi Parliament, was paid ID 1,000 a month from Iraqi secret service funds, was paid 2% of the salary of every Iraqi government official, including the Military and Police (all stopped at source). . . . In addition, authoritative sources now claim he was paid ID 60,000 by the Germans and ID 40,000 by the Italians.[68]

The Mufti had the political clout, the organizational ability, and the financial resources to foster his primary objective, to align Iraq with the wartime Axis powers. He was also able to gather his own circle of followers from Palestine and Syria and provide many of them with good jobs in the Iraqi government. His network included badly needed professionals, many of whom were unemployable at home because of their political activities. Their influence quickly spread throughout Iraq. As 1940 drew to a close, the Mufti had become a dominant power in Iraq's domestic politics.

Adopting an initial posture of neutrality, Rashid 'Ali proceeded cautiously in spite of his pro-German sympathies. However, the Mufti and four highly influential officers known as the "Golden Square" were determined openly to align Iraq with the Axis. Even before Rashid 'Ali took office, Hajj Amin was in contact with German authorities. On June 21, 1940, the week during which France surrendered to Hitler's Germany, the Mufti wrote to Franz von Papen, German ambassador to Turkey, to introduce Naji Shawkat, the new Iraqi justice minister. Hajj Amin requested that von Papen convey to "His Excellency the Great Chief and Leader" the "most cordial congratulations for the great political and military victories which he had just realized by his clear thinking and his great

Spirit (*par sa clairvoyance et son Grand Génie*)." The Mufti further asked von Papen to convey to Hitler "my compliments (*mes hommages*) and my best wishes for the work undertaken in preparation for the creation of a new order of things."[69] A month later the Mufti sent his German-speaking personal secretary, Uthman Kama'al Hadda'ad, to continue talks aiming at German-Arab wartime cooperation with von Papen in Istanbul and Foreign Minister Joachim von Ribbentrop in Berlin.[70]

On January 20, 1941, the Mufti wrote directly to Hitler from Baghdad setting out the shared interests and objectives that bound the Arabs to the Axis. He stated that Britain had spared no effort in frustrating Arab efforts toward national liberation because of their strategic location at the crossroads of the British Empire's lines of communications to the East. Echoing his objections to British support of Jewish settlement, he complained that Britain had unsuccessfully planned to import into Iraq from British India "several million Hindus and settle them among the indigenous population." He declared that the "Palestine problem united all of the Arab states in a mutual hatred of the English and the Jews." He further stated that "The warm sympathy felt by the Arab peoples towards Germany and the Axis is an established fact" and that "the Arab peoples will be ready . . . to take their place alongside of the Axis in order to fulfill their part in bringing about the well-deserved defeat of the Anglo-Jewish coalition."[71]

There was as yet no hint that the Mufti was contemplating involvement in an outright campaign of genocide. Nor was Hitler ready to order the implementation of the Final Solution of the Jewish Problem although his infamous Reichstag "prophecy" of January 31, 1939, indicated that he was clearly thinking about it.[72] Initially, the Mufti seems to have had more modest aims. He wrote to Hitler that aid extended:

> to the Arabs in their war against the Zionist aspirations will, therefore, cause the Jews to lose heart. The Jews of America especially, seeing their dream shattered to pieces, will be so discouraged that they will cease to support Britain with such enthusiasm and will reconsider their position before the catastrophe.[73]

The Mufti may have been exercising caution in his first letter to Hitler.[74] However, as the war continued and implementation of the Final Solution became a realistic possibility, the Mufti came to welcome it as the way to rid Palestine of its Jews.

When Rashid 'Ali returned to office on April 3, 1941, his regime became openly pro-Nazi. Encouraged by German victories in Greece and Crete, as well as by the possibility of German aid, he abrogated the Anglo-Iraqi Treaty of 1930 that had given Britain almost unlimited rights to base military forces in Iraq and to move its troops in and through Iraq. On

April 30, 1941, Iraqi troops besieged the Royal Air Force (RAF) base at Habbaniya.[75] Although the Iraqi regime received modest Luftwaffe support and the pro-Axis Vichy French permitted the Germans to send some military equipment through Syria, German aid was insufficient. The Germans were in the final preparatory stages for Operation Barbarosa, the monumental invasion of the Soviet Union that began on June 22, 1941, and were severely limited in the aid available for Iraq.

In October 1940, recognizing the extent to which the Mufti's activities threatened Britain's vital interests, Winston Churchill approved a plot to assassinate him. Fearing the proposed assassination's effect on Arab opinion, the Colonial Office objected.[76] When Rashid 'Ali returned to power a second time, an assassination attempt was approved. The British secured the cooperation of elements of the right-wing Zionist organization, Irgun Zvi Le'umi, committed to wartime cooperation with England in spite of the white paper. On May 17, 1941, the RAF flew David Raziel, the Irgun commander, and three associates to the Habbaniya air base, to carry out the assassination. The plot was terminated the next day when a Luftwaffe fighter plane destroyed the car carrying Raziel and a British officer.

Rashid 'Ali's return to power was accompanied by a sharp intensification of anti-Semitic violence. By May 29 the pro-Axis coup had failed and the Mufti, Rashid 'Ali, and other coup leaders left the country. The next day Yūnis al-Sabcāwī, Rashid 'Ali's minister of economics and a militant pro-Nazi, declared himself military governor of Baghdad. In 1933 and 1934, Yūnis had translated Hitler's *Mein Kampf* into Arabic and published it in serial form in a newspaper. He had also been the head of *Futtuwa* youth, a government-sponsored, pro-Nazi, paramilitary organization, modeled after Germany's Hitler Youth, one of the many to spring up in Arab countries after Hitler's rise to power.[77] As military governor, he ordered the Jewish community to remain in their homes for the next three days and refrain from using their phones or communicating with each other in any way.[78] Concurrently, he prepared a broadcast calling for an uprising that would cleanse the city of the enemy within. His intent was obvious; he was preparing the way for the wholesale slaughter of Baghdad's Jewish population. Arrested by the Council for Internal Security, he was expelled from the country before his plans could be brought to fruition. The council also ordered paramilitary groups allied to him to turn in their weapons.

This apparently fortunate turn of events gave the Jewish community a false sense of security.[79] Sunday June 1, 1942, was the first day of the Jewish festival of *Shavu'ot*. Mistakenly believing the Nazi danger had passed, Jews ventured out of their homes to celebrate the festival. Riots broke out, incited by soldiers, police, and *Futtuwa* youth. The rioters were joined by civilians and Bedouins seeking booty and a cheap victory over the Jews to compensate for Rashid 'Ali's defeat. The violence turned into a *Farhud*, Arabic for "violent dispossession" or "pogrom," that lasted for forty-eight hours, while British troops stood by passively on the outskirts of Baghdad. Between 150 and 180 Jews were murdered and 600 injured. An undetermined number of women were raped and fifteen hundred homes and stores were looted.[80]

The *Farhud* marked the beginning of the end for Iraq's twenty-five-hundred-year-old Jewish community of 125,000 that began with the Babylonian Captivity under Nebuchadnezzar in 586 B.C.E. and culminated in total expulsion in 1951.[81] By the mid-1950s the fate of Iraq's ancient Jewish community was replicated in every Arab country. There was simply no longer any place for Jews in the Arab-Muslim world. In 1948 it was conservatively estimated that there were approximately 856,000 Jews in Arab lands; in 2004, there were approximately 7,635, many too old to leave. According to the Report of the Iraqi Commission of Inquiry on the *Farhud*, issued in July 1941, the most important causes of the *Farhud* were (a) Nazi propaganda disseminated by the German Legation through the Italian embassy after Iraq severed diplomatic relations with Germany[82] and (b) the activities of "Hajj Amin al-Husseini and his entourage." The report describes the activities of the Mufti and his associates:

> Once he was firmly established, he began disseminating Nazi propaganda with great cunning, while decrying the injustice done to Palestine under the guise of Pan Arabism and the Islamic Religion. He exerted a considerable influence upon people in authority and positions of military leadership—to such a degree that orders were issued from his home. His entourage also engaged in wide-scale anti-Jewish and anti-British propaganda activities among all classes.[83]

The *Farhud* was Hajj Amin's parting gift to Iraq's Jews.

With the restoration of a pro-British regime in Iraq, the Mufti fled to Iran where Riza Shah Pahlavi, Iran's ruler, granted him political asylum. Although officially neutral, wartime Iran was strongly pro-German.[84] On June 22, 1941, three weeks after the Mufti's arrival in Iran, Nazi Germany attacked the Soviet Union. When the war began, most informed Iranians expected Germany speedily to defeat Russia, capture Ukraine and the Baku oil fields, and enter Iran at a later time.[85] Both the British and the Russians regarded the possibility of a German breakthrough to Iran as a catastrophic strategic threat. In addition, the shah had issued a Declaration of Neutrality, which prevented the use of Iran as a transit corridor for the shipment of British arms aid to the Soviet Union. On August 25, 1941, the British and the Russians jointly invaded Iran. Russia occupied the north, Britain Tehran and the south. Once again the Mufti eluded the British. Disguised, he made his way through Turkey to the Balkans, Rome, and finally Berlin.

After the war, some Arabs accused the Mufti of harming the Arab cause by siding with Hitler and Mussolini. Almost thirty years later, Hajj Amin still felt the need to respond to such accusations.[86] In 1969 he argued that, unlike Britain and France, "Germany had not harmed a single Arab or Muslim state" and added that *"I was, and continue to be, convinced that, had Germany and the Axis been victorious, then no remnant of Zionism would have remained in Palestine or the Arab states* (emphasis added)."[87] As we shall see, he meant exactly what he said when he wrote that "no remnant of Zionism would have remained."

To the end of his life, the Mufti never ceased to regret Hitler's defeat and to hope that it could be reversed. Yet, in spite of his record, many Arabs claim that he was anti-Zionist but not anti-Jewish. After the war, the Mufti denied any wartime knowledge of the Holocaust. Nevertheless, the weight of evidence, both documentary and photographic, appears to contradict him. For example, according to Wolfgang Schwanitz, the Mufti claimed in his published memoirs that he often met Himmler for tea and that in the summer of 1943 Himmler told him that 3 million Jews had been liquidated.[88]

Even Philip Mattar characterizes the Mufti's denial as "false." Given the Mufti's "penchant for ferreting out information and his contacts with Heinrich Himmler," Mattar argues that it is "possible" that Hajj Amin knew about the "extermination camps."[89] In reality, Himmler was by no means the only Nazi involved in the extermination process with whom the Mufti was in contact. Nevertheless, I believe the claim that the Mufti played a role in the *decision* to exterminate Europe's Jews exaggerates his actual involvement. He undoubtedly welcomed the so-called Final Solution, but the decision to proceed from ghettoization and expulsion to extermination needed no help from him.

The Mufti arrived in Rome on October 11, 1941. He remained there less than a month during which time the Italian government treated him as a most important dignitary. He met with Benito Mussolini on October 27 and sought a public declaration of support from him for the Arab cause. Mussolini spoke of his unconditional opposition to a Jewish state and declared that there would be no place for the Jews in Europe. "If the Jews want it [a Jewish state]," he said, "they should establish Tel Aviv in America. . . ."[90] The Mufti also met with Count Galeazzo Ciano, Italy's foreign minister and Mussolini's son-in-law. Although the Mufti was encouraged by their pro-Arab, anti-Zionist positions, he did not get the public declaration of support he sought. On November 5, he left for Berlin, the real center of Axis power.

The day after his arrival, the Mufti met with Ernst von Weizsäcker, secretary of state of the German Foreign Office, to discuss his proposed public declaration of Axis support for the Arab cause. He also met with

Foreign Minister Joachim von Ribbentrop and other high-level Nazi officials. On November 28, he met with Hitler for ninety-five minutes. Also present were von Ribbentrop and Dr. Fritz Grobba, the German minister in Iraq from 1932 to 1941. The Mufti told Hitler that the Arabs "were striving for the independence and the unity of Palestine, Syria, and Iraq" and that they were "Germany's natural friends because they had the same enemies." As he did with Mussolini, he asked Hitler for a public declaration of support but Hitler was no more forthcoming than Mussolini. Hitler told the Mufti that "Germany was resolved, step by step, to ask one European nation after another to solve its Jewish problem, and at the proper time direct a similar appeal to non-European nations as well."

Several highly regarded scholars, among them Christopher Browning and Christian Gerlach, differ concerning when Hitler made known his binding decision to exterminate all of Europe's Jews. Browning argues that by mid-October 1941, "Hitler, Himmler, and Heydrich—and a widening circle of initiates thereafter were aware that the ultimate goal or vision of Nazi policy was now the systematic destruction of . . . all European Jews."[91] According to Gerlach, Hitler communicated the decision to some of his oldest and most trusted associates on December 12, 1941.[92] Whoever is correct, Hitler's decision took place in the same time period that he met with the Mufti. Moreover, several months before that meeting, Hermann Goering, then Hitler's designated successor, instructed SS *Gruppenführer* Reinhard Heydrich, head of the *Reichssicherheitshauptamt*, to draw up "an overall plan covering the organizational, technical and material measures necessary for the accomplishment of the total solution of the Jewish problem (*Gesamtösung der Judenfrage*) of which we desire."[93]

Like the Germans, the Mufti saw the Soviet Union as a mortal enemy. A Soviet victory would have been disastrous for his plans to include the Soviet Union's Muslims in an independent, greater Muslim state.[94] Although pleased when he learned of Hitler's plans for the Jews, he wanted the German leader to issue a public declaration formally recognizing the right of Arab states to attain full independence. Hitler refused, pointing out that "Germany was now engaged in severe battles to force the gateway to the northern Caucasus region." He explained that the German plan involved a *Wehrmacht* sweep through southern Russia and the Caucasus into Iran, Iraq, and the Middle East on one side while, in a vast pincer movement, Field Marshal Erwin Rommel's *Afrika Korps* conquered Northern Africa, Egypt, Palestine, and Syria from the other. Had Hitler succeeded, Germany would have gained control of this strategic region with its petroleum reserves, Britain would have lost her empire, and Germany would have become the dominant world power.[95] With a collaborationist Vichy French regime in control of Syria and Lebanon, Hitler did not want to create problems for Vichy or for Italy, which would have opposed the creation of a potentially strong Arab entity on the southern shores of the Mediterranean, Mussolini's *Mare Nostrum.*

Hitler told the Mufti that he would "carry on the battle to the total destruction of the Judeo-Communist empire in Europe" and that when "Germany's tank divisions and air squadrons" reached the southern end of the Caucasus, he would give the Arab world "the assurance that its hour of liberation had arrived." The Mufti would then be "the most authoritative spokesman for the Arab world." When the Mufti asked whether Hitler could at least enter secretly into an agreement "of the kind just outlined," Hitler replied that he had just given the Mufti "precisely that confidential declaration."[96]

In addition to his meetings with Himmler, the *Reichsführer SS,* during his sojourn in wartime Nazi Germany, the Mufti was in close contact with officers of the *Reichssicherheitshauptamt,* the SS organization directly responsible for the implementation of the so-called Final Solution. Shortly after the Mufti's arrival in Germany, the RSHA assigned *Obersturmführer* Hans Joachim Weise, a seasoned SS professional, to serve as liaison officer with the Mufti responsible for his personal safety. Weise accompanied the Mufti on his trips in Germany, Italy, and the occupied territories.[97]

EINSATZKOMMANDO EGYPT AND THE JEWS OF PALESTINE

In May 1942 Weise was instructed to set up a mobile extermination unit, *Einsatzkommando* Egypt, for Field Marshal Erwin Rommel's *Afrika Korps.* Weise was later replaced as commander by *Obersturmbannführer* Walther Rauff, but remained a member of the unit. Thereafter, Weise's principal responsibility was to serve as a liaison with Arab collaborators.[98]

Rauff was a mass-murder expert. Before assuming command of *Einsatzkommando* Egypt, Rauff had served on Heydrich's personal staff as head of the Criminal Technical Institute of the Reich Security Main Office (RSHA). He supervised the modification of scores of trucks from normal usage into mobile gas chambers capable of efficiently asphyxiating between twenty-five and sixty people at a time as the vehicle traveled to the burial site.[99]

Students of the Holocaust first became aware of the *Einsatzkommando* Egypt in 2006 when historians Klaus-Michael Mallmann of the University of Stuttgart and his assistant Martin Cüppers published their findings based on hitherto unknown or ignored German plans to exterminate the Jews of Palestine during the war.[100] Their findings were drawn from previously undisclosed documents in the archives of the Reich Security Main Office, which, as noted, had the responsibility for implementation of the Final Solution, as well as from the Foreign Office. Rauff's unit had been assembled in occupied Greece in June 1942 in anticipation of Rommel's victory in North Africa. The unit had the same function as the *Einsatzgruppen* that murdered approximately 1.25 million Jews in Eastern Europe by the spring of 1943.[101] It was attached to Rommel's command and was answerable to him. Contrary to his relatively favorable reputation even among his allied opponents, until 1944 Rommel never opposed Hitler's programs and offered no objection to the proposed extermination of Palestine's Jews under his command. In May 2007, Germany's ZDF television channel presented a two-part series on "Rommel's War," written by historians Jörg Müllner and Jean-Christoph Caron and largely based on the findings of Mallmann and Cüppers. Commenting on Rommel's role in the plan to export the Holocaust from Europe to the Muslim world, the authors dismissed as a "myth" the notion that Rommel had fought a clean war. "With his victories, he was simply preparing the way for the Nazi extermination machine."[102] Thus we see that it was altogether possible to join the German resistance, as did Rommel in 1944, yet assume command of an SS unit whose purpose was genocide.

Mallmann and Cüppers also report that the plan for the extermination of the Yishuv was coordinated with Hajj Amin al-Husseini who had conferred on the subject with Heinrich Himmler, Adolf Eichmann, and other Nazi leaders. During his meeting with Hitler, the Mufti told him that the Arabs were prepared to participate in the war in acts of sabotage and in the formation of an Arab Legion that would draw volunteers from Muslim North Africa as well as the Middle East. The Mufti's offer of Arab volunteers was arguably more important than the Mufti may himself have realized. Anticipating an ample supply of Arab volunteers, Rauff's *Einsatzgruppe* consisted of a skeleton crew of twenty-four experienced genocide professionals. In an information booklet written by the army general staff *(Generalstab des deutschen Heeres)* to prepare Rommel's troops for the conquest of Palestine, the troops were told, "Those fighting Jewry can always rely on the sympathy of the Arab population."[103]

Montgomery's victory over Rommel in the Second Battle of El Alamein (October 23–November 5, 1942) effectively put an end to Hajj Amin's plans for North Africa. It also saved the Yishuv from the fate of European Jewry at the hands of *Einsatzkommando* Egypt. Nevertheless, Rauff still had work to do in North Africa. On November 9, 1942, one week after the British breakthrough at El Alamein, the Germans invaded Tunisia. By December 12, 1942, the Germans possessed the eastern third of the country where most of the country's eighty thousand to ninety thousand Jews were to be found. From July 1942 to May 1943, Rauff was the head of the Reich Security Main Office in Tunis and leader of an *Einsatzkommando* unit. Lacking available rail connections to European extermination centers and meeting with some opposition from the Italian government, the

Germans were unable to implement the Final Solution in North Africa, although Rauff imposed on the Jewish community humiliating conditions, a punitive indemnity, and brutal slave labor in which more than twenty-five hundred Jews perished. The worst was finally over when the Allies entered Tunis on May 7, 1943.[104]

THE MUFTI'S PRO-AXIS ACTIVITIES

Rashid 'Ali also made his way to Berlin from Iran. Both men quickly began to compete for Nazi support and recognition as the leader of the Arab cause. Since both believed, as did most Arabs, that an Axis victory was inevitable, much was at stake. Although Hitler refrained from choosing between them, the Italians favored Hajj Amin.[105] In September 1942, the Mufti reached an agreement with Italian military intelligence, approved by the Italian Foreign Office, that he would set up a propaganda and intelligence center in North Africa. He also proposed to establish Arab army units under his command for active combat and sabotage behind British lines. Because of the deteriorating Axis military situation in North Africa, the plans had to be "postponed."

In spite of Rommel's defeat, the Mufti's commitment to the Nazi cause remained unwavering. The extermination of Europe's Jews offered him hope that there would be a permanent cessation of Jewish immigration into Palestine. The Nazis provided him with a special office in Berlin, the *Büro des Grossmufti*, from which he carried out his many pro-Axis activities.

Among his contributions to the Axis cause were his supervision and delivery of propaganda broadcasts. Using the facilities of German and Italian shortwave radio, he broadcast frequently to the Arab world. His Arabic speeches and sermons broadcast from Berlin were transmitted by the Zeesen (Germany) shortwave transmitter, and relayed by a powerful transmitter at Bari in southern Italy. He repeatedly called for *jihad* against both the Yishuv and world Jewry, conveying the message that fundamental Arab objectives such as the destruction of the Jewish homeland were dependent upon a Nazi victory.

Even before arriving in Germany, the Mufti had broadcast a *fatwa* from Iraq on May 10, 1941, proclaiming *jihad* against Britain. He called on his "Muslim Brothers" to join him in a *"jihad* for God, for the defense of Islam" and to fight "the tyranny that always had as its aim the destruction of Islam in every land." He complained that, having brought about the dissolution of the Ottoman Caliphate and India's Muslim Empire, the British Empire included more than 220 million Muslims. His bitterest complaint, however, was reserved for Palestine, where, he alleged, the English were guilty of "unheard of barbarisms" including the profanation of the *al-Aqsa* Mosque. The Mufti reminded his listeners of an alleged comment that Prime Minister William Gladstone (1809–1898) is reported to have made in Parliament that the world would never see peace as long as the Qur'an existed. The Mufti claimed that Britain's attitude toward Islam had not changed since Gladstone's era.[106]

Apart from his usual expressions of hostility to England and the Zionists, this particular accusation is interesting for what it reveals about Hajj Amin's worldview. On this occasion, as well as many others, he was playing fast and loose with the truth. Gladstone made no such statement. He was reacting to a special case, Turkish brutality in suppressing the Bulgarian Rebellion of April 1876.[107] He wrote a pamphlet dated September 6, 1876, attacking the Benjamin Disraeli government for its lack of interest in the violent Ottoman repression of the rebellion, but he was very careful to state that he was not making a statement about Islam in general:

> It is not a question of Mahometanism simply, but of Mahometanism compounded with the peculiar character of a race. They are not the mild Mahometans of India, nor the chivalrous Saladins of Syria, nor the cultured Moors of Spain.[108]

Undoubtedly, British imperial policy had Christian overtones, but Britain had no interest in "destroying Islam." The British had powerful economic and political motives for maintaining their empire, which would have been seriously imperiled by an assault on Islam. This did not prevent the Mufti from seeing the British Empire as involved in a crusade against Islam. Given his religious inheritance, the idea that the political and religious orders could be discrete realms made no sense to him. Hence, he saw the British Empire's expansion as fundamentally a religio-political rather than an economic assault. And, as we have seen, he saw Zionism in similar terms.

His mindset was evident in a broadcast address to the wider Muslim world that he delivered as the principal speaker at a protest rally in Berlin's Luftwaffe Hall on November 2, 1943, the anniversary of the 1917 Balfour Declaration.[109] The event was attended by senior Nazi officials, both civilian and military, as well as members of the diplomatic corps and pro-Nazi Muslims from the Middle East, Iran, and Asia. Messages of greeting and support were sent by such senior members of the Nazi hierarchy as von Ribbentrop and Himmler in which they affirmed their commitment to "the obliteration of the Jewish National Home" (von Ribbentrop)[110] and "the fight against world Jewry (*den Kampf gegen das Weltjudentum*)" (Himmler).[111]

In keeping with the occasion, the Mufti began with an attack on the Balfour Declaration which, he claimed, was the result of a "British-Jewish conspiracy" in which "this Arab-Islamic land" with the *al-Aqsa* Mosque and other Islamic sanctuaries were treacherously "handed over" to the Jews. He alleged that this took place one year after Emir Hussein ibn Ali, sharif of Mecca, agreed to support Britain in its war against the Ottoman Empire in exchange for British support of his efforts to restore the caliphate and assume leadership of the Arab world. The agreement was spelled out in an exchange of letters between the emir and Sir Henry McMahan, the high commissioner for Egypt, during 1915 and 1916. Although Palestine is nowhere mentioned in the correspondence, the Arabs believed that it was part of the agreement.[112] The Balfour Declaration was seen as a duplicitous betrayal and part of a wider British-Jewish conspiracy.[113] In his speech, the Mufti quoted an unnamed Arabic poet to express the Arab mood:

> We expected a share of the booty when we entered the struggle
> But we ourselves became the booty.
>
> (*Wir erwarten einen Anteil an der Beute, Als wir wurden selbst die Beute.*)

The Mufti then launched into a bitter diatribe against Jews and Judaism. Claiming that the Arabs had suffered a great calamity "through the Jews," he spoke of their "depraved belief" that they are the Chosen People of God which, he claimed, had earned them the enmity and resentment of the world. As proof, he quoted the Qur'an: "You will find that the most hostily inclined toward the believers are the Jews" (5:82) and asserted that the hostility has endured for over thirteen hundred years. That verse has been a perennial favorite among anti-Semitic Muslims as "proof" of implacable Jewish hostility toward Islam.

The Mufti also asserted that the Jews had had a nefarious plan to establish a national home in Palestine and dominate the Middle East long before Lord Balfour addressed his declaration in the form of a letter to Lord Lionel Walter Rothschild. According to the Mufti, Lionel Rothschild, mistakenly identified by the Mufti as Nathaniel Rothschild, gave the "Jewish-British" prime minister Benjamin Disraeli (1804–1881) the capital with which to purchase shares in the Suez Canal Company from the bankrupt Khedive of Egypt, thereby harming Egypt and giving Britain the possibility of ruling the country. In reality, as a consequence of the financial imprudence of Ismail Pasha, Khedive of Egypt, the ruler was compelled discreetly to put his shares in the Suez Canal Company up for sale in 1875. Because of the importance of the canal to the strategic interests of the British Empire, Disraeli acted swiftly and secretly in November 1875 to acquire the shares for his government without parliamentary approval. He obtained a loan from Lionel de Rothschild to make the purchase. The banker was later reimbursed by Parliament.[114]

In the same radio tirade, the Mufti accused the Ottoman Empire's Jews of being the most important driving force in the destruction of the "Empire of the Islamic Caliphate." In effect, the Mufti was accusing the Jews of the former Ottoman Empire of having violated the *dhimma*, the Muslim pact of submission and protection imposed upon the "peoples of the Book." Such violation entailed automatic loss of all protection by the Muslim majority, with all of the hazards, not excluding loss of life, such outlaw status entailed. Amin's accusation was based upon the charge, often employed by contemporary Islamists to discredit Islamic modernization, namely, that Mustafa Kemal Attaturk (1881–1938), founder and first president of the modern secular Turkish republic, was in reality a member of the Dönmeh sect and, as such, a false Muslim and a real crypto-Jew who aimed at the destruction of Islam.[115] The Mufti's accusation was similar to the Nazi accusation that the Jews conspired to bring about Germany's defeat in World War I and in its own way was equally poisonous.

The Mufti also included in the speech the accusation, long a staple of Islamist anti-Jewish propaganda, that the Jews wanted to destroy the *al-Aqsa* Mosque and restore the ancient Jerusalem sanctuary. Insofar as he regarded the conflict with the Jews as, at bottom, a war of religion, this was potentially one of the most serious charges against Zionism he could make. As noted, from the start of his career the Mufti depicted the conflict as a *jihad* over sacred space, a view that continues to this day among radical Islamists and is expressed in the Charter of Hamas. As noted elsewhere in this work, Article 11 of the charter states that "The land of Palestine is an Islamic *Waqf* [an inalienable religious endowment] consecrated for future Muslim generations until the day of Resurrection. . . ."[116]

Actually, Muslim fears were not without a tenuous basis in fact. After the Romans destroyed the Jerusalem Temple in 70 C.E., the rabbis taught Jews to pray for its restoration and to study the laws of the Temple sacrifices in anticipation of its eventual restoration. For most traditional Jews, restoration came to be thought of as inseparable from Israel's final messianic redemption and not a matter of human agency.[117] In the aftermath of Israel's victory in the 1967 war, a small number of religious Jews experienced intense messianic enthusiasm, a development both Israel's secular government and its leading rabbis discouraged.[118] Nevertheless, Jewish messianic extremists and Christian end-timers, sometimes working together, regarded the *al-Aqsa* Mosque and the Dome of the Rock as an abomination whose destruction would be an indispensable prelude to redemption.[119] One group of extremists, whose number included army officers with a competent knowledge of explosives, attempted to dynamite the *al-Aqsa* Mosque and the Dome of the Rock on January 27, 1984. They were stopped by Israeli police.[120] When one of the plotters, Yehudah Etzion, was tried for his part in the plot and for placing bombs in the cars of the mayors of Nablus and Ramallah, he defended his actions as "the purification of the Temple Mount . . . from the structure now located upon it, on the site of the holy of holies, the building known as the Dome of the Rock."[121]

The plotters acted on their own, but they were not fringe people and their views resonated with a messianic-apocalyptic reading of traditional Jewish theology. Unlike some of the other accusations the Mufti customarily made against the Jewish people, his claim that the Yishuv constituted a potential threat to the Muslim holy places in Jerusalem was not entirely without foundation. The overwhelming majority of Jews have every motive to protect the *Haram al-Sharif* and its sanctuaries, but in a catastrophic existential crisis there is no way of predicting what an extremist fringe might attempt.

There was another reason why the fears the Mufti stirred up were not entirely groundless. *Muslims know what they had done to major Christian religious structures whenever they prevailed in battle.* At the very least, defeat in a religious war entails losing control of one's holy places. For example, Constantinople's Hagia Sophia, originally constructed from 532 to 537 C.E. on orders of the Emperor Justinian and considered the greatest and the most beautiful cathedral in Christendom in its time, was immediately converted into an Imperial Mosque when that city was conquered by Muslims in 1453. Similarly, the great cathedral of Cordoba, *La Mesquita* (Spanish for "mosque" from the Arabic "*Masjid*") had its origins in the Aljama Mosque whose construction was begun in 784 C.E. under the first emir of Cordoba, Abd ar-Rahman I (731–788 C.E.) and was for a time the world's second largest Muslim religious structure. When Cordoba was reconquered by King Ferdinand III of Castile in 1236, the mosque was converted into a cathedral.

The Mufti continued his radio address, asserting that the Jews wanted to erect their kingdom in Palestine, a danger for all of humanity, but a greater, more significant danger for the Arab and Muslim world, for this kingdom will be a "partition wall" (*Scheidewand*) separating the Muslims of Asia from those in Africa. "It is a bloody dagger in the heart of the Arab fatherlands." (*Er ist ein blütiger Dolch im Herzen des arabischen Vaterlandes.*) Moreover, the Mufti claimed that the Jews would not rest content until they controlled "Syria, Transjordan, Iraq, a part of Saudi Arabia and a part of Egypt." Hajj Amin went so far as to say that the "lusts" (*Begierden*) of the Jews had exposed "the holy states of the Hijaz to the greatest danger and would deprive the Arabs and Islam of the 'flower' (*Blüte*) of their lands which for thirteen centuries they had defended with the blood of martyrs."[122] He concluded the speech by stating that "I have not the slightest doubt that we will achieve victory over them in spite of the help of their cruel allies. God aids those who help him."

In reality, the Mufti's claim that the Jews had any interest in possessing the Hijaz was mendacious nonsense. In 641, the second caliph, Umar, decreed that Jews and Christians should be removed from Arabia to fulfill the Prophet's deathbed injunction, "Let there not be two religions in Arabia."[123] The Jews have had no interest in the Hijaz for almost fourteen hundred years and certainly no desire to return there.

The Mufti employed the same kind of inflammatory rhetoric in dozens of other speeches and writings he gave in the service of Nazi Germany.[124] According to Moshe Perlman, one of the earliest biographers of the Mufti, the Balfour Declaration anniversary speech contained an even more ominous note which Gerard Höpp has omitted from the collection of the Mufti's papers he published in Germany in 2001:

> The Treaty of Versailles was a disaster for the Germans as well as for the Arabs. But *the Germans know how to get rid of the Jews*. That which brings us close to the Germans and sets us in their camp is that up to today, the Germans have never harmed any Muslim, and they are again fighting our common enemy (applause) who persecuted Arabs and Muslims. But *most of all they have definitely solved the Jewish problem*. These ties, and especially the last, make our friendship with Germany not a provisional one, dependent on conditions, but a permanent and lasting friendship based on mutual interest (emphasis added).[125]

This statement is consistent with the Mufti's own "solution" to the "Jewish problem." The human equation was simple: no Jews, no Jewish Palestine. Moreover, he delivered this speech and others like it almost two years after Hitler had decided upon the Final Solution at a time when millions of Jews had already been murdered.

As we have seen, the circles in which the Mufti traveled or to which he had access in Germany included some of the *Shoah*'s most important perpetrators. These included *Obersturmbannführer* Adolf Eichmann, one of the leading perpetrators and head of the Gestapo's Jewish Bureau (Section IV b 4—Jewish Affairs and Expulsions). There are conflicting opinions concerning how well the Mufti knew Eichmann. Mallmann and Cüpers report that the Mufti met with Eichmann on several occasions to discuss plans for the Holocaust. They state that "The most important collaborator with the Nazis and at the same time a rabid anti-Semite was Hajj Amin al-Husseini."[126] The Mufti was "a prime example of how the Arabs and the Nazis became friends out of a hatred for the Jews."[127]

Their findings are consistent with the signed deposition submitted to the Nuremberg tribunal on July 26, 1946, by former SS *Hauptsturmführer* Dieter Wisliceny, Eichmann's deputy for Slovakia, Hungary, and Greece, concerning the wartime collaboration of the Mufti and Eichmann, as well as the Mufti's role in the *Shoah*.[128] In his deposition, Wisliceny declared that from his own activities at the head office of the *Sicherheitsdienst* (SD, the security service of the SS) in Berlin, he knew that there was an "intelligence link" between the SD and the Grand Mufti in Jerusalem in 1937 through the DNB (*Deutsche Nachrichten Büro*/German News Agency). The Jerusalem DNB bureau chief was Dr. Franz Reichert. The post was in reality a cover for Reichert's work as an SD agent. In the fall of 1937, Eichmann, accompanied by Herbert Hagen, his SS superior, visited Palestine to secure information on Zionist issues and meet with the Mufti. The meeting did not take place because the British decided to restrict the visit to forty-eight hours. However, Eichmann did meet in Cairo with a Jerusalem journalist who belonged to the circle of the Mufti.[129] As noted, when the Mufti arrived in Germany, he called on Heinrich Himmler. Shortly thereafter, either in late December 1941 or early January 1942, he met with Eichmann, Himmler's subordinate.

Although Wisliceny does not mention it, the Mufti's first encounters with the Nazi governing elite, including Hitler, Himmler, and von Ribbentrop, took place not long before the Wansee Conference of January 20, 1942, at which Heydrich, in his capacity as head of the Reich Security Main Office, called together fourteen senior German officials and announced that Hitler had decided upon the implementation of the Final Solution. Eichmann served as secretary and took notes. Wisliceny relates that Eichmann told him about the Mufti's visit a few days later:

> Eichmann lectured to the Grand Mufti in his Map Room . . . in detail about the solution of the Jewish Question in Europe: The Grand Mufti . . . was most impressed and said to Eichmann that he had already asked Himmler and had in fact secured Himmler's consent . . ., that a representative of Eichmann should come to Jerusalem as his personal adviser when he, the Grand Mufti, returned. Eichmann was greatly impressed. . . . He repeatedly said to me, both then and on a later occasion, that the Mufti had made a powerful impression on him, and also on Himmler, and that he had an acknowledged influence in Arab-Jewish affairs.[130]

We also have the Nuremberg Tribunal deposition of Dr. Rudolph Kasztner, a controversial Hungarian Jewish leader who negotiated with Eichmann during the summer of 1944 concerning the emigration of 1,685 Hungarian Jews in exchange for a bribe of $2,000 a person.[131] Kasztner claimed that on June 4, 1944, Eichmann stated in his Budapest office that he would be willing to recommend the emigration provided that Palestine was not their destination. According to Kasztner, Eichmann explained: "I am a personal friend of the Grand Mufti. We have promised him that no European Jews would enter Palestine any more."[132]

Kasztner further testified that several days later, also in Budapest, Wisliceny confirmed Eichmann's statement and added that in his opinion the

Mufti "played a role in the decision of the German government to exterminate the European Jews, the importance of which must not be disregarded."
Wisliceny added that the Mufti was "one of Eichmann's best friends" and
that he had "constantly incited him to accelerate the extermination measures." Kasztner's deposition is largely consistent with Wisliceny's.

When Eichmann was shown a copy of Wisliceny's deposition during
his pre-trial interrogation in Jerusalem in the spring of 1961, he did not
question its authenticity. During the trial, which began April 14, 1961,
he claimed that he met the Mufti only once at a reception in the latter's
residence arranged by the SD at which "most of the heads of the Reich
Security Main Office . . . were presented to him." Beyond that single encounter, Eichmann denied that he had any close relations or had cooper-
ated with him. For his part, the Mufti insisted that he had never met Eichmann and that he bore no responsibility for the extermination of Europe's
Jews. Nevertheless, Eichmann's admission of even a single contact with
the Mufti is not without significance. This was not a reception arranged
by the *Auswärtiges Amt*, the German Foreign Office. By Eichmann's own
admission, the *Sicherheitsdienst*, the intelligence sector of the SS, arranged
a reception at which most of the senior officials responsible for the implementation of the Final Solution were presented to the Mufti. It is hardly
likely that the leaders of the RSHA gathered in wartime for a social gathering with a foreign dignitary. It is far more likely that the reception was
for the purpose of acquainting themselves with an important personage
who was unconditionally committed to their fundamental objective, the
Final Solution of the Jewish Problem.

The testimonies of Wisliceny and Eichmann obviously contradict each
other. When asked at his trial about Wisliceny's possible motive, Eichmann
suggested that Wisliceny may have been seeking to curry favor with the
Nuremberg Tribunal. Wisliceny was, in any event, tried and executed as a
war criminal by Czechoslovakia in 1948. There was, however, further cor-
roboration of Wisliceny's deposition, a notarized statement, dated February 12, 1946, by Endre Steiner, an engineer who negotiated with Wisliceny
in 1943 and 1944 on behalf of the Jewish community of Slovakia concerning
the possible emigration to Palestine of Jewish children under adult supervision from Slovakia, Poland, and Hungary.[133] Approached by Steiner, Wisliceny told him that he agreed in principle to the proposal and was willing
to pass it on to Eichmann, but that Eichmann had indicated that under no
circumstance could Palestine be the destination "or at least that it should
not be openly indicated." Wisliceny added that "the Mufti was in the closest contact and collaboration with Eichmann and, in order not to have this
action disapproved by the Mufti, Palestine could not be accepted as a final
destination by a German authority." Wisliceny stated that the Mufti had
visited Auschwitz incognito accompanied by Eichmann. When shown

Steiner's affidavit, Wisliceny confirmed its accuracy, save for Steiner's statement that Wisliceny had said Eichmann had been born in Palestine.[134] Writing in 1947, Simon Wiesenthal asserted that the Mufti was on good terms with Rudolf Hoess, commandant of Auschwitz; Franz Ziereis, commandant of Mauthausen; Siegfried Seidl, commandant of Theresienstadt; and Josef Kramer, commandant of Belsen.[135]

If, according to Eichmann, Wisliceny had his motives for testifying about the alleged connection between the Mufti and Eichmann, Eichmann may have had his motives for an alternative narrative. Nothing in Eichmann's testimony in Jerusalem suggests that Eichmann had any regret about his role in the *Shoah*. Knowing that the Mufti was alive, Eichmann might not have wanted to add to the Mufti's jeopardy by describing details of their collaboration. We do not have a simple case of Eichmann's word against Wisliceny's. We have the testimony of Wisliceny, Kasztner, and Steiner, none of whom appear to have been in contact after the war.

A month before the Eichmann trial, the Mufti denied in a press interview in Beirut that he had ever met Eichmann or advised him on the extermination of Europe's Jews. The Mufti was, of course, aware that the Israelis had extensively interrogated Eichmann in advance of the trial and undoubtedly wanted to make his own interpretation of his wartime activities widely known. He told reporters in Beirut: "The Nazis needed no persuasion or instigation either by me or anyone else to execute their program against the Jews."[136] The Mufti's claim has been seconded by many of his defenders. Nevertheless, Mallmann and Cüppers find Wisliceny's testimony entirely credible and dismiss as "defensive" Eichmann's claim that he met the Mufti only once.[137] Elpeleg argues, cogently in this writer's opinion, that the Mufti's denials were motivated more by the fear that he might be brought to trial as a war criminal than by the truth.[138]

What the Mufti did readily admit was that he had taken strenuous diplomatic action to prevent the immigration of Jews of any age or condition to Palestine and that he was quite proud of having done so. On May 6, 1943, he sent the foreign minister of Bulgaria a strongly worded letter that began with a comment:

> The Jewish danger for the entire world, and particularly for those lands that Jews inhabit (*die von Juden bewohnten Ländern*), has for most nations become an objective fact and causes them to take measures of self-defense. The Axis powers and their allies count among the first to have recognized that one must as a vital national necessity take active measures so that this hostile element and her ideas and paralysis of economic life be brought to a halt.[139]

The Mufti then alluded to negotiations between the British and Bulgarian governments by which Bulgaria would have permitted the emigration of four thousand Jewish children and five hundred adult chaperones

(*Begleiter*) to Palestine. The Mufti requested that the Bulgarian government refuse permission. As a final thought, he added that it would be more desirable to send them to Poland "where they can be placed under stronger control (*unter starker Kontrolle*)."

A week later, the Mufti seems to have felt that further pressure on Bulgaria was necessary. He wrote to von Ribbentrop demanding that Germany use its influence to prevent Bulgaria from permitting the emigration. In the same letter, he requested that von Ribbentrop "do the utmost" (*das Äusserste zu tun*) to prevent Hungary and Romania from implementing similar emigration plans.[140] On June 10, 1943, he again wrote to von Ribbentrop spelling out in some detail pending plans for the emigration of Jews from Romania, Hungary, and Bulgaria and requesting that Germany take the necessary measures to "prevent the departure of these Jews and to obstruct the efforts of the Jews, the British and their allies." The same day he sent an identical letter to Count Galeazzo Ciano.[141] On June 28, 1943, he sent similar letters from Rome to the Romanian and Hungarian foreign ministers requesting that their governments prevent the emigration of Jewish groups to Palestine.

At a time when millions of Jews were powerless to prevent their own destruction, the Mufti retained the mindset of *The Protocols of the Elders of Zion*. In his letters to the foreign ministers, he accused the Jews of promoting emigration from Europe and the Near East in order to set up a "strategic center" in Palestine for "the domination of the world." He concluded, as he did in his letter to the Bulgarian foreign minister, by stating that if it is necessary to send the Jews away, it would be "indispensable and infinitely preferable" that their destination be Poland where "they will find themselves under active surveillance."[142] Given the Mufti's ties to the Nazi organizations responsible for the implementation of the Final Solution, it stretches the limits of credibility to think that he was ignorant of the fate that awaited Jews in Nazi-controlled Poland.

On July 25, 1944, he sent von Ribbentrop a letter protesting the fact that some Jews had been included in an exchange arrangement for Germans living in Palestine and Egypt. Once again, he demanded that Jews be prevented from emigrating from Europe.[143] He wrote:

> This exchange on the part of the Germans would encourage the Balkan countries likewise to send their Jews to Palestine. This step would be incomprehensible to the Arabs and Muslims after your Excellency's declaration of November 2, 1943 that "the destruction of the so-called Jewish national home in Palestine is an immutable part of the policy of the greater German Reich" and it would create in them a feeling of keen disappointment.[144]

Two days later, he sent a similar request to Himmler. The decision to exchange European Jews for Germans in Palestine required his approval.[145]

On this occasion, Himmler was more willing to let a small number of Jews to escape from Nazi-dominated Europe than Hajj Amin. The Mufti made many such interventions, all having one purpose, to keep Europe's Jews bottled up in Europe where Hajj Amin knew Germany's extermination machine would eliminate them. To repeat, the Mufti's rationale was simple: no Jews, no Jewish Palestine.

THE MUFTI IN THE BALKANS

Wherever possible, the Mufti sought active Muslim participation in Hitler's war. He was especially active in the Muslim areas of Bosnia. On April 6, 1941, the Germans and their Italian allies, together with some Hungarian and Bulgarian forces, invaded Yugoslavia. Four days later, the Germans divided the country into two major areas, Serbia and the "independent" state of Croatia which included Bosnia with its large Muslim population. Serbia was regarded as an enemy state and treated as such. Many, but by no means all, Bosnian Muslims welcomed their nation's incorporation into the pro-Nazi, Croatian Ustaše (Croatian fascist) state.[146] On April 17, 1941, a Muslim mob burned down and looted Sarajevo's Sephardic synagogue.

On February 10, 1943, Hitler approved the formation of a Muslim Waffen SS division, the 13th *Gebirgs [Mountain] Division der "Handzar."* Himmler was confident that the Bosnian Muslims would make good soldiers in large measure because of their performance in Austria-Hungary's Imperial Army during World War I and earlier. He also believed that Islam is an ideal religion for a soldier and told Joseph Goebbels that he had "nothing against Islam because it educates the men in this Division for me and promises them heaven if they fight and are killed in action; a very practical and attractive religion for soldiers!"[147]

Two months later, Himmler dispatched the Mufti to Sarajevo to recruit Muslims and help organize the division. Hajj Amin was greeted by cheering Muslim crowds and met with prominent Bosnian and Nazi leaders.[148] At its peak, the division consisted of 21,065 men, approximately 18,000 of whom were Muslim. As *Reichsführer SS,* Heinrich Himmler visited the unit at least twice. In January 1944 the Mufti spent three days with the unit in Germany where it had been training. He addressed the unit about the shared hatred of the Jews in both Islam and National Socialism and of the SS Handzar division as a "visible and practical expression" of the unity of both movements. On May 22, 1944, Hitler approved a second Muslim Waffen SS division, "Kama" (dagger), but because of the retreat of German forces in Yugoslavia, the unit was disbanded after five months. Muslim members of Kama were told to report to the Handzar division.[149]

Some scholars have argued that the Handzar division participated directly in the extermination of Croatian Jews. Undoubtedly, they would have if they could, but the division was not deployed in Croatia until early 1944 after Ustaše forces, which included Muslim volunteers, had done the grisly job. The last Jewish deportations from Zagreb, Croatia's capital, took place in May 1943 and from Sarajevo in the Italian zone of occupation in September and early October 1943. Nevertheless, it is very likely that Handzar personnel were involved in "the capture and murder of Jews found in hiding or captured as partisans."[150]

Hajj Amin was thus an integral part of a highly important SS operation to exterminate Croatia's Jews in which Himmler was directly involved. As the Mufti made clear in his messages to the unit, they were involved in *jihad*. That the unit that the Mufti helped to organize did not do the actual killing was due to a lack of opportunity not will. It had already been done for them.

Some Bosnian Muslims were aware that the Ustaše regime, in its quest for racial and religious homogeneity, might someday inflict upon them the same fate the regime intended for Jews and Serbs. Hence, some Bosnian Muslims were sympathetic neither to the Ustaše regime nor the German cause.[151] Nevertheless, even before the Mufti arrived on the scene, many Muslims volunteered for service in Croatian or German military units, which included serving in the Croatian brigade alongside of the Germans at Stalingrad. They were wiped out.[152] Moreover, many Muslims willingly participated in the obscene atrocities committed by the Ustaše. For example, the *Crna Legija*, the notorious Ustaše Black Legion responsible for some of the worst atrocities, recruited many Muslims.[153] The Ustaše atrocities were seen by Wehrmacht officers as a threat to public order that had to be stopped.[154]

The Handzar division surrendered to the British on May 8, 1945. In the 1990s, Bosnia's Islamist president, Alija Izetbegovic, reconstituted the Handzar division. In a 1993 interview, members of the reconstituted division told Robert Fox, a correspondent for London's *Daily Telegraph*, that they see themselves as the heirs of the SS Handzar division and affirmed that "their spiritual model was Mohammed Hajj Amin al-Husseini, the Grand Mufti of Jerusalem."[155]

As the war ended, the Mufti retained his VIP status in Hitler's collapsing empire. A German military aircraft flew him to Switzerland where authorities denied his request for political asylum. Returning to Germany, he prudently chose the French zone of occupied Germany. The French took him to a Paris prison and then to luxurious confinement in a villa in Varennes, eight miles outside of Paris. When the Allied High Command and the British demanded his extradition, the French, with their own postwar Middle East agenda, were unwilling to comply. The Mufti later wrote that French authorities sought to protect him from the moment he made contact with them and that Charles de Gaulle had personally intervened to allow him to remain politically active.[156] After an interlude in Varennes, he managed once again to "escape" from French confinement. The French Foreign Ministry issued a statement that the Mufti had not been under house arrest and that the measures taken by the government were only to ensure his safety. Nor did Britain long retain an interest in trying him as a war criminal. At the war's end, he was an enormously popular figure in the Arab and Muslim world.[157]

The Mufti arrived in Cairo May 29, 1946, determined to continue the fight against the Zionists and to establish an Arab Palestinian state. However, he delayed making his presence known publicly for several weeks since the Egyptian government was negotiating the withdrawal of British troops from that country. On June 19, he was received at the royal palace by King Farouk who provided palatial accommodations for him and his entourage. On June 20 the government officially announced his arrival.

When Hajj Amin arrived in Egypt, which was becoming a haven for Nazi war criminals, the Yishuv was in open rebellion against the British colonial government. From 1945 to 1952 more than 250,000 Holocaust survivors and other Jewish refugees were languishing in displaced persons camps and urban centers in Germany, Austria, and Italy. Because of implacable Arab opposition, the British were unwilling to permit the entry of more than a trickle to Palestine.[158] A number of attempts to resolve the crisis came to naught. Finally, on April 7, 1947, Britain requested that the UN call a special session of the General Assembly to make recommendations to the next meeting of the General Assembly concerning the future of Palestine.[159] On November 27, 1947, the General Assembly voted to partition Palestine into a Jewish and an Arab state. Immediately thereafter, the UN delegates of the Arab states declared their unconditional opposition to partition and their intention to fight it by force if necessary.

Having fought for an independent Arab Palestine for thirty years, the Mufti would have appeared to be the natural leader of the Palestinian cause, but it was not to be. The very extremism that had served him well as the leader of a movement failed him when confronted with British postwar opposition and the ambitions of an Arab head of state, King Abdullah of Transjordan. The British were in no mood to permit the Mufti's return to Palestine. This crippled his efforts to create a Palestinian military force under his command. Moreover, Abdullah had long harbored the ambition of uniting Greater Syria, including Palestine, under his crown. Abdullah had the advantage of the longest border with Palestine of any Arab country, the best trained army, the Arab Legion, led by Sir John Bagot Glubb, known as Glubb Pasha, and between fifty and seventy-five experienced British officers and noncommissioned officers.[160] Abdullah was supported by Iraq which was also ruled by members of the Hashemite family. The Hashemites had bitter memories of the Mufti's role in the 1941 pro-Nazi coup.[161] According to Israeli historian Benny Morris, during the 1948 war, Abdullah's Arab Legion had no interest in invading the predominantly Jewish areas of Palestine. Abdullah had had secret, on-and-off negotiations with the Jewish Agency for two years and preferred a Jewish state to one governed by Hajj Amin. By 1950 when the dust finally settled, the Palestinian territories conquered by the Arab Legion became known, not as Palestine, but as the West Bank of the Jordanian Hashemite Kingdom. Egypt controlled Gaza. The Mufti controlled nothing.

Hajj Amin had long been fearful of such an outcome which may explain his one futile attempt to negotiate with the Jewish Agency. On November 27, 1947, he sent a message to Dr. Mordecai Eliash, a leader of Mizrachi (the religious Zionist party), asking him to propose secret talks prior to the final vote on partition of the UN General Assembly, "without the mediation of any Arab country." David Ben Gurion responded on behalf of the Jewish Agency executive, declaring that the agency was prepared to meet with any Arab leader but the Mufti.[162]

Some Arab leaders saw partition of Palestine as the only viable solution, but none felt free to speak publicly and frankly.[163] There were elite families and clans, such as the Nashashibis and their allies in Hebron, Nazareth, and Nablus who took a somewhat more conciliatory approach than did the Mufti. Much of the opposition to the Mufti faded in 1947–1948 when the Husseini clan took to assassinating, Mafia-style, some of their opponents.[164] As Benny Morris has argued, all hope of a peaceful solution vanished with the United Nations Partition resolution of November 29, 1947, that completely ignored the problem of population transfer that left close to four hundred thousand Arabs alongside five hundred thousand Jews in the area designated for the Jewish state. "Once the battle was joined," Morris comments, "it was a recipe for disaster—and for refugeedom for the side that lost."[165] Paradoxically, by its silence on the subject of population transfer at the very same time that one of the largest population transfers in human history was taking place, namely, the transfer of as many as 13 million *Volksdeutsch* (ethnic Germans) from Eastern Europe to the rump postwar German state, the United Nations raised the stakes in Palestine to the point where compromise was no longer possible, if indeed it ever was.

There are Palestinians who hold that the Mufti's rejectionism contributed to the Palestinian failure in 1948 and claim that his policies "unwittingly contributed to the dispossession of the Palestinians."[166] In spite of having been expelled from Palestine in 1937, with the publication of the British white paper of 1939 the Mufti appeared to have achieved his major political objective, assurance of an independent state in Palestine with a permanent Arab majority within ten years. Facing imminent war with Germany and Italy, Great Britain reneged on commitments made to the Jews in the Balfour Declaration. In spite of what *Kristallnacht*, the monumental pogrom of November 9–10, 1938, revealed about German intentions toward the Jews, the white paper was Britain's response to the 1936–1939 Arab Revolt. Had the Mufti accepted the white paper, there would, in all likelihood, have been no Jewish state. Nevertheless, in spite of this apparent success, the Mufti's response was unconditional rejection, a response characterized by Mattar as "short-sighted and irresponsible."[167] As a territorial conflict, rejection may have been irresponsible, but, the Mufti was not conducting a territorial conflict; he was conducting a *jihad* and could not sign a document ceding *any* territory in Palestine to the infidel Jews.

THE FATE OF PALESTINE

In spite of the presence in Palestine of eighty thousand British military personnel and local police, in 1947 security had virtually collapsed, undermining Britain's domestic economy. On April 2, 1947, Britain formally turned the fate of Palestine over to the General Assembly of the United Nations. On August 31, 1947, the eleven-nation United Nations Special Committee on Palestine (UNSCOP) issued a majority report calling for partition of Palestine and the creation of independent Arab and Jewish states. After much violence, military preparation, committee hearings and diplomatic maneuvering, including a recommendation on March 19, 1948, by Warren Austin, the American ambassador to the UN, that action on partition be "suspended" and a temporary trusteeship over Palestine be established to determine "the character of the eventual political settlement," on November 29, 1947, the UN General Assembly voted to establish independent Jewish and Arab states in Palestine. Reconstituted after the war, the Mufti's Arab Higher Committee condemned the decision as "null and void" and announced a policy of noncooperation in its implementation. The group also declared that it would request the British government to hand over Palestine forthwith to its Arab people.[168]

The Arab Higher Committee's rejection was an accurate reflection of Arab sentiment. At the time, *New York Times* correspondent Clifton Daniel reported that "every class in Palestine, with or without political ties" rejects partition and follows the Grand Mufti.[169] Nevertheless, the Mufti had some inkling of what the Arab states, especially Egypt and Abdullah's Transjordan, had in store for him. They had no intention of letting him rule an independent Palestine. As noted, Abdullah was determined to take over the West Bank and, save for Jerusalem, leaving the territory occupied by the Jews essentially untouched. Hajj Amin had neither the resources nor the military force necessary to stop Abdullah, although it is likely that, in revenge, he arranged for Abdullah's assassination on July 20, 1951, while the king was at Friday prayer in Jerusalem's *al-Aqsa* Mosque.[170]

Hajj Amin could only have ruled an independent Palestine by lowering his expectations and accepting a truncated Palestinian state. Such a state would have had whatever legitimacy its UN-sponsored creation would have accorded it. Unless he moved aggressively to attack the Jewish state, there was little likelihood that a Zionist state could have expanded its territory at the expense of a state whose borders had been ratified by the UN.

Admittedly, such a compromise would, as noted, have been politically impossible for the Mufti. As noted above, *he was, above all, a Muslim religious leader.* By virtue of his office, compromise was impossible. As an Arab nationalist, he might have accepted what is today called the "two-state solution" if the terms were sufficiently advantageous. As Palestine's senior Muslim religious leader, he did not have that option. Throughout his career, he called his fellow Muslims to *jihad* against the Jews; during the Second World War, he also called for *jihad* against Great Britain. Because Muslims consider all of Palestine to be an inalienable part of *dar-al-Islam,* they are obliged, at least in theory, to wage *defensive jihad* against the Zionists whom they regarded as having forcibly "invaded" the land. According to a strict interpretation of Islamic jurisprudence, the obligation to expel the Jews was and remains a non-negotiable religious imperative.

Moreover, throughout his career, the Mufti regarded the Jews as Islam's most devious, dangerous, and demonic enemy. Like Adolf Hitler, and for similar reasons, he regarded *The Protocols of the Elders of Zion* as a verifiably accurate description of Jewish power and intentions. So too, do all too many contemporary Muslims including al Qaeda's Osama bin Laden and Ayman al-Zawahiri. With his *Protocols-of-Zion* mindset, he saw hidden Jewish power as the ultimate mover behind just about every misfortune that had befallen the Muslim world from the French Revolution to the Zionist settlement in Palestine. As with Hitler's insistence that World War I was lost and the Bolshevik Revolution won as a result of the surreptitious betrayal of Imperial Germany and Tsarist Russia by a secret Jewish conspiracy, so too the Mufti, lacking even a hint of critical self-reflection, could not conceive of the Islamic failure to prevail in modern times as due to any failing in that "most noble of all peoples," the Muslims. As noted, for the Mufti, as well as many other Muslims, the worst shock was the success of the Jews, looked upon with condescension or contempt by Muslims for almost fourteen hundred years, in prevailing militarily and in creating a modern society in their ancestral homeland.

We have argued that, at least theoretically, Muslims are obliged to wage *jihad* until unbelievers either become Muslim or acknowledge Islam's supremacy by accepting their subordinate status as a religious minority or *dhimmis*. Yet, as humiliating as was *dhimmi* status, Hajj Amin intended a far more dire fate for the Jews. The Mufti's whole life was devoted to permanently eliminating the Zionist settlement in Palestine. That could not be done by defeating the Jews militarily and then granting them *dhimmi* status. There would always be the possibility, small though it might be, that the *dhimmis* might someday overturn their subordination. Nor could the Jews of the rest of the world be permitted *dhimmi* status. They constituted a population reservoir from which future Zionist experiments might be launched. The only way permanently to put an end to Zionism and the threat it poses to Islam was to cut off by extermination the human flow at its source, as indeed Hitler was doing, and to work for a Nazi victory in North Africa that would bring Rommel and *Einsatzgruppe* Egypt into Palestine where they would do to the Jews of Palestine what other *Einsatzgruppen* had done to the Jews of Eastern Europe.

There is, of course, a difference between plan and implementation. The Mufti knew from Islamic tradition how in Medina in 627 C.E. the Prophet ordered the public beheading of the men and the enslavement of the women and children of the Jewish clan of Banu Qurayza. Nor is the Banu Qurayza massacre the only one in Islamic tradition the Mufti could have used as his model. The massacre is especially important because in it the Prophet himself provides the model for what Muslims consider religiously legitimated mass killing. Nor was the Mufti alone in recognizing that the Nazis, and they alone, were capable of putting an end to the threat of a Jewish state. As we have seen, admiration for Hitler and National Socialism was widespread among Arab leaders, many of whom were all too willing to provide a safe haven for Nazi war criminals after Germany's defeat. When the war was over, the Arab press frequently expressed regret that the Nazis had not finished the job of exterminating the Jews.[171]

Some of the Mufti's defenders claim that there was little ideological affinity between the Mufti and National Socialism. They claim that he understood better than most that the Arab-Zionist conflict was a zero-sum game in which a Zionist victory would ultimately spell the end of a significant Arab presence in Palestine through expulsion, population transfer, or emigration. They further assert that he turned to an alliance with Nazi Germany only after he realized that the policy of defending the interests of his community through moderation, diplomacy, and cooperation had failed utterly.[172]

The difficulty with that position is that it minimizes the Mufti's publicly stated, pro-Nazi sentiments and his role in fostering them among Muslims. On numerous occasions, he spoke of the strong ties binding Islam and National Socialism. We have already noted his radio address from Luftwaffe Hall on November 2, 1943, in which he stated that *"the Germans know how to get rid of the Jews"* and that *"most of all they have definitely solved the Jewish problem."* He added that "especially" this fact makes "our friendship with Germany" permanent and lasting. He made similar remarks in an address on October 4, 1944, before the imams serving with the Bosnian SS division. Once again, the Mufti spoke of the bonds that bind Muslims to National Socialist Germany. These included common enemies that would alone suffice as "a healthy basis for the creation of friendly relations and the development of collaborative efforts," but more was involved. He told the Muslim SS chaplains that *"The friendship and common effort of Muslims and Germans have become stronger since the rise to power of the National Socialist party, because the latter is developing in many respects parallel to the Muslim worldview* (emphasis added)."[173]

The Mufti cited the idea of "unity of leadership" (*Einheit der Führung*) or *Führerprinzip* as the "foundational idea" (*Hauptgebot*) in both Islam and National Socialism as the most important parallel. In Islam, the idea is expressed in the office of the caliph as the "sole ruler" who possesses the "power to govern Muslims' spiritual, political, military, and social interests." In National Socialism, the "party is built on this *Führerprinzip* . . . and seeks to centralize all authority in the hand of the *Führer*." As in the Luftwaffe Hall address, the Mufti saw the strongest parallel in their common combat (*Bekämpfung*) against Judaism. He reminded the imams that "Islam and the National Socialists come very close together in their battle against Judaism." He also reminded them that "Nearly one-third of the Qur'an concerns the Jews" and "the Qur'an . . . calls upon all Muslims to fight them wherever they may meet them."

The Mufti's war clearly transcended the issues of Zionism and the Jewish settlement in Palestine. As he said repeatedly, his was a war against "world Judaism, the hereditary enemy of Islam (*das Weltjudentum, den Erbfeind des Islams*)." And it is here that he finds the closest affinity between Islam and National Socialism. To repeat, his war was not only a conflict over territory but a nonnegotiable religious war that can have only two acceptable outcomes: The Jews must either be converted to Islam or be eliminated altogether.

Nor was the Mufti alone in seeing a deep affinity between Islam and National Socialism. Karl Barth, arguably the twentieth century's greatest Christian theologian, wrote: "It is impossible to understand National Socialism unless we see it in fact as a *new Islam* [emphasis in original], its myth as a new Allah, and Hitler as this new Allah's Prophet."[174] About the same time Carl Gustav Jung, one of the twentieth century's most prolific psychiatric pioneers, wrote:

> We do not know whether Hitler is going to found a new Islam. (He is already on the way; he is like Muhammad. The emotion in Germany is Islamic; warlike and Islamic. They are all drunk with the wild god). That can be the historic future.[175]

As noted, Hitler and National Socialism were enormously popular both in the "Arab street" and among many very important Arab leaders, including the young Anwar Sadat, Gamal Abdul Nasser, and Hassan al-Banna, founder of the Muslim Brotherhood.[176] After World War II some of the most vicious Holocaust perpetrators found a welcome haven and new opportunities in Egypt and other Muslim countries. For example, Walther Rauff was recruited by Syrian intelligence in 1948 although he subsequently fell out of favor and emigrated to Chile.[177] Alois Brunner, characterized by *The Guardian* (UK) in 2001 as "the world's highest-ranking Nazi fugitive," found Syria more congenial.[178] Although he organized the deportation to death camps of more than one hundred thousand Jews, in a *Chicago Sun-Times* telephone interview in October 1987 he said of his victims, "All of them deserved to die because they were the devil's agents and human garbage. I have no regrets and would do it again."[179] Other Nazi war criminals found havens in Spain, Latin America, and, if sufficiently talented, in the United States.[180] Nevertheless, whatever Nazi sentiments those who found a haven in North or South America retained, most were no longer actively involved in continuing their war of annihilation against the Jews.

There was, however, one region where Nazis were openly recruited in order to continue their destructive labors, the Arab Middle East. Among the high-level Nazis who came to Egypt was professor and honorary SS *Sturmbannführer* (Major) Dr. Johann von Leers (1902–1965).[181] Von Leers was one of Hajj Amin's friends and collaborators in Nazi Germany and in the Egypt of Gamal Abdul Nasser; he was an *Altekämpfer*, one of the earliest members of the Nazi Party, who joined the Nazi Party out of conviction in 1929 rather than out of convenience in 1933 or later. Although a professor at the University of Jena, "the brownest of German universities," he devoted a good deal of his efforts to writing anti-Semitic propaganda for schoolchildren and teachers because of his desire to see his brand of anti-Semitism take root in future generations.

Von Leers was one of the Third Reich's most brilliant, prolific, and vicious anti-Semitic propagandists. Like Alois Brunner and unlike most Holocaust deniers, von Leers insisted that "the extermination of the Jews in Europe was fully justified as a form of retribution and self-defense."[182]

In a personal communication to theologian Emil Fackenheim, Harvard historian Erich Goldhagen wrote that "among the Nazis von Leers had the unusual distinction of not bothering to veil his call for mass murder in euphemistic language."[183]

After a stint in the Argentina of Juan Perón (1952–1956), Nasser offered von Leers a position in 1956 as propaganda adviser on Jewish affairs in the Information Department of the Ministry of Guidance.[184] When von Leers arrived in Egypt, he was publicly welcomed by his old friend Hajj Amin al-Husseini with the words, "We thank you for venturing to take up the battle with the powers of darkness that have become incarnate in world Jewry."[185]

To the end of his life, von Leers remained an unwavering, unapologetic, radical anti-Semite. That was the tie that united him with Hajj Amin. There was also another tie, religion. Already in the 1930s, citing Qur'anic verses, von Leers praised Islam because it "has always seen Judaism as its enemy."[186] Other essays followed, including "Judaism and Islam as Opposites" which was published in 1942 in *Die Judenfrage*, a Nazi journal devoted, as its title indicates, to the "Jewish question."[187] Claudio Mutti, a spokesman for the pro-Muslim radical right in Italy who converted to Islam, writes that:

> numerous German and non-German patriots . . . requested the Egyptian government to grant them political asylum to escape the repression that was raging in Germany and to continue the battle against the same enemies; usually they were assigned to the ministries of propaganda, the interior, or war.[188]

Mutti further comments that "Like most of them, von Leers also adopted Islam, taking the name of Omar Amin." The latter name was in honor of the Mufti. Clearly, von Leers, one of the Third Reich's most unrepentant propagandists of genocide, found in radical Islam the faith most compatible with his genocidal project. There were others. Many, if not most, found their way to Egypt.

Islam's most important Nazi admirer was none other than Adolf Hitler. In his book *Inside the Third Reich*, Albert Speer, who had been close to Hitler since 1930 and served as his wartime minister of armaments and war production, recounted that a "delegation of distinguished Arabs" had told Hitler that the Arabs had been "driven back" at the Battle of Tours (France) in 732, but had they won the battle, "the world would be Mohammedan (sic) today. For theirs was a religion that believed in spreading the faith by the sword and subjecting all nations to that faith." According to Speer, on a number of occasions in his "teatime conversations," Hitler commented on "the scrap of history he had learned" from the Arabs saying that because of their "racial inferiority" the Arabs would have been unable to keep down the "more vigorous natives" or contend with the harsher climate so that "ultimately not the Arabs but the Islamized Germans could have stood at the head of the Mohammedan Empire."[189]

Hitler usually concluded this teatime "historical speculation" by saying,

> *You see it's been our misfortune to have the wrong religion.* Why didn't we have the religion of the Japanese, who regard sacrifice for the Fatherland as the highest good? *The Mohammedan religion too would have been much more compatible to us than Christianity.* Why did it have to be Christianity with its meekness and flabbiness? (emphasis added)

Nor was the sense of affinity between radical Islam and Western political extremism, especially Nazism, an evanescent phenomenon characteristic of the first half of the twentieth century. If anything, the mutual feeling of affinity between radical Islam and contemporary Nazism is stronger than ever, for contemporary Islam is the one movement that has the numbers and the power seriously to offer an alternative to Western civilization that both the extreme right and left despise.

It has often been said that one can tell much about a man by the company he keeps. We have seen that Hajj Amin's "company" included leaders of the Nazi apparatus unwaveringly committed to the extermination of the Jews. His claims of innocence and ignorance of the extermination of Europe's Jews defies all canons of credibility. Is it possible that the Mufti never discussed the *Shoah* in wartime with obsessed zealots like Johann von Leers? Could it really be that the man who worked so zealously at the highest levels of state and party authority to prevent Jews from leaving Europe for Palestine and who could only suggest Poland as an alternative "where they can be placed under stronger control (*unter starker Kontrolle*)" was not entirely cognizant of the effect of his activities? If we apply to the Holocaust the principle of *cui bono*, "for whose benefit?" apart from the Nazis, did any group stand to gain more from the *Shoah* than the Mufti and his Arab followers? As we have stated, it is not our intention to suggest that the Mufti was responsible for *initiating* the *Shoah*. It is, however, patently clear that he and his followers welcomed it and did everything in their power to facilitate it. Once the opportunity arose, the Mufti seized it. For Hajj Amin and his followers *jihad had indeed become genocide.*

4

On *Jihad*, Oil, and Anti-Semitism

A sea change has occurred in Europe. The post-Holocaust taboo on anti-Semitic speech and incitement—long respected by Europe's mainstream media and her political, religious, and intellectual leaders—has been effectively broken, opening the way for a plethora of vulgar, anti-Semitic cartoons and caricatures in the media, as well as statements by some European leaders of a kind seldom uttered publicly since the fall of the Third Reich.

If there had been any doubt about the prevalence of hate speech and behavior among a growing number of Europeans, the response of European institutions, media, and elites to the Israeli action in Gaza in late December 2008 through early January 2009 should remove that uncertainty. Elsewhere in this work, we take note of the hate-ridden, protest rallies that took place in European and American cities in response to Israel's actions in Gaza. All too often, the demonstrations resounded with cries of "Kill the Jews," "Hamas, Hamas, Jews to the gas!" "Long live Hitler!" and "Put Jews in Ovens."[1] The degree of violence, both verbal and physical, expressed at these events far exceeded in intensity any protest on behalf of Darfur or, at an earlier time, Rwanda. Long before Gaza, the demonization of Israel in mainstream European media had been pervasive. Israel has been repeatedly likened to Nazi Germany; her response to rocket attacks and terrorism against her civilians depicted as "genocide," with no regard for the tragic character of the conflict or its complexity.

This unnuanced portrayal of the conflict has been especially evident in cartoons and posters. Cartoons have long been one of the most effective means of demonizing Jews and fostering anti-Semitism. Such cartoons have once again surfaced in mainstream European journals such as *The Guardian* (UK), *Le Monde* (France), and *El Pais* (Spain).[2] As one example among many, the Holocaust theme appears in a Spanish cartoon depicting three completed buildings and one under construction. The signs in front of the completed buildings read "Museum of the Jewish Holocaust," "Museum of the Bosnian Holocaust," "Museum of the Chechen Holocaust." The sign on the building under construction reads, "Future Museum of the Palestinian Holocaust." (*La Vanguardia*, Spain, May 25, 2001). In an image worthy of Julius Streicher's *Der Stürmer*, former Israeli prime minister Ariel Sharon is depicted as a fat, ugly, hook-nosed Jew wearing a skullcap and saying, "From bad can come good. At least, Hitler taught me to invade a country and exterminate every living vermin." Characteristically, Sharon is depicted wearing a swastika within a Star of David on his chest. (*Cambio 16*, Spain, June 4, 2001). *El Pais*, arguably Spain's most influential newspaper, published a cartoon depicting a small figure flying toward Sharon. The caption reads "Clio, the muse of history, placing the mustache of Hitler on Sharon." (May 22, 2001). During the 1982 war in Lebanon, an earlier Israeli prime minister, Menachem Begin, received similar cartoon treatment. *Labor Herald*, a left-wing British newspaper, depicted him "wearing Nazi jackboots, a Death's Head insignia, and a Star of David armband, raising his right arm in a *Sieg Heil* salute over a mountain of skulls, Lebanon lying bleeding at his feet. The headline, in Gothic script, reads: 'The Final Solution.'" (June 25, 1982, 7).[3]

One of the most venomous cartoons appeared in *The Independent* (UK) on January 27, 2003, the week of Ariel Sharon's reelection. It depicts a fat, slovenly, naked Sharon, his private parts covered only by a small sign that reads "Vote Likud," voraciously biting off the head of a Palestinian baby. In the left hand corner four Israeli helicopters are attacking a bombed-out Palestinian town. Sharon is depicted as saying "What's wrong? You've never seen a politician kissing babies before?" In the lower right-hand corner is the phrase, "After Goya," an indication that the cartoon is modeled after one of Francisco Goya's most gruesome paintings, "Saturn Devouring His Children." Both the cartoonist, Dave Brown, and the editor of the *Independent*, Simon Kellner, are Jewish and denied any anti-Semitic intent. If indeed there is a new anti-Semitism, one of its defining characteristics has been the willingness of deracinated, left-wing Jews to foster it. The *Independent*'s cartoon image elicited powerful associations with one of the most durable of all anti-Semitic canards, the blood libel that Jews allegedly require the blood of Christian boys for their religious rites. And, indeed, blood libel cartoons appear frequently in Muslim newspapers and journals. What is shocking was its appearance in a supposedly respectable, mainstream British newspaper. Inevitably, the crucifixion of

Jesus has also been assimilated to the Palestinian struggle, as if the Palestinians were a Christ among the nations and the Jews once again Christ's crucifiers. One cartoon depicts a young, innocent Palestinian boy nailed not to a cross but to a Star of David. (*El Periodico de Catalunya,* Spain, October 6, 2000). There is no caption. None is needed.

The politics of oil and migration can at least partly explain the shift. During the Yom Kippur War of October 6–24, 1973, the Organization of Petroleum Exporting Countries unleashed its "oil weapon" by embargoing critical oil exports to the United States and Western Europe in order to induce the major oil-consuming nations to abandon support of Israel, and require that nation to withdraw unconditionally from all territories occupied in the Six-Day Arab-Israeli War of 1967.

The United States rejected Arab demands, but the European Community (EC, later European Union, or EU), more dependent at the time on Arab oil than America, decided on a policy of outright appeasement. According to Bat Ye'or, a pathfinding authority on the subject, this led to a series of quasi-official meetings between European and Arab officials and experts that culminated in a meeting at the ministerial level in Paris on July 31, 1974. There, an agreement was reached to initiate the Euro-Arab Dialogue (EAD), an ongoing series of closed, high-level meetings between senior EC and Arab officials designed to formulate a new understanding on economic, cultural, and diplomatic issues.[4] At the time, an important EAD objective was the eventual replacement of the United States as the dominant influence in the Middle East by the French-led European Community. Over time, the EAD instituted a number of long-term policy agreements that guaranteed the Europeans both an uninterrupted oil supply and lucrative export contracts from oil-rich Arab states. In return, the Europeans were expected to facilitate international recognition of Yassir Arafat's Palestine Liberation Organization (PLO) at a time when its charter unambiguously called for Israel's destruction. The Europeans were also expected to enable Arab religious, cultural, and intellectual institutions to achieve unprecedented influence in Europe.[5]

The Arabs also pressured the EC to relax its immigration rules and permit a massive, unprecedented influx of Muslims into Europe. From its inception, every EAD meeting passed resolutions in support of Muslim immigration to Europe.[6] The numbers tell the story. In 1952, the French National Office of Immigration put the number of Muslims in France at five hundred thousand; in 2006 estimates place their number at between 4.5 million and 6 million.[7] According to the U.S. Department of State's *Annual Report on International Religious Freedom 2005,* excluding Turkey, 23.2 million Muslims resided in Europe. And, as the Muslim population in Europe increased, so too did its political clout and anti-Semitism.

The stage had already been set for Europe's return to mainstream anti-Semitism by France's Charles de Gaulle when he asserted at a November 28, 1967, press conference that "Jews are still what they had always been—an elite people, sure of themselves and domineering" and responsible for "provoking ill-will in certain countries and at certain times."[8] Breaking the post-Holocaust taboo, he deliberately stirred up anti-Semitic sentiments in an effort to curry favor with the Muslim world at a time when Arabs were still in a state of rage and shock over their humiliating defeat by the Israelis in the Six-Day War of June 1967. The distinguished French-Jewish social theorist Raymond Aron, who had previously been sympathetic to de Gaulle, immediately understood the import of de Gaulle's attack. Characterizing de Gaulle's comment "as ludicrous as it is hateful," Aron, a highly assimilated French Jew, rightly concluded that "General De Gaulle knowingly and deliberately initiated a new phase of Jewish history."[9]

Until the end of France's war with Algeria in 1962, France's ties with Israel had been exceptionally close, so close that France agreed in 1956 and 1957 to construct for Israel a twenty-four-megawatt nuclear reactor and a chemical reprocessing plant at Dimona.[10] With Franco-Algerian peace at hand, de Gaulle decided to terminate those ties and seek an alliance with the Arab-Muslim world as a rival power center to the United States and the Soviet Union.[11] De Gaulle's decision to reverse course was fully consistent with his hostility to the United States already manifest during World War II. As historian Edward A. Kolodziej and others have pointed out, de Gaulle regarded it as inconsistent with the *grandeur* of France that Franklin Roosevelt, Winston Churchill, and Joseph Stalin denied him a role in their deliberations at which the future of Europe was decided.[12]

Even after terminating its ties with Israel, France continued to supply Israel with the Mirage jets and other armaments that were crucial to its victory in June 1967, although during the war de Gaulle denounced Israel as the aggressor and imposed a strict arms boycott.

As war clouds gathered in the spring of 1967, there was widespread apprehension that the world was about to witness a second Holocaust. This view was rendered plausible by statements by Arab leaders such as Egypt's president Gamal Abdul Nasser, who told Arab trade unionists on May 26, 1967, "The battle will be a general one and our basic objective will be to destroy Israel."[13] At the time, European public opinion was largely pro-Israel. Jews and pro-Israel non-Jews tended to identify Israel with the victims of the Holocaust and the Arabs as perpetrators. European attitudes began to change when Israel won a swift and sweeping victory. What did not change was the use of the Holocaust and genocide as a metaphor for the Arab-Israeli conflict. Arab, Gaullist, and left-wing media quickly perceived that they could turn the memory of the Holocaust into a powerful propaganda tool *against* Israel. No longer viewed as powerless, the Israelis were depicted in pro-Arab propaganda as perpetrators and the Arabs as their innocent victims, implicitly identifying the Israelis as the new Nazis and the Palestinians as victims of a new Holocaust, a theme that has acquired ever greater potency over the years.[14] There is an unpleasant subtext to such accusations: If the Israelis are the new Nazis, they deserve no better fate than Nazi Germany—utter destruction. *This would allow anti-Semites something denied to them in the Shoah, genocide without guilt.*

DEPLOYING THE ARAB OIL WEAPON

On Yom Kippur, October 6, 1973, Egypt and Syria attacked Israel. Ten days later, in the midst of the war, Saudi Arabia, Iran, Iraq, Abu Dhabi, Kuwait, and Qatar announced a stunning 70 percent rise in the price of oil, from $3.01 to $5.12 a barrel. On October 17, the Arab oil producers reduced production by 5 percent and threatened further cuts of 5 percent a month until Israel withdrew completely from the occupied territories. A day later, October 18, Saudi Arabia announced that it would cut production 10 percent until Arab terms were met. On October 19, Saudi Arabia, Libya, and other Arab oil producers imposed a total oil embargo on the United States and the Netherlands in retaliation for their support of Israel during the war. France and Great Britain were effectively exempt from the embargo—a reward for having denied their NATO (North Atlantic Treaty Organization) ally access to their airfields to resupply Israel. In addition, the Arab attack on Israel was supported by a massive Soviet arms airlift to Egypt. As Henry Kissinger, then U.S. secretary of state, later explained, the United States began an equally massive weapons airlift to Israel to maintain a military balance between the warring parties and to counter the threat of Soviet dominance in the Middle East. According to Kissinger, the warring Arabs and Israelis had become proxies in a contest between the Soviet Union and the United States.[15]

The European response to the Arab oil weapon was swift. Meeting in Brussels on November 6, 1973, two weeks after the war's end, the nine foreign ministers of the European Economic Community (EEC) issued an unambiguously pro-Arab statement listing what they regarded as essential requirements for Middle East peace. These included the termination of Israel's 1967 occupation of Arab territory and recognition of the "legitimate rights of the Palestinians," a condition mild by today's standards but not so in 1973 when the PLO was actively engaged in international terror. The European foreign ministers also asserted the "inadmissibility of acquiring territory by force," a doctrine they applied exclusively to Israel. And, as Bat Ye'or has pointed out, employing an old trick in diplomacy—mistranslation—the foreign ministers distorted the intent of UN Resolution 242 that marked the official end of the Six-Day War.[16] Originally formulated in English, the resolution referred only to an unspecified Israeli "withdrawal from territories" in exchange for an end to the Arab-Israeli conflict. The French translation improperly altered the original meaning to "from the territories" (*des territories*), creating the false impression that under the UN resolution Israel had no legitimate claim to any part of the occupied West Bank. The statement's final paragraph took note of "the ties of all kinds which have long linked" the EEC members to the states "of the south and east of the Mediterranean."[17] In spite of American opposition, the EEC had signaled to the Arabs that it would meet their demands.

The Europeans also attempted to convince the United States to join them in pressuring Israel to withdraw from the occupied territories. According to Kissinger, European leaders complained that the United States was itself to blame for the Yom Kippur War of 1973 because of its failure to force Israel into a settlement. In their view, America had put vital European interests at risk because of "domestic politics." In reality, this was a nasty bit of code language in which the Europeans blamed the United States for allegedly pandering to the Jewish lobby at Europe's expense. Nor has this view lost any of its potency in circles hostile to Israel to this day. European anti-Americanism has a strong and not always latent anti-Semitic component.[18]

On December 4, 1973, the Dutch, badly in need of Arab oil, bowed to Arab pressure, denounced Israel's occupation of Arab territories as "illegal" and demanded a total withdrawal. The change of policy had been prompted by a meeting in The Hague three days earlier of the Saudi and Algerian oil ministers with the Dutch minister of commerce. The oil ministers requested a special anti-Israeli "gesture" as the price of lifting the embargo.[19]

The Nixon administration rejected the European position. The United States insisted that capitulating to the Arabs under pressure would signal weakness and lead to demands for further concessions. Instead, Washington sought a unified response by the oil-consuming nations to counter the Arab oil weapon. Speaking in London on December 12, 1973, Kissinger called for the establishment of "an Energy Action group of senior and prestigious individuals with a mandate to develop within three months an initial action program for collaboration in all areas of the energy problem."[20] Kissinger reasoned that the embargo had been the result of unified action by the producing nations and that only the unified response of the consumers offered any hope of coming to a mutually satisfactory agreement.

Led by the French, the Europeans would have none of it. On December 20, 1973, French president Georges Pompidou told Kissinger that France would not run the slightest risk of an oil cutoff; nor would it participate in any action or policy that might provoke a confrontation with the Arab states.[21]

In mid-September 1974, emboldened by their diplomatic successes, Arab delegates attending a conference of European and Arab parliamentarians in Damascus demanded that the Europeans agree to four points as a precondition for economic cooperation: 1) unconditional Israeli withdrawal to the 1949 armistice lines; 2) Arab sovereignty over the old city of Jerusalem; 3) the participation of the PLO and Arafat in any negotiations; and 4) EEC pressure to detach the United States from Israel "and bring its policies closer to those of the Arab states."[22]

Over time the Europeans agreed to the Arab demands. A common, pro-Arab Middle Eastern policy was formulated that sought to create "a global alternative to American power."[23] The EAD was assigned the task of creating institutional structures to facilitate the integration and harmonization of European and Arab policies in international affairs, culture, education, and the media. Although there was no time limit, the Arabs confidently expected the Europeans to comply. Their confidence was rooted in the credibility of the oil weapon and Europe's surrender to it.[24] The Europeans had unmistakably signaled that they had abandoned all pretense of impartiality and that hostility to Israel, especially from France, would be a cornerstone of European diplomatic policy. Commenting on the creation of the EAD, Kissinger observed that "it was France that acted as the spearhead of the so-called Europe-Arab dialogue, the European alternative to our Middle East diplomacy, whose rationale—never made explicit—could only be dissociation from the United States."[25]

The Arabs also initiated a major effort to gain Christian support for their cause, stressing the theme of the Palestinians as innocent victims and Israel as their oppressors. On November 25–27, 1980, speakers at an Arab Summit meeting in Amman, Jordan, stressed the need for contacts with the Vatican and other Christian organizations, such as the World Council of Churches, to ensure support for "the recovery of full Arab sovereignty over Jerusalem."[26] Even as the mainstream churches, both Catholic and Protestant, continued interfaith dialogue with Jews in the Diaspora, all too often they favored the Palestinians in the ongoing conflict. Unfortunately, the bias against Israel is consistent with a reading of Christian theology that remains deeply rooted in hearts and minds of many clergy and laity, namely, that the Jews have been punitively exiled from their land for rejecting Christ. Replacement theology is an influential, albeit radical, version of that theology with its claim that Jews have been replaced by Christians in God's favor and that all of God's original promises to the

Jews, including the land of Israel, have been inherited by Christianity. Some Arab Christians claim that the Palestinians are the "true Israel" and, whether Christian or Muslim, they alone are entitled to possess the Holy Land. From such ideas to a total demonization of Jews and Judaism is an easy step and often taken. For such Christians, and unfortunately their numbers may be considerable, Israel's unmitigated defeat in a war of survival resulting in genocide would be a fulfillment of biblical prophecy.

The EU's policy reversal was formulated with little public input. Even after the 1973 oil embargo, European public sentiment remained pro-Israel, but with official encouragement, the media played an enormously important role in eventually bringing public opinion in line with EAD policy.[27]

THE NEW EUROPEANS

Georges Montaron, the influential director of *Témoignage Chrétien*, a Catholic weekly newspaper with a strong pro-Arab bias, had anticipated this problem. In a 1970 lecture in Cairo, he advised his Arab audience: "If you succeed in making from authentic Oriental Arabs authentic Frenchmen and Englishmen, what an influence you would yield in Europe."[28] A wave of Arab immigration to Europe, Montaron realized, could turn the tide of public opinion against Israel, as indeed it has.

In effect, Montaron had invited the Arabs to consider immigration to Europe as a weapon in what was, in effect, their *jihad* against Israel. He was well aware that, beginning with Germany's *Gastarbeiter* (temporary guest worker) program in the 1950s, Western Europe was already recruiting Arabs, Turks, Kurds, and other Muslims to solve the labor shortage that had developed during the postwar reconstruction period.[29] However, the temporary workers were expected to return home when no longer needed. Permanent residence would be assured only when either the workers or their children became eligible for citizenship. As in the United States, citizenship in France and Great Britain is governed by *ius soli* ("the law of the soil"), by which citizenship is automatically granted to anyone born in the country. In Germany, citizenship was based on blood kinship (*ius sanguinis*) rather than place of birth, but this changed on January 1, 2000, when new citizenship laws were enacted making it possible to acquire citizenship simply by having been born in Germany, and in some cases through naturalization.[30] Although the Arabs took no reciprocal measures, the Europeans agreed through the EAD to the establishment and financial support of Muslim religious, educational, and cultural institutions for the newcomers.[31]

Ironically, while de Gaulle sought a Franco-Arab alliance before his death in 1970, he was firmly opposed to large-scale Muslim immigration.

In spite of the bitter opposition of the *pieds noirs*, the Algerian settlers of European descent, and much of France's military leadership to an independent Algeria, an important motive for de Gaulle's willingness to separate Algeria from France was his belief that *Algerie française*, the political union of France and Algeria, would eventually lead to a Muslim majority in metropolitan France. On March 5, 1959, de Gaulle told his confidant Alain Peyrefitte:

> Try to mix oil and water. At the end of a moment they will separate again. The Arabs are the Arabs, the French are the French. Do you believe that the French body politic can absorb ten million Muslims, who tomorrow will be twenty million and the day after tomorrow forty million? . . . If all the Arabs and Berbers of Algeria are to be considered French, how could one prevent them from installing themselves in metropolitan France? . . . My village will no longer be called *Colombey-les-Deux-Églises* but *Colombey-les-Deux-Mosquées!*[32]

Had de Gaulle lived, in all likelihood, he would have regarded the EAD-sponsored immigration as a defeat for France and a victory for the Arabs.

With EAD encouragement, Muslim immigration to Europe soared, and with the advent of a new generation, so too did the number of European Muslim citizens. In 2003, for example, only 15 to 20 percent of Germany's Muslims were citizens, but a recent study by the Konrad Adenauer Foundation found that the majority of Muslims are planning to apply or are in the process of applying for citizenship.[33] Writing in the *Washington Quarterly* in 2004, Timothy M. Savage, division chief of the U.S. Department of State's Office of European Analysis, concluded that "these figures indicate that Germany could soon have up to 2.4 million new [Muslim] citizens and, significantly, potential voters."[34] The addition of so many Muslim citizens to the voting rolls could have a major impact on future national elections. With the Christian Democrats and Social Democrats equally divided, Muslim voters, who are overwhelmingly anti-American and anti-Israel, could tip the scales with serious strategic consequences.

Most Germans are far more sympathetic to the Palestinians than to the Israelis. According to a 2004 University of Bielefeld opinion poll, 68 percent of "non-immigrant" Germans believe Israel is waging a "war of extermination" against the Palestinians, while 51 percent believe there is not much difference between what the Israelis are doing to the Palestinians and what the Nazis did to the Jews.[35] In reality, had the Jews of Palestine dealt with the Palestinians as the Nazis dealt with them, few Palestinians would have escaped extermination. There may indeed be a self-exculpatory element in those Germans who liken Jews to Nazis.

By contrast, in her first address to the German Parliament as chancellor, Angela Merkel declared that Germany will stand by Israel and sell the Jewish state two advanced long-range submarines at a cost of $1.17 billion, with Germany sharing one-third the cost. Still, on December 1, 2005, when the UN General Assembly voted overwhelmingly in favor of six one-sided resolutions critical of Israel, Germany, along with every other EU member, voted with the majority. Only the United States and Australia were among the nations voting against the resolutions. In addition, as of this writing, as Iran's leading European trading partner, Germany has done much to strengthen that country industrially and technologically.[36]

A similar surge in Muslim voting power is expected in Spain; Italy, where 10 percent of the approximately 1 million Muslims currently hold Italian citizenship; and the Scandinavian countries, where the percentage of Muslims who are citizens is expected to increase significantly from the current 15 to 30 percent levels. Moreover, as Michel Gurfinkiel, editor-in-chief of *Valeurs Actuelles,* the French conservative journal, has pointed out, "One citizen or resident of France out of five has Islamic and/or Third World roots. No political party or leader in France can ignore it any more. Not even [Nicolas] Sarkozy." Gurfinkiel also commented that the non-Muslim, "Neo-French" with Third World roots tend to identify with their Muslim counterparts because of a common alienation from the French mainstream.[37] As the immigrant population increased in size, it has reinforced Europe's anti-Israel policy; it has also become the seedbed for the renewal of a virulent strain of anti-Semitism throughout Europe.

Montaron was by no means alone in calling for Muslim immigration. As Bat Ye'or has shown, many of the calls for large-scale Muslim immigration into Europe were first floated in *Eurabia,* a journal initiated in the mid-1970s by the European Committee for the Coordination of Friendship Associations with the Arab World. In a July 1975 issue, Tilj Declerq, a Belgian member of the Parliamentary Association for Euro-Arab Cooperation,[38] advanced the view that "policy must be formulated in order to bring about economic cooperation through a combination of Arab manpower reserves and raw materials and European technology and 'management.'"[39] Declerq saw the sharing of technology and manpower as gradually bringing about "as complete as possible an economic integration" between an Arab world with a surplus population and a technologically competent Europe with a declining birthrate.

Clearly, the introduction of so massive an immigrant population into Europe was bound to have revolutionary consequences for the political and religious life, as well as the foreign policy, of the nations of Western Europe. In the aftermath of the Madrid and London bombings, as well as the gruesome murder in broad daylight of Theo van Gogh by a

Muslim extremist on the streets of Amsterdam, and the riots of Muslim youth in France in October and November 2005, there is today much question whether this population can successfully be integrated. Even if one assumes that the majority of Europe's Muslims desire integration, a segment of unknown size not only disdains integration but dreams of a "New Andalusia," a new era of Muslim dominance on the European continent.[40]

ANTI-SEMITIC ATTACKS ACCELERATE

As Montaron had foreseen, massive Muslim immigration has had a profound impact on European sentiment toward Israel and Jews, ranging from the widespread pro-Arab slant in the news media, increased aggression against Jews and Jewish institutions, to Muslim efforts to eliminate Holocaust education in public schools and turn Holocaust commemorative events into propaganda opportunities for the Palestinian "victims" of alleged Israeli genocide. In January 2005, for example, Sir Iqbal Sacranie, OBE, then secretary general of the Muslim Council of Britain, wrote to Charles Clarke, the British home secretary, saying that the Muslim Council would not attend Holocaust Memorial Day, a national observance under the patronage of the Queen, unless it included the "holocaust" of the Palestinian Intifada.[41] In July 2005, some members of the prime minister's all-Muslim advisory committee on Islamic affairs called for the abolition of Holocaust Memorial Day altogether "because it is offensive to Muslims."[42] Continued observance, they warned, would encourage extremism among young Muslims, a not very veiled threat coming shortly after the London subway bombings. In its place, they advocated the creation of a day commemorating all genocide victims, including the Palestinians.[43]

Given their numbers, Muslims have already achieved significant clout in local elections, especially in France and England. To curry favor, some British politicians, such as George Galloway, member of Parliament, and Ken Livingstone, London's mayor from May 4, 2000, until May 4, 2008, have publicly expressed hostility toward Israel. On July 21, 2005, for example, Galloway made an incendiary speech on Syrian TV in which he declared:

Two of your beautiful daughters are in the hands of foreigners—Jerusalem and Baghdad. The foreigners are doing to your daughters as they will. The daughters are crying for help, and the Arab world is silent. And some of them are collaborating with the rape of these two beautiful Arab daughters. Why? Because they are too weak and too corrupt to do anything about it.[44]

In July 2004, Livingstone officially received as an honored guest Sheikh Yusuf al-Qaradawi, the celebrity satellite TV preacher who makes his home in Qatar. In honoring al-Qaradawi, Livingstone ignored the fact that his guest has openly advocated the killing of gays and has expressed approval of suicide bombings targeting civilians in Israel and the indiscriminate killing of Americans in Iraq. From al-Qaradawi's point of view, such attacks constitute defensive *jihad* and, hence, are obligatory for all Muslims capable of carrying out such acts. Characteristically, in a September 2005 interview, Livingstone likened al-Qaradawi to Pope John XXIII.[45] Galloway and Livingstone are but the tip of the iceberg. Many other European politicians seek to curry favor in less obvious ways, especially in foreign policy. In London as well as elsewhere in the West, far Left politicians like Livingstone have joined forces with Islamists in an informal political alliance, bound together by the demonization of Israel and, in the case of the extreme Left, by anti-Semitism.

Other European politicians have looked the other way when attacks on Jews multiplied after the beginning of the second intifada in 2000. This was especially true of former Socialist prime minister of France Lionel Jospin. As of this writing, France has the largest Muslim population in Europe, numbering between 4.5 and 6 million, of which more than three-fifths are citizens.[46] The much smaller Jewish community of approximately 650,000 has increasingly been the target of Muslim extremists. According to a 2004 report by S.O.S. Vérité-Sécurité, an anti-Semitism watchdog organization, 147 Jewish institutions—schools, synagogues, community centers, and businesses—have been attacked. The slogan *"Mort aux juifs"* (Death to the Jews) has been scribbled on school blackboards and uttered at mass rallies. Rabbis have been assaulted. Under pressure from Muslim students, secondary school teachers have canceled classes on the Holocaust.[47]

One of the most savage incidents was the ritualistic near-decapitation on November 19, 2003, of Sebastien Sallam, an Algerian Jew and one of the country's most popular disk jockeys. Sallam's killer was a neighbor who told his mother that he had fulfilled a praiseworthy religious obligation: "I have killed my Jew. I can go to paradise." Nor was Sallam's gruesome murder of interest to the mainstream journals, *Le Monde, Figaro,* and *Libération.* It was reported by only one minor French newspaper, the tabloid *Le Parisien.*[48] Moreover, Sallam's ritualistic near-decapitation resembled that of Theo van Gogh in Amsterdam and that of Ariel Sellouk, a twenty-three-year-old Jew of North African descent murdered by his "friend" Mohammed Ali Alayed, also twenty-three, in Houston, Texas, in August 2003.[49]

These proud, unrepentant killers believed that in killing their Jew they were carrying out their individual obligation as Muslims to conduct *jihad.*

Their behavior was consistent with the al Qaeda document, "Declaration of the World Islamic Front for Jihad against the Jews and the Crusaders," which we cite elsewhere in this work.[50] Although most Muslims domiciled in Europe and North America are unlikely to commit acts of homicidal *jihad,* these quasi-sacrificial killings reveal that there are extremists among them willing to commit such deeds in God's name and nobody can possibly identify all of them.

The revival of European anti-Semitism was long ignored or denied in official circles, but in early 2002 the issue could no longer be swept under the rug. A series of anti-Semitic incidents in early 2002 prompted the European Monitoring Centre on Racism and Xenophobia, an EU-sponsored institution, to commission the Center for Research on Anti-Semitism (CRA) of the Technical University of Berlin to conduct a study on the prevalence of physical and verbal violence against Jews and Jewish institutions. The CRA submitted its 112-page report in October 2002.[51] Despite the CRA's impeccable reputation for objective scientific research, the EU withheld publication of the report, deeming "inflammatory" one of its key conclusions—namely that Muslim and pro-Palestinian groups were largely responsible for the new and violent wave of Jew hatred in Europe. According to the study, of the "191 violent attacks on synagogues, Jewish schools, kosher shops, cemeteries, and rabbis in 2002," most had been perpetrated by "youth from neighborhoods sensitive to the Israeli-Palestinian conflict."[52]

The EU's attempt to suppress the report backfired when it was leaked to the press by an unknown source. In July 2003, U.S. congressman Robert Wexler (D-Florida) wrote to Javier Solana, the EU's foreign policy chief, demanding its release.[53] Forced to respond, the EU issued a revised report in March 2003, claiming that the original was of "poor quality and lacking in empirical evidence." Refuting this claim, the CRA published a detailed account both of its dealings with the EU commission and its research methods, noting: "There is some evidence that it was . . . political pressure from various EU countries on the management board that had led to its [the original report's] non-publication. . . ."[54]

The new version of the EU report blatantly contradicted one of the key conclusions of the carefully researched original. Acknowledging that some of the perpetrators were young Muslims and "people of North African origin," the revised report stated that the largest group of perpetrators of anti-Semitic activities appeared to be young, disaffected white Europeans influenced by extreme right ideas on Jews. This statement was at odds with the original study's findings that in 2002 "the percentage [of anti-Semitic activities] attributable to the extreme right was only nine per cent."[55] The findings of the original EU report have since been corroborated by the U.S. State Department "Report on Global Anti-Semitism," issued on January 5, 2005,[56] as well as by the Anti-Defamation League's (ADL) survey of *Attitudes Toward Jews in Twelve European Countries.*[57]

THE FUTURE OF EUROPE

As its Muslim population increases, Europe faces a growing threat from Islamic extremists. According to Bassam Tibi, A. D. White Professor-at-Large at Cornell University and professor of political science at Germany's Göttingen University, "The goal of the Islamic fundamentalists is to abolish the Western, secular order and replace it with a new Islamic divine order. . . . The goal of the Islamists is a new imperial, absolutist Islamic power."[58] Professor Tibi tells us that, while about half of the world's Muslim population may hope for the future supremacy of Islam, only between 3 and 5 percent are willing to resort to violence and, if necessary, suicide attacks. Unfortunately, his estimates are hardly reassuring; 3 to 5 percent of the world's Muslim population ranges from 39 to 65 million people.

Tibi's assessment of Islamic fundamentalism's goals was confirmed by Sheikh Omar Bakri Muhammad, an extremist Muslim leader formerly domiciled in London. In an interview in *Al-Sharq al-Awsat* (London), July 7, 2006, the sheikh declared that the Islamist movement "will see the banner [proclaiming] 'There is no God but Allah' flying over Big Ben and the British Parliament, with Allah's help."[59] As noted above, similar positions have been expressed by other highly influential Muslim leaders, including Sheikh Yusuf al-Qaradawi, Mayor Ken Livingstone's honored guest in London, Saudi Sheikh Muhammad bin Abd Al-Rahman 'l-'Arifi, imam of the mosque of the King Fahd Defense Academy, and Osama bin Laden.

All authorities agree that European Islam is by no means a monolith. Nevertheless, younger European-born Muslims tend to be more alienated from the dominant culture than are their parents and grandparents. According to a 2003 *Le Figaro* survey, three-fourths of French Muslim respondents regarded the values of Islam as compatible with those of the French Republic, but only one-fourth of those under twenty-five concurred.[60] These alienated European-born Muslims constitute a fertile recruiting group for extremists who openly call for the Muslim conquest of Europe.

Harvard historian Niall Ferguson has observed that "the whole of Western Europe is entering a new era of demographic transformation without parallel in modern times."[61] Mahmoud M. Ayoub of Temple University has projected that "by the early decades of the twenty-first century, Muslims will constitute half the population of France"[62] In a July 28, 2004, interview in *Die Welt*, Princeton professor Bernard Lewis predicted that "Europe will be Muslim by the end of the century."[63] No one can be sure whether such projections will actually come to pass, but regardless of whether Muslims achieve a numerical majority, there can be no doubt that their power and influence in Europe is in the ascendancy. And if present trends continue, we can expect to see an intensification of anti-Israel sentiments and policies as well as a proliferation of attacks against European Jews. Indeed, as Manfred Gerstenfeld, director of the Institute for Global Jewish Affairs, has commented in the aftermath of the Gaza conflict of 2009, "Anti-Semitic and anti-Israeli manifestations reached post–Second World War highs during Israel's recent Gaza campaign."[64]

There is a further potential danger to Europe's Jews. As noted above, as of this writing, there are more than 23 million Muslims in Western Europe. Elsewhere in this work, we noted the widespread protests and riots that took place in the Western world in response to Israel's 2009 incursion into Gaza and suggested that they would be as nothing compared to the violence that would follow a major confrontation between Israel and Iran. Unlike Europe's aging indigenous population, a larger proportion of Muslims than other Europeans are in their late teens and early twenties. Enraged young Muslims could inflict terrible harm on Europe's unarmed Jews who could expect little protection from police reluctant to put themselves at risk. Nor is it likely that the enraged Muslims would stop at the Jews. After the accidental death of two Muslim youths in Clichy-sous-Bois, a working-class suburb of Paris, on October 27, 2005, France experienced its worst civil unrest since the riots of 1968. Were major damage done to Muslims, the violence could easily spill over to the general population.

In the final analysis, the revival of European anti-Semitism is the result of a foreign policy rooted in European dependence on Arab oil and the fatal inability of Europe's indigenous population to reproduce itself. Some forty-odd years ago, in response to a temporary crisis, Europe's leaders made the fateful decision to appease the Arab League and open their gates to a population that includes elements which pose a serious threat not only to Jews but, as the Madrid and London bombings and the November 2005 riots in France demonstrate, to all Europeans.

5

Iran: Apocalyptic Nuclear Genocide?

On June 7, 1981, Israeli F-15 and F-16 jets destroyed Osirak, the French-built, Iraqi nuclear reactor. In September 2007, the Israelis took out a Syrian nuclear site under construction with North Korean assistance.[1] Israel was responding to a potential threat to its very existence. Israel's suspicions concerning Syria's intentions were confirmed on February 19, 2009, when the International Atomic Energy Agency (IAEA) reported that analysis of environmental samples taken from the site "revealed a significant number of anthropogenic natural uranium particles (i.e. produced as a result of human processing)."[2]

Ironically, by taking out Osirak in 1981, Israel was serving not only its own interests but those of the Islamic Republic of Iran, its most dangerous adversary. At the time, Iran was in the midst of a war with Iraq. On September 21, 2004, Iran celebrated her "Sacred Defense Week" with a military parade commemorating Iraq's 1980 attack and the eight-year war that followed, in which over a million people are estimated to have perished.[3] A principal feature of the parade was the display of Iran's Shahab-2 ballistic missile and the introduction of the newly developed Shahab-3. A banner was draped over the side of the Shahab-2 with the message, "ISRAEL MUST BE UPROOTED AND WIPED OFF [THE PAGES OF HISTORY]"[4]; another banner was draped over the side of a trailer carrying the more advanced Shahab-3 missile. It read "WE WILL CRUSH AMERICA UNDER OUR FEET."

The threatening messages were not new nor were the threats idle. They directly contradicted Iran's statements to the international community that it was developing nuclear energy facilities for peaceful civilian purposes. Nor did Iran make any attempt to disguise her real intentions. Iranian State Television broadcast an official commentary of the event stating: "These missiles enable us to destroy the enemy with missile strikes wherever he is."[5] The Shahab-3, based on a North Korean update of a Soviet Scud missile, is one of Iran's most advanced missiles. With a range of 800 miles and a payload of 1,540 pounds, it is capable of striking almost any Middle Eastern target, including Tel Aviv, Ankara, Riyadh, Cairo, and the U.S. Fifth Fleet in the Persian Gulf. Iran also possesses the more powerful Shahab-4 missile and is working on a missile with a range of 1,875 miles. Such a missile would put every major European capital within range.[6] Moreover, on February 3, 2009, Iran successfully launched its first domestically produced satellite.[7] In effect, the Islamic Republic of Iran has been threatening Israel with nuclear *jihad*.

That threat was significantly increased when Iran successfully launched its new Sejil-2 two-stage, solid-fuel missile with a range of 2,000 kilometers on May 20, 2009. Its accuracy in destroying its target was especially impressive. According to Western military sources cited by DEBKA/file, an unofficial Israeli intelligence source, "Iran is at least two or three years ahead of Israel's missile defenses." As of this writing, Israel relies on the Arrow 2 antimissile system to intercept incoming missiles, but the system works only when missiles are dangerously close. The Arrow 3 system, which is designed to take out longer-range missiles, will not be ready for several years.[8]

From the start of the 1979 revolution, enthusiastic crowds have responded to the Ayatollah Khomeini's characterization of America as the "Great Satan" and Israel as the "Little Satan," by chanting "Death to America; Death to Israel." On September 25, 1979, the Ayatollah Khomeini called on Muslims to "prepare themselves for the battle against Israel."[9] Khomeini and the Iranian leadership have consistently held that the destruction of Israel is a nonnegotiable, religious imperative. In the eyes of the Iranian leadership, no action by Israel could alter its indelible illegitimacy.

The most extreme threats have come from religious and political radicals, one of the most important being President Mahmoud Ahmadinejad. On October 26, 2005, during the final week of Ramadan, Ahmadinejad told Tehran university students "Our dear imam [Khomeini] ordered that this Jerusalem-occupying regime [Israel] must be erased from the pages of time. This was a very wise statement."[10] Ahmadinejad has repeated the threat on a number of occasions, including Tehran's infamous Holocaust Denial Conference in December 2006. In the same university address, Ahmadinejad added a rhetorical question and gave his own answer: "Is it possible to witness a world without America and

Zionism? You had best know that this slogan and this goal is attainable and surely can be attained."[11]

At the time, more cautious elements in Iran sought to distance themselves from Ahmadinejad's threat, but the Iranian president had no intention of being explained away. Two days later, he reminded the world of his official status and repeated the threat, cheered on by thousands of supporters: "My words," he said "are the Iranian nation's words."[12]

Unfortunately, some words, once spoken, alter both the military and political landscape. They can neither be lightly dismissed nor easily explained away. There was nothing new in the Iranian president's threats. Other Muslim leaders, both Sunni and Shi'ite, have made similar threats for decades. For example, on June 1, 1967, five days before the start of the Six-Day War, Ahmad Shuqayri, Yasser Arafat's predecessor as chairman of the PLO, was queried by reporters concerning the fate Israelis might expect in the coming war. He replied, "Those who survive will remain in Palestine. I estimate that none of them will survive." However parsed, this was a genocidal threat, the promise of a second Auschwitz. In the case of the Islamic Republic of Iran, the threats have been reinforced by the nation's military capabilities, made possible by its oil wealth, and by the contempt implicit in its official sponsorship of an international Holocaust-denial conference, the so-called "International Conference to Review the Global Vision of the Holocaust," December 11–13, 2006. At the conference, Ahmadinejad again declared: "Israel will soon be wiped out."[13] Those who deny the Holocaust are all too often the ones seeking its repetition.

Ahmadinejad's was one of the more recent Iranian threats promising Israel's destruction. On December 14, 2001, also at Tehran University, the allegedly "moderate" Ali Akbar Hashemi Rafsanjani, Ahmadinejad's predecessor as Iran's president, stated, "If one day, the Islamic world is also equipped with weapons like those that Israel possesses now, then . . . [their] global arrogance would come to a dead end because the use of a nuclear bomb in Israel will leave nothing on the ground, whereas it will only damage the world of Islam."[14]

Rafsanjani's threats have been backed up by deeds. He played a singularly important part in creating Iran's nuclear weapons program. Consistent with the Shi'ite belief in the superlative virtue of martyrdom, Rafsanjani indicated a willingness to sacrifice millions of his own people in a catastrophic nuclear exchange in order to obliterate Israel. In effect, Rafsanjani declared that, unlike the United States and the Soviet Union during the Cold War, *because of the losses Iran was willing to accept, it was undeterrable.* We return to that crucial issue below.

Six days before Rafsanjani spoke, Ayatollah 'Ali Meshkini, former chairman of the powerful Assembly of Experts, declared in a sermon

in the Holy City of Qum, "You should make the world understand that
. . . Israel must be destroyed."[15] Speaking on al-Aqsa TV on February 29,
2008, Dr. Walid al-Rashudi, head of the Department of Islamic Studies at
King Saud University, Saudi Arabia, claimed that no more than "50–60
Jews" died in the Holocaust in "Germany or Switzerland" and these
numbers cannot be compared to the number that allegedly died at the
hands of the Israelis in the "the real Holocaust in Gaza." Al-Rashudi then
asked rhetorically, "What compensation will satisfy us?" Answering his
own question, he declared, "By Allah, we will not be satisfied even if all
the Jews are killed."[16]

An even more ominous threat was uttered on January 31, 2002, by
Ahmadinejad's superior, Supreme Leader Ayatollah Ali Khamenei, who
called for continued terrorism against the "cancerous tumor of Zionism
. . .," a biological metaphor often used by political leaders to express
genocidal intent.[17] Khamenei's threat was by far the most serious. He,
not Ahmadinejad, has ultimate authority over any Iranian decision to use
weapons of mass destruction.

THE IRANIAN PERSPECTIVE

At one level, possession of nuclear weapons is a matter of national sovereignty for Iranians. In spite of having signed the Nuclear Non-Proliferation Treaty (NPT), Iranians tend to regard restrictions on their country's
ability to acquire or create nuclear weapons as an unacceptable limitation
on its national sovereignty with few, if any, compensating benefits.[18]
*Moreover, in view of the fact that Iran is a self-proclaimed theocracy, subordi-
nation to any non-Islamic or infidel norm, institution, or organization may be
temporarily necessary but ultimately unacceptable.* In addition, many Iranians
see Western attempts to prevent their acquisition of weapons of mass
destruction (WMD) as both self-serving and hypocritical. During the Iraq-
Iran War of 1980–1988, Saddam Hussein launched poison gas attacks on
a number of Iranian villages in which hundreds of civilians of all ages
were killed. Not only was there no protest by the Western powers or the
UN, but much of Iraq's weaponry equipment was supplied by the United
States and other Western nations.[19]

Initially, Khomeini opposed nuclear weapons on religious grounds.
After Iraq's weapons of mass destruction were employed against Iranian
civilians, Khomeini concluded that Iran's survival depended on developing its own WMD. He directed Rafsanjani to initiate such a program.

As of this writing, Iran appears to be on the threshold of success in
creating nuclear weapons and the means with which to deliver them and
President Barack Obama appears to have decided that his administra-

tion can do little to forestall this development. Indeed, in his address to the Muslim world at Cairo's al-Azhar University on June 4, 2009, the president stated that Iran, like all other nations, should have the right to access peaceful nuclear power as long as all proliferation concerns are put to rest.[20] The next day the International Atomic Energy Agency (IAEA) reported that Iran had increased the number of its installed centrifuges to seven thousand, "more than enough . . . to make fuel for up to two nuclear weapons a year. . . ."[21] The Israeli government reacted swiftly to the report, declaring that Tehran had acted despite three sets of UN Security Council sanctions designed to compel Tehran to freeze such activities. Israel further stated that the IAEA statement revealed that "neither the international community, nor Israel, could rely on IAEA supervision inside Iran."[22]

America's response to the nuclear programs of both Iran and North Korea have been marked by considerable confusion. On the one hand, successive American administrations have declared the programs unacceptable and threatened sanctions if Iran and North Korea refused to desist, to no avail. On the other hand, influential American voices have recommended a phased withdrawal from Iraq and a reversal of American policy toward Iran. This was evident both in the report and the reactions to it of the Iraq Study Group (ISG), also known as the Baker-Hamilton Commission, after its cochairmen, former secretary of state James A. Baker and Lee Hamilton, president and director of the Woodrow Wilson Center of Scholars.[23] The ISG recommended that:

> the United States should engage directly with Iran and Syria in order to try to obtain their commitment to constructive policies toward Iraq and other regional issues. In engaging Syria and Iran, the United States should consider incentives, as well as disincentives, in seeking constructive results.[24]

It would appear that many of the recommendations of the ISG have been adopted by the Obama administration.

The most influential rebuttal to the ISG report was Frederick Kagan's *Choosing Victory in Iraq: A Plan for Success in Iraq.* Kagan essentially recommended the addition of twenty-five thousand American troops in Iraq and the adoption of what became known as the surge strategy. Kagan also rejected the idea that negotiating with Iran and Syria would stop the violence.[25] Some commentators advocated an American understanding with Iran that, in effect, left Israel to face a nuclear-armed Iran alone. That, in fact, was implicit in the National Intelligence Estimate on Iran of 2007 and was the import of the Baker-Hamilton report.[26]

At first, the George W. Bush administration appeared to reject the ISG recommendations, but it soon began to reverse course in the hope that negotiations with Iran would yield a positive result. The appointments of Robert M. Gates as secretary of defense by both Presidents Bush and Obama, and Leon E. Panetta as Obama's director of the Central Intelligence Agency were important indications of the policy change. Both had been members of the Baker-Hamilton Commission. Gates had also been cochair with Zbigniew Brzezinski, national security adviser under President Jimmy Carter, of a 2004 Council on Foreign Relations report, *Iran: Time for a New Approach,* that, in effect, called for the United States to draw closer to Iran at Israel's expense.[27]

Even those who argue that diplomatic compromise is possible between the United States and Iran see little hope for compromise between Iran and Israel. After thirty years in power, most informed observers agree that the Iranian regime's hostility toward Israel remains the most unshakable element in its foreign policy and the least likely to change. Iranian hostility has been manifest in support and subsidies that country has given to Hezbollah in Lebanon, Hamas in Gaza and the West Bank, Islamic Jihad in Palestine, a variety of terrorist organizations globally, as well as the Syrian government of Bashar al-Assad. Moreover, the posture of unremitting hostility toward Israel serves important Iranian strategic interests. As an uncompromising supporter of the Palestinian cause, Iran has been able to transcend the Sunni-Shi'ite divide even as it fosters the rise of Shi'ite power in the larger Muslim world against the opposition of Arabia's Sunni rulers.[28] It gives Iran tremendous power and prestige in the "Arab street" and binds together the disparate elements in both Iran's ruling religious elite and some relatively secular elements in the Iranian body politic. Rejection of Israel's legitimacy thus becomes the test of fidelity to the Iranian revolutionary tradition and the glue that binds together the disparate elements that are heir to the Iranian Revolution.[29]

THE AUSCHWITZ FACTOR

Iran's hostility toward Israel is very largely grounded in religion. The two countries do not have a common border and economic issues do not play an important role between them. This gives Iran's leadership the ability to adopt a more radical posture than would be the case were the two countries physically contiguous. Nevertheless, were Iran to continue to threaten Israel's existence while making progress toward the acquisition of a nuclear arsenal, the "Auschwitz factor" will very likely come into play. For many Jews, one of Auschwitz's most enduring lessons can be expressed in a single sentence: *Believe those who promise to kill you, especially when they seek the weapons with which to do it.* After Auschwitz, many, perhaps most Jews regard this as prudent counsel.

Auschwitz has other lessons: *Unless a strategic national interest is at stake, no nation will risk its blood and treasure to rescue citizens of another country.* Indeed, the Zionist quest for sovereignty stemmed in large measure from that perception. In the case of Iran, many who argue that the United States can resolve its problems with Iran diplomatically also say—some openly, some covertly—that Israel's survival is not a strategic national interest. This could mean that Israel may have to cope with Iran's existential threat unaided, in spite of the fact that there are circumstances in which a successful Israeli attack on Iran's nuclear facilities might serve the strategic interests of the United States, the European Union, and even Sunni Muslim countries such as Saudi Arabia, Egypt, and the Gulf States.

ISRAEL'S COPING RESOURCES

Israel is not without coping resources with which to meet an Iranian threat. According to the *Wall Street Journal*, when Admiral Mike Mullen, chairman of the Joint Chiefs of Staff, was asked at a meeting with the *Journal's* editorial board on April 2, 2009, "whether Israel was capable of inflicting meaningful damage to Iran's nuclear installations, his answer was a simple 'Yes.'"[30]

According to one scenario, Israel perceives a nuclear-armed Iran poised to launch a nuclear strike. Unable to wait for irrefutable evidence of a launch, the Israel Defense Force (IDF) launches a crippling preemptive strike before Iran's weapons are fully activated. Carrying out such an attack would not be easy. Nevertheless, some security analysts regard it as feasible. For example, Whitney Raas and Austin Long, both affiliated with the Massachusetts Institute of Technology (MIT), came to that conclusion in an analysis published in the journal *International Security*.[31] According to Raas and Long, several conditions would have to be met for an Israeli attack to succeed: Three Iranian facilities would have to be taken out of action: (a) the heavy water plant and plutonium production reactors under construction at Arak, (b) a uranium conversion facility in Isfahan, and (c) a uranium enrichment facility at Natanz. Destruction of the Natanz site is critical.[32] Effectively to damage all three sites would require twenty-four five-thousand-pound and twenty-four two-thousand-pound bombs. Given the limited capacities of Iran's ground and air defenses, Raas and Long believe the Israeli Defense Force will require twenty-five F-15Is and twenty-five F-16Is.[33]

Raas and Long calculate that twenty-four Israeli planes must reach Natanz, six must reach Isfahan, and five Arak. Israeli aircraft would have to traverse great distances over hostile airspace to reach their destination, but Raas and Long estimate that the distances are manageable.

For the Iranian defense to prevail, Raas and Long estimate that the Iranians would have to destroy at least one-third of the Israeli force before it reached its targets. Raas and Long do not regard this outcome as likely. Israeli aircraft or missiles might also reach Kharg Island, through which 90 percent of Iran's oil is exported, thereby doing serious damage to Iran's economy.

Raas and Long do not discuss the possibility that Russia might deliver its most-advanced surface-to-air missile system, the SA-20 system, also known as the S-300, to Iran. This system is reportedly capable of tracking up to one hundred targets while engaging up to twelve at one time.[34] Moreover, experts claim that the system is far more resistant to electronic countermeasures than earlier Russian systems. On December 18, 2008, RIA, the Russian News Agency, announced that Russia was in the process of delivering the system to Iran.[35] Operational deployment would present "a nearly insurmountable obstacle" for the conventional aircraft of the Israeli Defense Forces.[36] Iranian acquisition of the system would also vastly complicate any plans the United States might have had to take out Iranian nuclear facilities with conventional weapons.

As of this writing, it is not at all certain that Russia has actually delivered the system to Iran. Russia has been promising to deliver nuclear technology to Iran for years, but has often delayed actual delivery. This puts the Russians in an advantageous position vis-à-vis the United States, which may be more concerned with Iran receiving a comprehensive air-defense system than the transfer of nuclear technology. According to one source, the Russians could be using the Middle East "as a lever to extract American concessions in their own near abroad."[37] The Russian invasion of Georgia in August 2008 was a reminder that the Russians want no serious American interference with their plans for Georgia, Belarus, Ukraine, and the central Asian lands that were formerly part of the Soviet Union. The threat to supply a highly effective surface-to-air missile system to Iran might be Russia's way of persuading America, mired in Afghanistan, not to interfere with its plans. Indeed, on February 17, 2008, a story appeared in *Pravda* stating that Russia was delaying the shipment of the S-300 missile system "hoping to improve ties with USA."[38]

It may also be possible for Israel to take electronic countermeasures to disable the S-300 system. In August 2008, a senior Israel defense official stated that "if the system is delivered, an EW [electronic warfare] system will likely be developed to neutralize it." He added that "No country will want to buy the system if it is proven ineffective."[39] We discuss the electronic measures Israel might take below.

Raas and Long argue that Iran might be deterred from proceeding with its weapons program because Israel has a "reasonable chance of success." From the perspective of any rational, cost-benefit analysis, it makes absolutely no sense for the Iranians to proceed with a nuclear weapons program in which Israel is the designated target. Some Israeli circles, primarily on the left, are willing to gamble that the Iranians can be deterred. They reject an Israeli preemptive strike as too risky and favor a MAD (mutually assured destruction) approach that determined U.S.-Soviet relations during the Cold War. An important expression of that approach appeared in *Haaretz* on May 15, 2009:

> Only a clear and credible signal to the Iranians, indicating the terrible price they will pay for attempting a nuclear strike against Israel, will prevent them from using their missiles. The Iranians have no logical reason to bring about the total destruction of their big cities, as could happen if Israel uses the means of deterrence at its disposal. Neither the satisfaction of killing Zionist infidels, nor, certainly, the promotion of Palestinian interests would justify that price. Israeli deterrence in the face of an Iranian nuclear threat has a good chance of succeeding precisely because the Iranians have no incentive to deal a mortal blow to Israel.[40]

This analysis in *Haaretz* is characteristic of Israel's secular left in its failure to recognize that Iran may indeed have incentives—religious incentives—"to deal a mortal blow to Israel."

Other Israelis may believe that a preemptive strike may be Israel's only option. Although such an attack would concentrate initially on military targets, the Iranians have made it clear that they would make no distinction between civilian and military targets. The Israelis must take into account the possibility that they could be the object of simultaneous missile strikes by Iran, Syria, Hezbollah, and Hamas.[41] Once the escalation begins, perceiving the threat to be existential, the Israelis might feel compelled to unleash their nuclear arsenal on civilian targets.

There would undoubtedly be an Iranian response. Both Israel and Iran have second-strike capability. On January 17, 2008, Israel Radio announced that Israel had successfully tested a long-range ballistic missile capable of carrying an "unconventional payload." The same day President Ahmadinejad stated in a newspaper interview that "the Zionist regime . . . would not dare attack Iran. The Iranian response would make them regret it, and they know this."[42] On other occasions, Iran has threatened to launch both its own missiles and those of Hezbollah in response to an Israeli attack.

In November 2007, Anthony Cordesman, a highly regarded security analyst at Washington's Center for Strategic and International Studies and former director of defense assessment for the secretary of defense, examined the consequences of the likely failure of diplomatic efforts to prevent Iran from acquiring a nuclear arsenal.[43] In March 2009 Cordesman and Abdullah Toukan, a senior associate at the center, completed yet another study on the subject.[44] Cordesman starts from the premise that the acquisition of nuclear weapons by Iran would leave the world with the constant prospect of a nuclear exchange between Israel and Iran. In the earlier study, Cordesman took issue with Rafsanjani who asserted that in such an exchange Israel would be completely wiped out while Iran, though severely wounded, would be capable of survival. Cordesman argued that the reverse would be true. According to Cordesman, Israel would be capable of inflicting vastly greater damage in a nuclear exchange on population centers. Between 16 million and 28 million Iranians would die in the first twenty-one days, with an incalculable long-term death rate. By contrast, Israel would be likely to suffer between two hundred thousand and eight hundred thousand dead. Beyond the first twenty-one days, Israel's toll could be much higher. The crucial factor in minimizing long-term casualties would be the competence of civil defense and public health facilities, where Israel has a considerable advantage. Theoretically, it would be possible for Israel to recover both demographically and economically. By contrast, "Iranian recovery is not possible in the normal sense of the term."[45]

According to Cordesman, the difference in possible outcomes can be attributed to the weapons disparity between the two nations. Iran is expected to have fewer than fifty bombs, predominantly fission, most with a yield of 20 to 30 kilotons, some with a 100 kiloton yield.[46] A 100 kiloton bomb can inflict third-degree burns at eight miles; a 1 megaton bomb can inflict third-degree burns at twenty-four miles; Israel is believed to have more than two hundred boosted and fusion nuclear weapons, most with a yield of between 20 and 100 kilotons and some with a yield of 1 megaton and with far more accurate and sophisticated delivery systems.[47] In the 2009 study, Cordesman and Toukan offered a more cautious view of Israel's ability to launch a successful nuclear strike against Iran:

> A military strike by Israel against Iranian Nuclear Facilities is possible and the optimum route would be along the Syrian-Turkish border then over a small portion of Iraq then into Iran, and back the same route. However, the number of aircraft required, refueling along the way and getting to the targets without being detected or intercepted would be complex and high risk and would lack any assurances that the overall mission will have a high success rate.[48]

In reality, neither side could "win" such a war. I seriously doubt Cordesman's scenario in which Israel could survive the loss of eight hundred thousand and the accompanying damage to its infrastructure even though Israel might be able to inflict greater damage than Iran. If Cordesman is correct about Israel's survivability, it would have to hold back part of its nuclear arsenal as "a reserve strike capability to ensure no other power can capitalize on strikes against Israel."[49] Were either Egypt or Syria tempted to attack or even make preparations for an attack, their population centers and resource facilities, such as the Aswan Dam and even the Suez Canal, would, in all likelihood, be destroyed with monumental loss of life.

The title of Raas and Lang's analysis "Osirak Redux? Assessing Israeli Capabilities to Destroy Iranian Nuclear Facilities," points to the difference in scope between their study and Cordesman's. Raas and Lang are primarily concerned with Israel's ability to take out Iran's nuclear sites, not its civilian population. Cordesman assumes that each side would quickly be compelled to target the other's civilian population. Regrettably, there are circumstances in which such a descent into unprecedented mass slaughter might be seen by some as Israel's most likely option when confronted with Iran's oft-repeated threats.

A more tentative but no less pessimistic scenario concerning Iran's persistent threats to destroy Israel is offered by Andrew F. Krepinevich, president of Washington's Center for Strategic and Budgetary Assessments.[50] Krepinevich calls his chapter on Israel and Iran "Armageddon: The Assault on Israel." He opens and closes the chapter with a reflection on the summer of 1914, when Europe's great powers drifted toward a war that nobody wanted and that almost everybody assumed would be of brief duration. Instead, "massed formations of soldiers on both sides were mowed down by modern firepower, leaving an indelible stain on the military profession and a lasting scar on European societies."[51] Krepinevich suggests that "recent events in the Middle East have put the region—indeed the world—on a path that promises, if not guarantees, an outcome similar to the cataclysmic events that were triggered a century ago. . . ." There would, however, be an important difference. The coming war, if indeed it does come, could be "the first in nearly seventy years in which nuclear weapons are used."[52]

In Krepinevich's scenario, Iran successfully triggers a nuclear device sometime in 2011. Failing to gain support for serious UN sanctions, the United States is reluctant to act alone. Initially, Hezbollah and Hamas, Iran's proxies, limit their attacks to sporadic, low-level missile strikes, but under the pressure of Iran's deteriorating economic situation, both step up their attacks using more long-range, precision, guided missiles supplied by Iran. An even more serious challenge confronts Israel when an Israeli combat ship is hit and severely damaged by a Chinese Silkworm, anti-ship, cruise missile launched by Hezbollah. Israel's seaborne commerce is endangered by the strike and Israel's enemies appear to have struck a decisive blow against her economy. Among the options considered by Israel is the Armageddon Option, which calls for retaliatory Israeli missile attacks on Iranian ports. As the Israelis mobilize, Iran threatens Israel with nuclear obliteration.

In the midst of the crisis, the Iranian president refers to the coming of the Twelfth Imam in a speech that some observers take to mean that Iran is willing to "light the fire of a large-scale conflagration . . . involving the possible—and perhaps the likely—use of nuclear weapons."[53] (It should be noted that Krepinevich's scenario is the only one that takes note of the apocalyptic element in the official narrative of Iran's leadership.) In an attempt to find a diplomatic solution, the president of the United States dispatches the secretary of state to Tehran, the first such visit since the Iranian Revolution, but the United States has little leverage. Nor can the United States deploy an advance missile defense system in the region as the Iranians would be likely to view the effort as an attempt to compromise its nuclear capability. Krepinevich then cites a statement by Najaf Ali Mirzai, a former Iranian diplomat, on the relative strength of Iran and the United States:

> Iran's supporters are widespread—they're in Iraq, they're in Afghanistan, they're everywhere. And you know, the American soldiers in the Middle East are hostages of Iran, in the situation where a war is imposed on it. They're literally in the hands of the Iranians. The Iranians can target them wherever, and Patriot missiles aren't going to defend them and neither is anything else.[54]

Nevertheless, in spite of Iran's apparent regional advantage, the major parties to the conflict slide toward a war that, like the war that began in 1914, "all will likely come to regret."

In all of the above scenarios, were Israel to rest content with taking out Iran's nuclear facilities, an effort whose success is by no means certain, it would not have removed Iran's long-term genocidal threat. In time, devastated weaponry and facilities could be rebuilt and/or replaced. The ensuing rage and humiliation would, in all likelihood, provide an effective goad for reconstruction and revenge. Yet, unless Iran is stopped before acquiring nuclear weapons, Israel will have few policy options, none good. In spite of obvious hazards, a preemptive strike targeting Iran's civilian population might appear to some Israelis to be their most rational option. I shudder when I write these words, but I must remind the reader that the leaders of Iran have repeatedly threatened to wipe out Israel, not the reverse. Under the circumstances, should diplomacy fail, the only way to prevent Iran from rising in revenge after an attack on its military facilities would be to take out its civilian centers first. In all likelihood, the closest Israel would come to such a preemptive strike would be to adopt a "fire-upon-launch" strategy in which Israel targets Iran's civilian centers the moment it learns that Iran has launched missiles at Israel.

Were Israel either to launch a preemptive strike or a fire-upon-launch attack on Iran's major civilian and industrial centers, it could do monumental damage. Nor would it necessarily have to depend on its air force. Israel possesses the Jericho-3 missile, a two-stage, long-range, ground-to-ground ballistic missile that can be equipped with a nuclear, chemical, or biological warhead and is said to have a range of up to 4,500 kilometers (2,800 miles). Such a missile could conceivably overcome the problem of penetrating unwelcome airspace. In addition, Israel has three German-built, Dolphin Class submarines that can fire nuclear-tipped cruise missiles. In 2003 they were reported to have a range of 1,500 miles.[55] Moreover, if Israel concludes that it must target major metropolitan centers, pinpoint accuracy will not be necessary.

About 20 percent of Iran's population, some 12 to 14 million people, live in metropolitan Tehran, an area Cordesman describes as a "topographic basin [with] mountain reflector" and a "nearly ideal nuclear killing ground."[56] Because of the horrendous loss of life and the monumental global economic dislocations such a strategy would entail, a "victory" would indeed be pyrrhic. If it survived Iranian retaliation, Israel's relations with every other country would be poisoned for years to come with the most damaging consequences to every aspect of Israeli life. Nevertheless, no matter how their words are interpreted, Iran's leaders have long been contemplating genocidal *jihad*. Having radically demonized Israelis for thirty years, neither Iran's leaders nor the partisans of Ahmadinejad who were responsible for his "reelection" on June 13, 2009, are likely to have any compunction about targeting Israel's civilian centers in a first-strike assault. Despite such threats, Israel cannot launch a preemptive nuclear strike at an Iranian civilian center without becoming a permanent international pariah. The anger and the violence manifest in the protests in the West during the Israeli incursion into Gaza would be as nothing in comparison to the massive violence that would be perpetrated by enraged Muslims and their extremist allies in the Western world in response to an Israeli attack, however necessary, against an Iran preparing to launch a nuclear attack. And the likelihood that such violence might spill over to assaults on the general population cannot be ruled out. Unfortunately, a crucial factor in Israeli calculations is that, after Hitler, they can neither ignore nor dismiss Iranian threats as hyperbole. In a nuclear crisis, inaction or ineffective action could conceivably be tantamount to national suicide.

The distinguished Israeli historian Benny Morris has suggested the bleakest scenario by far. There is an Arab saying: "Eat them for lunch before they eat you for dinner."[57] Although that may be the grim choice facing Israel in the not-too-distant future, Morris has expressed the opinion that Israel cannot make that fateful choice and that Iran will employ its Shahab III and IV ballistic missiles to inflict a second, even more de-personalized Holocaust on Israel:

> One bright morning, in five or ten years . . . a day or a year or five years after Iran's acquisition of the bomb, the mullahs in Qom will convoke a secret session . . . and give President Ahmadinejad, by then in his second or third term, the go ahead.[58]

Unlike Anthony Cordesman, who believes that Israel can better survive a nuclear attack than Iran, Morris believes that Israel will be incapable of surviving a well-planned, coordinated Iranian nuclear assault. According to Morris, unlike the first Holocaust, the second Holocaust will be devoid of guilt for the perpetrators and bystanders alike. Indeed, it is likely to be the occasion of great rejoicing in much of the Muslim world. Both the Muslim "street" and the Muslim elite have been "taught" by a monumental, ongoing propaganda effort of ever-increasing effectiveness that Jews and Zionists are the absolute "embodiment of evil" and that, as a supreme religious imperative, "Israel must be destroyed." In a parallel effort aiming at Israel's demonization, much of the Western media, especially in Europe, has defamed Israel as a "racist oppressor state" and that in a multicultural age, Israel "is an anachronism and superfluous."[59]

Morris argues that Israel, isolated internationally, will be paralyzed by indecision, hoping against hope that Iran will act "rationally." But, such a hope will prove to be a chimera. According to Morris, "the Iranians will launch their rockets. And, as with the first Holocaust, the international community will do nothing. It will all be over, for Israel, in a few minutes."

Morris's scenario is by far the grimmest and the bleakest. Yet, it must be taken seriously. Morris has been an informed student of Israel and its conflicts for decades. He knows his people and their leaders better than do most outsiders. He does not discuss Israel's second-strike, submarine capability, perhaps because of his conviction that the Iranians will proceed to annihilate Israel at a time of their own choosing, no matter what the costs to their own people, believing that Allah will protect Iran or that Israel's destruction is worth any price.

Nor does Morris discuss the "Samson option."[60] From the birth of the State of Israel, there have been Muslim leaders who have not hesitated to threaten "Zionists," the State of Israel, and its people with extermination, albeit without the capabilities Iran possesses or will possess in the foreseeable future. It was inevitable that Israeli leaders would reflect on possible responses to a worst-case scenario. One response was ruled out. There would be no second Holocaust such as that envisioned by Morris. No enemy would do to the Israelis what the Germans did to Europe's Jews.

There was a moment during the 1973 war when some Israeli leaders feared the worst but rejected Masada as a model. After the Romans destroyed the Second Temple in 70 C.E., surviving Zealots made their way to the fortress of Masada where they held out for three years against the Tenth Roman Legion. When further resistance was seen as useless, they killed themselves, their wives, and children rather than surrender and endure slavery or worse at the hands of the Romans. In all, 960 Jews died on Masada.[61] Those who died there did not take the enemy with them. Samson, blinded by the Philistines, did. Scripture depicts Samson's revenge:

> And Samson said, "Let me die with the Philistines!" And he bent with all his might so that the house [the temple of Dagon, the principal Philistine deity] fell on the lords and all the people who were in it. So the dead whom he killed at his death were more than those whom he killed in his life.[62]

If the Samson option were employed in a nuclear age, a doomed Israel could take down much of the Middle East with it. To threaten any nation with extermination is dangerous, especially one armed with weapons of mass destruction. To do so with the Israelis after the Holocaust borders on insanity!

Finally, we consider a somewhat more optimistic scenario suggested by Jerome Gordon, a respected former military intelligence officer.[63] Noting that the scenarios suggested by Cordesman and Toukan in their 2009 report involve refueling over the Turkish-Syrian border both to and from Iran, Gordon argues that "The IAF [Israeli Air Force] will have a hard time locating an area above which the tankers can cruise without being detected by the Syrians or the Turks." Gordon contends that Israel's successful attack on the Syrian nuclear reactor on September 6, 2007, "demonstrated IAF mastery of ECM [electronic countermeasures] and the ability to knock out radar countrywide." He further comments that "The joint IAF-Greek air maneuvers of last summer [2008] indicated the ability of the IAF to spook [disarm by electronic means] the Russian S-300 anti-air missile system. . . ."[64]

Gordon goes on to suggest that Typhoon-class cruise missiles, which the Israeli navy has equipped with both conventional and non-conventional (nuclear) warheads might be launched against Iranian targets from Israel's 800 ton Dolphin class submarines positioned in either the eastern Mediterranean or the Arabian Sea beyond the Straits of Hormuz.[65]

He further argues that with its Jericho II and III ballistic missiles, Israel could launch an electronic magnetic pulse (EMP) attack on Iran's electrical grid and its command-and-control net, disrupting the country's entire economy, especially its nuclear development program.[66] The Jericho III would carry a low-yield nuclear warhead—less than 3 kilotons to be detonated in a low orbit of say fifty miles. The collateral damage from an Israeli EMP assault on Iran might involve the destruction of satellites in low orbit in the vicinity of such an attack and the disabling of electrical grid complexes of adjacent Arab states in the Gulf. If successful, such an attack would minimize the risk to Israel's military assets.

Gordon concludes his analysis with a reflection on another Israeli asset:

> The other non-conventional option may be already in hand in Israel, given its world-ranked prowess in cyber-warfare—a hacking attack on the Power grid supporting the Iranian nuclear development facilities. That would have the benefits of targeting these facilities and the Revolutionary Guards command-and-control net, while avoiding the losses using aircraft and missiles of the IAF conventional attack force.

IRAN: DOES RELIGION TRUMP POLITICS?

No one knows whether and under what circumstance Iran might launch a nuclear attack on Israel. *A fundamental issue is whether religion trumps politics and national interest or national interest trumps religion in Iran's attitude toward Israel.* Ironically, before the Iranian Revolution, Iran and Israel had reason to cooperate as non-Arab communities. Under the Shah, Iran supplied Israel with 75 percent of its petroleum supplies.[67] During the Iraq-Iran War, in spite of Ayatollah Khomeini's vitriolic animosity, Israel considered Iraq the greater danger. Although there is no evidence of coordination, Iranian Air Force F-4 fighter jets bombed the Osirak Reactor on September 30, 1980, less than a year before Israeli jets took out the reactor.[68] Moreover, between the outbreak of the Iran-Iraq War in September 1980 and the end of 1983, Israel sold weapons to Iran with covert American approval in what became known as the Iran-Contra Affair.[69]

Iran participated in an arms deal with Israel out of desperation. Iraq was winning the war with both financial and material help from the United States and other Western powers, including the sale of poison gas. Yet, even as Israel served as a conduit supplying Iran with American-made weapons, Iranian leaders continued to vilify Israel and call for its destruction.

There was a time during the presidency of Mohammad Khatami (1997–2005) when Iran's position toward Israel appeared to soften slightly. Partly in response to the widespread publicity accorded Samuel J. Huntington's book, *The Clash of Civilizations,* Khatami proposed a "Dialogue of Civilizations" in which artists, intellectuals, politicians, and writers would gather together and discuss those elements in their cultures that they shared.[70] Khatami pointedly suggested that Jewish scholars might participate.[71]

When asked in a CNN interview on January 7, 1998, about Iran's opposition to the Middle East peace process, Khatami qualified that opposition by stating, "we don't intend to impose our views on others or to stand in their way."[72] When in 2002 the Arab League endorsed Saudi Crown Prince Abdullah's resolution calling for collective recognition of Israel if it withdrew from the occupied territories and recognized the Palestinian "right of return," Khatami took the unprecedented step of declaring "We will honor what the Palestine people accept." Although Abdullah's proposals were unacceptable to Israel, they did represent a small step in a very different direction from the league's habitual rejection of any recognition of Israel. Instead of opposing the Saudi initiative, Khatami indicated that his government was prepared to change its position.

Nevertheless, many experts on contemporary Iran have questioned the sincerity of his alleged moderation.[73] Even so, whatever doubts may have surfaced concerning Khatami's moderation, his successor Mahmoud Ahmadinejad sought to revive Khomeini's revolutionary extremism and reverse the "Khatami compromise." Referring to Khatami's very modest steps toward a less hostile attitude toward Israel, on October 28, 2005, Ahmadinejad declared, "Anybody who takes a step toward Israel will burn in the fire of the Islamic nations' fury."[74]

Apart from religious and ideological considerations, Iran's uncompromising public hostility to Israel has yielded, as noted above, important strategic benefits and would yield even more were it to succeed in destroying Israel. A genocidal strike against Israel would be welcomed by large segments of the Arab and the larger Muslim world, especially the Arab "street." As Ray Takeyh has observed, "Iran's ardent embrace of the Palestinian cause allowed an isolated Shiite regime to project its influence in the heart of the Arab world and mobilize regional opinion behind its claims."[75] As of this writing, the benefits of a policy of unremitting hostility far outweigh the costs.

EXCURSUS

The National Intelligence Estimate of 2007: An Invitation to Genocide?

Prior to December 3, 2007, there appeared to be something close to unanimity among American and other Western intelligence analysts concerning Iran's active involvement in the acquisition of nuclear weapons. On that date, sixteen American intelligence agencies issued an unclassified summary of the National Intelligence Estimate's (NIE) *Iran: Nuclear Intentions and Capabilities*.[76] On first reading, the NIE summary looked as if it had reversed the judgment of the May 2005 NIE which assessed "with *high confidence* that Iran is currently determined to develop nuclear weapons despite its international obligations and international pressure . . . (emphasis added)." By contrast, the first sentence of the 2007 NIE states: "We judge with *high confidence* that in fall 2003 Tehran halted its nuclear weapons program (emphasis added)." Such an apparently extreme reversal of judgment was bound to attract maximum media attention and obscure any qualifications that followed in the body of the text. As the editors of the *Wall Street Journal* commented, "only in a footnote" did the NIE qualify its definition of Iran's "nuclear weapons program" to exclude "Iran's declared civil work related to uranium conversion and enrichment."[77] In reality, as the authors of the NIE knew, the very same process of uranium enrichment and conversion may be used for the creation of *both* civilian nuclear power stations *and* nuclear weapons.[78] Thus, there are good reasons to question both the validity of the NIE's distinction between Iran's civilian and military nuclear energy programs and the motives of its authors.

In spite of UN resolutions to desist, as noted above, Iran has continued to enrich uranium. On July 26, 2008, Ahmadinejad declared that Iran was employing six thousand centrifuges, double the previously assumed number. At the same time, Iranian officials declared that Iran plans to employ as many as fifty-four thousand centrifuges for uranium enrichment.[79]

Thus, Iran has continued to use an ever-increasing number of centrifuges to enrich uranium in spite of repeated UN resolutions to desist. The enrichment has no civilian purpose and is in violation of the Nuclear Non-Proliferation Treaty to which Iran is a signatory. Apart from Iran's huge petroleum reserves, Iran will have all the fuel it needs for civilian nuclear power with the completion of the nuclear reactor constructed by Russia at Bushehr.[80]

The timing of Ahmadinejad's announcement of the additional centrifuges was significant. It came a week after the United States had reversed course and sent a top American diplomat to participate in one of a seemingly endless series of negotiations to get Iran to desist from its nuclear weapons program or face serious UN sanctions. Iran's response was to announce a further enhancement of its weapons program.

The NIE states that "until fall 2003, Iranian military entities were working under government direction to develop nuclear weapons."[81] Put differently, the NIE concedes that, until discovered in 2003, Iran repeatedly lied about its clandestine nuclear activities in violation of its obligations as a Nuclear Non-Proliferation Treaty signatory. Moreover, the very same group, the National Council for Resistance in Iran (NCRI) that exposed Iran's nuclear weapons program in 2002, rejected the findings of the 2007 NIE or, more precisely, the misleading first sentence of the document.

The NCRI has had an excellent track record of exposing both Iran's clandestine nuclear activities and Iran's state-sponsored terror attacks. On the basis of its informants within Iran, the NCRI claims that Iran did indeed shut down its nuclear fuel program in 2003 but only to disperse the installations and resume the program in 2004.[82] Nor was British intelligence impressed with the 2007 NIE. According to the *Daily Telegraph* (UK), a "senior British intelligence official" let it be known that his agency believes that "the CIA has been hoodwinked by Teheran (sic)."[83] British analysts believe that "Iranian staff, knowing their phones were tapped, deliberately gave misinformation." The official stated that "British spies shared the concerns of Israeli defense (sic) chiefs that Iran was still pursuing nuclear weapons." Apparently, French analysts also had their doubts. On January 31, 2008, during a visit to Washington, French defense minister Hervé Morin told reporters: "'Coordinated information from a number of intelligence services leads us to believe that Iran has not given up its wish to pursue its (nuclear) program' and is 'continuing to develop' it."[84] Most surprising was the skepticism expressed by staff members of the UN's International Atomic Energy Agency (IAEA). Speaking on condition of anonymity, an IAEA official noted that the analysis in the report twice described the Iranian enrichment program at Natanz as civilian and omitted the observation, often previously cited by the United States, that "that there is no logical application for enriched uranium other than eventual military use." Referring to the finding's characterization of uranium enrichment as civilian, the official allied with the international agency said, "We wouldn't go that far."[85]

There may also be a question of the reliability of the current NIE given the dismal track record of the U.S. intelligence community, including past NIE assessments made "with high confidence."[86] If the 2007 NIE is accurate, the 2005 NIE was dead wrong. To take but one past example, a special NIE, dated September 19, 1962, dismissed the possibility that the Soviet Union would deploy nuclear ballistic missiles in Cuba. Twenty-five days later, a U-2 spy plane photographed a Soviet missile site in Cuba and the Cuban Missile Crisis began in earnest.[87] And there have been other mistaken or misleading NIEs.[88]

If the 2007 NIE was deliberately misleading—and we do not know that it was—why would its authors have set forth a misleading report? Admittedly, few officials outside of the closed circle of those who formulated the NIE can claim knowledge of what actually transpired. Nevertheless, the issues involved are so fraught with danger for peace in the region, and perhaps beyond, that to seek a plausible narrative is neither futile nor frivolous.

In one grim scenario, those responsible for the NIE, namely the Office of the Deputy Director of National Intelligence for Analysis (DDNI/A), may have known exactly what it was doing and may have welcomed the likely outcome of its publication. In the fall of 2006, there was considerable talk that the George W. Bush administration was preparing to bomb or otherwise attack Iran. The highly publicized NIE rendered that outcome just about impossible.[89] The document represents the consensus of sixteen intelligence agencies, led by Dr. Thomas Fingar, the DDNI/A. Dr. Fingar is superbly trained academically with an impressive publication record. (Cornell, BA; Stanford, MA and PhD in political science). An expert on China, he speaks Chinese.[90] Moreover, the professionals who worked with Dr. Fingar are also highly intelligent men and women who must have been aware of the likely consequences of publication of the 2007 NIE. At the very least, publication relieved Iran of the pressure of Security Council sanctions and would have left Iran "free to pursue its military-nuclear ambitions."[91]

In this scenario, *the State Department, the Office of the Director of National Intelligence, and America's European allies may have conceivably regarded the benefits of a nuclear-armed Iran either as inevitable or as outweighing any possible cost.* The NIE team may have had no illusions that Iran would abandon either its military-nuclear program or its intention to "wipe Israel off the map." With effective UN sanctions no longer possible, Israel might find itself compelled to take the risks of attempting to eliminate Iran's nuclear weapons single-handedly. Put differently, *the NIE may have placed Israel in the position of having to do the dirty work for all of Iran's potential adversaries or of having to risk the prospect of national annihilation.* In any event, as noted, Iranian retaliation would be swift and multifaceted. In addition to Iranian nuclear strikes, the rockets of Hezbollah in the north and Hamas in the south would be unleashed, and perhaps chemical and biological weapons from Syria.[92] As noted above, really to be effective, an Israeli strike might entail targeting Iran's civilian population centers, bringing upon Israel even stronger international condemnation than it received for taking out Iraq's Osirak nuclear reactor and for stopping Hamas's Gaza rockets in 2009.

There could be an even grimmer scenario: Some members of the NIE team *may actually have welcomed the possibility that Iran might develop the capacity to lay waste to Israel.* The plausibility of such a scenario rests on the assumption that if one wishes to know what intelligent people really want, the likely consequences of their behavior is a good place to start. Offering up Israel to Iran would "solve" the Arab-Israeli problem in a manner not unlike Hitler's Final Solution and might conceivably even be followed by a "punitive" American retaliatory strike against Iran to prevent any menace to Saudi Arabia and America's oil supply. Such a strike might enable the United States to reestablish its hegemony in the Middle East.[93] If there were something approaching an unspoken consensus on this issue, there would be no need for a paper trail that future historians might chance upon.

While this scenario is only a speculation, it is not without precedent in World War II. By 1943 the magnitude of the Nazi Final Solution had become known to British and American leadership circles. On March 23, 1943, the late William Temple, archbishop of Canterbury, pleaded in the House of Lords that immediate steps be taken to rescue Europe's Jews. In response, the Foreign Office proposed to the U.S. Department of State that "an informal United Nations Conference" be held to consider what steps could be taken for refugees from Nazi extermination, but insisted that *no special preference be given to Jewish refugees.* Confident of a sympathetic re-sponse, the Foreign Office candidly informed the State Department why it did not want to pressure Nazi Germany to stop the slaughter:

> There is the possibility that the Germans or their satellites may change over from the policy of extermination to one of extrusion, and aim as they did before the war at embarrassing other countries by flooding them with alien immigrants.[94]

The conference was held in Bermuda April 19–29, 1943. Exactly as planned, nothing was accomplished. *The responsible officials of both nations preferred to let genocide take its course rather than attempt any effort at allevia-tion that might risk an immigrant flood.* Moreover, the Foreign Office was well aware that the real danger Britain, an island nation, might face was not the flooding of Britain with unwanted refugees but Palestine.

At the end of the war, the sheer horror visited upon Europe's Jews resulted in a primordial resolve on the part of the majority of the world's Jews to bring into being a sovereign Jewish state in Palestine. Traditional Judaism had always regarded existence outside of the Land of Israel as *galut*, exile. Both the Holocaust and the increasingly murderous Euro-pean anti-Semitism of the last decades of the nineteenth century and the first half of the twentieth century had demonstrated how irredeemably murderous *galut* could be.[95] For most of Europe's surviving Jews, the continent had become a veritable charnel house and the movement of *return* from exile had become unstoppable for both secular and religious survivors, regardless of any and all obstacles.

Nevertheless, there were obstacles. As we have seen, the prospect of an independent Jewish state in Palestine with the will and the resources to welcome the survivors and other Jews was anathema to both the gov-ernments and the peoples of the Arab world. Moreover, the Arabs had and still have very powerful American allies. These included executives of the major oil companies, many of the military and civilian leaders of what is now the Department of Defense, and the Arabists of the State

Department. The latter were the mediating link between the Arab world and their own government.[96] At Israel's birth, the State Department's Arabists were vehemently opposed to American support or even recognition of an independent Jewish state, as were George Marshall, secretary of state; James V. Forrestal, secretary of defense; and the influential group of public officials who later were to become known as the "wise men": Robert Lovett, Dean Acheson, Charles Bohlen, George Kennan, and Dean Rusk. All viewed Israel as an intrusive, alien presence in an Arab-Muslim world with which they felt more or less comfortable. They also regarded President Harry Truman's support of the infant Jewish state as that of a small-time Midwestern politician who placed his own political interests above America's national interests. Had they won over Truman, there would have been no Jewish state. [97]

There has, in any event, often been a divide between the support accorded to Israel by American political leaders and disapproval of that support by an influential group of diplomats and career civil servants. One way of looking at the NIE was that it was an effort by career civil servants and their public allies to wrest control of Middle Eastern policy from a weakened, lame-duck president. They succeeded with George W. Bush. A comparable effort failed during the presidency of Harry Truman. No such effort seems necessary for Barack Hussein Obama.

Could there be today officials within the State Department, the CIA, and other branches of government who might be willing to create a situation that could predictably result in genocide? There is a difference between actually implementing a program of genocide and creating a situation in which one becomes an indirect accessory to it. The latter is the more likely alternative. For example, in 1943 a group of senior aides to Secretary of the Treasury Henry Morgenthau Jr., none of whom was Jewish, discovered a consistent pattern of obstruction by the State Department of any and all efforts to rescue Europe's Jews. They also found that the State Department had, in effect, surreptitiously blocked Gerhardt Riegner of the World Jewish Congress from using the cable facilities of the American Legation in Bern, Switzerland, to convey to Rabbi Stephen S. Wise and other American Jewish leaders "information concerning the murder of the Jewish population in Europe."[98] At the time, Riegner had no other means of communicating with the United States.

On January 24, 1944, Josiah DuBois, one of Morgenthau's senior aides, submitted the group's findings to him in a document, "Report to the Secretary on the Acquiescence of this Government in the Murder of the Jews."[99] Morgenthau in turn submitted it to Franklin Roosevelt as "Personal Report to the President." Morgenthau also accused the State Department of supporting the British policy of thwarting all efforts aimed at saving Jews, lest the unwanted survivors find their way to Palestine, the United States, or Great Britain. Nazi propaganda minister Joseph Goebbels was by no means in error, at least as far as the Foreign Office and the State Department were concerned, when he wrote in his diary on December 13, 1942, "I believe that both the English and the Americans are happy that we are exterminating the Jewish riff-raff."[100] "Happy" was perhaps too strong a term. Nevertheless, these officials undoubtedly felt that Hitler's Final Solution was also *their* solution to the Jewish problem. Moreover, as is well known, American planes bombed sites within five miles of Auschwitz but the War Department adamantly refused the urgent requests of Jewish and other organizations to bomb the camp so that the killing might be slowed down if not halted altogether.[101]

When the British government refused admission to Palestine of all but a very small number of Jews during World War II in full knowledge of the ongoing Holocaust, it was not actively implementing a program of genocide and, as we see elsewhere in this study, Bernard Law Montgomery's victory over Erwin Rommel at El Alamein saved the Jews of Palestine from the fate of the Jews of Europe. Nevertheless, with the full support of the State Department, Britain had indirectly but knowingly fostered extermination as the policy most likely to prevent further immigration of Europe's Jews to Palestine. The formula was simple: The more Jews who went up in smoke, the fewer Jews would reach Palestine. That policy was not all that different from the policy followed by Hajj Amin al-Husseini during the war.

After receiving Morgenthau's report and with the 1944 presidential elections approaching in which irate Jewish voters in key states might make a difference in the outcome, Roosevelt's policies did change. Until then, there was little if any difference between British and American policy toward Europe's rapidly declining Jewish population. Three years later, the same State and War Department officials who had worked so hard to block all avenues of escape for the remnant of Europe's Jews now opposed the creation of a Jewish state in a partitioned Palestine.

There have been other situations in which State Department officials have preferred to let genocide take its course. In an unpublished paper entitled "The Pin-Stripe Approach to Genocide," dated January 1, 1994, Richard Johnson, head of the Yugoslavia Desk of the State Department from 1990 to 1992, accused his superiors of deliberately ignoring genocide in Bosnia. Johnson's paper had been circulating in Washington for several weeks when the *New York Times* reported its existence.[102] At the time, I was able to obtain a copy of the original manuscript, which begins, "My thesis here is a simple one: senior U.S. government officials know that Serb leaders are waging genocide in Bosnia, but will not say so in plain english [sic] because this would raise the pressures for U.S. action."[103] After detailing the evasions and obfuscations deliberately practiced by the State Department under both the Bush I and Clinton administrations, Johnson concluded by quoting statements made by Undersecretary of State Peter Tarnoff and Department Counselor Timothy Wirth at a State Department luncheon for Elie Wiesel, at which Johnson was present, on April 28, 1993:

> Weisel [sic] argued that whether or not genocide was underway in Bosnia, the Serb concentration camps and mass murders there constituted a moral imperative for decisive outside intervention. Tarnoff took Weisel's point but noted that failure in Bosnia would destroy the Clinton Presidency. *Wirth agreed that the moral stakes in Bosnia were high, but asserted that there were even higher moral stakes at play, "the survival of the fragile liberal coalition represented by this Presidency."*[104]

It would seem that as far as Wirth was concerned, a Democratic victory in 1996 was more important than the death of hundreds of thousands of Bosnian Muslims. Moreover, Wirth was a figure of considerable importance in American life, having previously served as U.S. senator from Colorado and as a member of the Harvard Board of Overseers.

The accuracy of the 2007 NIE was further challenged on February 19, 2009, when the International Atomic Energy Commission announced in Vienna that it had discovered an additional 460 pounds of low-enriched uranium, a third more than Iran had previously disclosed, and that Iran had now amassed more than a ton of uranium, a quantity sufficient, with added purification, to produce at least one bomb.[105]

In December 2007, officials in the Departments of State and Defense, as well as the intelligence agencies, may have knowingly produced a misleading document that had the effect of compelling Israel to face the risks of a nuclear exchange with Iran and Iran's satellites in Gaza, Lebanon, and Syria unaided. It may be that some traditions never die.

RELIGION, MENDACITY, AND TERROR

Given the present Iranian regime's record for mendacity and terror, it is difficult to understand why the NIE's reversal of judgment should be regarded as credible. Iran is still governed by the same leaders who were responsible for its very serious nuclear-proliferation deceptions, as well as manifold programs of state-sponsored terrorism. To take but one example among many, on March 17, 1992, an Iranian-funded Hezbollah team carried out the bombing of the Israeli embassy in Buenos Aires that killed 29 people and wounded 292. An even worse attack took place in Buenos Aires on July 18, 1994. An Iranian-organized suicide bombing leveled the seven-story building of the Asociación Mutual Israelita Argentina (AMIA), Buenos Aires's Jewish community center. Eighty-five men, women, and children were killed and more than 300 wounded, all of whom were civilians participating in recreational or social activities. It was the greatest single assault on a Jewish target since World War II.

The Islamic Republic of Iran was almost immediately suspected of having been responsible, but it took a decade before an Argentine court finally charged Iran's leaders with having used their very considerable resources to shift the blame away from themselves to corrupt Argentine officials. At one point, an attempt was even made to suggest that the bombing was an inside job perpetrated by the Israelis.[106]

The most visible culprit in the cover-up appears to have been Federal Judge Juan José Galeano, the Argentine official assigned to investigate the case in 1994. In seven fruitless years, Galeano's deliberately incompetent investigation yielded no credible results. This generated considerable anger in the Argentine public which did not fail to notice the speed and effectiveness of investigations into the terror bombings in New York, London, and Madrid. For example, Spanish police were able to destroy the terror network responsible for the Madrid terror bombings of March 11, 2004, in less than a week.[107]

Because of the egregious irregularities in his investigation, Judge Galeano was finally removed from the case in December 2003.[108] On September 2, 2004, the court charged that:

> Judge Galeano left the way of finding truth and engaged in behavior contrary to the law, behavior in which he had the collaboration, by action or by omission, of several organs in the three branches of government that gave him political support and cover for his irregular and unlawful acts.[109]

On August 3, 2005, Galeano was formally impeached and removed from his position as a federal judge for mishandling the investigation. Galeano and Hugo Anzorreguy, the director of intelligence in the government of former President Carlos Saul Menem, were charged with obstruction of justice.[110]

It was only possible to get to the bottom of the case after Nestor Kirchner became president of Argentina in May 2003. Kirchner branded the failed investigation a "national disgrace," waived the protection of the Government Secrets Act, and ordered several intelligence officers to be interrogated by the Third Federal Criminal Oral Tribunal.[111] Many of the facts had been leaked earlier, but President Kirchner's action stripped the veil of secrecy from intelligence officers, making it possible to compel them to testify in open court and for the court to find that the state itself was responsible for much of what happened, especially the tainted, fruitless, multiyear investigation.

In 1998 National Council for Resistance in Iran (NCRI) members came forward with evidence that the Iranian government at the very highest level had planned and orchestrated the attack. This information was submitted to a bipartisan group of members of U.S. Congress who shared it with the Department of State. The department later confirmed the accuracy of the evidence.[112] It should be noted that in August 2002 the NCRI delivered to the International Atomic Energy Agency hitherto unknown but highly accurate information that Iran was building two nuclear sites, a uranium enrichment plant in Natanz and a reactor in Arak to produce plutonium.[113]

In 2003 Miguel Ángel Toma, director of Argentina's *Secretaria de Intelligencia del Estado* (Secretary of State Intelligence or SIDE), confirmed Iran's role in the Buenos Aires bombings when he presented a secret report containing thousands of pages of evidence of Iran's role to his Israeli counterpart, Meir Dagan, then head of Mossad. Toma was appointed in 2002 by President Eduardo Duholde to replace his tainted predecessor Carlos Soria. The SIDE report tallied with investigations by the Mossad, the Federal Bureau of Investigation (FBI), and the CIA.[114] According to the report, the attacks were partly in revenge for the Israeli assassination in March 1992 of Abbas Mussavi, Hezbollah's first leader. Both attacks were approved at a meeting on August 14, 1993, in Mashad, Iran's second largest city, by Ayatollah Ali Khamenei, Iran's supreme leader, and Ali Akbar Hashemi Rafsanjani, then Iran's president. Also present were Foreign Minister Ali Velayati and Intelligence Minister Ali Fallahin.[115] According to Toma, Iranian authorities began working with Hezbollah to implement the attack following the meeting.[116]

I cannot stress strongly enough that the decision to carry out this mass murder 8,569 miles distant from Tehran ultimately came from the theocracy's highest religious leader, Ayatollah Ali Khameini. Article 109 of the Islamic Republic's constitution stipulates that "the essential qualifications and conditions for the [supreme] Leader" must include:

1. Scholarship, as required for performing the functions of mufti in different fields of *fiqh* [Islamic jurisprudence].
2. Justice and piety, as required for the leadership of the Islamic *Ummah*.[117]

These provisions are in accord with the theory of *velayat-e faqih*, first formulated by Ayatollah Khomeini, whereby an unelected religious leader would have supreme authority over all of Iran's national affairs.[118]

The mass-murder operation carried out at the behest of Iran's supreme religious leader, with its bribery and corruption of Argentine public officials, resembled nothing so much as a large-scale Mafia operation, save that the Mafia was never known deliberately and randomly to select targets with whom it had no grievance. Nor did the Mafia bestow upon its actions the aura of religious sanctity. It should be obvious that the Ayatollahs dwell in an entirely different moral universe than any we in the West have had to deal with. Even when agents of the KGB or the clandestine sections of Western security services engaged in operations aimed at eliminating opponents, they used the rationale of *raisons d'état* or national interest to justify their actions. Rarely, if ever, did they justify mass murder of human beings of all ages as a sanctified act in the service of God.

Such behavior would seem to call into question the value of entering into dialogue with the Islamic Republic or their clients, Hamas, Hezbollah, and Islamic Jihad, as recommended by the Baker-Hamilton Study Group and apparently adopted by the Obama administration, in order to achieve a genuinely peaceful settlement of the outstanding issues in the conflicts of the Middle East. Conceivably, one could come to an agreement on a *hudna*, or truce, but that would at best be a temporary arrangement in which concessions would have to be carefully calibrated. In such a truce, one rule ought to be paramount: *Paper promises can always be broken; territory, once surrendered, can only be repurchased with a nation's blood.*

Further confirmation of Iran's role in the bombings came from three depositions by a former senior official in Iran's intelligence agency, Abdolghassem Mesbahi. According to Mesbahi, Carlos Menem, Argentina's president from 1989 to 1999, was deeply involved in the official cover-up. In one of his depositions, Mesbahi declared that Iran had deposited $10 million in a Menem-designated, numbered Swiss bank account to guarantee that Iran's involvement in the bombing would not emerge from the investigations.[119] In return, Menem agreed to "make declarations that there was no evidence that Iran was responsible."[120] Mesbahi further stated that the money came from a $200 million account controlled by Rafsanjani and a son of Ayatollah Ruhollah Khomeini.[121] Argentine officials claim that Mesbahi's account was confirmed by a second Iranian who twice visited the Argentine Embassy in Tehran. Responding to an Argentine inquiry, Swiss authorities confirmed that a deposit had been made in a bank account controlled by Menem for the amount specified by Mesbahi.[122] In any event, Menem's term in office was marked by an unusually high number of corruption scandals involving over one hundred government officials and business leaders, including members of the former president's own family.[123]

Why did Iran choose Buenos Aires for an attack on Jewish targets? Apparently, it was partly in revenge for Menem's reneging on an agreement to transfer nuclear technology to Iran and train Iranian nuclear technicians in Argentina.[124] Menem had been raised as a Muslim by his immigrant parents, but converted to Roman Catholicism in 1966. Thereafter, he spoke of himself as a "Christian of Syrian Ancestry."[125] Before becoming president, Menem was quite open in proclaiming his anti-Zionist commitments. While adult apostasy from Islam is normally considered a capital offense, Menem's conversion did not prevent him from having warm relations with secularist Baathist Syria and, at times, Islamist Iran. In a 2002 interview, Menem's ex-wife, Zulema Fatima Yoma, stated that he had only converted to Christianity because he wanted to become president. Until 1994 Argentina's constitution required the president to be a Roman Catholic. One recalls the statement of Henry IV of France (r. 1589–1610), *"Paris vaut bien une messe."* (Paris is well worth a mass.) Yoma also said that she considers him to be a Muslim, a view widely shared by the Argentine public.[126] However, once in office, Menem yielded to American and Israeli pressure and terminated the agreements with Iran. Menem was also the first Argentine head of state to visit Israel.[127] His *volte face* aroused considerable Muslim anger and resentment.

Iran first lobbied Menem to honor the agreements and then threatened him. When threats failed, Iran's senior leadership decided to punish Argentina. By hitting Jewish targets in Buenos Aires, Iran was in effect killing two birds with one stone. It was punishing Argentina and demonstrating to Israel and to the Jews of the world that there were few places in the world beyond the reach of an avenging Iran.

In July 2005, the Kirchner government issued a decree formally accepting a share of the blame for the failure of the investigations into the AMIA bombing. On October 25, 2006, prosecutors in Buenos Aires accused Iranian authorities of directing Hezbollah to carry out the attack. The prosecutors formally charged Iran and Hezbollah with the bombing. Argentina's chief prosecutor, Alberto Nisman, declared, "We deem it proven that the decision to carry out an attack July 18, 1994 on the AMIA was made by the highest authorities of the Islamic Republic of Iran which directed Hezbollah to carry out the attack."[128] Nisman also identified Ibrahim Hussein Berro, twenty-one, a member of Hezbollah, as the suicide bomber who blew up the community center, a view in which the FBI concurred.[129] Nissim called for the arrest of former president Rafsanjani and seven others, most of whom still hold high office in Iran as of this writing. Not surprisingly, a spokesman for Iran's foreign ministry called the accusations "a Zionist plot" and both Hezbollah and Iran denied any involvement in the bombing.

On November 8, 2006, Judge Rudolfo Canicoba Corral ordered the issuance of international arrest warrants for Rafsanjani and eight other Iranians in connection with the 1994 bombing. The others included Ali Fallahian, former intelligence chief, Ali Akbar Velayati, former foreign minister, two former commanders of Iran's Revolutionary Guard, Mohsen Rezai, and three former officials of the Iranian Embassy in Buenos Aires including Hadi Soleimanpour, ambassador of Iran to Argentina at the time. Soleimanpour was arrested in Britain, but was later released for "lack of evidence."[130]

On September 25, 2007, Kirchner addressed the UN General Assembly stating that Iran had failed to cooperate with Argentina in her probe of the terror bombing.[131] This was first time Kirchner mentioned Iran in connection with the bombing at the United Nations. Several days earlier, Mohsen Baharvand, Iran's top diplomat in Buenos Aires, told *Clarín*, Argentina's largest-circulation daily newspaper, that if Kirchner delivered a speech critical of Iran at the UN, Iran would interpret it as an indication that Argentina supports war against Iran. "For our country," Baharvand said, "this assembly is very important, it will show which countries are for or against war. It is possible that if President Kirchner accuses Iran, many countries will interpret Argentina as being for war."[132]

Less than two months later on November 7, 2007, Interpol's General Assembly met in Marrakech, Morocco, and voted to place on its most-wanted list Ali Fallahian, former Iranian intelligence chief; Mohsen Rabbani, former cultural attaché at the Iranian Embassay in Buenos Aires; Ahmad Reza Asghari, an Iranian diplomat; Mohsen Rezaei, former leader of the elite Revolutionary Guards; and Hezbollah militant Imad Mughniyeh, one of the world's most wanted terrorists. The vote was 78–14 with 26 abstentions.[133] Interpol declined to issue warrants for Rafsanjani, Velayati, or Soleimanpour. As of this writing, they are still wanted by Argentina, save for Imad Mughniyeh who was assassinated by a car bomb in Damascus on February 12, 2008.

The AMIA bombing was one of the worst terror attacks ascribed to Iranian state authorities, but there have been many others. For example, on September 17, 1992, agents of the Islamic Republic of Iran murdered three leaders of the Democratic Party of Iranian Kurdistan (PDKI) and one of their supporters in a private dining room of the Mykonos Restaurant in Berlin.[134] The getaway car was driven by Farajollah Haidar, a Lebanese national and a key member of Hezbollah in Osnabrück. Haidar abandoned the car and a sports bag containing the murder weapons. The bag was found five days later, enabling German police speedily to identify the perpetrators.[135]

The trial of the five Mykonos bombing suspects began in the Berlin Court of Appeal on October 28, 1993, and lasted three and a half years. The court heard 176 witnesses and examined documentary evidence that included secret intelligence files and tapes of Iranian television broadcasts. Abdolhassan Banisadr, Iran's exiled, first post-revolutionary president, testified that the Mykonos murders had been personally ordered by Ayatollah Khamenei, Iran's supreme leader.[136] Banisadr also testified about the role of Iran's elite Special Affairs Committee in "commissioning and overseeing political assassinations." According to Banisadr, such assassinations required the approval of both Khamenei, committee chairman, and Rafsanjani, a committee member.[137]

A key prosecution witness, first identified as witness "C" and subsequently as Abolghassen Mesbahi, a former high-level Iranian intelligence operative, described in meticulous detail how assassination targets beyond Iran's borders required the approval of the committee and the signatures of both Ayatollah Khamenei and Rafsanjani. Mesbahi also supplied eyewitness accounts of discussions by the committee that preceded the attack at Berlin's Mykonos restaurant in September 1992. His testimony was checked by Germany's foreign intelligence service, the *Bundesnachrichtendienst*, or BND, which was reputed to have the best information on Iran among Western intelligence agencies.[138] Mesbahi's testimony was further corroborated by the tape shown to the court of a remarkably frank interview given by Ali Fallahian, Iran's minister of intelligence and head of its National Security Council, on Iranian television station IRB on August 30, 1992. In the interview, Fallahian claimed that Iran's agents had struck "decisive blows" at the regime's enemies both within and beyond that country's borders. Fallahian explicitly mentioned the Democratic Party of Iranian Kurdistan (PDKI).[139]

The court found four men, three of whom were Lebanese nationals affiliated with Hezbollah, guilty of murder.[140] Judge Frithjof Kubsch declared that "The Iranian political leadership ordered the crime. They made a decision to silence an uncomfortable voice. This is an official liquidation measure ordered without a verdict."[141] Chief Federal Prosecutor Kay Nehm issued an international arrest warrant for Fallahian. German authorities concurred with Mesbahi's testimony that the action was authorized by the Special Affairs Committee and that Ayatollah Ali Khamenei and Rafsanjani had ordered the killings. Ali Fallahian and Foreign Minister Ali Akbar Velayati, also committee members, were charged with having supervised the actual operation. The same four were accused of authorizing and organizing the Buenos Aires bombing.[142]

On June 25, 1996, members of *Hizballah al-Hijaz* (Saudi Hezbollah), detonated a twenty-five-thousand-pound truck bomb that utterly destroyed Khobar Towers, which was part of a housing complex near Dhahran, Saudi Arabia, for foreign, predominantly American, military personnel. Nineteen American airmen were killed and more than four hundred additional military and civilian personnel were wounded, many seriously, in the meticulously planned attack.[143] Subsequent investigations by the *Mahabeth*, the Saudi secret police, and the FBI revealed that the actual attack was carried out by Saudi Hezbollah members, but that the entire operation was "planned, funded and coordinated by Iran's security services, the IRGC (Iranian Revolutionary Guard Corp) and the MOIS (Ministry of Intelligence and Security), acting on orders from the highest levels of the regime in Teheran."[144] As was the case in many other Iranian terror attacks, authorization came from Ayatollah Ali Khamenei and Rafsanjani.

In response to questions at a meeting of the Council on Foreign Relations on June 7, 2007, William E. Perry, secretary of defense in the first Bill Clinton administration, stated that although he initially believed that Iran was responsible for the Khobar Towers bombing, he had concluded in retrospect that it was "probably masterminded by Osama bin Laden."[145] Perry appears to be echoing a suggestion made by the 9/11 Commission that al Qaeda may have "played a 'yet unknown role' in aiding Hezbollah militants in the 1996 bombing of the Khobar Towers complex. . . ."[146] There have been a number of situations in which hatred of a common foe has overcome the Sunni/Shia split between al Qaeda and Iran. For example, the Jerusalem, or Quds, Force of Iran's Islamic Revolutionary Guards Corps heeded the request of Ayman al-Zawahiri, al Qaeda's second-in-command, to provide sanctuary in the guise of "house arrest" to Saad bin Laden, Osama's son, and two dozen al Qaeda leaders trapped in Tora Bora, Afghanistan, by the American offensive in December 2001.[147]

Secretary Perry admitted that his revised views were a matter of "belief" and that he had no proof. Former FBI director Louis Freeh and other former FBI officials, who were personally involved in the Khobar Towers investigation, have testified in public that "There is absolutely no doubt either today, or in the months following the Khobar Towers attack, that the attack was ordered, funded, and orchestrated by the Islamic Republic of Iran."[148] Moreover, substantial evidence of "Iran's direct, material involvement" was aired in the lawsuit brought by the families and estates of seventeen of the nineteen servicemen killed in the bombing in the Federal District Court of the District of Columbia against the Islamic Republic of Iran, the Iranian Ministry of Information and Security (MOIS), and the Iranian Islamic Revolutionary Guard Corp (IRGC, or "the Pasdaran") "for damages from the [Khobar Towers] attack because these institutions provided material support and assistance to Hezbollah, the terrorist organization that orchestrated and carried out the bombing."[149] On December 22, 2006, Federal Judge Royce Lamberth ruled that the Iranian government financed the Khobar Towers bombing and must pay $254 million to the victims' families.

Perhaps the earliest attack organized by Iran against American armed forces occurred in Beirut, Lebanon, on October 23, 1983. A suicide bomber crashed his truck, loaded with twenty thousand pounds of TNT, through the external barriers of the U.S. Marine barracks and detonated in the lobby. Two hundred forty-one American servicemen were killed and sixty Americans wounded. The Marines had been assigned to Lebanon as peacekeepers during the Lebanese Civil War (1975–1990). Two minutes later a second suicide bomber drove his truck into the underground garage of the eight-story building housing French peacekeepers. Fifty-eight French paratroopers were killed and fifteen injured.[150] Suspicion quickly fell on Islamic Amal and a group identified as the "party of God." Both were militant Lebanese Shi'ite splinter groups allied to Iran and Syria.[151] The designation of the latter group appears to be an early reference to Hezbollah, which means the "party of God" in Arabic. Imad Mughniyeh was largely responsible for planning and implementing the attack, as he was for many other Iranian-sponsored terror attacks.[152] As noted above, in November 2007 Interpol issued a warrant for Mughniyeh's arrest for his part in the AMIA bombing in Argentina.

Two decades after the bombing of the U.S. Marine barracks, the families of the 241 U.S. servicemen killed in the attack brought suit in the U.S. District Court of the District of Columbia for compensatory and punitive damages. On September 7, 2007, after a very lengthy judicial procedure, Judge Royce C. Lamberth concluded that the attack was carried out by Hezbollah which "was formed under the auspices of the Iranian government, was completely reliant on Iran in 1983, and assisted Iranian Ministry of Information and Security (MOIS) agents in carrying out the operation."[153]

A critical issue in determining whether the plaintiffs had legal standing to sue Iran was whether the Marines' mission involved combat. The judge ruled that the bulk of the evidence in the case pointed clearly to a peacekeeping mission operating on stringent peacetime rules of engagement.[154] After hearing the testimony and considering the evidence, Judge Lamberth ruled that Iran must pay $2.65 billion for the support it gave to Hezbollah, the organization that carried out the actual attack.[155] There was, of course, little likelihood that Iran will pay that sum. Nevertheless, it was considered an important moral victory by the victims' families.

Judge Lamberth's ruling concerning Iran's complicity was partly based on the testimony of Admiral James A. Lyons Jr., deputy chief of Naval Operations for Plans, Policy, and Operation from 1983 to 1985. On October 25, 1983, two days *after* the bombing, the chief of naval intelligence notified Admiral Lyons of an intercept of a message between Tehran and Damascus sent on or about September 26, 1983, from MOIS to the Iranian ambassador to Syria, Ali Akbar Mohtashemi, who played a crucial role in the creation of Hezbollah.[156] The message directed Mohtashemi to contact Hussein Musawi, the leader of Islamic Amal, and instruct him to have Amal instigate attacks against the multinational coalition in Lebanon and "take a spectacular action against the United States Marines." Admiral Lyons testified that he has absolutely no doubt of the authenticity or reliability of the message, which he took immediately to the secretary of the navy and chief of naval operations. Evidence was presented at trial that Mohtashemi proceeded to contact a member of the Iranian Revolutionary Guard (IRG), and instructed him to instigate the Marine barracks bombing. The bombings followed.

Perhaps the most shocking aspect of Admiral Lyons's testimony was the fact that the intercept was received a month *before* the bombing, but nothing was done to warn the Marines "even though there was specific intelligence in hand about the identities of both the prospective sponsor—the Iranian government and the perpetrators, Islamic Amal."[157] Nor was anyone held accountable for this monumental intelligence failure. There was neither an investigation nor any meaningful American action against either Amal/Hezbollah or Iran. In an interview with ABC-News correspondent John Miller on May 28, 1998, Osama bin Laden took note of America's failure to act and drew his own conclusions:

> We have seen in the last decade the decline of the American government and the weakness of the American soldier who is ready to wage Cold Wars and unprepared to fight long wars. This was proven in Beirut when the Marines fled after two explosions.[158]

CAN IRAN BE DETERRED?

In the fall of 2007, Economist.com published an assortment of views on the subject of "Is Iran Suicidal or Deterrable?"[159] No conclusion was reached but the editors did identify what may prove to be a crucial issue confronting the world in the face of a nuclear Iran. As noted above, Benny Morris does not believe that Iran can be deterred. The most important reason for believing that Iran may not be deterrable is that the Islamic Republic is not a normal state. As the German scholar Matthias Küntzel and others have pointed out, during the Cold War it would have been unthinkable for a gang of Soviet students to seize the American Embassy in Moscow and under humiliating conditions hold captive the embassy staff for 444 days. To have disrupted the embassy's ability to function would have meant the abandonment of diplomacy by what was, in effect, an act of war.[160]

Küntzel further states that approval of the embassy seizure by the supreme leader, Ayatollah Ruhollah Khomeini, made it clear that the West was facing a radically different enemy than the Soviet Union, one that rejects the traditional system of international relations and sees the West as engaged in a "Christian-Jewish conspiracy" that continues the millennial conflict between Christianity and Islam.[161] This same view of international relations is to be found in Ahmadinejad's threats against the State of Israel which he sees as "a front of the World of Arrogance in the heart of the Islamic world."[162] For Ahmadinejad, the State of Israel is no normal community but the Christian world's "crusader base for the domination of Islam." According to Ahmadinejad, Israel's survival threatens the security of the entire Islamic world. Moreover, Khomeini explicitly rejected the priority of "national interest" over religion: "We do not worship Iran, we worship Allah," he wrote. "For patriotism is another name for paganism. I say let this land [Iran] burn. I say let this land go up in smoke, provided Islam emerges triumphant in the rest of the world."[163] For Khomeini, as for Ahmadinejad, the real struggle is not between the West and the Iranian state but between the West and Islam. However, the "Islam" for which Khomeini claimed he would be willing to sacrifice Iran is his own distinctive version of Shi'ite Islam.

Historically, the Shi'ite movement has been quietist, enduring evil while awaiting the return of the Twelfth Imam. According to Shi'ite tradition, legitimate Islamic rule will only be established *after* the reappearance of the Twelfth Imam. By teaching that the *Twelfth Imam will only emerge when true believers vanquish evil* Ayatollah Khomeini introduced an element of radical activism into his version of Shi'ite Islam. This gave a new meaning to the Shi'ite martyrdom tradition that became manifest in the role of the Basiji, the thousands of Iranian children who perished clearing the minefields with their own bodies during the Iraq-Iran War of 1980–1988.[164] Faced with the possibility of military defeat because of the superiority of Iraqi equipment, a law was passed stipulating that children as young as twelve could be used to clear minefields, even against the objections of their parents. Before entering the fields, each child was given a small yellow plastic key imported from Taiwan to be worn around the neck. They were told that the key would open the gates to paradise to them. The children and young men were part of the "Basij" movement created by the Ayatollah Khomeini in 1979. Against all instincts of self-preservation, they went enthusiastically to their own destruction by the thousands. One veteran of the war later recalled, "It was sometimes like a race. Even without the commander's orders, everyone wanted to be first."[165]

The minefield martyrs were soon followed by the first *religiously* motivated suicide-bombing attack against Israel, which took place in Tyre, Lebanon, on November 11, 1982.[166] The perpetrator was a fifteen-year-old Lebanese Shi'ite, Ahmad Qusayr, a member of the newly emerging Shi'ite militia, Hezbollah. Qusayr had been inspired by the Basiji model. It was only a matter of time before Sunni Islamists also began to employ suicide bombing as a weapon against their enemies in Israel and the West Bank. No longer was the martyr expected to die at the hands of those regarded as evil-doers; now the martyr died *fighting them*. Intention trumped results. In September 1980, Khomeini explained that the Basiji "must understand that he is a 'soldier of God' for whom it is not so much the outcome of the conflict as the mere participation in it that provides fulfillment and gratification."[167] Neither the Basiji nor later suicide bombers had to achieve victory to gain paradise; all that was required was that they perish in the attempt.

Just as the Iranians would be likely to sacrifice the lives of Muslims in Israel, Gaza, and the West Bank in a nuclear attack in order to destroy the State of Israel, so too it is conceivable that they might also sanction a comparable sacrifice of a segment of their own people in a mutually assured destruction (MAD) nuclear exchange with Israel to achieve the latter's demise and the inauguration of a universal reign of perfect peace and justice under Allah. What gives this scenario a measure of plausibility is the fact that Ahmadinejad is a fervent disciple of Khomeini and believes in the imminent return of the Twelfth Imam or Mahdi, the messiah of Shi'ism. He also believes that it is the responsibility of his government to prepare its citizens for that singularly auspicious event. Unfortunately, the "return" of the Mahdi may be an apocalyptic nuclear event that some Iranian hardliners like Ahmadinejad might conceivably welcome.[168] Ahmadinejad has been deeply involved in the Basij movement from its inception in the Iranian revolution to the present. During the Iran-Iraq war, he served as a Basiji instructor teaching children and young men how to achieve martyrdom. In 2005 his election as president was largely due to the support of the Basiji that had over the years grown into a mass movement. Once in office, he proclaimed a "Basiji Week." It is estimated that 9 million Basiji responded. They formed "a human chain some 8,700 kilometers long. . . . In Tehran alone, some 1,250,000 people turned out."[169] In his speeches, Ahmadinejad praises the "Basiji culture" and the "Basiji power" with which "Iran today makes its presence felt on the international and diplomatic stage." In a sermon delivered December 2, 2005, a like-minded Ayatollah Ahmad Jannati, secretary of Iran's Guardian Council, the twelve-member upper house of the Iranian parliament, described the very existence of Iran's nuclear program as a triumph of those who "serve the Basiji movement and possess the Basiji-psyche and Basiji-culture."[170]

As we have suggested above, there is a possible way out for Israel: Adopt an "Eat them for lunch before they eat you for dinner" strategy and cripple or destroy Iran as a nation before Iran is capable of taking out Israel. Put differently, to survive, Israel may have to adopt a very distinctive *ethic of reciprocity*. Just as Iran plans to exterminate the people of Israel through a nuclear attack, Israel must be prepared to do the same with the population of Iran's civilian centers before that happens. The scenario to be preferred is one in which Israel cripples Iran's war making capability electronically, as suggested above by Jerome Gordon. Conceivably, that might allow time for regime change and a less ideologically governed, destructive Iran. Nevertheless, in the final analysis, if Israel wants to avert a second Holocaust, it may only have the choice of kill first or wait to be killed. It could be the price of survival, but hardly a survival that any sane person could wish for.

No one really knows whether the nuclear plans of Ahmadinejad or his superior, the Ayatollah Khameini, include an apocalyptic finale in which millions of Iranians might be sacrificed in order to destroy Israel or, alternatively, to make good their predictions of a world without America. Nevertheless, in both propaganda and ritual, Ahmadinejad's government, acting under Khameini, has glorified martyrdom for the sake of the return of the Twelfth Imam. And, as we have also seen, his threats to destroy Israel have introduced an element of radical instability into the region and the world. Moreover, the Iranian motivation is the same as that of Haj Amin al-Husseini: Exterminate the Jews and the Palestinian problem will be solved. *Jihad* was genocide for the Grand Mufti. At least rhetorically, this is also true of Ahmadinejad.

6

The Fruits of Rage

Sheer rage has become an important element in the behavior of a size-able number of Muslims toward non-Muslims, especially but by no means only Jews. Rage itself has been characterized as a "shame-based expression of anger."[1] To experience shame, a person must compare his actions with some standard, either his own or another's, and he must regard himself as having failed to meet that standard. Moreover, shame is the product of the very self that it condemns.[2] In those societies in which the military caste enjoys dominant status, defeat in war can result in shame so painful that death may be deemed preferable to life after defeat.

Rage has also been understood as "anger out of control."[3] Frequently, this kind of anger is related to "a perceived *loss of control* over factors affecting our integrity—*our beliefs and how we feel about ourselves*."[4] Put differently, rage is a response to the subject's perception of his/her own impotence. Guilt is different. Like shame, it involves recognition of the fact that I have violated a standard, but, unlike shame, guilt focuses on those undesirable actions I seek to end and for which I would make amends.[5] By contrast, *shame is not about specific actions but about myself*. In shame I judge myself to be without worth. Shame is thus a painful, narcissistic injury in which corrective action is paralyzed and I am left only with an anguished sense of self-contempt.[6]

In the past, Muslim anti-Jewish hostility could be characterized as the *condescension or contempt of a dominant power toward a useful but powerless inferior*. Today, Muslim anti-Jewish hostility partakes of something entirely novel in the history of Islam, *the rage of the defeated in the face of an enemy's military victories and economic success*. The situation was difficult

155

enough when Christendom reversed centuries of Muslim dominance; Jewish military victories were far less tolerable. Even the ability of Hezbollah's forces to hold their own against Israeli armed forces during the 2006 war in Lebanon has not really dissipated that rage.

Bernard Lewis took note of this phenomenon almost two decades ago in an *Atlantic Monthly* article, "The Roots of Muslim Rage: Why so many Muslims deeply resent the West and why their bitterness will not be easily mollified."[7] Long a knowledgeable observer of the world of Islam, the Princeton historian took note of the fact that the rejection of the West by an important segment of the Muslim world had generated emotions that could only be characterized as rage. Indeed, this rejection was becoming so unconditional that radical Muslims could think of no more fitting characterization of the West than "enemies of God."[8]

According to Lewis, in its heyday the Muslim world saw itself as "the center of culture and enlightenment, surrounded by infidel barbarians whom it would in due course civilize."[9] I would add that, at least among Islamists, the same self-perception remains valid today. As Lewis has commented, the struggle between Islam and Christendom has consisted in "a long series of attacks and counterattacks, jihads and crusades, conquests and reconquests" that have lasted for fourteen hundred years. It was not until the failure of the second Turkish siege of Vienna in 1683 that the world of Islam found itself on the defensive vis-à-vis the world of Christendom.

Particularly humiliating was the fact that Christian empires came to dominate much of the world of Islam. This was equally true of the expansion of the Tsarist Empire in the East and the Western European powers in the Middle East, Africa, India, and Indonesia. In the nineteenth century, Britain, France, Spain, Italy, and Holland divided up much of the Muslim world almost at will. The nineteenth-century efforts of the European powers to secure equal rights for Christians and Jews in the Ottoman Empire were especially galling. The world of Islam had been built upon a hierarchical system of structured inequality in which the religious and social dominance of Muslims over unbelievers was the uncontested first premise. Built into the very structure of Muslim identity was the system of dhimmitude, namely "the comprehensive legal system established by the Muslim conquerors to rule the native non-Muslim populations subdued by *jihad* wars."[10] No matter how brilliant, talented, or wealthy an unbeliever might be, the humblest believing Muslim was regarded as superior to all unbelievers, at least in the eyes of Allah.

In the nineteenth and much of the twentieth centuries, Westerners tended to regard their influence on Islam as essentially beneficial. The French, for example, spoke of their colonial expansion as a *une mission civilatrice*. By contrast, traditional Muslims regarded Western influence as disorienting. Confronted with the movement toward gender equality in the West, traditional Muslim societies have tended to react harshly. For example, the program of gender control under the auspices of the Taliban Ministry for the Promotion of Virtue and the Prevention of Vice (*al-Amr bi al-Ma'ruf wa al-Nahi `an al-Munkir*) was one of the most draconian in modern times.[11] Moreover, the Taliban ministry was itself modeled after a similarly named Saudi agency and the Islamic Republic of Iran has its own version of religious police (Arabic, *mutaween*). One of the worst cases of *mutaween* abuse occurred in Mecca, Saudi Arabia, on March 11, 2002, when members of the Saudi religious police prevented schoolgirls from leaving their burning school building because they were not wearing headscarves and black robes and were not escorted by a male guardian. Fifteen girls died and fifty were injured in the incident.[12]

Other examples of gender control include so-called "honor-killings." In April 2001, a representative of Human Rights Watch took note of this phenomenon before the UN Commission on Human Rights:

> Honor crimes are acts of violence, usually murder, committed by male family members against female family members who are perceived to have brought dishonor upon the family. A woman can be targeted by her family for a variety of reasons including, refusing to enter into an arranged marriage, being the victim of a sexual assault, seeking a divorce—even from an abusive husband—or committing adultery. The mere perception that a woman has acted in a manner to bring "dishonor" to the family is sufficient to trigger an attack.
>
> The ramifications for women of this impunity are significant. For example, a woman in an abusive marriage must make the choice of staying in the marriage, hoping that the violence will end, or leaving the marriage, hoping that neither her husband nor any male relatives will kill her. A woman who is raped, even if she can prove that she was the victim, may be killed by her husband, father, son, brother or cousin.[13]

Honor killings can thus be seen as an attempt to erase the stigma of shame from a family by eliminating the allegedly offending member. No act of contrition will do. Only the death of the alleged offender will suffice.[14] Some of the "offenses" seem trivial by Western standards. According to the *Daily Telegraph* (UK), a young Saudi woman was murdered by her father for chatting on Facebook, a social networking website. She was beaten and shot after her father found her in the middle of an Internet conversation with a man.[15] In a particularly bizarre case, a sixteen-year-old Jordanian woman was murdered by her brother because another brother had raped her.[16] The victim, not the rapist, was seen as having brought shame upon the family. While such killings are not officially sanctioned and cases of domestic violence are by no means confined to

Islam, the official penalties incurred for such crimes tend to be exception-ally light when and if applied. Moreover, honor killing currently appears to be far more prevalent among Muslims than among other faiths.

At the heart of all such behavior, there appears to be masculine *fear of loss of control,* with all that such loss entails for personal identity. This is especially apparent among the kind of men most likely to insist on main-taining such control, such as the Taliban. According to Ahmed Raschid:

> The Taliban's uncompromising attitude [toward women] was also shaped by their own internal political dynamic and the nature of their recruiting base. Their recruits—the orphans, the rootless, the lumpen proletariat from the war and the refugee camps—had been brought up in a totally male society. In the *madrassa* milieu, control over women and their virtual exclusion was a powerful symbol of manhood and a reaffirmation of the students' commit-ment to jihad. Denying a role for women gave the Taliban a kind of legiti-macy among these elements.[17]

The social stratum from which the Taliban recruiting base is drawn consists largely of boys and young men at the very bottom of the ladder. As individuals, they are powerless and count for little. As members of the Taliban, they count for a great deal. The very fact that women are subject to their authority infuses their identities with a sense of power otherwise unavailable to them. Few things are as likely to enhance the Taliban sense of power than the power of life and death over another human being.

We need not enter into psychoanalytic reflection about masculine fear of the feminine to explain the need for control over women found in strongly patriarchal cultures. When unable to control their women, some men in traditional societies are likely to experience feelings of impotence and rage. Unfortunately, impotent rage can often be sated, if only tem-porarily, by injury and murder. All too often *men deny their impotence by their power to kill.*

GERMAN DEFEAT AND THE BIRTH OF HITLER'S RAGE

In important respects, Muslim rage as characterized by Bernard Lewis is not unlike what Adolf Hitler and many right-wing German nationalists experienced in the face of Germany's defeat in the First World War. Be-fore the war, Hitler had drifted for years without any definite vocation. The war gave Hitler his calling by giving him a "chance to defend his beloved Motherland,"[18] In the early 1920s, Hitler described his feelings when Germany declared war on Russia and France in August 1914:

> To me these hours seemed like a release from the painful feelings of my youth. Even today I am not ashamed to say that, overpowered by stormy

enthusiasm, I fell down on my knees and thanked Heaven from an over-flowing heart for granting me the good fortune of being permitted to live at this time.[19]

For Hitler, the stakes could not have been higher:

Destiny had begun its course . . . this time not the fate of Serbia or Austria was involved, but whether the German nation was to be or not to be.[20]

Imperial Germany declared war on Russia on August 1, 1914, and on France two days later. On August 5, 1914, Hitler volunteered for service and served with the Second Reserve Battalion of the Second Bavarian Infantry, known as the List Regiment, for the duration of the war. The unit first saw combat on October 29, 1914. After four days of fighting, the regiment was reduced in number from 3,600 to 611.[21] The depressingly high casualty rate did not dampen Hitler's enthusiasm for combat. He identified with Germany's struggle in a deeply personal way. He found his element in his regiment and in the war itself. He was apparently content to serve as a dispatch runner for the duration.

According to Ian Kershaw, one of Hitler's most authoritative biographers, "from all indications, Hitler was a committed, rather than simply conscientious and dutiful, soldier, and did not lack physical courage."[22] Wounded slightly by shrapnel in October 1916, he was hospitalized in Berlin until December 1, 1916. He returned to his regiment on March 5, 1917.[23] On August 4, 1918, he received the Iron Cross, First Class, a rare achievement for a corporal. On the night of October 13, 1918, Hitler was painfully wounded in a British gas attack. By the next morning he was blind and was shipped to a hospital in Pasewalk near Stettin. It was there that he learned "the shattering news of defeat and revolution," what he called "the greatest villainy of the century."[24] Hitler described his reaction upon learning of the way the war ended:

I could stand it no longer. It became impossible for me to sit still one minute more. Again everything went black before my eyes. I tottered and groped my way back to the dormitory, threw myself on my bunk, and dug my head into my blanket and pillow. I had not wept since the day when I had stood at my mother's grave. . . . The more I tried to achieve clarity on the monstrous event in this hour, the more the *shame of indignation and disgrace* burned into my brow (emphasis added).[25]

Germany's defeat was his personal defeat. For him the war would never end. He described his reaction when he first learned of the defeat:

And so it had all been in vain. In vain all the sacrifices and privations; in vain the hunger and thirst of months that were often endless; in vain the hours in which, with mortal fear clutching our hearts, we nevertheless did our duty; and in vain the death of two million who died.[26]

Unable to bear the shame of military defeat, Hitler concluded that Germany had not been defeated but betrayed:

> I knew that all was lost. Only fools, liars, and criminals could hope in the mercy of the enemy. In these nights hatred grew in me, hatred for those responsible for this deed.

According to Hitler, Jews and Marxists, the so-called "November criminals," were responsible for Germany's ultimate disgrace, surrender. Since Hitler had no intention of accepting the "Versailles *Diktat*" as the permanent basis for Germany's relations with its enemies, another war was inevitable were he ever to gain power, And, in such a war, there would be no place for Jews once again to "betray" Germany.

Hitler's response to Germany's defeat in November 1918 was a private matter. The official response of the German high command was not very different. On March 3, 1918, Bolshevik Russia signed a peace treaty with Imperial Germany. Less than three weeks later, General Erich Ludendorff launched the first of four German offensives against the Allies in the west. By July 1918 the German offensive had spent itself.[27] On September 29, 1918, Ludendorff summoned Germany's political leaders and demanded that they ask for an immediate armistice.[28] In seeking an armistice, Ludendorff and Field Marshal Paul von Hindenburg, the Chief of the General Staff, were partly driven by fear of the imminent collapse of German arms and its likely consequences, the worst being a Russian-type revolution in Germany.[29] Nevertheless, with the German army still in northern France, Belgium, and the former Tsarist Empire defeated, a number of senior officers strongly opposed the armistice initiative.[30] Their resolve was strengthened after receiving Woodrow Wilson's uncompromising replies to the German armistice request between October 10 and 14. Ludendorff and Hindenburg became convinced that the Allies would never offer peace terms Germany would deem acceptable.[31]

According to historian Michael Geyer, the High Command became convinced that surrender was incompatible with German honor that could only be saved by an apocalyptic *Endkampf* (terminal struggle) involving the systematic devastation of the population and infrastructure of occupied French and Belgian territory, as well as a possible war to the death involving the entire German population. The *Endkampf* would be both a war of annihilation against the enemy and the self-annihilation of the German nation.[32]

German defeat did not result in an *Endkampf* because the government of the newly appointed chancellor, Prince Max von Baden, and the Reichstag majority rejected the High Command's plans. Prince Max pointed out that the first responsibility of the government was to ensure the *survival* of the nation. If that meant acknowledging defeat, the humiliation had to be accepted. By contrast, the High Command insisted that the Allied terms were dishonorable. Hence, total military catastrophe was to be preferred to a humiliating surrender.

In late October, Hindenburg and Ludendorff attempted to persuade the Kaiser to reject the armistice and call for a *Volkskrieg*, a total "people's war." The Kaiser refused and sent them with several other senior commanders to meet with the Imperial Vice Chancellor Friedrich von Payer, Prince Max being unavailable because of illness. Ludendorff sought to persuade Payer to abandon peace negotiations and call for a popular insurrection. The issue for both the military and the German ultra-right was no longer victory or even territorial defense but the "honor" involved in preferring catastrophic national destruction to surrender.

Von Payer rejected Ludendorff's demand for an end to peace negotiations whereupon Ludendorff declared, "Then, your Excellency, *I throw the entire shame of the Fatherland into your and your colleague's faces* (emphasis added)."[33] In his memoir of the war years, Payer spelled out his fundamental disagreement with Ludendorff:

> An army commander with his entourage may well end his illustrious career [*Ruhmeslaufbahn*] with a ride into death [*Todesritt*], but a people of seventy million cannot make the decision about life and death according to the terms of honor of a single estate [i.e., the military].[34]

Geyer recounts that Rear Admiral Magnus von Levetzow, chief of staff of the Naval High Command, was also present at the meeting. In his memoirs, Levetzow described Ludendorff as "a majestic man, a representative of German honor" and described von Payer as "a small, crappy party hack without a sense of national dignity and honor . . . weighing everything only from a petit bourgeois point of view . . . sitting there cowering, with his beady, hate-filled eyes and clasped hands, under the powerful blows of the general."[35]

Geyer comments on this encounter, "*One could call this* [the encounter between Ludendorff and von Payer] *the pivotal scene in the formation of the stab-in-the-back legend.*"[36] Although von Payer was not Jewish, von Levetzow used classical anti-Semitic stereotypes to characterize him. According to historian Peter Pulzer, "In the eyes of the extreme Right [von] Payer had long counted as an honorary Jew."[37]

Neither Hitler nor the World War I German High Command invented the tradition of the ignoble betrayer who in stealth and treachery brings defeat upon the German military. It was deeply embedded in their cultural world. Although more Jews proportionally than their fellow citizens made the supreme sacrifice for what they mistakenly thought was their Fatherland, that sacrifice was invisible to Hitler, the German High Command, and, increasingly, the German public. On the contrary, in October1916, the German High Command ordered a *Judenzählung*, a "Jew census," to demonstrate that Jews were less patriotic than what at the time were considered their "fellow Germans." The findings demonstrated the opposite. Approximately 80 percent of the Jews in the German army served in the frontlines. Over 100,000 Jews served out of a total German Jewish population of 550,000; 12,000 died in battle; 30,000 were decorated for bravery.[38] Disappointed, German military officials suppressed the findings.

To repeat, a person who experiences guilt can make reparation for *specific* acts whereas a person who experiences shame cannot. In shame, reparation seems impossible as the *whole person* condemns him/herself as worthless. Hence, the *temptation to evade self-condemnation by projecting one's shame onto another is almost irresistible*. Instead of punishing oneself, one punishes another for one's failings.

This was especially true of Imperial Germany, a society in which the warrior caste stood at the very apex of the social hierarchy and military prowess was the emblem of superlative masculine virtue. By failing to achieve victory and by impotently standing by while Imperial Germany's civilian authorities consented to what amounted to *unconditional surrender,* leaving the nation at the mercy of its enemies, the German warrior caste had failed its ultimate test. Nothing could be more shameful than to have been vanquished in a war in which approximately 2 million of their comrades were killed and 4,814,557 were reported wounded.[39]

THE STAB-IN-THE-BACK LEGEND: PRELUDE TO GENOCIDE

As the war came to a close, Germany's military leaders prepared to reject responsibility for their catastrophic failure. It seemed inconceivable to them that Europe's most advanced industrial power, with the best universities and scientific personnel, could collapse and surrender while the German army, numbering in the millions, still occupied the soil of its enemies. Moreover, the greatest humiliation was arguably yet to come. Article 231, the "war guilt clause" of the Treaty of Versailles, signed on June 28, 1919, stipulated that:

> Germany accepts the responsibility of Germany and her allies for causing all the loss and damage to which the Allied and Associated Governments and

their nationals have been subjected as a consequence of the war imposed upon them by the aggression of Germany and her allies.[40]

During the 1920s, the Treaty of Versailles, especially Article 231, was viewed by the majority of Germans as a "dictate of shame" whose purpose was to keep Germany from regaining the status of a great European power. The compulsory signing was especially bitter because Germans of all political persuasions "had rushed to arms in 1914 in the sincere conviction that they were fighting a war of self-defense."[41]

The stab-in-the-back (*Dolchstoß in den Rücken*) legend offered an enormously potent means of shifting responsibility so that German "honor" could be preserved. Nor was it difficult to identify a suitable "betrayer." The legend had its roots in two powerful traditions, the *Nibelungen* Saga in which Siegfried, the dragon-slaying hero, is stabbed in the back by Hagen von Tronje, and the New Testament narrative in which Jesus is betrayed by Judas Iscariot for money with a loving kiss.[42] Over the centuries, Jews have been identified with Judas as the paradigmatic betrayer within Christendom. More often than not, whenever the stronger community met with grave misfortune, Jews were punished as calamity's alleged authors.

Apart from its sources in myth and legend, the stab-in-the-back legend gained enhanced credibility in the German Right from the presence of left-wing Jews in the leadership of revolutionary movements that sought to end the war and establish socialist or communist regimes in its aftermath. Although Jewish loyalty to the Fatherland was real, it was all but invisible to right-wing German nationalists. What was visible was the Jewish presence in the Bolshevik leadership and in the left-wing regimes that managed to seize power temporarily in Bavaria and Hungary. For example, on November 7, 1918, Kurt Eisner, a socialist Jewish writer from Berlin, found himself at the head of the provisional revolutionary government of predominantly Catholic Bavaria. After Eisner's assassination, a number of other Jewish intellectuals, *literati*, and revolutionaries took highly visible leadership roles in the succeeding revolutionary regimes in Munich.[43] At the time, Munich was home to Adolf Hitler and the embryonic National Socialist Party.

As noted, advocates of peace negotiations came to be characterized as either "Jewish" or influenced by "a Jewish mentality."[44] By 1919 Ludendorff was committed to the "destruction of the 'internationalist, pacifist, defeatists,' namely, the Jews and the Vatican, people who 'systematically destroyed' our 'racial inheritance and national character.'"[45] Not surprisingly, Ludendorff took part with Hitler in the Munich Beer Hall Putsch of 1923. A year later, the general wrote that Germany must be made *judenrein,* "free of Jews," before the next war.[46] *The stab-in-the back legend thus became a prelude to genocide.* If, as the legend asserted, the Jews had succeeded in bringing down the mighty German nation by treachery and deceit, it was imperative to eliminate them for Germany to achieve success in the coming war.

Hitler saw the war's outcome as did Ludendorff. He had no doubt that the cause of Germany's defeat had not been the failure of German arms but betrayal by Jews and Marxists. He was resolved to enter politics to prevent a repetition of the alleged betrayal. Thus, the Jews of Europe were ultimately to pay with their lives for the monumental, and indeed cowardly, evasion of responsibility by Germany's World War I military leadership in seeking to preserve their "honor." In his Political Testament, written on April 30, 1945, the day before he killed himself, Hitler persisted in that evasion. "It is untrue," he claimed, "that I or anyone else in Germany wanted the war in 1939." On the contrary, "It was desired and instigated exclusively by those international statesmen who were either of Jewish descent or worked for Jewish interests."[47] From 1919 to 1945, a rage-obsessed Adolf Hitler gave powerful expression to that emotion for himself and his followers. His rage unappeased even by genocide and his own *Endkampf*, Hitler concluded his testament by charging "the leaders of the nation and those under them . . . to merciless opposition to the universal poisoner of all peoples, international Jewry." To the bitter end, Hitler saw himself as the innocent victim of those who had conspired to bring him and Germany down.

DEFEAT AND MUSLIM RAGE

Like the rage of Hitler and the German ultra-right, the rage of contemporary Islamists and their fellow travelers against Jews, Zionism, America, and, ultimately, the entire Western world has its roots in military defeat. In the case of rage against the West, the roots can be found in the Battle of Lepanto (1571), the lifting of the Ottoman siege of Vienna by the Polish King Jan III Sobieski on September 12, 1683, and the Treaty of Karlowitz (1699). At Karlowitz, the Ottomans signed a peace treaty for the first time on terms "basically determined by their victorious enemies."[48] The treaty set the pattern of Muslim retreat and defeat that continued until the middle of the twentieth century.

As noted above, no defeat visited upon Muslims by unbelievers has ever been as deeply felt as an offense against Muslim honor as the twin defeats inflicted upon the Arabs in the 1948 Israeli War of Independence and the Six-Day War of 1967. This has been cogently expressed by the Israeli historian Benny Morris in the concluding paragraphs of his book on the first Arab-Israeli War:

But 1948 has haunted and still haunts, the Arab world on the deepest level of collective identity, ego, and pride. The war was a humiliation from which that world has yet to recover—the antithesis of the glory days of Arab Islamic dominance. . . . The 1948 War was the culminating affront, when a community of 650,000 Jews—Jews, no less—crushed Palestinian Arab society and then defeated the armies of the surrounding states. The Arab states had failed to "save" the Palestinians and failed to prevent Israel's emergence and acceptance into the comity of nations. And what little Palestine territory the Arabs had managed to retain fell under Israeli sway two decades later.[49]

Since the 1930s there have been numerous attempts to "solve" the Arab-Israeli conflict. In recent years, there has been much talk about a "peace process." Almost immediately after assuming office, President Obama let it be known that he intended to pursue it energetically. Perhaps in anticipatory compliance, Israel's outgoing prime minister Ehud Olmert gave an interview on September 21, 2008, to the Israeli daily newspaper *Yedioth Aharonoth* outlining the territorial concessions he believed Israel must make for the sake of peace with its neighbors.[50] Yet, no attempt to resolve the conflict has ever succeeded.

This writer is convinced that a fundamental flaw in all such efforts is the failure of both Western and Israeli policy makers to take into account the religious dimension of the conflict. This is especially true in the Middle East where Islamists regard their ongoing struggle with Israel and, for that matter, the entire non-Muslim Western world, as a *jihad,* a religiously sanctioned war with ostensibly religious ends. Although two Muslim countries, Egypt and Jordan, have signed "peace" treaties with Israel, a critical mass among both educated professionals and the "Muslim street" in Egypt and Jordan remain completely unwilling to accept any "solution" to the conflict other than Israel's annihilation.

According to Gilles Kepel, a French authority on radical Islam, Anwar Sadat's address to the Israeli Knesset on November 20, 1977, and the subsequent signing of a peace treaty with Israel on March 26, 1979, marked a decisive turning point for radical Islam. There was a widespread consensus among the Islamists that "a shameful peace with the Jews" must be rejected.[51] Nor were they alone in rejecting peace. The treaty was hugely unpopular throughout the Muslim world. For a time, it resulted in the expulsion of Egypt from the Arab League. Sadat himself was gunned down on October 6, 1981, for having signed the treaty by Lieutenant Khalid al-Istambouli during the annual parade commemorating Egypt's "victory" over Israel in the 1973 war. Al-Istambouli, a member of the Egyptian Islamic Jihad movement, was condemned to death by an Egyptian court and executed on April 15, 1982. He has since been widely venerated by Islamists as a *shaheed,* a witness and a martyr in the cause of Islam. A Tehran street has been named after him.

Islamists make no secret of the religious dimension of the conflict. An extraordinary range of sermons, essays, newspaper columns, TV broadcasts, websites, and other material in Arabic, Persian, Turkish, and Urdu-Pashto has been translated into English, German, Hebrew, Italian, French, Spanish, Russian, Chinese, and Japanese by MEMRI, the Middle East Media Research Institute, and made available on the Institute's website.[52] This site is an invaluable resource for both the professional researcher and the informed layman.

Few of these sources convey the depth of uncompromising, religiously legitimated hatred toward Jews and Israel as the Covenant of the Islamic Resistance Movement, known by its acronym Hamas (*Harakat al-Muqāwama al-Islāmiyya*). The covenant has been made available on the Web in a reliable translation by the Avalon Project of the Yale Law School.[53] Hamas itself has been designated by the U.S. Department of State as a Foreign Terrorist Organization. There is no doubt that the designation is well deserved insofar as Hamas has used and continues to use terrorism against civilians of all ages to achieve its political and diplomatic objectives.[54] Nevertheless, while accurate, the designation may obscure the degree to which Hamas's long-term objective, the destruction of the State of Israel and its people, is grounded in an unconditional religious imperative it regards as binding on all Muslims.

In the preface to the covenant, Hamas spells out the radical difference between Muslims and nonbelievers. Muslims are described as "the best nation that hath been raised up unto mankind" whereas non-Muslims are depicted as "smitten with vileness wheresoever they are found." (Preamble). The only exceptions are those who submit to Islamic domination as *dhimmis*, thereby obtaining "security by entering into a treaty with Allah." Hassan al-Banna, founder of the Muslim Brotherhood in Egypt, is then quoted in the text as promising the destruction of Israel which "will continue to exist until Islam will obliterate it, just as it obliterated others before it." Lest there be any illusion that Hamas could be induced to make peace with Israel, the document explicitly asserts that "The Islamic Resistance Movement believes that the land of Palestine is an Islamic *Waqf* [an inalienable religious endowment] consecrated for future Muslim generations until Judgment Day." (Article 11, Hamas Covenant.) Hence, "*there is no solution for the Palestinian question except through Jihad*. Initiatives, proposals and international conferences are all a waste of time and vain endeavors" (emphasis added) (Article 13).

Moreover, the Hamas Covenant rejects any distinction between anti-Zionism and anti-Semitism. Although some contemporary writers allege that Muslim anti-Semitism is a recent development fostered by National Socialist influence, Hamas regards Muhammad himself as looking forward to a genocidal ending of the Muslim-Jewish conflict.[55] The covenant cites a *Hadith* of Muhammad ibn Ismail al-Bukhari (810–870), the editor-collector of what is considered one of the most trusted collections of oral traditions concerning the life of Muhammad. In the *Hadith*, the Prophet is depicted as declaring "The Day of Judgment will not come about until Muslims fight the Jews (killing the Jews), when the Jew will hide behind stones and trees. The stones and trees will say O Muslims, O Abdulla, there is a Jew behind me, come and kill him. Only the Gharkad tree, (evidently a certain kind of tree) would not do that because it is one of the trees of the Jews." (Article 7.)

In keeping with the spirit of al-Bukhari's *Hadith* and in complete disregard for the truth, Hamas includes many of National Socialism's most vicious, anti-Semitic falsehoods in its covenant:

> With their money they stirred revolutions in various parts of the world. . . . They were behind the French Revolution, the Communist revolution and most of the revolutions we heard and hear about. With their money they formed secret societies, such as Freemasons, Rotary Clubs, the Lions and others in different parts of the world for the purpose of sabotaging societies and achieving Zionist interests. With their money they were able to control imperialistic countries and instigate them to colonize many countries in order to enable them to exploit their resources and spread corruption there. . . . They were behind World War I, when they were able to destroy the Islamic Caliphate, making financial gains and controlling resources. They obtained the Balfour Declaration, formed the League of Nations through which they could rule the world. They were behind World War II, through which they made huge financial gains by trading in armaments, and paved the way for the establishment of their state. It was they who instigated the replacement of the League of Nations with the United Nations and the Security Council to enable them to rule the world through them. There is no war going on anywhere, without having their finger in it. (Article 22)

Hamas predicts that once the Zionists digest Palestine, "they will covet expansion," first "from the Nile to the Euphrates" and then "they will look forward to more expansion." As evidence, Hamas identifies the notorious forgery, *The Protocols of the Elders of Zion*, as its authoritative source.[56] This is hardly surprising. For those who have experienced defeat or identified themselves with those who have, whether Germans after World War I or Muslims after 1948, the claim that defeat came from a deceitful, underhanded secret conspiracy rather than honorable combat mitigated the disgrace and shame of defeat and was a source of enormous consolation.

The worldwide success of the *Protocols* as an anti-Semitic tract dates from the post–World War I period. From 1919 to 1945 the *Protocols* were taken by German right-wing nationalists as "proof" of the stab-in-the-back legend, that the Jews were the hidden force that betrayed Germany and brought about her downfall in World War I. The pamphlet was also used to show that the Bolshevik revolution was the result of an alleged Jewish conspiracy to enslave the world and destroy Christianity.[57] Such beliefs gave a delusional coherence to Germany's shattering experience of World War I defeat.

However, in 1921 Philip Graves, an English journalist writing in the *Times* of London, offered convincing evidence that the *Protocols* was a forgery. He pointed to the close resemblance between the text of the *Protocols* and a mid-nineteenth-century, political pamphlet *Dialogue aux Enfers entre Machiavel et Montesquieu, ou la politique au xixe siècle* (*Dialogue in Hell between Machiavelli and Montesquieu or the Politics of the Nineteenth Century*, 1864).[58] The pamphlet ascribed to Emperor Napoleon III the ambition to dominate the world. It contained no reference to Jews or Judaism. However, in the last decade of the nineteenth century the pamphlet was transformed into an anti-Semitic tract by an unknown author working for the *Okhrana*, the Tsarist secret police. The "dialogue" became the "protocols" in 1905, the year of Russia's defeat in the Russo-Japanese War and the first Russian Revolution. In its revised form, the *Protocols* described an alleged conference of the leaders of world Jewry who claimed that, under the cloak of democracy, they already controlled a number of European states and were close to their ultimate objective, world domination. In his *Times* article, Graves succinctly described the *Ohkrana*'s motives in publishing the *Protocols* in 1905:

> They were designed to foster the belief among Russian conservatives and especially in court circles, that the prime cause of discontent among the politically minded elements in Russia was not the repressive policy of the bureaucracy, but a worldwide Jewish conspiracy. They thus served as a weapon against the Russian Liberals, who urged the Czar to make certain concessions to the intelligentsia.[59]

Put differently, then as now, the *Protocols* served as an ideal vehicle by which decision makers and those dependent upon them could evade responsibility for disastrous decisions and blame others, especially but not exclusively the Jews, for their catastrophic mistakes. In the case of the Tsarist government in 1905, it was responsible for the first major defeat of a European power by an Asian nation. The *Protocols* served as a relatively cost-free means of deflecting the anger and bitter resentment of the victims of those mistakes to a group unable to retaliate.

To make matters worse, the *Protocols* has historically served as a support for the conviction that genocide is a *moral* imperative. It has rightly been called a "warrant for genocide."[60] Daniel Pipes has described the power of the *Protocols* as a propaganda tool:

The great importance of the *Protocols* lies in its permitting antisemites (sic) to reach beyond their traditional circles and find a large international audience, a process that continues to this day. The forgery poisoned public life wherever it appeared; it was "self-generating; a blueprint that migrated from one conspiracy to another." The book's vagueness—almost no names, dates, or issues are specified—has been one key to this wide-ranging success. The purportedly Jewish authorship also helps to make the book more convincing. Its embrace of contradiction—that to advance, Jews use all tools available, including capitalism and communism, philo-Semitism and antisemitism, democracy and tyranny—made it possible for the *Protocols* to reach out to all: rich and poor, Right and Left, Christian and Muslim, American and Japanese.[61]

The fundamental objective of the *Protocols* was to depict the Jews—not just Zionists but all Jews—as the clandestine enemy of all humanity and thereby a legitimate target of all attempts to eliminate them. This in itself was an incitement to genocide. For example, Joseph Goebbels reported a conversation about the *Protocols* with Hitler on May 13, 1943, in which Hitler expressed the conviction that "the *Protocols* were absolutely genuine" and drew the conclusion that *"Es bleibt also den Modernen Völkern nichts anderes übriges, als die Juden auszurotten."* (There is therefore no other recourse left for modern nations except to exterminate the Jew. . . .)[62]

In the twenty-first century, the *Protocols* have again been put in the service of a radical assault on Jews, Judaism and the State of Israel throughout the Arab and Muslim world, this time on satellite TV. The subtext remains the same: Jews, Judaism, and Israel must be destroyed. On November 6, 2002, at the beginning of the holy month of Ramadan, Egyptian State Television Channel 2, Dream TV (a privately owned Egyptian satellite network), Abu Dhabi TV, Hezbollah's al-Manar TV, Yemen TV, and others, all began screening *Horseman without a Horse*, a forty-one-episode "historical" series covering the Middle East from 1850 to 1948. The entire series emphasizes *The Protocols of the Elders of Zion* as "proof" of an alleged Jewish plot to dominate and enslave the world and depicts the founding of the State of Israel as a major step toward that end.

The unprecedented use of the *Protocols* in a television series, reaching perhaps as many as 200 million Muslims continuously for forty-one days, constitutes a radical escalation of both the scope and intensity of anti-Jewish propaganda in the Muslim world. No scholarly essay or newspaper article exposing the lie can possibly match the power of a widely promoted, prime-time TV series scheduled immediately after the nightly meal that breaks the fast of the holy month of Ramadan. The Nazis and other earlier anti-Semites had recourse solely to widely circulated print editions. The producers of *Horseman without a Horse* possessed a far more potent propaganda medium that combined visual and dramatic power and was capable of influencing millions possessed of varying degrees of literacy. The potentiality of the series for hateful damage was understood by Samir Raafat, a writer and chronicler of life in Cairo, who wrote: "Once it goes on television it enters everyone's living room, and that's where the danger is. . . . You are spoon-feeding them more hate propaganda."[63] By contrast, Nabil Osman, an Egyptian government spokesman, rejected criticism of the series. Although, like the original *Protocols*, the series deals with an alleged Jewish conspiracy for world domination, Osman insisted that "There is a world of difference" between anger at Israeli policies and anti-Semitism. He added that the program had been reviewed by a government broadcasting committee that vets all television programs for pornography or the "desecration of religion."[64]

As we note in our chapter on "The Nazi-Muslim Connection and Hajj Amin al-Husseini, the Mufti of Jerusalem," both Adolf Hitler and National Socialism have long been held in high esteem in the Arab world and after the war many of the most vicious Nazi war criminals found a welcome haven in Egypt, Syria, and other Arab countries as well as new opportunities to attempt to finish Hitler's assault on the Jews. The objective of the Islamists was and remains genocidal.

GAZA

On December 18, 2008, Hamas declared an end to the six-month-old ceasefire with Israel. Six days later it indiscriminately ratcheted up its mortar and rocket fire against civilian targets in southern Israel. To end the attacks, Israel launched air strikes on December 27 at targets in Gaza. Almost immediately, French president Nicolas Sarkozy, speaking as president of the European Union, criticized Israel for a "disproportionate use of force."[65] Often repeated, Sarkozy's complaint failed to confront a crucial issue in the conflict: *What is the appropriate response of any community to an enemy on its borders that has openly and unconditionally stated that it is under a divinely sanctioned mandate utterly to destroy that community and its people? Would any of the states condemning Israel for its alleged "disproportionate" use of force tolerate such aggression?* How indeed does one relate to a group that uses hospitals as its military headquarters and mosques, schools, refugee camps, and civilian housing to store and fire its weapons?[66] Would *any* other government add to the hazards facing its own people by permitting the enemy's civilian population, deliberately placed in harm's way by its own rulers, to dwell in safety? Just how many deaths and injuries is Israel expected to sustain before retaliating?

The fundamental cause of the Gaza war of 2008–2009 was Hamas's use of its rockets to make normal life untenable in an ever-expanding area of Israeli territory. Both the UN and the so-called "international community" have acted as enablers by routinely condemning any serious Israeli attempt to defend its citizens and its territory. In spite of having been labeled a terrorist organization by the United States and other Western powers and widely distrusted by many Sunni Arab governments, Hamas has largely succeeded in garnering widespread, tacit international support for its attacks against Israel. For example, on January 4, 2009, Sandro Magister, an Italian authority on the Vatican, commented in *Chiesa,* his daily blog, that while the Vatican had condemned the "massive violence" in Gaza, it did not exhibit a comparable concern for "the existence of Israel—which its enemies want to annihilate, and is ultimately at stake in the conflict." Magister added that, in spite of having diplomatic relations with Israel, "Every time a conflict erupts, the [Vatican's] judgment is that the Arabs are the victims. Even Islamist terrorism is traced back to this basic cause."[67] Magister makes the seldom discussed point that one reason for the Church's pro-Arab stand is that it believes Israel's existence is "temporary" and that only its military superiority guarantees its survival.

A similar, if not more hostile, attitude has long pervaded the halls of the UN with its more than fifty Muslim member states as well as the foreign offices, media, churches, and relief organizations of most Western European countries. Implicit in their one-sided complaints is the conviction that without Israel, there would be no Middle East conflict and the influence of radical Islam would be greatly diminished.[68]

When one compares the inaction of the West and the UN when actual mass murder and genocide took place in Rwanda, where in 1994 an estimated eight hundred thousand were killed in one hundred days, and in Darfur, where three hundred thousand are estimated to have been killed and 2.5 million displaced, with the eagerness with which Israel has been repeatedly singled out for condemnation and vilification, *it would appear that something other than rational political behavior is operative.*[69] At one level, such behavior seems to reflect the fact that there are far more Muslims in the world than Jews and that close to 25 million Muslims live in Western Europe.

Sandro Magister's observation that the Vatican regards the existence of the State of Israel as a transitory phenomenon may offer a clue concerning the root of the issue, at least in the predominantly Christian world. I would like to suggest that there is a religious element in this widespread bias and that long after *literal religious belief* has lost much of its credibility, it can nevertheless retain a powerful subterranean influence on culture. I would further suggest that this subterranean religious influence is especially prevalent in the persistent tendency of European governments, civic institutions, and media to ignore historical context and consistently to judge Israel guilty in its conflicts with the Palestinians and the larger Muslim world.

The work of the Protestant theologian Stephen R. Haynes may help us to understand this phenomenon. In his book *Reluctant Witnesses: Jews and the Christian Imagination,* Haynes writes of the "witness-people myth" which he describes as "the belief that whatever happens to the Jews, for good or ill, is an expression of God's providential justice." As such, it is a sign "for God's church."[70] According to Haynes, the witness-people myth is "a deep structure in the Christian imagination . . . a complex of ideas and symbols that, *often pre-critically and unconsciously,* informs ideas about Jews among persons who share a cultural heritage (emphasis added)."[71] Moreover, Haynes argues that "Jews must always be special cases in products of the Christian imagination, because of the uniquely ambivalent place which the Jewish people inhabit there."[72] He notes that this is also true of Israel as a nation among nations.

Haynes's insights go a long way to explain Christian and post-Christian attitudes toward contemporary Israel. In the perennial Christian narrative, *the unbelieving Jewish community is destined sooner or later to lose unless and until it accepts Christ as its Savior.* In this narrative, which has its roots in the religious thinking of St. Augustine, a remnant will "survive but not thrive" as "witnesses to the prophecies which were given beforehand [i.e. before Christ's coming] concerning Christ."[73] And there is one location where Jewish good fortune is especially problematic, the Holy Land, known to the medieval Church as "Christ's patrimony."[74]

From the time of the Fall of Jerusalem in 70 C.E., *Jewish misfortune and defeat has historically been understood in Christian thought as divine chastisement for Jewish unbelief and as evidence that Christ is Lord and Savior.* Toward the end of the nineteenth century a number of Jewish leaders became convinced that the Jews of Europe were fated for elimination one way or another, the most influential leader being the journalist Theodore Herzl (1860–1904), the father of political Zionism. Herzl became convinced that only mass emigration and resettlement in a territory of their own could save Europe's Jews. He devoted the rest of his life to the realization of that goal. There was much that was problematic in Herzl's thinking, but his prescience concerning the impending doom of Europe's Jews is undeniable.[75]

One of the earliest Christian responses to Herzl's project was published in the authoritative Jesuit journal, *Civiltà Cattolica,* four months before the meeting of the First Zionist Conference in Basel, Switzerland, August 29–31, 1897:

> 1827 years have passed since the prediction of Jesus of Nazareth was fulfilled, namely that Jerusalem would be destroyed . . . that the Jews would be

led away to be slaves among all the nations, and that they would remain in the dispersion till the end of the world. . . . *According to Sacred Scriptures, the Jewish people must always live dispersed and wandering among the other nations, so that they may render witness not only by the Scriptures . . . but by their very existence.* As for a rebuilt Jerusalem, which would become the center of a reconstituted state of Israel, we must add that this is contrary to the prediction of Christ Himself (emphasis added).[76]

Civiltà Cattolica's editorial is an important example of the witness people myth. Pope Pius X expressed a similar sentiment in the audience he granted Theodore Herzl on January 25, 1904. When Herzl requested the Pope's support for Zionism, the Pontiff replied:

We are unable to favor this movement. We cannot prevent the Jews from going to Jerusalem—but we could never sanction it. *The ground of Jerusalem, if it were not always sacred, has been sanctified by the life of Jesus Christ.* As the head of the Church I cannot answer you otherwise. The Jews have not recognized our Lord, therefore we cannot recognize the Jewish people.[77]

Much of this theology is shared by traditionally oriented Protestant and Orthodox churches. Even ardently pro-Israel Evangelicals concur, although they add that the return of the exiles to Zion and the establishment of the State of Israel are preconditions for the second coming of Christ. Save for pro-Israel Evangelicals, there was not much *theological* support for the establishment of a Jewish state in Palestine although some Christians did support the creation of the State of Israel for humanitarian reasons, especially in the years immediately after World War II.

The Vatican and the State of Israel finally entered into diplomatic relations in 1993. The State of Israel had demonstrated its durability and it was the political authority in a region of historical importance to the Church. As it had accommodated itself to a wide array of regimes, not all to its liking, so the Church finally accommodated itself to diplomatic relations with Israel, but the *theological rejection* of a sovereign Jewish state never ceased.

In reality, there should be little reason for surprise at the growing chorus of anti-Israel hostility. Latent attitudes and emotions can often surface after relatively long periods of dormancy. One does not have to be a doctrinaire Freudian to see the "return of the repressed" at work in the so-called "new anti-Semitism," especially in relation to the State of Israel and its conflicts. I would like to suggest that what had been repressed for decades was *the darker side of Christian ambivalence toward Jews and Judaism* that resulted from knowledge of and horror concerning the Holocaust. Undoubtedly, that is an important reason why Holocaust denial has been fostered by the government of Iran and Islamist writers and thinkers while, at the same time, threatening a new Holocaust. Holocaust denial facilitates the reawakening of that dark side by alleging that the historical reality was a devilish Jewish hoax to extort political and financial support for Israel and other Jewish causes from unduly guilt-ridden Christian nations.

Implicit in the claim that Israel's response to Hamas in Gaza was disproportionate, if the criticism is serious, is the expectation that the Israeli government will act as if Hamas were a rational political actor whose covenant does not mean what it plainly says when it declares that the destruction of Israel and its people is a fundamental objective of the "Palestine Resistance Movement." Unfortunately, after Auschwitz it is difficult to see how such an explicitly stated threat can be dismissed, at least by Jews, especially when it is endlessly repeated by the Muslim "street" and by some of Islam's most prominent religious leaders. We need not offer a complete catalogue. A representative sample will have to suffice.

We take as examples of clerical concord with the Muslim street, Sheikh Amin al-Ansari, an Egyptian Sunni Islamist, and the better known Sheikh Yusuf al-Qaradawi. On January 26, 2009, the day before International Holocaust Remembrance Day, *al-Rahma* (Mercy) TV, the Egyptian Sunni Islamist channel, broadcast its own version of the Holocaust featuring al-Ansari.[78] Unlike Iranian president Mahmoud Ahmadinejad, al-Ansari makes no attempt to deny the Holocaust. On the contrary, he glorifies it as Allah's "way of wreaking vengeance" on the Jews and offers graphic film images of the most inhumane Nazi cruelty as the behavior Allah expects from pious Muslims. In al-Ansari's narrative, the Germans are the innocent victims and the Jews the evil oppressors.

After cursorily examining alleged Jewish wickedness throughout history, al-Ansari offers his justification for the Holocaust: "The corruption spread by the Jews was very great. Very great. It got to the point that the rulers themselves had no solution but to annihilate them." Some very gruesome clips of death-camp scenes are exhibited as al-Ansari comments: "Let us watch how oppressors are killed by the people they oppressed." Skeleton-like Jews are shown awaiting their turn to be burned to death. There are also horrific scenes of Jews being tortured after which Al Ansari addresses the TV audience: "The [Jews] are oppressors. They are being deported." When a film clip shows mounds of Jewish corpses being bulldozed into mass graves, al-Ansari exults: "Ibn Mas'oud was right when he said: 'All the oppressors are killed by those they oppress.'" Close-ups of dead bodies are shown. Al-Ansari tells his viewers: "These are bodies, these are dead people, these are skulls. These are the bodies of the Jews being loaded like animals. Watch this tractor clearing away the corpses of the Jews, and these are the refugees awaiting their turn to be killed." As a Muslim religious leader, he expresses the pious hope: "*This is what we hope will happen, but, Allah willing, at the hand of the Muslims* (emphasis added)."

Al-Ansari's Holocaust propaganda actually exceeds in viciousness anything Joseph Goebbels, Hitler's propaganda minister, ever contrived. The Nazis were careful to hide their extermination program from public view. By contrast, al-Ansari and *al-Rahma* TV offer for public viewing some of the worst examples of the Nazi extermination program and torture as models of Allah's vengeance with the prayer that Muslims be permitted to repeat and complete the Nazi performance. This is both an expression of and an incitement to hatred, rage, and genocide as a holy act. Unfortunately, the average Muslim does not possess the kind of knowledge with which to recognize the viciousness and mendacity of such TV programs while the politicians who talk of "peace in the Middle East" ignore the power of this kind of propaganda.

When we turn to Yusuf al-Qaradawi, we find a similar message without the Nazi trappings. Al-Qaradawi is the author of over one hundred books on Islam and Islamism and is one of the most widely read contemporary Islamic scholars. He also has had a weekly program on Al Jazeera TV, *al-Shari'a wal-Hayat* (Shari'a and Life) and is the cofounder and president of the International Association of Muslim Scholars and the European Council for Fatwa and Research. He has, however, been refused entry into the United States and has been barred from entering the United Kingdom as a "threat to peace and security."[79] Although controversial, al-Qaradawi is not a fringe figure but a major Islamic leader capable of influencing millions.[80]

During the Israeli action against Hamas in Gaza, al-Qaradawi delivered a TV sermon on Friday, January 9, 2009, in which he called for the complete extermination of the Jews:

Oh Allah, take your enemies, the enemies of Islam. Oh Allah, take the Jews, the treacherous aggressors. . . . this profligate, cunning, arrogant band of people. Oh Allah, they have spread much tyranny and corruption in the land. Pour Your wrath upon them, oh our God. Lie in wait for them. Oh Allah, You annihilated the people of Thamoud at the hand of a tyrant, and You annihilated the people of 'Aad with a fierce, icy gale . . . and You destroyed the Pharaoh and his soldiers—oh Allah, take this oppressive, tyrannical band of people. Oh Allah, take this oppressive, Jewish, Zionist band of people. *Oh Allah, do not spare a single one of them. Oh Allah, count their numbers, and kill them, down to the very last one* (emphasis added).

Having implored Allah to destroy the Jews, al-Qaradawi urges his fellow Muslims to join in Allah's work:

We wait for the revenge of Allah to descend upon them, and, Allah willing, it will be by our own hands: "Fight them, Allah will torment them by your hands, and bring them to disgrace, and will assist you against them, and will heal the hearts of the believers, and you will still the anger of your hearts." This is my message to the treacherous Jews, who have never adhered to what is right, or been true to their promises, who violate each time the promises they make to you.

Al-Qaradawi's call to genocide was not an angry, momentary outburst. On the contrary, the sermon is an Islamic legal argument that carefully leads to the conclusion that the extermination of all Jews is not only justified but mandatory under Islamic law. He begins the argument by reminding his viewers:

The Islamic Countries . . . Received [the Jews] with open arms [when they were banished from Europe] . . . [but the Jews] turned their backs on [us], and we have become their victims.

Al-Qaradawi then characterizes the Zionist settlement in Palestine as the work of "plunderers, who acted arrogantly toward the servants of Allah in the land of Allah." He reminds his listeners that Allah has already punished the Jews for spreading "corruption in the land twice." He first sent Nebuchadnezzar, king of Babylon, "who . . . destroyed their homes, razed their temples, and burned their Torah, and took them into captivity in Babylon for 70 years." When they repeated their offense at a later date, Allah sent the Romans "as masters upon them."

He then complains of the Jewish ingratitude:

The Jews have lived as *dhimmis* in our land for a long time, and no Muslim violated the covenant with them. . . . Despite this, they were not faithful to the [covenant]. When they were banished from Europe, they found no compassionate bosom, no cave to shelter them, except for the lands of Islam . . . but when [the Jews] gained influence, they turned their backs on them, and we have become their victims.

In essence, al-Qaradawi's complaint is that the Jews have broken the *dhimma*, the pact of surrender and submission which they or their ancestors had concluded with their Muslim overlords in exchange for the right of "protected" domicile. Since even minimal human rights for *dhimmis* in Islam are conditional upon fulfillment of the conditions of the *dhimma*, Muslims are no longer under obligation toward them. Their lives and property are now forfeit.

In reality, none of the Jews who migrated to Palestine in the twentieth century ever agreed to any pact of subordination by which they would have become *dhimmis*. They came to the land from Christian Europe to escape the ever more dangerous hazards of powerlessness and subordination. Those who came from Muslim countries after World War II did so to escape the persecution, pogroms, and expulsions that were visited upon them. None of that mattered to al-Qaradawi. In his narrative, all Jews were or should have been *dhimmis*. Facts were of no importance. He wanted to give the *umma*, the worldwide community of Muslim believers, a license to kill all Jews. On January 9, 2009, he conveyed that message on Al Jazeera TV to Muslims throughout the world.[81]

JIHAD, RAGE, AND THE MUSLIM "STREET"

On September 30, 2005, the *Jyllands-Posten*, a Danish daily newspaper, published twelve editorial cartoons most of which depicted Muhammad. The editors explained that they were attempting to contribute to the debate concerning the limits of freedom of expression in dealing with criticism of Islam. A discussion of that important issue is beyond the scope of our inquiry, but many Muslims regarded the cartoons as an insult to their religion and were enraged by their publication. Their sense of outrage intensified as the cartoons came to be reprinted in newspapers in more than fifty countries.[82] Many Westerners suspected that some Muslims were using the incident to control what non-Muslims could write about Islam. The protests simmered for a time, together with boycotts and threats of boycotts of Denmark and other Western governments that insisted on the right of free expression. In London the situation came to a head on February 3, 2006, when Muslims marched through the city's streets chanting and carrying posters threatening Denmark, the Jews, and the West in general. A collection of photographs taken at the demonstration and others like it is available on the Web.[83]

The following is a brief description of such photographs. They are a representative sample:

- A woman wearing a *hijab*, a head cover, stands next to a London policeman holding a poster with the message, "Europe You Will Pay; Your 9/11 Is On Its Way!!!"
- A person hidden behind two policemen holds up a sign reading "Kill Those Who Insult Islam."
- Woman dressed in black with black *hijab* carries a sign that reads, "Be Prepared for the Real Holocaust!"
- A young man holds a sign that reads "Islam Will Dominate the World"
- A poster carries the message, "Behead Those Who Insult Islam"
- A woman wearing a *hijab* carries a sign reading, "Freedom Go To Hell"

- A group picture with several signs. One sign reads: "Europe, You'll Come Crawling When the *Mujahadeen* [a Muslim involved in *jihad*] Come Roaring!"
- In a photograph taken at a Melbourne, Australia demonstration, a woman in a *hijab* carries a sign that reads, "Cleanse the earth from dirty Zionists."[84]

As chilling as are the photographs, they do not convey the atmosphere of rage and visceral hatred nearly as well as do video clips taken at such events and made available on YouTube. Most of the clips cited below were taken at demonstrations that occurred during the Gaza war of December 2008 and January 2009. However, we begin with demonstrations protesting the *Jylands-Posten* cartoons. Like the photographs, the video clips are representative of Muslim "street" reaction in Western countries to the cartoons and Israeli response to Hamas's rockets in 2008–2009. In the West, the Muslim "street" is, at least in appearance, solidly middle class. The people shouting threats and curses do not appear to be fringe people:

- London, February 24, 2006: Demonstration at the Danish Embassy. Numbering several hundred, the crowd chants *"Allah hu Akbar"* in front of the Danish Embassy. A poster is held high reading, "Europe, You will pay. Your annihilation is on the way!!!" Other signs read: "Death to you, by God, May Allah Bomb You, May Usamah bin Laden Bomb You," "We Love Usama. Usama bin Laden, we love you!" "Usamah and [Ayman] al-Zawahiri-They Are Men. They Will Bomb You. Allah Will Be With Them." "[May they] bomb Denmark so that we can invade their country and take their wives as war booty," "Europe. You'll Come Crashing When The *Mujahadeen* Come Roaring," "Annihilate Those Who Insult Islam," "You have Declared War Against Allah And His Prophet." Someone shouts, "You have declared war against the Muslim *ummah* . . . for which you will pay a heavy price. Take the lesson of Theo van Gogh. Take the Lesson of the Jews of Khaybar for You will pay with your blood." The crowd responds by repeating, "With your blood, with your blood" and "Down, down Denmark, Burn Burn, Denmark, Burn, Burn France, Burn, Burn Spain, *Allah hu Akbar*," "Denmark, Watch your back, Bin Laden's coming back." The crowd repeats, "Kill, kill Denmark, UK you will pay, 7/7 [date of the London bombings] On its Way. Jihad is on its way. We want Danish blood." A boy of about 11 shakes his fist and holds up sign reading, "Europe, you will pay, your 9/11 is on its way."[85]
- London, January 3, 2009: There are a disquieting series of video clips taken during London demonstrations in which Muslims chase

as many as fifty policemen through the streets. The Muslims chant "Free speech, Palestine" and *"Allah hu Akbar"* as the police retreat, ceding control of the streets to the demonstrators. A demonstrator leader shouts at the retreating police, "Run you, f---ing cowards, *kuffar*, and swine, pigs."[86]

- Washington, D.C., January 10, 2009: Video clips taken at Lafayette Park, opposite the White House, followed by clips taken at other locations. Thousands gathered at the Lafayette Park demonstration sponsored by allegedly "mainstream" Muslim organizations, such as the Muslim America Society and the Council on American Islamic Relations. In the first clip the crowd chants "From the river to the sea, Palestine will be free." In another Washington clip taken the next day, a typical sign reads, "The cancer of the Middle East, Israel Must not Exist!" In a clip taken at a pro-Hamas rally in Manhattan on January 11, 2009, a man holds a poster with the message "Death to the juice," an intentional misspelling. In another clip taken at the same demonstration, a woman in a *hijab* carries a large sign with the message, "Zionism: Go back to the oven; we need another Hitler!" In a clip taken in Washington on December 30, 2008, the message, "Holocaust, It's Time to Open the Ovens Again!" is painted on the back of a male figure's white outer garment while the crowd chants, "Down, down Israel, free, free Palestine!" In other demonstrations in Chicago, New York, Houston, and Oklahoma City, the crowd chants, *"Khaybar, Khaybar, ya, Yahud,"* and *"Khaybar, Khaybar ya Yahud, jaysh Muhammad sauf ya'ud"* ("Khaybar, Khaybar, O You Jews, the army of Muhammad shall return."[87] In a Montreal clip, children scream, "Palestine is ours; the Jews are our Dogs." In a Los Angeles clip, January 6, 2009, the crowd chants repeatedly, "Long live Hitler! Long live Hitler!" and "Put Jews in Ovens."[88]
- Amsterdam, January 3, 2009: In one clip, the crowd, numbering several hundred chants, "Hamas, Hamas, *joden aan het gas!*" (Hamas, Hamas, Jews to the gas!). In the foreground, Harry van Bommel, a Socialist member of Parliament chants repeatedly, "Intifada, Intifada!" The crowd repeats the chant in unison.[89]
- Fort Lauderdale, Florida, December 30, 2008: A clip shows several hundred people in the city center. A much smaller group of pro-Israel counter demonstrators are on the sidewalk behind a police barrier. A Muslim girl in *hijab* shouts "You're losing, you're losing, you're dead! Your mother is a whore! Yes, you're losing!" Then lifts up a sign, "Nuke Israel" and screams ""Nuke, nuke Israel. Yes, there is no Israel!" Muslims shout at the pro-Israel demonstrators who carry signs and Israeli flags but do not answer them when they shout "Go to Hell, Go to Hell, Israel!"[90]

- Copenhagen, January 10, 2009, "Pro-Arabisk Demonstration": The clip begins with a chant: "Down, down Israel, down, down USA, down, down Denmark!" Later, the crowd chants, "Denmark: Heil! Down with democracy. All the Jews should be killed, *Allah hu Akhbar!*" As in many other demonstrations globally and over the decades, the crowd repeatedly shouts, *"Khaybar, Khaybar, ya, Yahud,"* and *"Khaybar, Khaybar ya Yahud, jaysh Muhammad sauf ya'ud."* ("Khaybar, Khaybar, O You Jews, the army of Muhammad shall return.) [91]
- Montreal, Quebec, January 4 and 11, 2009: The crowd demands the murder of the Jews and chants in French, *"Khaybar, Khaybar, Ô Juifs, l'armée de Mohammad va revenir"* and in Arabic, *"Khaybar, Khaybar, ya Yahud."* The scene is repeated the following Sunday. The crowd is angrier and louder than the previous week. "Chavistas," followers of Hugo Chavez of Venezuela, join the demonstration and chant in Spanish, "The people united will never be defeated." There are also Arabic chants addressed to Hezbollah's leader, Hassan Nasrallah, "Oh Nasrallah, Oh beloved, Strike, Strike Tel Aviv!"[92]

There are laws prohibiting "hate speech" in the Netherlands, Canada, France, and Italy, and for the past ten years the Saudi-based Organization of the Islamic Conference has pushed the UN to adopt a universal ban on defaming Islam.[93] The chief complainants demanding prosecution for what they perceive to be hate speech have been Muslims, as in the Canadian prosecution of serious writers such as Mark Steyn and Ezra Levant.[94] At the same time, we see that a critical mass of Muslims feels free to call for mass murder and genocide and in the case of Amin al-Asari, shows films of the Holocaust as a model for Muslim behavior while public authorities are loath to enforce the same hate speech laws against Muslim offenders. These scenes were reported neither by Britain's mainstream media nor by CNN.[95]

MUSLIM RAGE IN ACTION

Between November 26 and 29, 2008, a gang of Islamist terrorists from Pakistan murdered at least 195 people and wounded several hundred others in Mumbai in a sixty-hour rampage. According to World Gazetteer, Mumbai is conservatively reckoned to be the world's second-largest city with a population in 2008 of 13,662,885.[96] Indian police claimed that ten terrorists took part in the attack, nine of whom were killed and one, Ajmal Amir Kasab, was captured. Given the meticulous planning that went into the attack, the number of participants seems doubtful. A columnist writing in *Asia Times*, a Hong Kong–based, English-language newspaper, claims he was "reliably informed" that the actual number was closer to thirty, "not counting support personnel in Mumbai who arranged safe houses with extra ammunition and explosives months in advance of the attack."[97] Kasab told the police that he was instructed to continue killing until he himself was killed. He also said that the terrorists planned to kill 5,000 people and completely destroy the luxurious, hundred-year-old Taj Mahal, the city's most prestigious hotel.

Whatever the strategic thinking of the Islamist leadership, at least ten terrorists were willing to go to their deaths in a sadistic orgy of indiscriminate murder and mayhem perpetrated against people they did not know and who had done them no personal harm. They were undoubtedly promised the heavenly rewards of numerous female companions—seventy-two virgins being the most frequently cited estimate—a rich, otherworldly compensation for lives lived "in pure frustration, with no opportunity to experience sex, love, tenderness or even understanding from the opposite sex."[98] Nevertheless, there were other, more this-worldly rewards, some psychic, others material, awaiting the terrorists. There is, for example, no greater assertion of power by one individual over another than the ability to take a life, especially when, rightly or wrongly, the attacker is convinced that he or she has been injured by the victim or what the victim represents. In preparation for the assault, Kasab and the other terrorists received months of training in the use of weapons and explosives. They were also drilled in close-quarters combat. [99] When captured, Kasab told his interrogators, "I have no regrets. . . . I have done right."[100] Kasab's pride in his murders is typical of all of the Islamist killers we examine here below. They feel no guilt. They are not reluctant to confess when apprehended for their confessions are in their eyes the record of divinely sanctioned achievements. They dwell in an utterly alien moral universe.

Most of the victims in Mumbai were attacked at random simply because they were not Muslim and happened to be unlucky enough to be at a location the terrorists planned to assault, such as the Taj Mahal and Oberoi hotels. There was, however, nothing random about the torture and murder of Rabbi Gavriel Holtzberg, his pregnant wife Rivkah, and four other Jews who were present at Nariman House, the Chabad community center in Mumbai. Before the rampage, Mumbai's Jewish population was estimated to be about four thousand.[101] Nariman House was hidden away on a narrow, remote side street. It was, however, as deliberately targeted as the five-star Taj Mahal hotel. Kasab is reported to have told police that, in order to familiarize themselves with the building, some of the terrorists disguised themselves as Malaysian students and rented rooms at the Chabad center before the attack.[102] If, as seems likely, Kasab's testimony is reliable, the terrorists had the information necessary to take over the Chabad center and its inhabitants well in advance of the attack.

According to Kasab, the Chabad group was singled out "to avenge atrocities on Palestinians."[103] Like many other Muslims, Kasab believes that Jews have no right to be in Palestine save as *dhimmis* under Muslim domination. Hence, they consider *any* warlike act by Israel, defensive or offensive, to be an atrocity. It is in that sense that we can understand Kasab's claim that the assault on the Chabad center was, in his mind, a legitimate act of vengeance.

Moreover, the Chabad Jews were obscenely tortured before being killed. Writing from Mumbai, Damien McElroy of the *Daily Telegraph* (UK) reported, "Doctors expressed horror at the condition of the bodies recovered from the Nariman building." The mortician who examined the bodies said, "I have seen so many dead bodies in my life, and was traumatised. It was apparent that most of the dead were tortured."[104] Regarded as *shaheeds*, martyrs, by the Islamists, the killers were actually torturers in the name of their God. Their behavior was consistent with that advocated by Sheikh Amin al-Ansari in his TV address we discuss above.

Seeking information and control, religious and political institutions have used torture as an instrument of compulsion for centuries. This was evident, for example, in the Albigensian Crusade (1209–1229), in which the newly established Inquisition played a major role in the destruction of the dualist Cathar sect in the Languedoc region of France.[105] The Inquisition sanctioned torture to identify and root out heresy. In our time, torture has been used to extract information such as an enemy's intentions or the identity of his clandestine agents. Nevertheless, such torture was seldom an end in itself and was normally terminated when the torturer achieved his objective. One of the reasons the torture, degradation, and murder of prisoners at Abu Ghraib elicited such widespread revulsion was that many, if not most, of the abuses were acts of pure sadism with no purpose. The torture was an end in itself perpetrated by military personnel who thought they could act with impunity. This was also the case at the Chabad center in Mumbai. Torture was inflicted on the young rabbi and his wife simply to intensify the pain of their deaths. If nothing else, such sadism demonstrates dominance, a dominance Islam has not achieved over the State of Israel. Moreover, as painful as was the torture inflicted on the young rabbi, the worst pain may have been watching helplessly as others, including his pregnant wife, were tortured. A vengeful sadist enjoys a symbolic victory when genuine victory is unattainable. Unable to defeat real enemies, he takes revenge on a defenseless surrogate. Nevertheless, such satisfaction is ephemeral and cannot alter the shame of real defeat.

One of the most obscene cases of rage-induced sadism occurred in Paris on January 21, 2006, when Ilan Halimi, a Jewish clerk, was abducted by a predominantly Muslim gang who appropriately called themselves "the

Barbarians." The gang demanded ransom money from Ilan's family, who were too poor to pay it. Losing interest in money, the gang then used their helpless victim to gratify their rage through three weeks of incessant beating, burning, and other forms of torture in the basement of the eleven-story apartment block in a predominantly Muslim area on the southern edge of Paris. Nor was the gang's treatment of Ilan unknown to many of the inhabitants of the block.[106] Finally released on February 13 as he was about to expire, he was found naked by a railroad track with 80 percent of his body covered with burn marks and knife wounds. He died on the way to a hospital. Although mainstream French Muslims have often massed in protest against perceived injustices, they had no interest in the Halimi case.[107]

Other examples of the same phenomenon include ritualistic decapitation and near decapitation of innocent victims in the name of Allah, such as *Wall Street Journal* reporter Daniel Pearl in Pakistan, French-Jewish disc jockey Sebastien Salem in Paris, Theo van Gogh in Amsterdam, and Ariel Sellouk in Houston, Texas. Pearl was the South Asia bureau chief of the *Wall Street Journal*, stationed in Mumbai. He came to Pakistan ostensibly to investigate possible connections between al Qaeda and Richard Reid, the "shoe bomber," who was arrested in December 2001 for attempting to ignite explosives hidden in his sneakers while on a Paris-to-Miami flight. There is some suspicion that Pearl's real interest lay in investigating links between al Qaeda and Pakistan's powerful Inter-Services Intelligence agency (ISI).[108] Pearl was kidnapped on January 23, 2002, while seeking an interview in Karachi with Mubarak Ali Shah Gilani, a radical Muslim cleric. On or about February 1, 2002, he was gruesomely murdered, an event that was recorded on videotape by his captors and released on the Internet under the title "The Slaughter of the Spy-Journalist, the Jew Daniel Pearl." The video lasts three minutes and thirty-six seconds. It includes Pearl's statement that he is a Jew and a Zionist.[109] One minute and fifty-five seconds into the video, Pearl is shown with his throat slit. An unidentified man then decapitates him. His body was subsequently found in a shallow grave and cut into ten pieces. A copy of the video was delivered to the U.S. consulate on February 21, 2002. On May 14, a thirty-second clip of the beheading was shown on CBS News in spite of appeals by the Pearl family and the Departments of State and Justice to CBS to refrain from showing it. CBS News reported obtaining the video from a dissident Saudi journalist who found it on an anti-American Arabic website *where it was being used by jihadists as a recruiting tool.*[110]

According to the *9/11 Commission Report*, "No one exemplifies the model of the terrorist entrepreneur more clearly than Khalid Sheikh Mohammed (KSM), the principal architect of the 9/11 attacks."[111] KSM was arrested by the ISI in Pakistan on March 1, 2003, and has been in American custody ever since. On March 10, 2007, KSM proudly declared at a Combatant Status Review Tribunal Hearing at Guantánamo Bay:

> I was the Operational Director for Sheikh Usama Bin Laden for the organizing, planning, follow-up, and execution of the 9/11 Operation. . . . I was the Military Operational Commander for all foreign operations around the world under the direction of Sheikh Usama Bin Laden and Dr. Ayman Al-Zawahiri. I was directly in charge, after the death of Sheikh Abu Hafs Al-Masri Subhi Abu Sittah, of managing and following up on the Cell for the Production of Biological Weapons, such as anthrax and others, and following up on Dirty Bomb Operations on American soil.

> I hereby admit and affirm without duress that I was a responsible participant, principal planner, trainer, financier (via the Military Council Treasury), executor, and/or a personal participant in the following:

KSM then listed twenty-nine major operations, not all of which were brought to fruition. Far from being a confession of wrongdoing, his admission was in reality a boastful claiming credit. The third item on his list was his statement about Daniel Pearl:

> I decapitated with *my blessed right hand* the head of the American Jew, Daniel Pearl, in the city of Karachi, Pakistan. For those who would like to confirm, there are pictures of me on the Internet holding his head (emphasis added).[112]

This was clearly an operation that gave him great satisfaction. KSM could make a claim because he was firmly convinced that his actions were those of a faithful Muslim fulfilling Allah's commandments. According to Ibn Ishaq, one of Muhammad's earliest biographers, at one point Muhammad told his followers, "Kill any Jew that falls into your power."[113]

Jews have by no means been the sole objects of Muslim rage. Apart from the 9/11 attack on the World Trade Center and the Pentagon with its huge loss of life, there have been other horrendous events on a smaller scale, among them the murder and mutilation of fifty-eight foreign tourists on November 18, 1997, at the site of Egypt's Luxor temple by six armed members of an Egyptian extremist, Islamist group led by Ayman al-Zawahiri, who was safely ensconced in Kandahar, Afghanistan, at the time.[114] We deal with this incident in greater detail in another chapter.

Both rage and pride in sacralized sadism were also evident in videos available for sale and viewing at London's Finsbury Park Mosque. In 2002, journalist Jason Burke reported on the sale and widespread distribution of such videos at the mosque. One video, *Algeria*, was produced by the *Groupe Salafiste pour Prédication et Combat* (Salafist Group for Preaching and War or GSPC). A second, *The Mirror of Jihad*, was produced by a group allied with the Taliban in Afghanistan.[115] According to Burke, the *Algeria* film consists of "graphic footage of the deaths of more than 20 young conscripts in an ambush." These were ordinary Muslims conscripted for military service by the Algerian government. There was no way they could have refused military service. The film shows the trucks that carried the conscripts hitting a GSPC mine and exploding. The Salafists then slit the throats and shot the survivors. Other pictures of dead soldiers were shown, some with skulls shot away and brains exposed, followed by images of joyful "Islamists congratulating each other and offering prayers of thanks." The murder scenes are preceded by the injunctions on the screen: "Fight them until the sentence of God is carried out on Earth" and "You have to kill in the name of Allah until you are killed. . . . The whole Islamic world should rise up to fight all the sick unbelievers. The flag *of jihud will* be forever held high." There is further commentary: "*God loves people who kill in his name.* The enemies of Islam are scared. The Jews and the Christians know that they have lost [the war] and want to stop us from spreading the truth (emphasis added)." The Taliban film was equally gruesome, featuring Taliban warriors torturing and decapitating Northern Alliance troops in Afghanistan. Far from disturbing the mosque's faithful, the films were freely available at the mosque for £10 each and, like the video of Daniel Pearl's beheading, were used as a recruiting device by Islamists. The Finsbury Park Mosque offered its believers multiple opportunities vicariously to enjoy unmitigated sadism and an imagined victory over imputed enemies, all in the name of God.

On March 3, 2006, Mohammed Reza Taheri-Azar, an American citizen of Iranian origin and a graduate student at the University of North Carolina at Chapel Hill, deliberately drove a rented four-wheel drive Jeep Grand Cherokee vehicle into a crowd in a pedestrian commons at the university at 11:45 A.M., a time and place where students customarily gather for lunch. He struck nine people. When asked later by reporters whether he intended to kill, he answered "Yes." He repeated his affirmation at his trial on August 12, 2006.[116] The police reported that he told them he had been planning the assault for two years and had rented a four-wheel drive vehicle because he could "run things over and keep going."[117] Fortunately, none of the victims was seriously hurt. Taheri-Azar also told the judge at the preliminary hearing, "I am thankful you're here to give me this trial and to learn more about the will of Allah."[118] In his value system, he had done nothing wrong and saw the trial as an opportunity to instruct nonbelievers in the true faith. He did, however, express some regret. He told the police that he regretted that there were not more people in the commons area when he struck and that he had not killed anyone, claiming that his attempt at mass murder was a divinely sanctioned act to "avenge the deaths of Muslims around the world."[119] Such thinking is, of course, consistent with the doctrine of *jihad* and of an Islamist tendency to see themselves as victims.

Effectively hiding his destructive intentions over a period of several years, Taheri-Azar's outburst can be seen as an example of cold rage. At Chapel Hill, he was an above-average student and had been admitted to a doctoral program at Nova University in Miami while surreptitiously planning the one event that, in his mind, would give his life meaning. Daniel Pipes has characterized such behavior, often perpetrated by isolated individuals, as terrorism and has identified it as "Sudden *Jihad* Syndrome." Pipes argues that Taheri-Azar "fits into a widespread pattern of Muslims who lead quiet lives before turning to terrorism" and that his behavior "represents the ultimate Islamist nightmare: a seemingly well-adjusted Muslim whose religion inspires him, out of the blue, to murder non-Muslims."[120] I would add that such behavior is only sudden from the point of view of its intended victims rather than the perpetrators. Like the perpetrators of 9/11 and the 2008 assault on Mumbai, Taheri-Azar's assault took time and planning. I would also add that such acts are impelled by rage so consuming that the perpetrator is more than willing to kill himself in the process of killing others.

In yet another instance of what Pipes has identified as Sudden *Jihad* Syndrome, on February 12, 2007, Sulejman Talović, a twenty-two-year-old Bosnian Muslim with a U.S. permanent residence card (green card), suddenly began firing into a crowd at the Trolley Square Mall in Salt Lake City, Utah. Before being stopped by two off-duty policemen, Talović had killed five people and wounded at least four others. Characteristically, neither the police nor the FBI agent involved in the case could find reason to label the attack as either a terror attack or religiously motivated. Indeed, unless the perpetrator openly proclaims his deed an act of vengeance, all too often public officials in the West have preferred to characterize such attacks as isolated incidents for which no motive can be assigned. Moreover, there has been a tendency on the part of the police and the FBI to deny that random acts of homicidal violence perpetrated by Muslims are religiously motivated even though the assailants themselves often assigned such motives for their deeds.[121]

Such expressions of rage often serve the strategic interests of the larger Muslim community in its relations with government and nongovernment institutions concerned with the maintenance of public order. This was certainly the case when angry Muslim mobs belatedly responded in February 2006 to the publication of the *Jyllands-Posten* cartoons in September 2005 and to Pope Benedict XVI's lecture at the University of Regensburg on September 12, 2006, in which he cited the negative opinions on Islam offered in 1391 by the Byzantine emperor Manuel II Paleologus. As noted above, in response to the Danish cartoons, more than two hundred people were killed in rampages throughout the world[122] Response to the Pope was of shorter duration but included the murder of an elderly Italian nun and her bodyguards in Somalia. Western institutions have been given graphic examples of the price to be paid for arousing Muslim ire. Unfortunately, Muslim ire has been aroused. At least among Islamists, it will not be calmed until they are convinced that the shame and disgrace of Muslim defeats from the Battle of Lepanto (1571) to the Israeli War of Independence (1948) and the Six-Day War (1967) have been erased. If we take the Islamists at their word, nothing less than genocide will suffice.

Notes

INTRODUCTION

1. Richard L. Rubenstein and John K. Roth, *Approaches to Auschwitz: The Holocaust and Its Legacy*, 2nd ed. (Louisville: Westminster John Knox Press, 2003).

2. Lawrence Wright, *The Looming Tower and the Road to 9/11* (New York: Vintage Books, 2007), 201–203.

3. I am grateful to Professor Roth for his e-mail of March 21, 2009 in which he helped to clarify our correspondence.

4. Richard L. Rubenstein, *Power Struggle: An Autobiographical Confession* (New York: Charles Scribner's Sons, 1974), 154–169.

5. "Transcript of President Bush's address to a joint session of Congress on Thursday night, September 20, 2001," CNN.com./U.S., http://archives.cnn.com/2001/US/09/20/gen.bush.transcript/ (accessed June 12, 2009).

6. Mary Habeck, *Knowing the Enemy: Jihadist Ideology and the War on Terror* (New Haven: Yale University Press, 2006), 41. See also the measured comments by Robert Spencer on the alleged "hijacking" of Islam, "Johns Hopkins professor: Jihadists' 'definition of jihad is quite different from that generally accepted by Muslims today,'" *Jihad Watch*, May 17, 2007, http://www.jihadwatch.org/archives/016497.php (accessed June 13, 2009).

7. Michael Oren, *Six Days of War: June 1967 and the Making of the Modern Middle East* (Oxford: Oxford University Press, 2002), 78.

8. The text of the Roadmap can be found at "A Performance-Based Roadmap to a Permanent Two-State Solution to the Israeli-Palestinian Conflict," United States Institute of Peace, April 30, 2003, http://www.usip.org/library/pa/israel_palestinians/ adddoc/roadmap_04302003.html.

9. "Statement by incoming Foreign Minister Avigdor Liberman at the ministerial inauguration ceremony," Israel Ministry of Foreign Affairs, April 1,

2009, http://www.mfa.gov.il/MFA/About+the+Ministry/Foreign_Minister/ Speeches/Statement_by_incoming_FM_Avigdor_Liberman_1-Apr-2009.htm>; see also Jeff Jacoby, "In Israel, A Voice of Realism," *Boston Globe,* April 5, 2009, http://www.jeffjacoby. com/5247/in-israel-a-voice-of-realism.

10. Ayman al-Zawahiri, "Loyalty and Enmity" in Raymond Ibrahim, ed. and trans., *The Al Qaeda Reader* (New York: Broadway Books, 2007), 93. Al-Zawahiri cites Ibn Taymiyya (1263–1328) as his authority.

11. The proceedings of one such conference, a Jewish-Muslim dialogue held in Cordoba, Spain, are to be found in Charles Selengut, ed., *Jewish-Muslim Encounters: History, Philosophy and Culture* (St. Paul, MN: Paragon House, 2001).

12. Ismail R. al-Faruqi, "Islam and Zionism," in John L. Esposito, ed., *Voices of Resurgent Islam* (New York: Oxford University Press, 1983), 265.

13. Jack O'Sullivan, "Zaki Badawi," *The Guardian,* January 25, 2005, http:// www.guardian.co.uk/news/2006/jan/25/guardianobituaries.religion.

14. Nevertheless, there was one genocide to which Zaki Badawi was indifferent. I was informed by a British friend who had been active in raising the awareness of the British public about the mass murder in Darfur that when he sought the support of Zaki Badawi, the latter responded that he had no interest in the sub-Saharan victims as they were in reality polytheists and not Muslim.

15. Ryan Jones, "French Official: Israel's Establishment a Historic Mistake," *Jerusalem News Wire,* June 20, 2004. http://www.jnewswire.com/article/128.

16. Barbara Amiel, "Islamists Overplay Their Hand, but London Salons Don't See It," *Daily Telegraph* (UK), December 21, 2001.

17. Jan T. Gross, *Fear: Anti-Semitism in Poland After Auschwitz* (New York: Random House, 2006).

18. Ya'akov Meron, "Why Jews Fled the Arab Countries," *Middle East Quarterly,* II, 3 (September 1995), http://www.meforum.org/263/why-jews-fled-the-arab-countries.

19. Henri Pirenne, *Mohammed and Charlemagne* (Mineola, NY: Dover Publications, 2001), 17.

20. For example, in the spring of 2009 Turkish prime minister Recep Tayyip Erdogan told a *New York Times* columnist, "Hamas must be represented at the negotiating table. Only then can you get a solution." Roger Cohen, "Turkey Wants U.S. 'Balance,'" *New York Times,* April 6, 2009, http://www.nytimes.com/2009/04/06/opinion/06iht-edcohen.html.

21. Eli Wiesel, *Night,* trans. Stella Rodway (New York: Avon Discus Books, 1969), 91–92.

CHAPTER ONE

1. A *hadith* is a saying or an action attributed by tradition to the Prophet Muhammad.

2. The sources on *jihad* are voluminous. I have found the insights of John Kelsay, Bassam Tibi, Andrew Bostom, and Bat Ye'or especially helpful. See Tibi, *The Challenge of Fundamentalism: Political Islam and the New World Disorder* (Berkeley: University of California Press, 2002), 54–55. See also Tibi, "War and

Peace in Islam," in Terry Nardin, ed. *The Ethics of War and Peace: Secular and Religious Perspectives* (Princeton. NJ: Princeton University Press, 1996), 128–45; John Kelsay, *Islam and War: A Study in Comparative Ethics* (Louisville: Westminster/John Knox, 1993); Kelsay, *Arguing the Just War in Islam* (Cambridge: Harvard University Press, 2007); Bat Ye'or, *Islam and Dhimmitude: Where Civilizations Collide* (Madison. NJ: Farleigh Dickinson University, 2002), 40–50; Andrew G. Bostom, *The Legacy of Jihad: Islamic Holy War and the Fate of Non-Muslims* (Amherst. NY: Prometheus Books, 2005); Rudolph Peters, *Jihad in Classical and Modern Islam: A Reader* (Princeton: Markus Weiner Publishers, 1996); David Cook, *Understanding Jihad* (Berkeley: University of California Press, 2005); John Kelsay and James Turner Johnson, eds., *Just War and Jihad: Historical and Theoretocal Perspectives on War and Peace* in *Western and Islamic Traditions* (Westport, CT: Greenwood Press, 1991).

3. Tibi, "War and Peace in Islam," in Bostom, *The Legacy of Jihad,* 327.

4. There was an intermediate category that also implied submission to the Muslim overlord, *dar al-Sulh* (House of Truce) or *dar al-Ahd* (House of Pact or Covenant). This was a region in which a non-Muslim sovereign agreed to protect his Muslim subjects and maintain their mosques. See Bernard Lewis, *Islam and the West* (New York: Oxford University Press, 1993), 50.

5. Kelsay, *Islam and War,* 34–35.

6. The saying is attributed to Umar ll (c. 682–720). See Cook, *Understanding Jihad,* 35, 217,9(N).

7. After an angry backlash, Yassin changed the title to the innocuous "A Faith and Citizenship."

8. Interview by Darryn Kagan of Zayed Yassin, aired June 5, 2002, CNN transcript, http://transcripts.cnn.com/TRANSCRIPTS/0206/05/lt.23.html.

9. See, for example, John Esposito, *The Islamic Threat. Myth or Reality* (New York: Oxford University Press, 1999), 30.

10. The exhortation has been removed from the website of the Saudi Embassy. It has, however, been retained by Steven Stalinsky, "The 'Islamic Affairs Department' of the Saudi Embassy in Washington, DC," MEMRI (Middle East Media Research Institute) Special Report no. 23 (November 26, 2003), http://www.memri.org/bin/articles.cgi?Page=archives&Area=sr&ID=SR2303#_ednref12 (accessed July 27, 2008).

11. *Encvclopedia of Islam,* new ed., s.v. "Djihad" (E. Tayan). For this reference, I am indebted to Cook, *Understanding Jihad,* 213, 1(N).

12. Cook, *Understanding Jihad,* 42.

13. Kelsay, *Arguing the Just War in Islam,* 102.

14. John Kelsay, *Arguing the Just War,* 100. Kelsay's chapter "Politics, Ethics and War in Premodern Islam," 97–124, offers a succinct and authoritative overview of the classical view of the justification and conduct of war in Islam.

15. There are Qur'anic verses that identify *jihad* as a means of persuading the nonbeliever to convert peacefully, such as the following: "Do not yield to the unbelievers and use the Qur'an for your *jihad* to carry through against them." (Qur'an, *al-Furqan* 25:52.) Scholars who interpret the Qur'an historically argue that this and similar verses come from the Mecca period of Islam's formative years, before the *Hijra* and the establishment of the Muslim city-state in Medina in 622.

The Meccan verses, they argue, contain no reference to *qital* because Muhammad and his followers were too few in number to employ force. Hence, they were compelled to employ persuasion to convince non-Muslims of the truth of the new faith. The situation changed when Muhammad became Medina's leader and military commander. Thereafter, *jihad* became *qital* when non-Muslims refused to submit to Islam peacefully or actively opposed it. See Bassam Tibi, "War and Peace in Islam," in Andrew Bostom, ed., *The Legacy of Jihad: Islamic Holy War and the Fate of Non-Muslims*, 330.

16. His exact words were, "Islam is peace," The White House, Office of the Press Secretary, September 17, 2001, http://www.whitehouse.gov/news/releases/ 2001/09/20010917-11.httml.

17. Bassam Tibi, "The Totalitarianism of Jihadist Islamism and Its Challenge to Europe and Islam," *Totalitarian Movements and Political Religions*, 8 (March 1, 2007):1, 45.

18. Majid Khadduri, *War and Peace in the Law of Islam* (Baltimore: Johns Hopkins University Press, 1955), 64.

19. Tibi, "War and Peace in Islam," 328.

20. Tibi, "War and Peace in Islam," 329.

21. An argument has been made that *jihad*, when initiated by legitimate authority and conducted in accordance with *shari'a* is, from an Islamic perspective, a "just war." See Kelsay, *Arguing the Just War*, 101–102. On the other hand, Tibi argues that the Western idea of a "just war" is meaningless in Islam since all wars against nonbelievers faithful to their own traditions are regarded as "just." See Tibi, "War and Peace in Islam," 329.

22. Tibi, "War and Peace in Islam," 331.

23. The "redemption of captives" *(pldyon shivuimj)* was regarded by Jewish communities as a primary responsibility.

24. George F. Natziger and Mark W. Walton, *Islam at War: A History* (Westport, CT: Praeger, 2003), 10.

25. Ibn Hashām, "The Extermination of the Banū Qurayza," in Hashām, *al-Sira al-Nabawiyya* (The Life of the Prophet), vol. 2, (Cairo: Mustafa al Babi al Hababi & Sons, 1955), 233–45; English translation in Norman Stillman, *The Jews in Arab Lands: A History and Source Book* (Philadelphia: Jewish Publication Society, 1979), 137–144.

26. For an apologetic defense of the slaughter, see Karen Armstrong, *Islam* (New York: The Modern Library, 2000), 19–23.

27. W. Montgomery Scott, *Muhammad: Prophet and Statesman* (Oxford: Oxford University Press, 1961), 175.

28. Watt, *Muhammad*, 173.

29. Sayyid Qutb, *Milestones*, vol. 1 (New Delhi: Islamic Book Service, 2001), 19, 6(N).

30. Absent the murders, something similar was involved both among the ancient Hebrews and the early Christians. The Hebrews were commanded: "Thou shalt have no other Gods before me."(Exodus 20:3). Paul of Tarsus proclaimed to the Galations: "There is neither Jew nor Greek, there is neither slave nor free. . . . For you are all one in Christ Jesus." (3:28). In each case, rejection of ancestral gods was followed by the creation of a new community bound to the monotheistic God.

31. For a succinct but authoritative account of the interpretative process on the subject of war and peace, see John Kelsay, *Arguing the Just War in Islam.*

32. For my interpretation of Qutb's views on *jihad*, I am indebted to Hendrik Hansen and Peter Kainz, "Totalitarian Movements and Political Religions," in *Totalitarian Movements and Political Religions*, vol. 8, no. 1, 56–63 (November 26, 2007); William E. Shepard, "Sayyid Qutb's Doctrine of *Jāhiliyya*," *Internaional Journal of Middle East Studies*, November 2003, vol. 35, no. 4, 521–545 (June 22, 2002); Gilles Kepel, *Muslim Extremism in Egypt: The Prophet and the Pharaoh*, trans. Jon Rothschild (Berkeley: University of California Press, 1993), 26–43.

33. Adnan A. Musallam, "Prelude to Islamic Commitment: Sayyid Qutb's Literary and Spiritual Orientation, 1932–1938," *The Muslim World*, 80, 3–4 (1990): 176; see also Yvonne Haddad, "Sayyid Qutb: Ideologue of Islamic Revival," in John Esposito, *Voices of Resurgent Islam* (New York: Oxford University Press, 1983), 68.

34. Stefan M. Aubrey, *The New Dimension of International Terrorism* (Zurich: vdf Hochschulerverlag, 2004), 89.

35. Haddad, "Sayyid Qutb," 69.

36. For an analysis of his poetry and his literary criticism up to 1938, see Musallam, "Prelude to Islamic Commitment," 176.

37. Sayyid Qutb, "The America I Have Seen, 1951," trans. Tarek Masoud and Ammar Fakeeh in Kamal Abdel Malek, ed., *America in an Arab Mirror: Images of America in Arab Travel Literature: An Anthology 1895–1995* (New York: St. Martin's Press, 2000), 9–28.

38. Emanuel Sivan, *Radical Islam: Medieval Theology and Modern Politics* (New Haven: Yale University Press, 1990), 29.

39. Among the Christians active in Arab nationalist movements were George Antonius (1891–1941), author of *The Arab Awakening*; Michel Aflaq (1910–1989), a founder of the Syrian Baath Party; George Habash, (1926–2008), founder of the Popular Front for the Liberation of Palestine (PFLP), a Marxist-Leninist terrorist group; Edward Said (1935–2003), University Professor at Columbia and for many years a member of the Palestine National Council; Tariq Azziz, Saddam Hussein's foreign minister.

40. Sivan, *Radical Islam*, 36.

41. Robert C. Doty, "Britain and Egypt in Accord on Suez," *New York Times*, October 19, 1954.

42. Gilles Kepel, *Muslim Extremism in Egypt*, 26–29; 38–43.

43. One prisoner noted, "Former rulers used to maltreat their adversaries, but not until the revolutionary [Nasserist] regime have we seen rulers who bring the wife and children of an opponent and torture them in his presence." Sivan, *Radical Islam*, 41; In August 1964, some Muslim Brotherhood prisoners refused to leave their cells in Kardasa fearing they would be killed while at work. Soldiers responded by breaking into their cells, killing twenty-three, injuring forty-six, and leaving some of the wounded to die unattended. See Lawrence Wright, *The Looming Tower: Al-Qaeda and the Road to 9/11* (New York: Alfred A. Knopf, 2006), 34.

44. Kepel, *Muslim Extremism in Egypt*, 26–29.

45. Kepel, *Muslim Extremism in Egypt*, 38.

46. Kepel, *Muslim Extremism in Egypt*, 42.

47. Lawrence Wright interview with Mahfouz Azzam, *The Looming Tower*, 36.

48. Wright, *The Looming Tower*, 36.

49. Sayyid Qutb, *Milestones*, (New Delhi: Islamic Book Service, 2001), I, 19, 6(N).

50. Shepard, "Sayyid Qutb's Doctrine of *Jāhiliyya*," 534; Kepel, *Muslim Extremism in Egypt*, 27–28.

51. *Jāhiliyya* is described as "the peculiar attitude of hostility and aggressiveness against the monotheistic belief of Islam" in Toshiko Izutsu, *Ethnico-religious Concepts in the Quran* (Montreal: McGill University Press, 1966), 35. For this reference, I am indebted to William E. Shepard, "Sayyid Qutb's Doctrine of *Jāhiliyya*," *International Journal of Middle Eastern Studies*, 35 (2003): 522.

52. Kepel, *Muslim Extremism in Egypt*, 13.

53. Qutb, *Milestones*, I, 11.

54. Shepard, "Sayyid Qutb's Doctrine of *Jahiliyya*," 527.

55. Qutb, *Milestones*, I, 21–22; Kepel, *Muslim Extremism in Egypt*, 53.

56. Qutb, *Milestones*, II, 21.

57. Qutb, Milestones, III, 51. For this citation, I am indebted to Hendrik Hansen and Peter Kainz, "Radical Islamism and Totalitarian Ideology: A Comparison of Sayyid Qutb's Islamism with Marxism and National Socialism," *Totalitarian Movements and Political Religions*, 8, 1 (March 1, 2007): 59.

58. Hansen and Kainz, "Radical Islamism and Totalitarian Ideology," 61.

59. Hansen and Kainz, "Radical Islamism and Totalitarian Ideology," 61.

60. Peter Berger, *The Sacred Canopy: Elements of a Sociological Theory of Religion* (Garden City: Doubleday, 1967), 107.

61. Qutb, *Milestones*, IV, 71.

62. Qutb, *Milestones*, IV, 61.

63. Bat Ye'or, *The Dhimmi: Jews and Christians under Islam*, trans. David Maisek, Paul Fenton, and David Littman (Rutherford, NJ: Fairleigh Dickenson University Press, 1985) and Bostom, *The Legacy of Jihad*.

64. Qutb, *Milestones*, IV, 72.

65. Qutb, *Milestones*, I, 15.

66. Qutb, *Milestones*, IV, 63.

67. Qutb, *Milestones*, IV, 63.

68. Shepard, "Sayyid Qutb's Doctrine of *Jāhiliyya*," 531; Abu A'la Mawdudi, *Jihad fi Sabilillah [Jihad in Islam]*, trans. Khurshid Ahmad, ed. Huda Khattab (Birmingham: U.K. Islamic Mission Dawah Centre, undated), www.ukim.org/dawah/jihad.pdf (accessed June 25,2008).

69. Qutb, *Milestones*, IV, 62–63; see Shepard, "Sayyid Qutb's Doctrine of *Jāhiliyya*," 531.

70. Shepard, "Sayyid Qutb's Doctrine of *Jāhiliyya*," 531.

71. For the formulation of the issues in this paragraph, I am indebted to Hansen and Kainz.

72. Hansen and Kainz, "Radical Islamism and Totalitarian Ideology," 61.

73. Hansen and Kainz, "Radical Islamism and Totalitarian Ideology," 61.

74. On "paranthropoid identity, see Gil Eliot, *Twentieth Century Book of the Dead* (New York: Charles Scribner's Sons, 1972), 41, 94, 124.

75. Sayyid Qutb, *Hadha al-Din* (Cairo: Dar Al-Qalam, 1962), 85. Cited in MEMRI, Special Report-No. 25, "Contemporary Islamist Ideology Authorizing

Genocidal Murder," http://memri.org/bin/articles.cgi?Page=archives&Area=sr &ID=SR2504. A useful discussion of Qutb can be found in Paul Berger, "The Philosopher of Islamic Terror," *New York Times Magazine*, March 23, 2003.

76. Nimrod Raphaeli, "Ayman Muhammad Rabi' Al-Zawahiri: The Making of an Arch-Terrorist," *Terrorism and Political Violence*, 14 (2002): 4, 3.

77. Montasser al-Zayyat, *The Road to Al-Qaeda: The Story of Bin Laden's Right-Hand Man*, ed. Sara Nimis, trans. Ahmed Fekry (London: Pluto Press, 2004), 24–25.

78. Wright, *The Looming Tower*, 44.

79. Wright, *The Looming Tower*, 43.

80. Raphaeli, "Ayman Muhammad," 5.

81. *Al-Sharq al-Awsat*, December 5, 2001, translated by Rafaeli, "Ayman Muhammad," 6. *Al-Sharq al-Awsat* is a London-based Arabic daily newspaper.

82. Al-Zayyat, *The Road to Al-Qaeda*, 51; Rafaeli, "Ayman Muhammad," 10.

83. Wright, *The Looming Tower*, 61.

84. Sivan, *Radical Islam*, 16.

85. For a brief review of the Egypt-Yemen War of 1962–67 in the larger context of Israeli-Arab conflict, see Michael B. Oren, *Six Days of War: June 1967 and the Making of the Modern Middle East* (New York: Random House, 2003), 15 (ff).

86. Sivan, *Radical Islam*, 17.

87. Peter Bergen, "Could It Happen Again?" *The National Interest*, Sept./Oct. 2006, http://www.nationalinterest.org/PrinterFriendly.aspx?id=12034 (accessed July 2, 2008).

88. Gilles Kepel, *The War for Muslim Minds: Islam and the West* (Cambridge: Harvard University Press, 2004), 83.

89. Steve Coll, "Young Osama: How he learned radicalism, and may have seen America," *The New Yorker*, December 12, 2005, http://www.newyorker.com/archive /2005/12/12/051212fa_fact?currentPage=all (accessed July 7, 2008).

90. Coll, "Young Osama."

91. Coll, "Young Osama."

92. Chris Suellentrop, "Abdullah Azzam: The Godfather of Jihad," *Slate*, April 16, 2002, http://www.slate.com/id/2064385/ (accessed July 6, 2008).

93. Andrew McGregor, "'Jihad and the Rifle Alone': 'Abdullah 'Azzam and the Islamist Revolution,'" *The Journal of Conflict Studies*, 23, 2 (Fall 2003): 98, http://www.lib.unb.ca/Texts/JCS/bin/get.cgi?directory=Fall03/&filename=mcgregor .htm (accessed July 11, 2008); see also *Article* "Abdullah Yusuf Azzam," *Indopedia*, http://www.indopedia.org/Abdullah_Yusuf_Azzam.html. This article is especially helpful in its overview of Azzam's career and its links to other sources of information about him.

94. McGregor, "Jihad and the Rifle Alone," 98.

95. Steven Emerson, *American Jihad: The Terrorists Living Among Us* (New York: Free Press, 2002), 130. I am indebted to McGregor, "Jihad and the Rifle Alone" 104–105 for this citation.

96. Abdullah Azzam, *The Defense of Muslim Lands (Ahle Sunnah Wal Jama'at)*, undated, Chapter 2, http://www.islamistwatch.org/texts/azzam/defe nse/chap2. html (accessed July 13, 2008).

97. Wright, *The Looming Tower*, 118.

98. Wright, *The Looming Tower,* 119 (ff).

99. Azzam, *The Defense of Muslim Lands,* Ch. 4, http://www.islamistwatch. org/texts /azzam/defense/chap4.html (accessed July 13, 2008).

100. Wright, *The Looming Tower,* 150.

101. Wright, *The Looming Tower,* 149.

102. Kepel, *Muslim Extremism in Egypt,* 32.

103. According to Kepel, *The War for Muslim Minds,* 174; Muhmmad Qutb's position was at Mecca's Umm al-Qura University; according to Wright, *The Looming Tower,* 91.

104. Interview with Khalifa by Lawrence Wright, Wright, *The Looming Tower,* 91.

105. Kepel, *Muslim Extremism in Egypt,* 61–67.

106. Wright, *The Looming Tower,* 92.

107. Wright, *The Looming Tower,* 290-291; see also Backgrounder, "Jamaat al-Islamiyya," *Council on Foreign Relations,* http://www.cfr.org/publication/9156/jamaat_alislamiyya.html (accessed July 4, 2008).

108. Wright, *The Looming Tower,* 290–294: Douglas Jehl, "70 Die in Temple Attack," *New York Times,* November 18, 1997 and "At Ancient Site Along the Nile, Modern Horror," *New York Times,* November 19, 1997.

109. Wright, *The Looming Tower,* 290–294; Douglas Jehl, "70 Die," and "At Ancient Site Along the Nile."

110. Jailan Halawi, "Bin Laden Behind Luxor Massacre?" *Al-Ahram Weekly,* 430 (May 20–26, 1999), http://weekly.ahram.org.eg/1999/430/eg21.htm (accessed July 5, 2008). For this citation, I am indebted to Wright, *The Looming Tower,* 293.

111. Wright, *The Looming Tower,* 293.

112. Wright, *The Looming Tower,* 293.

113. Al-Zawahiri explores the permissibility of killing innocents in "defensive *jihad*" in the treatise "Jihad, Martyrdom, and the Killing of Innocents" in Raymond Ibrahim, ed. and trans., *The Al Qaeda Reader* (New York: Doubleday Broadway Books, 2007), 137–171.

114. See note 46.

115. The text is available on the World Wide Web at http://www.fas.org/irp/world/para/docs/980223-fatwa.htm.

116. Andrew Bary, "Bountiful Barrels: Where to Find $140 Trillion," *Barrons,* July 16, 2008.

117. Osama bin Laden, "Why We Are Fighting You," in Ibrahim, *The Al Qaeda Reader,* 204.

118. When the war ended in 1991, thousands of American troops stayed on partly to enforce UN Security Council Resolution 688 imposing a "no-fly" zone in northern Iraq to protect the Kurds. A second "no-fly" zone was added in the south. By the beginning of the second Iraq war approximately 286,000 flight missions had originated from Prince Sultan Air Base to enforce the no-fly zone.

119. Don Van Natta Jr., "The Struggle for Iraq; The Last American Combat Troops Quit Saudi Arabia," *New York Times,* September 22, 2003, http://query.nytimes.com/gst/fullpage.html?res=990CEFDB1E3AF931A1575AC0A9659C8B63&sec=&spon=&pagewanted=all (accessed July 31, 2008).

120. Peter Bergen, *Holy War: Inside the Secret World of Osama bin Laden* (New York: The Free Press, 2001), 76–78.

121. Bernard Lewis, "License to Kill: Usama bin Laden's Declaration of Jihad," *Foreign Affairs*, 77, 6 (November/December 1998): 14–19.

122. Lewis, "License to Kill," 15.

123. The links to the letter and all of the posted responses can be found at http://www.americanvalues.org/html/follow-up.html.

124. See Mahan Abadin, "The Face of Saudi Opposition," *Asia Times Online*, April 20, 2006, http://www.atimes.com/atimes/Middle_East/HD20Ak02.html (accessed August 3, 2008). This is an interview with Dr. Saad al-Faqih, leader of the movement.

125. The letters and the responses are posted at http://www.americanvalues .org/html/follow-up.html.

126. "Moderate Islam is a Prostration to the West." The original title was "Al Qaeda's Declaration in Response to the Saudi Ulema: It's Best That You Prostrate Yourselves in Secret" in Ibrahim, *Al Qaeda Reader*, 17–62.

127. Ibrahim, *Al Qaeda Reader*, 18–19.

128. Ibrahim, *Al Qaeda Reader*, 23.

129. For the discussion of "Loyalty" and "Emnity," I am indebted to Ibrahim, *Al Qaeda Reader*, 63.

130. Osama bin Laden, "Moderate Islam Is a Prostration to the West," in Ibrahim, *Al Qaeda Reader*, 43.

131. Ibrahim, *Al Qaeda Reader*, 43.

132. Ibrahim, *Al Qaeda Reader*, 63.

133. Ibrahim, *Al Qaeda Reader*, 32.

134. Osama bin Laden, in Ibrahim, *Al Qaeda Reader*, 47

135. Ibrahim, *Al Qaeda Reader*, 49.

136. Ibrahim, *Al Qaeda Reader*, 51.

137. Ibrahim, *Al Qaeda Reader*, 46–47.

138. Ibrahim, *Al Qaeda Reader*, 57–58.

139. An English translation of the letter was subsequently posted on the London *Observer*'s website. "Full text: bin Laden's 'letter to America,'" *Observer* (UK), November 24, 2002, http://www.guardian.co.uk/world/2002/nov/24/theob-server. The text can also be found as "'Why We Are Fighting You': Osama bin Laden's Letter to Americans," Ibrahim, *Al Qaeda Reader*, 197–208.

140. Ibrahim, *Al Qaeda Reader*, 197. Direct quotations from Bin Laden's letter are cited from Ibrahim.

141. Ibrahim, *Al Qaeda Reader*, 197.

142. Nazila Fathi, "Iran's President Says Israel 'Must Be Wiped Off The Map,'" *New York Times*, October 26, 2005, http://www.nytimes.com/2005/10/26/ international/middleeast/26cnd-iran.html (accessed August 2, 2008).

143. Although the Qur'an states that Abraham was commanded to sacrifice his son, the son is not named (Qur'an 37:99–113). In early Islam, there was some doubt over the son's identity but the belief that the son was Ishmael prevailed.

144. Camilla Adang, *Muslim Writers on Judaism and the Hebrew Bible: From Ibn Rabban to Ibn Hazm* (Leiden: Brill, 1996), 223.

145. Ibrahim, *Al Qaeda Reader*, 198.

146. Ibrahim, *Al Qaeda Reader*, 199.

147. Bin Laden refers to the UN Security Resolution 661, adopted August 6, 1990 following the Iraqi invasion of Kuwait on August 2 of that year. The sanctions imposed a full-trade embargo, save for medical supplies, food, and other items of humanitarian necessity. After the war ended, the sanctions were continued and remained in effect until the termination of the U.S.-led invasion of Iraq from March 20, 2003 to May 1, 2003. The sanctions were intended to topple Saddam Hussein or at least prevent him from once again attempting to build weapons of mass destruction. They were controversial. Bin Laden's estimate of the number of victims is far higher than the estimates of others who have examined the issue. For a defense of the sanctions, see David Cortright and George A. Lopez, "Containing Iraq: Sanctions Worked," *Foreign Affairs* 83, 4 (July/August 2004): 90–103. For a critical evaluation of sanctions, see David Rieff, "Were Sanctions Right?" *New York Times Magazine*, July 27, 2003, http://query.nytimes.com/gst/fullpage.html?res=9E06E7 DF163FF934A15754C0A9659C8B63&scp=1&sq=W ere%20Sanctions%20Right?&st=nyt. Reiff accepts the UNICEF estimate that the deaths attributable to the sanctions were approximately five hundred thousand, a far lower figure than Bin Laden's.

148. Ibrahim, *Al Qaeda Reader*, 200.

149. David Blankenhorn, "Reading an Enemy: Analyzing Al Qa'ida's Letter to America," February 18, 2003, http://www.americanvalues.org/html/reading_an _enemy.html (accessed July 31, 2008).

150. Ibrahim, *Al Qaeda Reader*, 202.

151. Ibrahim, *Al Qaeda Reader*, 207–208.

152. Kelsay, *Arguing the Just War in Islam*, 2.

153. "La Lettre de Mahmoud Ahmadinejad à George Bush," *Le Monde.fr.* May 9, 2006, http://www.lemonde.fr/iran-la-crise-nucleaire/article/2006/05/09/la-lettre-de-mahmoud-ahmadinejad-a-george-w-bush_769886_727571_100.html. According to the White House, the English translation of Ahmadinejad's letter published in *Le Monde* is exactly the same as the one they received.

154. Robert Spencer, "Ahmadinejad's Letter a Call to Accept Islam?" *Jihad Watch*, May 9, 2006, http://www.jihadwatch.org/archives/011363.php.

155. The Qur'an translation is by Ibrahim, *Al Qaeda Reader*, 72.

156. The Qur'an translation is by Ibrahim, *Al Qaeda Reader*, 72.

157. Ibrahim, *Al Qaeda Reader*, 73. The underlined passage is underlined in the original Arabic text.

CHAPTER TWO

1. On the Adana massacres of 1909, see Vahakn N. Dadrian, *The History of the Armenian Genocide: Ethnic Conflict from the Balkans to Anatolia to the Caucasus*, 3rd rev. ed. (Oxford: Berghahn Books, 1997), 179–184, and Peter Balakian, *The Burning Tigris and America's Response* (New York: Harper Collins, 2003), 144–157. For a contemporary account, see James Creelman, "The Slaughter of Christians in Asia Minor," *New York Times*, August 22, 1909, http://query.nytimes.com/mem/archive-free/pdf?res=9F02E3DE143EE033A25751C2A96E9C946897D6CF.

2. Dadrian, *The History of the Armenian Genocide*, 179–184.

3. Ronald Grigor Suny, "Religion, Ethnicity, and Nationalism: Armenians, Turks, and the End of the Ottoman Empire" in Omar Bartov and Phyllis Mack, eds., *In God's Name: Genocide and Religion in the Twentieth Century* (London: Berghahn Books, 2001), 44.

4. Suny, "Religion, Ethnicity," 50–52; Bat Ye'or, *The Decline of Eastern Christianity under Islam: From Jihad to Dhimmitude* (Rutherford, NJ: Fairleigh Dickinson University Press, 1996), 195.

5. Dadrian, *The History of the Armenian Genocide*, 4.

6. Bat Ye'or, *Islam and Dhimmitude: Where Civilizations Collide* (Madison, NJ: Fairleigh Dickinson University Press, 2002), 37–38.

7. Suny, "Religion, Ethnicity," 30–31.

8. On the *Tanzimat* Reforms, see Dadrian, *The History of the Armenian Genocide*, 25–27, 32–33.

9. Benjamin Braude and Bernard Lewis, *Christians and Jews in the Ottoman Empire: The Functioning of a Plural Society* (New York: Holmes and Meier Publishers, 1982), 30.

10. J. C. Hurewitz, *Diplomacy in the Near and Middle East, A Documentary Record: 1535–1914*, vol. 1 (Princeton, NJ: Princeton University Press, 1956), 1, 154.

11. See "Infidel Status in the Ottoman Empire" in Balakian, *The Burning Tigris*, 40–43.

12. Bat Ye'or, *The Dhimmi: Jews and Christians under Islam* (Rutherford, NJ: Fairleigh Dickinson University Press, 1985), 101.

13. Balakian, *The Burning Tigris*, 41–42.

14. Lord Kinross (John Balfour, 3rd Baron Kinross), *The Ottoman Centuries: The Rise and Fall of the Turkish Empire* (New York: William Morrow, 1977), 556–557.

15. Dadrian, *The History of the Armenian Genocide*, 45–47.

16. For an exploration of the phenomenon of market-dominant minorities, see Amy Chua, *World on Fire: How Exporting Free Market Democracy Breeds Ethnic Hatred and Global Instability* (New York: Doubleday, 2003).

17. Suny, "Religion, Ethnicity," 39.

18. On the origins of the Sasun massacres, see Balakian, *The Burning Tigris*, 54–56, and Dadrian, *The History of the Armenian Genocide*, 114–116.

19. Kinross, *The Ottoman Centuries*, 559.

20. Dadrian, *The History of the Armenian Genocide*, 147.

21. Kinross, *The Ottoman Centuries*, 560.

22. Dadrian, *The History of the Armenian Genocide*, 149.

23. Dadrian, *The History of the Armenian Genocide*, 150.

24. Abraham H. Hartunian, *Neither to Laugh Nor to Weep: A Memoir of the Armenian Genocide* (Boston: Beacon Press, 1968), 12–14.

25. Suny, "Religion, Ethnicity," 46–47.

26. Suny, "Religion, Ethnicity," 47.

27. Braude and Lewis, *Christians and Jews*, 418.

28. David Fromkin, *A Peace to End All Peace: The Fall of the Ottoman Empire and the Creation of the Modern Middle East* (New York: Henry Holt, 1989), 152–153.

29. Balakian, *The Burning Tigris*, 178.

30. Balakian, *The Burning Tigris*, 178.

31. Suny, "Religion, Ethnicity," 52.

32. Balakian, *The Burning Tigris*, 179.

33. Henry Morgenthau, *Ambassador Morgenthau's Story* (New York: Doubleday, Page, 1919), 299. For an American eyewitness's account of the events in Van in 1915, see Grace Higley Knapp, "The American Mission in Van" in Viscount Bryce, *The Treatment of Armenians in the Ottoman Empire 1915–1916: Documents Presented to Secretary of State for Foreign Affairs by Viscount Bryce*, 2nd ed. (Beirut: G. Doniguian & Sons, 1972), 21–47.

34. Dadrian, *The History of the Armenian Genocide*, 221.

35. Mark Mazower, "The G Word," *London Review of Books*, 23, 3 (February 8, 2001), http://www.lrb.co.uk/v23/n03/mazo01_.html.

36. Dadrian, "The Secret Young-Turk Ittihadist Conference and the Decision for the World War I Genocide of the Armenians," *Holocaust and Genocide Studies*, 7, 2 (Fall 1993): 173–201; and Michael J. Arlen, *Passage to Ararat* (New York: Farrar Strauss and Giroux: 1975), 343–344.

37. Taner Akçam, "The Genocide of the Armenians and the Silence of the Turks," http://www.omroep.nl/human/tv/muur/artikel2.htm.

38. Bryce, *The Treatment of Armenians*, 84. This information was also presented by Professor R. Hrair Dekmejian of the University of Southern California at the Seminar in Commemoration of the 65th Anniversary of the Armenian Genocide, St. Vartan's Cathedral, New York, NY, April 25, 1980.

39. The telegram is quoted in Manuel Sarkisianz, *A Modern History of Transcaucasian Armenia* (Privately printed by the author, Nagpur, India: Udyama Commercial Press, 1975 [Distributed by E. J. Brill, Leiden]), 196.

40. According to Mark Mazower, "Deportation—a traditional instrument of imperial rule—had little to do with it: the old-fashioned version [of deportations], which valued subject populations for economic reasons, aimed to relocate rather than destroy them." Mazower, "The G Word."

41. Bryce, *The Treatment of Armenians*, 648.

42. For an early example of the Turkish justification of the slaughter, see the interview granted by Halil Bey, the Turkish foreign minister, to the Associated Press representative at Vienna, October 25, 1915. Halil attempted to throw the blame for the massacres of Armenian men, women, and children upon the Armenians themselves, asserting that they had risen in revolt when the Russians invaded the country. "Turkish Foreign Minister's Defense of the Armenian Massacres," *Current History Magazine* (December 1915), http://www.cilicia.com/armo10c-nyt191612.html.

43. Richard L. Rubenstein, *The Cunning of History* (New York: Harper and Row, 1975), 11–12 and *The Age of Triage: Fear and Hope in an Overcrowded World* (Boston: Beacon Press, 1983), 12–19.

44. Morgenthau, *Ambassador Morgenthau's Story*, 162–163. See also Balakian, *The Burning Tigris*, 169–170.

45. Balakian, *The Burning Tigris*, 183.

46. Richard Kloian, ed., *The Armenian Genocide: News Accounts from the American Press: 1915–1922* (Richmond, CA: Anto Publishing, 1988), XIII.

47. Ara Sarafian, "The Absorption of Armenian Women and Children into Muslim Households as a Structural Component of the Armenian Genocide," in Bartov and Mack, *In God's Name*, 210.

48. Sarafian, "The Absorption."

49. Oscar Heizer, "Report on the treatment of Trebizond" to Ambassador Henry Morgenthau, July 15, 1915, forwarded to the Secretary of State, July 20, 1915, www.armeniangenocide.org/us-7-20-15-text.html.

50. Sarafian, "The Absorption," 212–213.

51. Sarafian, "The Absorption," 217.

52. Suny, "Religion, Ethnicity," 50.

53. Bernard Lewis, *Islam and the West* (New York: Oxford University Press, 1993), 132–143.

54. Yigal Carmon, "Contemporary Islamist Ideology Authorizing Genocidal Murder," MEMRI (Middle East Research Institute), January 27, 2004, Special Report No. 25, http://memri.org/bin/articles.cgi?Page=archives&Area=st&ID=SR2504#_edu2.

CHAPTER THREE

1. See, for example, Joseph B. Schechtman, *The Mufti and the Fuehrer: The Rise and Fall of Hajj Amin el-Husseini* (New York: Thomas Youseloff, 1965); Moshe Pearlman, *Mufti of Jerusalem: Hajj Amin El Husseini* (Philadelphia: Pavillion Press, 2006) (1947); Lukasz Hirszowicz, *The Third Reich and the Arab East* (London: London, Routledge & Kegan Paul, 1966); Zvi Elpeleg, *The Grand Mufti: Hajj Amin al-Hussaini, Founder of the Palestinian National Movement*, trans. David Harvey, ed. Shmuel Himelstein (Portland, OR: Frank Cass, 1993); Jennie Lebel, *The Mufti of Jerusalem Hajj Amin el-Husseini*, trans. Paul Münch (Belgrade: Čigoja Štampa, 2007); Klaus-Michael Mallmann and Martin Cüppers: *Halbmond und Hakenkreuz. Das Dritte Reich, die Araber und Palästina* (Darmstadt: Wissenschaftliche Buchgesellschaft, 2006); Gerhard Höpp, ed., *Mufti-Papiere. Briefe, Memoranden, Reden und Aufrufe Amīn al-Hussainis aus dem Exil, 1940–1945* (Berlin: Klaus Schwarz Verlag, 2001); Yehuda Taggar, *The Mufti of Jerusalem and Palestine: Arab Politics, 1930–1937* (New York: Garland Press, 1986); Klaus Gensicke, *Der Mufti von Jerusalem, Amin el-Husseini, und die Nationalsozialisten* (Frankfurt a/Main: Peter Lang, 1988); Philip Mattar, *The Mufti of Jerusalem: Al-Hajj Amin Al-Husayni and the Palestinian National Movement* (New York: Columbia University Press, 1988); David G. Dalin and John F. Rothmann, *Icon of Evil: Hitler's Mufti and the Rise of Radical Islam* (New York: Random House, 2008); J. C. Hurewitz, *The Struggle for Palestine* (New York: Schocken Books, 1976). For a recent examination of National Socialism, Hajj Amin al-Husseini, and anti-Semitism, see Mattias Künzel, "National Socialism and Anti-Semitism in the Arab World," *Jewish Political Studies Review* 17 (Spring 2005): 1–2.

2. A Mufti is a Muslim religious expert empowered to give legal opinions on sacred law.

3. I. A. Abbady, "Will Massacre All Zionists, Said the Mufti 30 Years Ago," *New York Post*, December 29,1947. See Schechtman, *The Mufti*, 18.

4. On the 1920 al-Nabi Musa events, see Tom Segev, *One Palestine, Complete: Jews and Arabs under the British Mandate* (New York: Henry Holt, 1999), 127–144.

5. Segev, *One Palestine*, 138–139; Elpeleg, *Grand Mufti*, 183, 14(n). Mattar claims that the Mufti's offense was to hold up a picture of King Faysal of Syria, a British ally, and stir up the crowd by proclaiming "This is your King." However, Mattar

does admit the Arab violence. Mattar, *Mufti*, 17–18.; Benny Morris, *Righteous Victims: A History of the Zionist-Arab Conflict, 1881–2001* (New York: Vintage Books, 2001), 95–97.

6. On Jabotinsky's role, see Joseph Schechtman, *Rebel and Statesman: The Vladimir Jabotinsky Story: The Early Years* (New York: Thomas Yoseloff, 1956), 322–337.

7. Joseph Schechtman asserts that "the Mufti's agitators were immediately busy fanning the flames of national antagonism." Schechtman, *The Mufti and the Fuehrer*, 29. Phillip Mattar, an Arab biographer, stresses the spontaneity of the outbreak. Mattar, *Mufti*, 27.

8. On Samuel's decision, see Bernard Wasserstein, "Herbert Samuel and the Palestine Problem," *The English Historical Review*, 91, 361 (October 1976): 765–766. See also Elpeleg, *Grand Mufti*, 9.

9. Howard M. Sachar, *A History of Israel: From the Rise of Israel to Our Time* (New York: Alfred A. Knopf, 1979), 170–171.

10. The campaign raised well over P£100,000 from Muslims from India to Egypt. Contributors included Egypt's King Fu'ad (P£ 10,000), the Nizam of Haydarabad (P£7,000) and King Faysal of Iraq (P£6,000). Yehoshua Porath, *The Emergence of the Palestinian-Arab National Movement, 1918–1929*, vol, 1 (London: Frank Cass, 1974), 205–206; Mattar, *Mufti*, 30. During the Mandate, the Palestine Pound was equal in value to the British Pound.

11. In 1921, Sir Arthur Mond, a Jewish philanthropist, British minister of health and later Lord Melchett, incautiously told the Palestine Foundation Fund that a new "edifice" should be erected "where Solomon's Temple once stood." Photomontages were also distributed by heads of Yeshivot showing the Star of David over the Dome of the Rock. From time to time, there was talk of taking over the Haram al-Sharif. In 1928, shortly after Passover, the Zionist leader Menachem Ussishkin was reported to have concluded an emotionally charged speech by saying: "Let us swear that the Jewish people will not rest and will not remain silent until its national home is built on Mt. Moriah," a clear reference to the Temple Mount. Segev, *One Palestine*, 304.

12. For the Hadith concerning Muhammad's night journey and al-Buraq, see http://hadith.al-islam.com/bayan/Display.asp?Lang=eng&ID=95. This is the official site of the Kingdom of Saudi Arabia's Ministry of Islamic Affairs, Endowments, Da'wah and Guidance.

13. Mattar, *Mufti*, 34.

14. Bernard Wasserstein, *The British in Palestine: The Mandatory Government and the Arab-Jewish Conflict 1917–1929* (Oxford: Basil Blackwell, 1991), 225–228; Morris, *Righteous Victims*, 112–113.

15. Mattar, *Mufti*, 38.

16. Morris, *Righteous Victims*, 113.

17. Morris, *Righteous Victims*, 114; Mattar concedes that the Mufti contributed to the politicization of the religious conflict and the ensuing tension but claims he "neither incited nor planned the August 1929 violence." Mattar, *Mufti*, 49.

18. At least some of Hebron's Orthodox Jews blame "the Zionists" for the trouble. In an interview posted on the ultra-Orthodox Neturei Karta website, Rabbi Baruch Kaplan, a survivor of the Hebron massacre, repeatedly claims that "the Arabs were very friendly people" and that the Zionists were wholly

to blame for the violence, http://www.nkusa.org/Historical_Documents/KaplanInterview.cfm.

19. Segev, *One Palestine, Complete*, 322–325.

20. Wasserstein, *British in Palestine*, 237.

21. One hundred sixteen Arabs were killed and 232 Arabs wounded, primarily by the British police. Wasserstein, *British in Palestine*, 237.

22. Wasserstein, *British in Palestine*, 237-238; Morris, *Righteous Victims*, 116.

23. Ronald J. Rychlak. "Hitler's Mufti: The Dark Legacy of Hajj Amin Al-Husseini," InsideCatholic.com, June 6, 2009, http://insidecatholic.com/Joomla/index.php?option=com_content&task=view&id=6174&Itemid=48 (accessed June 11, 2009).

24. Shaw Commission Report, Cmd. 3530, 163; Morris, *Righteous Victims*, 116.

25. Lord Curzon was one of the most important critics of Zionism and the Balfour Declaration. See David Gilmour, "The Unregarded Prophet: Lord Curzon and the Palestine Question," *Journal of Palestine Studies*, 25, 3 (Spring, 1996): 60–68.

26. A synopsis of the report, John Hope Simpson, "Palestine. Report on Immigration, Land settlement and Development," October 1930, Cmd. 3686, H. M. Stationery Office, is to be found at http://www.mideastweb.org/hopesimpson.htm.

27. The text of the Passfield white paper, "Palestine: Statement of Policy by His Majesty's Government in the United Kingdom," Cmd. 3692, H. M. Stationery Office, October 1930, is to be found at http://www.mideastweb.org/passfieldwp.htm.

28. The text of the letter is to be found at http://www.zionism-israel.com/macdonald_letter_text_1931.htm.

29. According to Timotheus Wurst, the German consul in Jaffa in 1935, Arab pro-German attitudes were primarily due to Hitler's anti-Jewish policies. He also noted that some were also impressed by the militarism and discipline of the Nazi party. Nicosia, 353–354.

30. In his annual report for 1933, Wolff stated that enthusiasm for and support of Nazi Germany was undiminished "in spite of Nazi emigration policies." Nicosia, 353–354.

31. In Twelver Shi'ism to which the Mahmoud Ahmadinejad of Iran subscribes, the "Twelfth Imam" is the messianic figure who will emerge from his thousand-year occultation at a time of immense crisis and persecution for Muslims, make war against the enemies of Islam, and transform the world into a perfect Islamic dominion.

32. The subject of the *Haavara* agreement is explored in detail by Edwin Black, *The Transfer Agreement: The Dramatic Story of the Pact Between the Third Reich and Jewish Palestine* (New York: Carroll and Graf, 2001).

33. See Richard L. Rubenstein and John K. Roth, *Approaches to Auschwitz: The Holocaust and Its Legacy*, 2nd ed. (Louisville: Westminster/John Knox, 2003), 140–141.

34. Basheer Nafi, "Shayk 'Izz al-Dīn al-Qassām: A Reformist and a Rebel Leader," *Journal of Islamic Studies*, 8, 2. (1997): 189, http://jis.oxfordjournals.org.proxy.lib.fsu.edu/cgi/reprint/8/2/185 (January 27, 2008).

35. Nafi, "Shayk 'Izz al-Dīn al-Qassām," 203;Yehoshua Porath, *The Palestinian Arab National Movement, 1929–1939: From Riots to Rebellion* vol. 2 (London: Frank Cass, 1977), 133.

36. This phenomenon is discussed in detail in Richard L. Rubenstein, *The Age of Triage: Fear and Hope in an Overcrowded World* (Boston: Beacon Press, 1983).

37. "In spite of the great effect left by the death of this one man, the fact remains that he was the only member of the whole elite to lay down his life." Bayan Nuweihid al-Hout, "The Palestinian Elite During the Mandate Period," *Journal of Palestine Studies*, 9, 1 (Autumn 1979): 109.

38. Shai Lachman, "Arab Rebellion and Terrorism in Palestine: The Case of Sheikh Izz al-Din al-Qassam and His Movement," in Elie Kedourie and Sylvia G. Haim, eds., *Zionism and Arabism in Palestine and Israel* (London: Frank Cass, 1982), 79–80.

39. Lachman, 66-67.

40. Mattar, *Mufti*, 67.

41. Segev, *One Palestine*, 361.

42. Nafi, "Shayk 'Izz al-Dīn al-Qassām," 212.

43. Nafi, "Shayk 'Izz al-Dīn al-Qassām," 212–213.

44. Kenneth W. Stein, "The Intifada and the 1936–39 Uprising: A Comparison," *Journal of Palestinian Studies*, 19, 4. (Summer 1990): 75.

45. Morris, *Righteous Victims*, 130.

46. Harold Callender, "British Setbacks Fan Arab Revolt," *New York Times*, October 16, 1938.

47. Lukasz Hirszowicz, *The Third Reich and the Arab East* (London: Routledge and Kegan Paul, 1968), 86.

48. John Marlowe, *Rebellion in Palestine* (London: Cresset Press, 1946), 157; Morris, 133; See Segev, *One Palestine*, 359.

49. Mattar, *Mufti*, 77.

50. Morris, *Righteous Victims*, 131; Christopher Sykes, *Cross Roads to Israel* (London: Collins, 1965), 219.

51. Peel Commission Report (Palestine Royal Commission Report: Presented by the Secretary of State for the Colonies to Parliament by command of His Majesty, July 1937, Cmd, 5479, Jerusalem: 1937, 100); Elpeleg, *Grand Mufti*, 46.

52. Ferdinand Kuhn, Jr., "Britain to Take Up Massacres in Iraq; Ruler Plans Flight," *New York Times*, August 17, 1933.

53. Peel Commission Report.

54. Benny Morris, *The Birth of the Palestinian Refugee Problem Revisited* (Cambridge: Cambridge University Press, 2004), 39–64. I am indebted to Morris for his citation of the Palestine Royal Commission Report, Cmd 5479 (London, July 1937), 389–391.

55. On the subject of population in Palestine, see Ari Shavit's interview with historian Benny Morris, "Survival of the Fittest," *HaAretz*, November 1, 2004, http://www.haaretz.com/hasen/pages/ShArt.jhtml?itemNo=380986&contrassID=2.

56. Elpeleg, *The Grand Mufti*, 47.

57. The incident is reported in some details in "British Chief in Galilee Killed by Arabs Near Nazareth Church," *New York Times*, September 27, 1937, http://select.nytimes.com/mem/archive/pdf?res=F70A10F73F59177A93C5AB1782D85F4383 85F9 (accessed June 11, 2009).

58. "British Chief," *New York Times*.

59. Joseph M. Levy, "Britain Deports Palestine's Arab Leaders; Mufti of Jerusalem a Refugee in Mosque," *New York Times*, October 1, 1937.

60. Elpeleg, *Grand Mufti*, 48–49.

61. Morris, *Righteous Victims*, 145; Mattar, *Mufti*, 89.

62. Elpeleg, *Grand Mufti*, 50.

63. The full text of the "British White Paper of 1939" is available on line at the website of the Avalon Project of Yale University Law School, http://www.yale.edu/law web/avalon/mideast/brwh1939.htm.

64. Mattar, *Mufti*, 88–89.

65. *The Arab War Effort: A Documented Account* (New York: The American Christian Palestine Committee, 1946), 35–40. For this citation, I am indebted to Schechtman, *The Mufti and the Fuehrer*, 96–97.

66. A variation on the Hitler theme appeared in some Syrian shops that showed posters in Arabic that read: "In heaven, God is your ruler; on earth Hitler." See Stefan Wild, "National Socialism in the Arab Near East between 1933 and 1939," *Die Welt des Islams*, New Ser., Bd. 25, Nr. 1/4. (1985), 128; Schechtman, *The Mufti and the Fuehrer*, 84; Norman A. Stillman, *Jews of Arab Lands in Modern Times* (Philadelphia: Jewish Publication Society, 2003), 115.

67. Elpeleg, *Grand Mufti*, 57–58.

68. Schechtman, *The Mufti and the Fuehrer*, 84. There appears to be conflicting reports concerning the sums paid to the Mufti. On page 103, Schechtman writes "The new administration provided Hajj Amin with an outright gift of £572,000 and a monthly stipend of £4,000. The Axis supplemented these gifts reportedly totaling £400,000, some 60 per cent coming from Germany." For these figures he cites The Nation Associates, *Arab Higher Committee, Its Origins, Personnel and Purposes: The Documentary Record Submitted in the United Nations* (New York: 1947).

69. Letter (in French) from Hajj Amin al-Husseini to Franz von Papen, German Ambassador to Turkey, June 6, 1940 in Höpp, ed., *Mufti-Papiere: Briefe*, 15–16.

70. See letter (in French) from Hajj Amin al-Husseini to Franz von Papen, July 22, 1940, in Höpp, *Mufti-Papiere*, 16; see also Mattar, *Mufti*, 101.

71. Letter (in French) from Hajj Amin al-Husseini to Adolf Hitler, January 20,1941, Höpp, *Mufti Papiere*, 17–19.; an English translation can be found in Elpeleg, *Grand Mufti*, 17–19.

72. In his address of 30 January 1939, Hitler told the Reichstag: "If the Jewish international financiers in and outside Europe should succeed in plunging the nations once more into a world war, then the result will not be the Bolshevization of the earth, and thus a victory of Jewry, but the annihilation of the Jewish race in Europe." An English translation of the text is to be found in J. Noakes and G. Pridham, eds., *Nazism: 1919–1945: A Documentary Reader*, Vol. 3. *Foreign Policy. War and Racial Extermination* (Exeter: Exeter Studies in History, No. 13, 1988), 1049.

73. Höpp, *Mufti Papiere*, 17–19.

74. For a comprehensive overview of this subject, see Christopher R. Browning, *The Origins of the Final Solution: The Evolution of Nazi Jewish Policy, September 1939–March 1942* (Lincoln and Jerusalem: University of Nebraska Press and Yad Vashem, 2004).

75. On the 1941 British intervention in Iraq, see Douglas Porch, "The Other Gulf War: British Intervention in Iraq, 1941," *Joint Force Quarterly* (Summer 2003), http://findarticles. com/p/articles/mi_m0KNN/is_35/ai_n8563331.

76. On the assassination attempt, see Elpeleg, *Grand Mufti*, 60; Mattar, *The Mufti*, 148.

77. On the Futtuwa (also spelled Futuwwah), see Wild, "National Socialism," 136, 137.

78. Esther Meir-Glitzenstein, Article "Farhud," *Holocaust Encyclopedia*, United States Holocaust Memorial Museum, http://www.ushmm.org/wlc/article.php? lang=en&ModuleId=10007277.

79. Stillman, *Jews of Arab Lands*, 117–118.

80. Meir-Glitzenstein, "Farhud." The figures are approximate. According to Mallmann and Cüppers, the figures are 110 Jews murdered, 240 wounded, 86 shops and workshops, destroyed as well as 911 houses and apartments. See Mallmann and Cüppers, "'Beseitigung der jüdisch-nationalen Heimstätte in Palästina': Das Einsatzkommando bei der Panzerarmee Afrika 1942," in Jürgen Matthäus and Klaus Michael Mallmann, eds., *Volkermord: Der Holocaust als Geschichten and Gegenwart* (Darmstadt: Wissenschaftlische Buchgesellschaft, 2006), 153–173.

81. Elie Kedouri, "The Sack of Basra and the Farhud in Baghdad," Kedourie, *Arabic Political Memoirs and Other Studies* (London: Frank Cass, 1974), 283–314; Joseph Schechtman, *On Wings of Eagles: The Plight, Exodus, and Homecoming of Oriental Jewry* (New York: Thomas Yoseloff, 1961); Hayyim Cohen, "The Anti-Jewish Farhud in Baghdad, 1941," *Middle Eastern Studies* (1966), 3:2–17; "The Farhood," *Holocaust Encyclopedia*, U.S. Holocaust Memorial Museum, http://www .ushmm.org/wlc/article. php?lang=en&ModuleId=10007277v; Edwin Black, "Dispossessed: How Iraq's 2,600 year-old-Jewish Community Was Decimated in One Generation," *Reform Judaism*, 33, 2 (Winter 2004), http://www.reformjuda-ismmag.net/04winter/black.shtml.

82. Britain and France declared war on Germany September 1, 1939. Prime Minister Nuri al-Sa'id declared Iraq a nonbelligerent but broke off diplomatic relations with Germany. It continued diplomatic relations with Italy which did not enter the war until June 10, 1940.

83. Stillman, "The Iraqi Government Committee for the Investigation of the Events of June 1 and 2, 1941," *Jews of Arab Lands*, 117–118, 414.

84. See Nikki R. Keddie, *Modern Iran: Roots and Results of Revolution* (New Haven: Yale University Press, 2006), 101–102; Arthur C. Millspaugh, *Americans in Persia* (Washington: The Brookings Institution, 1946), 8. I am indebted to Schechtman, *On Wings of Eagles*, 117, for this citation.

85. F. Eshraghi, "Anglo-Soviet occupation of Iran in August 1941," *Middle Eastern Studies*, 20:1, 28.

86. Elpeleg, *Grand Mufti*, 64–65.

87. Elpeleg, *Grand Mufti*, 65.

88. Wolfgang G. Schwanitz, "Amin al-Husaini and the Holocaust. What Did the Grand Mufti Know?" *World Politics Review*, May 13, 2008, http://www.gloriacenter.org/index.asp?pname=submenus/articles/2008/schwanitz/5_13.asp (accessed July 21, 2008); The memoir cited by Schwanitz is Abd al-Karim al-Umar (ed.), *Mudhakkirat al-Hajj Muhammad Amin al-Husayni* (Hajj Amin al-Husseini Memoirs) (Damascus: al-Ahali, 1999), 126.

89. Mattar, *Mufti*, 148.

90. Elpeleg, *Grand Mufti*, 65.

91. Christopher Browning, *Nazi Policy, Jewish Workers, German Killers* (Cambridge: Cambridge University Press, 2000), 51–52.

92. Christian Gerlach, "The Wannsee Conference, the Fate of German Jews, and Hitler's Decision to Exterminate All European Jews,"*Journal of Modern History* 70 (December 1998), 784–785, http://www.jstor.org/stable/2990683 (accessed June 11, 2009).

93. An English translation of Goering's directive is to be found in Noakes and Pridham, *Nazism*, vol. 2, 1104. A photocopy of Goering's original letter can be found at http://www.ghwk.de/engl/authorization.htm (accessed June 11, 2009).

94. Anthony R. De Luca, "'Der Grossmufti in Berlin: The Politics of Collaboration," *International Journal of Middle East Studies*, 10, 1 (February 1979): 129–130, http://links.jstor.org/sici?sici=0020-7438%28197902%2910%3A1%3C125%3A%2 7GIBTP%3E2.0.CO%3B2-W (accessed January 27, 2008).

95. On July 9, 1942, in a discussion with Japanese Ambassador Oshima, German Foreign Minister von Ribbentrop discussed the plan: ". . . if we can succeed in eliminating Russia as the principal ally of England and the U.S., and can advance through the Caucasus to the south, while Rommel on the other side is pressing forward through Egypt into the Near East, then the war will have been won. In any case, in the last four weeks we have come closer to this goal than the German leadership, even in its greatest optimism, could ever have hoped to achieve." Klaus-Michael Mallmann and Martin Cüppers, "Beseitigung der jüdisch-nationalen Heimstätte in Palästina," 160; Mallmann and Cüppers, "'Elimination of the Jewish National Home in Palestine': The Einsatzkommando of the Panzer Army Africa, 1942," *Yad Vashem Studies*, XXXXV (2007), 14. http://www1.yadvashem.org/about_holocaust/studies/vol35/Mallmann-Cuppers2.pdf (accessed June 11, 2009).

96. Walter Laqueur, ed., *The Israel-Arab Reader*, 111.

97. Mallmann and Cüppers, "Beseitigung," 6–7.

98. Mallmann and Cüppers, "Beseitigung," 156–157; "Elimination of the Jewish National Home in Palestine," 6–7.

99. Article "Gas Chambers," in Walter Laqueur and Judith Tydor Baumel, eds., *The Holocaust Encyclopedia* (New Haven: Yale University Press, 2001), 230.

100. Klaus-Michael Mallmann and Martin Cüppers, *Halbmond und Hakenkreuz. Das Dritte Reich, die Araber und Palästina* (Darmstadt: Wissenschaftliche Buchgesellschaft, 2006), Volume 8 of the Publications of the Ludwigsburg Research Institute of the University of Stuttgart.

101. Article "Einsatzgruppen," *Concise Encyclopedia of the Holocaust*, The International School of Holocaust Studies, Yad Vashem, http://www1.yadvashem.org/education/entries/english/16.asp (accessed June 11, 2009).

102. See the ZDF website, "*ZDF Zeitgeschichte-Mythos und Wahrheit*." Complete videos of both segments of the presentation, "*Rommels Krieg*" and "*Rommels Schatz*" are available at the site. See also Tony Patterson, "'Chivalrous' Rommel Wanted to Bring Holocaust to Middle East," *The Independent*, 25 May 2007; Jan Friedmann, "New Research Taints Image of Desert Fox Rommel," *Der Spiegel Online*, May 23, 2007, http://www.spiegel.de/international/germany/0,1518,484510,00.html (accessed January 27, 2008) .

103. Friedmann, "New Research."

104. Stillman, *Jews of Arab Lands,* 130–133; for the text of report of the meeting of the Chief Rabbi and the president of the Tunis Jewish Communal Council with Rauff concerning the requisition of Jewish laborers and other documents concerning Jewish disabilities in Nazi occupied Tunis, see Stillman, 435–436.

105. Habib Cana'an, Interview with Fritz Grobba, HaAretz, March 1, 1970; Elpeleg, *Grand Mufti,* 68.

106. Radio broadcast by Hajj Amin al-Husseini, May 10, 1941, *Oriente Moderno* (Rome: Istituto per L'Oriente, 1941), 552–553. I am indebted for this citation to Perlman, *Mufti of Jerusalem,* 53–54.

107. For an eyewitness report of the atrocities, see "J. A. MacGahan on Turkish Atrocities in Bulgaria," *London Daily News,* August 22, 1876, http://www.attackingthedevil. co.uk/related/macgahan.php. For a defense of Turkish behavior by Hobart Pasha, an Englishman serving as an admiral in the Turkish Navy, see "The Bulgarian Atrocities: An Extraordinary Letter from a Turkish Admiral," *New York Times,* September 10, 1876, http://query.nytimes.com/mem/archive-free/pdf?res=9D0CEED81F3FE73BBC4852DFBF66838D669FDE (accessed August 16, 2008). See R. W. Seton-Watson, *Disraeli, Gladstone and the Eastern Question: A Study in Diplomacy and Party Politics* (London: MacMillan, 1935).

108. William Ewart Gladstone, *Bulgarian Horrors and the Question of the East* (London: John Murray, 1876), 9; pamphlet digitized by Google from the Harvard University Library, December 19, 2005, http://books.google.com/books?hl=en&id=Ev9wkUr1UloC&dq=%22Bulgarian+Horrors+and+the+Question+of+the+East%22&printsec=frontcover&source=web&ots=GbFI8Mm_Zq&sig=bNhJAHUogHu1_qc3My870eMkCxQ&sa=X&oi=book_result&resnum=1&ct=result#PPA1,M1 (accessed August 16, 2008).

109. For the German text of Amin's speech, see "Rede zum Jahrestag der Balfour-Erklärung, 2.11.1943" Höpp, ed., *Mufti-Papiere,* 193.

110. Perlman, *Mufti of Jerusalem,* 61.

111. Heinrich Himmler telegram to Hajj Amin al-Husseini, November 2, 1943. A photocopy of this telegram is found at http://www.eretzyisroel.org/~jkatz/nazis.html. A cautionary note concerning the translation of this telegram in Perlman, *Mufti of Jerusalem,* 61. Perlman translates Himmler's key sentence as "The National Socialist Party has inscribed on its flag: the extermination of world Jewry." There is no doubt that extermination was National Socialism's most important objective. Accurately translated, the sentence should read "The National Socialist Party has inscribed on its flag the struggle against world Jewry" (*den Kampf gegen das Weltjudentum*). There is absolutely no documentary justification for Perlman's translation of Kampf as "extermination."

112. The text of the Hussein-McMahan correspondence is to be found in "Hussien (sic) ibn Ali and Sir Henry McMahan Letter Exchange," http://web. ics.purdue.edu/~fop/pages/exchange.html. See also Laqueur, *The Israel-Arab Reader,* 33–35.

113. For a discussion of the issues involved in McMahan's "promises" to the Arabs and the Balfour Declaration, see David Fromkin, *A Peace to End All Peace: The Fall of the Ottoman Empire and the Creation of the Modern Middle East* (New York: Henry Holt, 1989), 173–187.

114. Caroline Shaw, "Egyptian finances in the nineteenth century: A Rothschild perspective," *The Rothschild Archive,* http://www.rothschildarchive.org/ib/articles/AR2006Egypt.pdf.

115. On the Dönmeh, see Gershom Scholem, Article, "Doenmeh," *Encyclopaedia Judaica* (Jerusalem: Keter, 1972); see also Jane Hathaway, "The grand vizier and the false Messiah: the Sabbatai Sevi controversy and the Ottoman reform in Egypt," *The Journal of the American Oriental Society* (October–December 1997), http://find.galegroup.com.proxy.lib.fsu.edu/itx/infomark.do?&contentSet=IAC-Documents&type=retrieve&tabID=T002&prodId=EAIM&docId=A20608605&source=gale&srcprod=EAIM&userGroupName=tall85761&version=1.0 (accessed May 27, 2007). The Dönmeh were crypto Jews, outwardly Muslim but inwardly committed to belief in Sabbatai Zvi (1626–1676) as Israel's Messiah. Before the post–World War I exchange of Greek and Turkish populations, Salonika was the most important Dönmeh center. The Dönmeh largely supported Turkish secularization. Ataturk came from Salonika but was not a Dönmeh. Nevertheless, the complex nature of Dönmeh loyalties inevitably led to wild conspiracy theories. On Islamist use of the Dönmeh accusation against Ataturk and other secularists, see Gilles Kepel, *Muslim Extremism in Egypt: The Prophet and Pharaoh,* trans. Jon Rothschild (Berkeley: University of California Press, 2003), 121–123.

116. Hamas Covenant, August 18, 1988, The Avalon Project at Yale Law School, http://www.yale.edu/lawweb/avalon/mideast/hamas.htm.

117. On the struggle for the Temple Mount, see Gershom Gorenberg, *The End of Days: Fundamentalism and the Struggle for the Temple Mount* (New York: Oxford University Press, 2000).

118. Gorenberg, *The End of Days,* 115.

119. In addition to Gorenberg, see Ian Lustick, *For the Land and the Lord: Jewish Fundamentalism in Israel* (New York: Council on Foreign Relations, 1988); Ehud Sprinzak, *Gush Emunim: The Politics of Zionist Fundamentalism in Israel* (New York: American Jewish Committee, 1986), http://www.geocities.com/alabasters_archive/zionist_ fundamentalism.html#21nl. Richard L. Rubenstein, *After Auschwitz: History, Theology, and Contemporary Judaism* (Baltimore: Johns Hopkins University Press, 1992), 210–233.

120. David Shipler, "Extremist Jews Blamed in Raid on Arab Shrine," *New York Times,* January 30, 1984.

121. Etzion's remarks are quoted in Lustick, *For the Land,* 97–98.

122. The Hijaz is that part of Arabia bounded by the Gulf of Aqaba and the Red Sea that contains the holy cities of Mecca and Medina.

123. Bernard Lewis, "License to Kill: Usama bin Ladin's Declaration of Jihad," *Foreign Affairs,* November/December 1998, 16.

124. For the most complete collection of the Mufti's wartime speeches and writings in European languages, see Höpp, ed., *Mufti-Papiere. Briefe.*

125. Excerpts from the speech are found in Perlman, *Mufti of Jerusalem,* 60, and in Schechtman, *The Mufti and the Fuehrer,* 149. The German translation of the Mufti's speech, which was originally delivered in Arabic, as found in Höpp's *Mufti-Papiere,* does not contain this material which appears in both Schechtman and Perlman. I find no reason to question the version by Schechtman and Perlman. This is not the only text in which Höpp has omitted important details.

126. Mallmann and Cüppers, "Beseitigung der jüdisch-nationalen Heimstätte in Palästina," 162; "Elimination of the Jewish National Home in Palestine," 19.

127. Allan Hall, "Hitler's holocaust plans for Jews in Palestine stopped by Desert Rats," *The Independent* (UK), April 14, 2006. http://news.independent.co.uk/europe/ article357644.ece.

128. Wisliceny's Nuremberg deposition concerning Eichmann was introduced as evidence at the trial of Adolf Eichmann on March 16, 1963. The minutes of that session, which include most of Wisliceny's deposition can be found at http://www.nizkor.org/ftp.cgi/people/e/eichmann.adolf/transcripts/ftp.py?people/e/eichmann.adolf/transcripts/Sessions/Session-016-03.

129. Hurewitz, *The Struggle for Palestine,* 87, 338, 15(n).

130. Hurewitz, *The Struggle for Palestine,* 87, 338, 15(n).

131. For a brief discussion of the Kasztner controversy see Leora Bilsky, "Judging Evil in the Trial of Kastner," *Law and History Review,* 19, 1 (Spring 2001), http://www.historycooperative.org/journals/lhr/19.1/bilsky.html; see also Tom Segev, *The Seventh Million: The Israelis and the Holocaust,* trans. Haim Watzman (New York: Hill and Wang, 1993), 255–320.

132. Perlman, *Mufti of Jerusalem,* 92–93.

133. Affidavit of Endre Steiner, May 5, 1946, deposed in the minutes of the Nuremberg Trial; Perlman, *Mufti of Jerusalem,* 90–91. Steiner also testified concerning his dealings with Wisliceny at the Eichmann trial, the text of which is to be found at The Nizkor Project, The Trial of Adolf Eichmann, Session 50, http://www.nizkor.org/hweb/people/e/eichmann-adolf/transcripts/Sessions/Session-050-07.html.

134. Perlman, *Mufti of Jerusalem,* 92.

135. Simon Wiesenthal, *Grossmufti-Grossagent der Achse: Tatsachenbericht* (Salzburg: Reid-Verlag, 1947).

136. "Arab Denies Aiding Nazi: Ex-Mufti of Jerusalem Says He Never Met Eichmann," *New York Times,* March 5, 1961, http://select.nytimes.com/search/restricted/article?res=FB0717FC34580C778DDDAC0894DC404482.

137. Mallmann and Cüppers, "Elimination of the Jewish National Home in Palestine," 27, 84(n).

138. Elpeleg, *Grand Mufti,* 71–72.

139. Höpp, ed., *Mufti-Papiere,* 163–164.

140. Höpp, ed., *Mufti-Papiere,* 164–165; Schechtman, *The Mufti and the Fuehrer,* 157.

141. Höpp, ed., *Mufti-Papiere,* 166–169. The letter to von Ribbentrop is in French; the Ciano letter is in English.

142. Höpp, ed., *Mufti-Papiere,* 179–181.

143. Höpp, ed., *Mufti-Papiere,* 215.

144. The text of the letter is to be found in Schechtman, *The Mufti and the Führer,* 157–158.

145. Höpp, ed., *Mufti-Papiere,* 216.

146. On the complex Bosnian Muslim response to the creation of the "Independent State of Croatia," see Yeshayahu A. Jelinek, "Bosnia-Herzegovina at War: Relations Between Moslems and Non-Moslems," *Holocaust and Genocide Studies,* 5, 3 (1990). Jelinek estimates that "at least half the Moslems" sided with the new state but that "precise data" is absent. (279).

147. I am indebted to Carl K. Savich for his e-mail correspondence on the Mufti in Bosnia and for his essay, "The Holocaust in Bosnia: Hercegovina: 1941–1945," *Serbianna*, 75(N), http://www.serbianna.com/columns/savich/006.shtml.

148. Carl K. Savich, "Islam Under the Swastika," http://www.serbianna.com/columns/savich/022.shtml.

149. "Waffen SS in Einsatz: Unfulfilled Hope," http://stosstruppen39-45.tripod.com/id8.html.

150. Francis R. Nicosia, Article, "Hajj Amin al-Husayni: The Mufti of Jerusalem," *Holocaust Enyclopedia*, United States Holocaust Memorial Museum, http://www.ushmm.org/wlc/article.php?lang=en&ModuleId=10007255. Referring to Handzar personnel participation Nicosia uses the phrase, "It is possible" that Handzar personnel participated in the "capture and murder" of Jews. I use the phrase "It is very likely."

151. Jelinek, "Bosnia-Herzegovina," 282–283.

152. Jelinek, "Bosnia-Herzegovina," 281.

153. Jelinek, "Bosnia-Herzegovina," 286; Carl Savich, "The Black Legion: A History of the First Ustacha Regiment," http://www.serbianna.com/columns/savich/049.shtml..

154. Save for Jews and Gypsies, the Wehrmacht leadership in Yugoslavia saw its policies of depopulation and enslavement as technological responses to the military problem of subduing a hostile population. They objected to the Ustaše effort to create an ethnically homogenous nation through genocide and the forced conversion of Orthodox Serbs to Roman Catholicism. They regarded such measures as "passionate and imprecise" resulting in the "breakdown of order and authority" in the targeted areas. See Jonathan Gumz, "'Pacified Areas' vs. 'Unheard of Bestialities:' Wehrmacht Perceptions of Mass Violence in the Independent State of Croatia," http://www.hks.harvard.edu/kokkalis/GSW1/GSW1/16%20Gumz.pdf (June 6, 2009).

155. Robert Fox, "Albanians and Afghans fight for the heirs to Bosnia's SS past," *Daily Telegraph* (UK), December 29, 1993, http://www.pogledi.co.yu/izetbegovic/articles/2-1993.php.

156. Elpeleg, *Grand Mufti*, 74–75.

157. The Mufti's "kid glove" treatment is hardly surprising. The CIA was known to have secretly enlisted known Nazi war criminals. The recruitment of Major General Reinhard Gehlen, head of Foreign Armies East section of *Abwehr*, the German high command's (O.K.W.) intelligence agency, was a glaring example. For decades the CIA covered up the fact that an impressive number of the Gehlen organization's personnel had been involved in the worst crimes of the Nazi regime. See Douglas Jehl, "C.I.A. Said to Rebuff Congress on Nazi Files," *New York Times*, January 30, 2005, http://select.nytimes.com/search/restricted/article?res=F60815FE3E5F0C738FDDA80894DD404482. It is now known that at least five associates of Adolf Eichmann, each of whom had a significant role in the Nazi campaign to exterminate the Jews, had worked for the CIA. Moreover, the CIA knew the whereabouts of Adolf Eichmann in Argentina and his pseudonym three years before his capture by Israeli agents, but kept it secret out of fear that, if captured, Eichmann might reveal the names of Nazi war criminals employed by the CIA. Only in recent years have some parts of the story finally been revealed in spite of strong CIA resistance. See Richard Breitman, et al., eds., *U.S. Intelligence*

and the Nazis (Washington: National Archives Trust Fund Board, 2004), 337–418; Tamara Feinstein, ed., *The CIA and Nazi War Criminals: Security Archive Posts Secret CIA History Released Under Nazi War Crimes Disclosure Act*, National Security Archive Electronic Briefing Book No. 146, 4 February 2005; Christopher Simpson, *Blowback: America's recruitment of Nazis and its effects on the Cold War* (London: Weidenfeld & Nicolson, 1988); Tim Wiener, *Legacy of Ashes: The History of the CIA* (New York: Doubleday, 2007), 39 (ff).

158. Article "Displaced Persons," *Holocaust Encyclopedia*, United States Holocaust Memorial Museum, http://www.ushmm.org/wlc/article.php?lang =en&ModuleId= 10005462.

159. Letter of Sir Alexander Cadogan to Dr. Victor Chi Tsai Hoo, Secretary General, April 2, 1947, Israel Ministry of Foreign Affairs, Historical Documents.

160. Morris, *Righteous Victims*, 223.

161. See Zvi Elpeleg, "Why Was an Independent Palestine Never Created in 1948," *The Jerusalem Report*, 50 (Spring 1989), http://www.mfa.gov.il/mfa/ peace%20process/guide%20to%20the%20peace%20process/why%20was%20- independent%20palestine-%20never%20created%20in%201.

162. Dan Kurzman, *Genesis 1948: The First Arab-Israeli War* (New York: World Publishing Company, 1970), 21–22. According to Kurzman, the story of the Mufti's attempt to negotiate with the Jews was published in *Al Youm*, July 27, 1950, an Arabic daily published in Jaffa. Kurzman reports that the Israelis do not deny the story.

163. According to British officials considered reliable, their number included Nuri Sa'id, a senior Iraqi politician and sometime prime minister, Arshad al-Umari, Iraqi foreign minister, Tawfiq Abdul Huda, Jordanian prime minister, Mustafa Nahas Pasha, Egyptian prime minister, and King Abdullah of Jordan. Morris in *The Birth of the Palestinian Refugee Problem Revisited*, 57–61.

164. Morris, *The Birth of the Palestinian*, 22.

165. Morris, *The Birth of the Palestinian*, 60.

166. Mattar, *Mufti*, 149.

167. Mattar, *Mufti*, 151.

168. Hurewitz, *The Struggle for Palestine*, 309–312.

169. Clifton Daniel, "All Arabs Oppose More Jews' Entry," *New York Times*, March 18, 1947, http://select.nytimes.com/mem/archive/pdf?res=F00614FF3C5 8147B93CBA81788D85F438485F9 (June 11, 2009).

170. Albion Ross, "Abdullah, Jordan King, Slain By an Arab in Old Jerusalem," *New York Times*, July 21, 1951, http://select.nytimes.com/mem/archive/pdf?res =F00B1EFD3D551A7B93C3AB178CD85F458585F9 (accessed June 6, 2009); Mattar, *Mufti*, 136.

171. Hannah Arendt, *Eichmann in Jerusalem* (New York: Viking Press, 1964), 13.

172. See, for example, Mattar, *Mufti*, 141–153. It should be noted, however, that Mattar is by no means an uncritical apologist for the Mufti.

173. Höpp, *Mufti-Papiere*. 219–221

174. Karl Barth, *The Church and the Political Problem of Our Day* (London, Hodder and Stoughton, 1939), 43; 64–65:

175. Carl Gustav Jung, *The Collected Works: Volume 18, The Symbolic Life* (Princeton: Princeton University Press, 1939), 281. I am indebted for this citation to

Andrew Bostom, *The Legacy of Islamic Anti-Semitism: From Sacred Text to Solemn History* (Amherst, NY: Prometheus Books, 2008), 150.

176. See Bernard Lewis, *Semites and Anti-Semites* (New York: W. W. Norton, 1999), 140–236; Matthias Küntzel, "Hitler's Legacy: Islamic antisemitism and the impact of the Muslim Brotherhood," Lecture Delivered at Leeds University, October 10, 2007, Texte von Matthias Küntzel, http://www.matthiaskuentzel .de/contents/hitlers-legacy-islamic-antisemitism-and-the-impact-of-the-muslim-brotherhood.

177. See *Disclosure: Newsletter of the Nazi War Crimes and Japanese Imperial Government Record Interagency Working Group,* November 2002, 2.

178. Jon Henley, "French Court Strikes Blow at Nazi Fugitive," *The Guardian,* March 3, 2001, http://www.guardian.co.uk/nazis/article/0,2763,445717,00.html.

179. Stuart Wavell, "The Tuesday People: The Cool Killer-Alois Brunner," *The Guardian* (UK), November 10, 1987.

180. On Wernher von Braun's complicity in abusive slave labor involving 12,000 people at the Peenemunde Missile Development center in wartime Germany, see Tony Paterson, "Germans at last learn truth about von Braun's 'space research' base," *Daily Telrgraph* (UK), June 14, 2001, http://www.telegraph. co.uk/news/main.jhtml?xml=/ news/2001/06/10/wnaz10.xml.

181. On von Leers, see Gregory Paul Wegner, "'A Propagandist of Extermination:' Johann von Leers and the Anti-Semitic Formation of Children in Nazi Germany," *Paedegogica Historica,* vol. 43, no. 3, 299–325, http://dx.doi .org/10.1080/003092307 01363625. In this writer's opinion, Wegner's is the best and most authoritative scholarly article on the subject currently available in English. See also Wegner, *Anti-Semitism and Schooling Under the Third Reich* (London: Routledge Falmer, 2002), 22–33, 145–147, 182–184; Claudio Mutti, "Il Gotteskampf di Johann von Leers," Prima Parte, http://www.centro studilaruna.it/johannvonleers.html, Seconda Parte, http://www.centrostudilaruna.it/joh annvonleers2. html. I am indebted to Dr. Andrew Bostom for calling my attention to Von Leers and for his help in securing documentation.

182. Wegner, "A Propagandist of Extermination," 300.

183. Emil L. Fackenheim, *To Mend the World: Foundations of Post-Holocaust Jewish Thought* (Bloomington: Indiana University Press, 1994), footnote to 184. For this reference, I am indebted to Joel Fishman, "The Big Lie and the Media War Against Israel: From Inversion of the Truth to Inversion of Reality," *Jewish Political Studies Review,* 19 (Spring 2007): 1–2, http://www.jcpa.org/JCPA/Templates/ShowPage .asp?DBID =1&TMID=111&LNGID=1&FID=388&PID=0&IID=1704.

184. Wegner, "A Propagandist of Extermination," 306.

185. Lewis, *Semites and Anti-Semites,* 207.

186. Johann von Leers, *Blut und Rasse in der Gesetzgebung. Ein Gang durch die Völkergeschichte* (Munich: J.F. Lehmanns Verlag, 1936), 49.

187. Von Leers, "Judentum und Islam als *Gegensätze," Die Judenfrage,* 6, 24 (December 15, 1942), cited by Fishman, "The Big Lie," and Jeffrey Herf, *The Jewish Enemy: Nazi Propaganda during World War II and the Holocaust* (Cambridge: Harvard University Press, 2006), 181.

188. Claudio Mutti, "Johann von Leers' Gotteskampf, Part Three: From the Andes to the Pyramids."

189. Albert Speer, *Inside the Third Reich: Memoirs,* trans. Richard and Clara Winston (New York: Macmillan, 1970), 96. Historian John Rosenthal questions the reliability of Speer's account. He comments: "Speer in particular was a notorious fabulist and his often farfetched inventions have been the subject of several books." John Rosenthal, "The Mufti and the Holocaust," *Policy Review,* April and May 2008, http://www.hoover.org/publications/policyreview/17089176. html#note6 (accessed July 25, 2008).

CHAPTER FOUR

1. See Chapter 6, pages 177–180 in this book.
2. David A. Harris, "Europe on Israel, 2000–2001: A Sampling of Words and Images," http://www.ajc.org/InTheMedia/PublicationsPrint.asp?did=474 (January 4, 2002).
3. Robert Wistrich, "Cruel Britannia: Anti-Semitism in Britain has gone mainstream,"*Azure On Line,* 1 (Summer 2005), http://www.azure.org.il/include /print.php?id=173.
4. The most reliable source on the EAD is Bat Ye'or, *Eurabia: The Euro-Arab Axis* (Madison, NJ: Farleigh Dickinson University Press, 2005); see especially 147–189. For a somewhat different Arab assessment of the EAD, see Saleh al-Mani and Salah al-Shaikhly, *The Euro-Arab Dialogue: A Study in Associative Diplomacy* (New York: St. Martin's Press, 1983). Many of the documents relating to the EAD are publicly available on the EU website where the EAD is referred to as the "Euro-Mediterranean Partnership" at http://europa.eu.int/comm/external_relations/ euromed/conf/index.htm.
5. On the difference between the American and European responses to the embargo and the initial American perception of the EAD as an attempt under French leadership to undermine American influence in Europe and the Middle East, see Henry Kissinger, *Years of Upheaval* (Boston: Little, Brown and Company, 1983), 874(ff), 928–930.
6. Bat Ye'or, *Eurabia,* 93.
7. A religious census is prohibited by law in France. Hence, the available figures are informed estimates. On the 1952 figures, see Soheib Bencheikh, *Marrianne et le prophète: l'islam dans la France laïque* (Marianne and the Prophet: Islam in lay France) (Paris: Bernard Grasset, 1998), 86–87. For this citation, I am indebted to Shireen T. Hunter, ed., *Islam, Europe's Second Religion: The New Social, Cultural, and Political Landscape* (Westport, CT: Praeger, 2002), 6. In 1978 one source placed the figure at 2 million. See Dominique Norbrook, *Passport to France* (New York: Franklin Watts, 1986). According to the U.S. Department of State's *Annual Report on International Religious Freedom 2005,* France's Muslim population is estimated to be between 5 and 6 million or between 8 and 10 percent of the population. In July 2008, the CIA estimated the population of metropolitan France to be 60,876,136 with the Muslim population estimated at between 3 and 6 million (5 percent to 10 percent). See CIA, *The World Factbook,* https://www.cia.gov/library/publications/the-world-factbook/geos/fr.html. The semiofficial Muslim website, Muslim Population Worldwide estimates that as of 2006 there were approximately 6

million Muslims in France or 10 percent of the population. http://www.islamic population.com/europe_general.html.

8. Henry Tanner, "French Chief Rabbi Sees Anti-Semitism in De Gaulle's Views," *New York Times,* November 30, 1967, http://select.nytimes.com/mem/archive/pdf?res=F10B16FE345813778DDDA90B94D9415B878AF1D3.

9. John Eric Lewis, "De Gaulle and the New Anti-Semitism," *Israel Insider,* November 28, 2003, http://web.israelinsider.com/bin/en.jsp?enPage=ViewsPag e&enDisplay=view&enDispWhat=object&enDispWho=Article%5El3017&enZon e=Views&enVersion=0&.

10. The story of Israel's development of nuclear weapons is told in Avner Cohen, *Israel and the Bomb* (New York: Columbia University Press, 1998).

11. Bat Ye'or, *Eurabia: The Euro-Arab Axis,* 39–41.

12. See Edward A. Kolodziej, *French International Policy Under De Gaulle and Pompidou* (Ithaca: Cornell University Press, 1973), 447–552.

13. "Statement by President [Gamal Abdul] Nasser to Arab Trade Unionists," May 26, 1967, *Jewish Virtual Library,* http://www.jewishvirtuallibrary.org/jsou rce/History/nasser1.html.

14. For an important exploration of the rapid transformation of French media attitudes from a pro-Israel to an anti-Israeli position, see Joan B. Wolf, "Anne Frank is Dead, Long Live Anne Frank: The Six-Day War and the Holocaust in French Public Discourse," *History and Memory,* 11 (1999): 104–141.

15. On October 26, 1973 Kissinger sent the following message to the West German government: "The U.S. G[overnment] believes that for the West to display weakness and disunity in the face of a Soviet-supported military action against Israel could have disastrous consequences." A similar note was sent to the British and other "allies." Kissinger, *Years of Upheaval,* 714.

16. Bat Ye'or, *Eurabia,* 78–79.

17. Al-Mani and Al-Shakli, *The Euro-Arab Dialogue,* 111; *Keesing's Contemporary Archives,* 19 (November 26–December 2, 1973), 9–10.

18. On the difference between the American and European responses to the embargo and the initial American perception of the EAD as an attempt by French leadership to undermine American influence in Europe and the Middle East, see Kissinger, *Years of Upheaval,* 874(ff), 928–930.

19. "Dutch See Israel in 'Illegal' Stand," *New York Times,* December 4, 1973, 17, http://select.nytimes.com/mem/archive/pdf?res=F60A16FA395D127A93C7A9 1789D95F478785F9.

20. Kissinger, *Years of Upheaval,* 897.

21. Kissinger, *Years of Upheaval,* 897.

22. Bat Ye'or, *Eurabia,* 55.

23. Bat Ye'or, *Eurabia,* 63.

24. The Europeans were initially reluctant to recognize the PLO officially although PLO representatives were included among the Arab representatives at EAD meetings. Nevertheless, the Arabs understood that the Europeans had little choice but to follow their lead. For example, in the midst of the turmoil of the Iranian Revolution of 1979, a conference was held at Rimini on the subject of petroleum and Europe Arab relations with the cooperation of the UN, the European Communities, OPEC (Organization of Petroleum Exporting Countries), and the

League of Arab States. In his conference address, Mana Ben Saceed Al-Otaiba, chairman of OPEC and minister of petroleum and mineral resources of the United Arab Emirates, told the European participants: "If there is no political harmony between us, how can we talk about commercial and economical harmony? Economics and politics are two sides of the same question. . . . All we ask is that Europe and the industrialized countries recognize Palestine as a nation and the Palestine Liberation Organization as its sole representative. . . . You all know that this [petroleum] is a highly volatile and inflammable product and that it is located in an area dominated by military and political disturbances. We must all work together to calm this situation—this smoldering in the oil fields must be damped down otherwise it will burst into flames and then there would be no more oil to supply the industrialized countries with. We must all face this reality if we want to find a peaceful solution to the Palestine problem and to the problem of the Middle East." *Europe Arab World: From Clashing on Petroleum to Cooperating for a New Economic Order* (Forli, Italy: Pio Manzu International Centre, December 1979), 77–79. For this citation I am indebted to Bat Ye'or, *Eurabia*, 81–82.

25. Kissinger, *Years of Upheaval*, 898.

26. "Final Declaration of the Eleventh Arab Summit Conference, held at Amman from 25 to 27 November 1980, UNITED NATIONS General Assembly Security Council, A/35/719, S/14289," December 8, 1980, http://domino.un.org/UNISPAL.NSF/9a798adbf322aff38525617b006d88d7/2d87441f82c77dd0052566c500577c9a!OpenDocument (accessed July 25, 2008).

27. Wolf, "Anne Frank Is Dead," 116(ff).

28. "Le directeur de 'Témoignage Chrétien' dénonce la propaganda sioniste," *Informations Arabes*, No. 15, Geneva, November 30, 1970, p. 6. For this citation, I am indebted to Bat Ye'or, *Eurabia*, 46, 328.

29. On Germany's *Gastarbeiter* program, see Charles Hawley, "Integration in Europe: How Germany failed its immigrants," *Der Spiegel Online*, December 21, 2004, http://service.spiegel.de/cache/international/0,1518,druck-333899,00.html; for France see Bencheikh, *Marrianne et le prophète: l'islam dans la France laïque* [Marianne and the Prophet: Islam in lay France], 86–87; for England see "Muslims in the West: Dim drums throbbing in the hills half heard," *The Economist*, August 8, 2002, http://www .economist.com/displaystory.cfm?story_id=1270416.

30. Details of the citizenship reform, "Reform of Germany's Citizenship and Nationality Law," are posted on the web page of the German Embassy to the United Kingdom, http://www.german-embassy.org.uk/reform_of_germany_s_citizenshi.html.

31. See Derek Hopgood, *Euro-Arab Dialogue: Relations between the Two Cultures: Acts of the Hamburg Symposium, April 11th to 15th 1983* (London: Croom Helm, 1983), 305–316; Bat Ye'or, *Eurabia*, 91–98.

32. Alain Peyrefitte, *C'Était De Gaulle* (Paris: Fayard, 1994), 52.

33. Ulrich von Wilamowitz-Moellendorff, *Türken in Deutschland* (Sankt Augustin, Germany: Konrad Adenauer Foundation, 2001), 18, www.kas.de/db_files/dokumente/ arbeitspapiere/7_dokument_dok_pdf_12_1.pdf (accessed July 25, 2008).

34. Timothy J. Savage, "Europe and Islam: Crescent Waxing, Cultures Clashing," *The Washington Quarterly* (Summer 2004): 26–27.

35. Robin Shepherd, "In Europe, an Unhealthy Fixation on Israel," *Washington Post*, January 30, 2005.

36. Jonathan Weckerle, "Germany's Special Relationship—with Iran," *Jerusalem Post*, August 19, 2008, http://www.jpost.com/servlet/Satellite?cid=1218710 408403&pagename=JPost%2FJPArticle%2FShowFull (accessed August 25, 2008).

37. Michel Gurfinkiel, "Special Report/Gaza and the Rise of the Neo-French," *Michel Gurfinkiel.com*, March 1, 2009, http://www.michelgurfinkiel.com/articles/ 223-Special-Report-The-Gaza-War-and-the-rise-of-the-Neo-French.html.

38. The Parliamentary Association continues to play an important role in the EAD. Its website is http://www.medea.be/index.html?page=0&lang=en&idx=0 &doc =1020&PHPSESSID=07b07f2ccf97a4734e2e86aef7516291.

39. Tilj Declerq, "A European point of view," *Eurabia* (magazine), Paris, July 1975; cited by Bat Ye'or, *Eurabia*, 64.

40. On the idea of the "new Andalusia" as the model for the Euro-Arab symbiosis in Europe, see Gilles Kepel, *The War for Arab Minds: Islam and the West*, trans. Pascale Ghazaleh (Cambridge: Harvard University Press, 2004), 293–295.

41. *The Sunday Times*, London, January 23, 2005.

42. Toby Helm, "Holocaust Memorial Day Must Be Scrapped, Say British Muslim Leaders," *Daily Telegraph Online* (UK), September 12, 2005, http:// www.telegraph.co.uk/news/main.jhtml?xml=/news/2005/09/12/nholo12. xml&sSheet=/news/2005/09/12/ixhome.html.

43. Abul Taher, "Ditch Holocaust memorial day, advisers urge Blair," *The Sunday Times*, London, September 11, 2005, http://www.timesonline.co.uk/tol/ news/uk/article565335.ece.

44. "British MP George Galloway in Syria: Foreigners are Raping Two Beautiful Arab Daughters," MEMRI Special Dispatch Series No. 948, August 3, 2005, http://memri.org/bin/articles.cgi?Page=subjects&Area=jihad&ID=SP94805.

45. On the killing of gays, see Jenny McCartney, "Livingstone Lauds the Man who advocates the killing of gays," *Daily Telegraph* (UK), November 7, 2004, http://www.telegraph.co.uk/opinion/main.jhtml?xml=/opinion/2004/07/11/ do1104.xml. On suicide bombers against Israelis, see "Al-Qaradawi Full Transcript," *BBC News*, July 8, 2004, http://news.bbc.co.uk/2/hi/programmes/ newsnight/3875119.stm. See also "Sheikh Al-Qaradhawi on Hamas Jerusalem Day Online" MEMRI, Special Dispatch No. 1051, December 18, 2005, http:// memri.org/bin/articles.cgi?Page=archives&Area=sd&ID=SP105105. On likening Qaradawi to Pope John XXIII, see Philip Johnston, "Radical Imam Like Pope, says Mayor," *Daily Telegraph* (UK), September 14, 2005, http://www.telegraph.co.uk/news/main.jhtml?xml=/news/2005/09/14/nliv14.xml&sSheet=/ news/2005/09/14/ixnewstop.html.

46. According to "Background Note: France" of the U.S. Department of State, dated January 2008, the Muslim population of France is estimated to be 10 percent of the total or approximately 6.1 million, http://www.state.gov/r/pa/ei/bgn/3842. htm (accessed July 19, 2008).

47. Fernanda Eberstadt, "A Frenchman or a Jew?" *New York Times*, February 29, 2004. See also Marie Brenner, "France's Scarlet Letter," June 2003, http://www .mariebrenner. com/articles/france/sl2.html.

48. See Alyssa A. Lappen, "Ritual Murders of Jews in Paris," *Front Page Magazine*, December 4, 2003, http://www.frontpagemag.com/Articles/ReadArticle.asp?ID=11062.

49. *Jewish Herald-Voice Online*, http://www.jhvonline.com/news/render.asp?a=357&print=yes. The *Jewish-Herald Voice* is a Houston Anglo-Jewish newspaper.

50. See Chapter 1, 30–32.

51. The original report, withheld by the EU, is available on the Web at http://uk-org-bod.supplehost.org/EUMC/EUMC.pdf.

52. Bertrand Benoit, "EU body shelves report on anti-semitism," *Financial Times*, November 21, 2003; Clifford D. May, "Hatred, European Style," *Washington Times*, December 3, 2003.

53. http://www.wexler.house.gov/press_releases/Nov_25_03.htm.

54. "Anti-Semitism in the Spotlight," *Newsletter*, Zentrum für Antisemitismusforschung (Center for Research on Anti-Semitism), Berlin 26 (December 2003).

55. Ambrose Evans-Prichard, "EU covered up attacks on Jews by young Muslims," *Daily Telegraph*, January 4, 2004, http://news.telegraph.co.uk/news/main.jhtml?xml=/news/2004/04/01/wsemit01.xml.

56. U.S. Department of State, "Report on Global Anti-Semitism," January 5, 2005, http://www.state.gov/g/drl/rls/40258.htm.

57. The report was independently prepared by First International Resources, LLC and issued on May 5, 2005, http://www.adl.org/PresRele/ASInt_13/4726_13.htm.

58. Cited by Lisbeth Lindeborg, "Osama's Library," *Dagens Nyheter*, Stockholm, Sweden, 25 October 2001, reprinted in *World Press Review* 49, 1 (January 2002).

59. "Exiled British Islamist Sheikh Omar bin Bakri in Beirut: We Will See the Banner of Islam 'Flying Over Big Ben and the British Parliament,'" MEMRI, Special Dispatch Series, No. 1203, http://memri.org/bin/articles.cgi?Page=archives&Area=sd&ID= SP120306#_ednref2. The sheikh's views have been consistent over time. In an interview in *Le Monde*, Paris, September 9, 1998, he declared that the goal of Islam was "to make the flag of Islam fly high at No. 10 Downing Street and at the Élysée Palace."

60. Thierry Portes and Cecilia Gabizon, "Sondage: pour les valeurs de la Republique, mais contre la victoire des Etats-Unis," *Le Figaro*, April 5, 2003, www.lefigaro.fr/cgi/perm/archives/find?url=http://newportal.cedromsni.com/httpref/intro.asp&user=lefigaro&part_ID=lefigaro. I am indebted to Timothy Savage, "Europe and Islam: Crescent Waxing," for this reference.

61. Niall Ferguson, "The Way We Live Now: 4-4-04; Eurabia?," *New York Times Magazine*, April 4, 2004, file:///C:/Users/RLR/Documents/Cambridge%202006/Ferguson%3b%20Eurabia%20-%20NYTimes.htm.

62. Willard G. Oxtoby, ed., *World Religions: Western Traditions* (New York: Oxford University Press, 2002), 449.

63. Wolfgang Schwanitz, Interview with Bernard Lewis, "Europa Wird Am Ende Des Jahrhunderts Islamisch Sein," *Die Welt*, July 28, 2004, http://www.welt.de/print-welt/article211310/Europa_wird_islamisch.html.

64. Manfred Gerstenfeld and Barzi, "The Gaza War and the New Outburst of Anti-Semitism," *Institute for Global Jewish Affairs*, 79, April 1, 2009 (published March 2009), http://www.jcpa.org/JCPA/Templates/ShowPage.asp?DRIT=3&DBID=1

&LNGID=1&TMID=111&FID=624&PID=0&IID=2895&TTL=The_Gaza_War_ and_the_New_Outburst_of_Anti-Semitism.

CHAPTER FIVE

1. See Uzi Mahnaimi and Michael Sheridan, "Israelis 'Blew Apart Syrian Nuclear Cache,'" *TimesOnline* (UK), September 16, 2007, http://www.timeson-line.co.uk/tol/news/world/middle_east/article2461421.ece; see also Mahnaimi and Sheridan, "Israelis hit Syrian 'nuclear bomb plant,'" *TimesOnline* (UK), December 2, 2007, http://www.timesonline.co.uk/tol/news/ world/middle_east/ article2983719.ece; for a report questioning whether the Israelis hit a Syrian nuclear site, see Seymour Hersh, "A Strike in the Dark: What Did the Israelis Bomb in Syria?" *New Yorker*, February 11, 2008, http://www.newyorker.com/ reporting/2008/02/11/080211fa_fact_hersh?printable=true. There has been some speculation that Syria may have intended to supply Iran with nuclear fuel rather than construct a nuclear weapon. See Ian Black, "Syria planned to supply Iran with nuclear fuel, Israel says," *The Guardian* (UK), June 25, 2008, http://www.guardian .co.uk/world/2008/jun/25/syria.iran.

2. IAEA Board of Governors, "Implementation of the NPT Safeguards Agreement in the Syrian Arab Republic," *Report by the Director General*, February 19, 2009, www.isis-online.org/publications/syria/IAEA_Report_Syria_19Nov2008.pdf.

3. "Iran-Iraq War," GlobalSecurity.org., http://www.globalsecurity.org/ military/world/war/iran-iraq.htm (August 20, 2008).

4. Most media sources translated the slogan as "Israel must be wiped off the map." Joshua Teitelbaum, with the assistance of Dr. Dennis MacEoin, who holds a PhD in Persian/Islamic Studies from Kings College, Cambridge University, argues that the correct translation is the one offered here. See Joshua Teitelbaum, "What Iranian Leaders Really Say about Doing Away with Israel," *Jerusalem Center for Public Affairs*, 2008, http://cddrl.stanford.edu/publica-tions/what_iranian_leaders_really_say_about_doing_away_with_israel/ 13, (accessed June 8, 2009).

5. Yossi Melman and Meir Javedanfar, *The Nuclear Sphinx of Tehran: Mahmoud Ahmadinejad and the State of Iran* (New York: Carroll and Graf, 2007), 133.

6. Dinshaw Mistry, "European Missile Defense: Assessing Iran's ICBM Capabilities," *Arms Control Today*, October 2007, http://www.armscontrol.org/act/ 2007_10/Mistry.asp; Ayelet Savyon, "The Internal Debate in Iran: How to Respond to Western Pressure Regarding Its Nuclear Program" MEMRI, *Inquiry and Analysis Series*, No. 181, http://memri.org/bin/articles.cgi?Page=archives&Area =ia&ID=IA18104.

7. "Pentagon: Iran Satellite Launch a Concern," *msnbc.com news services*, February 3, 2009, http://in.reuters.com/article/asiaCompanyAndMarkets/ idINDAH217783 20090222; see also Reuters India, "Iran to Mark Satellite Launch with new bank note," February 22, 2009, http://in.reuters.com/ar-ticle/asiaCompanyAndMarkets/idINDAH21778320090222.

8. "Israel has no adequate interceptor for Iran's new long-range missile," DEBKA/file Special Report, May 20, 2009, http://www.debka.com/headline_ print.php?hid=6086.

9. Ray Takeyh, *Hidden Iran: Paradox and Power in the Islamic Republic* (New York: Council on Foreign Relations/Holt, 2006), 196. The statement appeared on September 25, 1979, 243, 12(n).

10. This is the Teitelbaum translation, "What Iranian Leaders Really Say," 7; there is debate concerning the translation of Ahmadinejad's threat to wipe Israel "off the face of the earth." The translation distributed by Iran Broadcasting of the Islamic Republic (IRIB) read, "Our dear Imam [Ayatollah Khomeini] said that the occupying regime [Israel] must be wiped off the map and this was a very wise statement." The *New York Times* and the Western media published the IRIB translation. (Nazila Fathi, "Iran's New President Says 'Israel Must Be Wiped Off the Map," *New York Times*, October 27, 2005, http://select.nytimes.com/search/ restricted/article?res=F10A17F83A5B0C748EDDA90994DD4044 82.) However, some scholars have challenged the translation's accuracy. For example, Professor Juan Cole of the University of Michigan, hardly a friend of Israel, has offered what he claims is a more accurate translation: "The Imam said that this regime occupying Jerusalem *(een rezhim-e eshghalgar-e qods)* must [vanish from] the page of time *(bayad az safheh-ye ruzgar mahv shavad)*." (Juan Cole, "Hitchens the Hacker and Hitchens the Oientalist, Informed Comment: Thoughts on the Middle East, History, and Religion," May 3, 2006, http://www.juancole.com/2006/05/hitchens-hacker-and-hitchens.html. On Cole's bias see Cinnamon Stillwell, "Juan Cole Peddles Hamas Propaganda," *Front Page Magazine*, February 4, 2008, http://www.front pagemag.com/Articles/Read.aspx?GUID=5199be45-43db-4130-91b2-9d2e72fcb8b9; see also Arash Norouzi, "Wiped off the Map—The Rumor of the Century," http://www.mohammadmossadegh.com/news/rumor-of-the-century/. This would suggest that Ahmadinejad's intent was not genocidal but an expression of the hope that the Israeli "regime" would collapse under pressure from the Palestinians and a united Muslim world. A number of sources within the Iranian government claimed that Ahmadinejad's statement had been "misunderstood" and that no genocidal intent was implied. ("Iran: Holocaust Remarks Misunderstood," CNN.com, December 16, 2005, http://memri.org/bin/articles.cgi?Page=archives&Area=sd&ID=SP101305.) MEMRI, the Middle East Media Research Institute whose mission is to bridge "the language gap between the Middle East and the West," offered the following translation: "Imam [Khomeini] said: 'This regime that is occupying *Qods* [Jerusalem] must be eliminated from the pages of history.' This sentence is very wise." MEMRI's translation is ambiguous. It could imply either genocidal intent or the collapse of the Israeli state under Muslim pressure. On June 11, 2006, Ethan Bronner, deputy foreign editor of the *New York Times*, took note of the translation controversy. He pointed out that "translators in Tehran who work for the president's office and the foreign ministry" disagree with Cole and others who have attempted to soften the meaning of Ahmadinejad's threat. According to Bronner, "All official translations of Mr. Ahmadinejad's statement, including a description of it on his website (www.president.ir/eng/), refer to wiping Israel away." Bronner cites two of Iran's most prominent translators, both of whom said that "wipe off" or "wipe away"" is more accurate than "vanish," Cole's term, "because the Persian verb is active and transitive." Bronner also noted that Ahmadinejad refused "even to utter the

name Israel," referring to it as the "occupying regime" and that "Ahmadinejad had called Israel 'a stain' on Islam that must be erased." Although conceding that the Iranian president "had never specifically threatened war," Bronner further observed, "When combined with Iran's longstanding support for Palestinian Islamic Jihad and Hezbollah of Lebanon, two groups that have killed numerous Israelis, and Mr. Ahmadinejad's refusal to acknowledge the Holocaust, it is hard to argue that, from Israel's point of view, Mr. Ahmadinejad poses no threat. . . . So did Iran's president call for Israel to be wiped off the map? It certainly seems so." See Ethan Bronner, "Just How Far Did They Go, Those Words Against Israel?" New York Times, June 11, 2006, http://www.nytimes.com/2006/06/11/weekinreview/11bronner.html?scp=2&sq=&st=nyt.

11. Transcript of keynote address of President Mahmoud Ahmadinejad at the World Without Zionism Conference, Tehran, October 26, 2005, http://www.iranfocus.com/modules/news/article.php?storyid=4164.

12. On Iranian attempts to moderate Ahmadinejad's rhetoric and his repetition of the threat, see Nazila Fathi, "Iran Does Damage Control," *International Herald Tribune*, October 29, 2005, http://www.iht.com/articles/2005/10/28/news/iran.php.

13. "Ahmadinejad at Conference: Israel Will 'Soon Be Wiped Out,'" *Haaretz*, December 13, 2006, http://www.haaretz.com/hasen/spages/800098.html.

14. The speech was reported in *Iran News* (English), *Kayhan* (Farsi), and *Al-Wifaq* (Arabic), December 15, 2001. Middle East Media Research Institute [MEMRI], Special Dispatch Series—No. 325, January 3, 2002, http://memri.org/bin/articles.cgi? Page=archives&Area=sd&ID=SP32502.

15. "Nuclear Weapons-Iranian Statements: Weapons of Mass Destruction (WMD)," *Global Security.org*, http://www.globalsecurity.org/wmd/world/iran/nuke2.htm.

16. MEMRI-TV, No. 1711, February 29, 2008. A video excerpt of al-Rashudi's comments is available at http://www.memritv.org/newsletter/AlAqsa.htm#.

17. Ayatollah Sayyid Ali Khamenei, "Address to Islamic World Media Conference," January 31, 2002, http://www.globalsecurity.org/wmd/library/news/iran/2002/020131-khamenei.htm.

18. Takeyh, *Hidden Iran*, 149.

19. Takeyh, *Hidden Iran*, 170–174.

20. "Text: Obama's Speech in Cairo," *New York Times*, June 4, 2009. http://www.nytimes.com/2009/06/04/us/politics/04obama.text.html?scp=5&sq=Cairo%20speech&st=cse.

21. William J. Broad and David E. Sanger, "Iran Has Centrifuge for Nuclear Arms, Report Says," *New York Times*, June 6, 2009, http://www.nytimes.com/2009/06/06/world/middleeast/06nuke.html.

22. Herb Keinon, "J'Lem rips Iran, Syria over IAEA reports," *Jerusalem Post*, http://www.jpost.com/servlet/Satellite?cid=1244035008964&pagename=JPost%2FJPArticle%2FPrinter.

23. For a description of the Iraq Study Group and access to the ISG's Official Report, see http://www.usip.org/isg/index.html.

24. James A. Baker, III, and Lee H. Hamilton, cochairs, *The Iraq Study Group Report* (Washington: United States Institute of Peace, 2006), 37, http://www.usip.org /isg/iraq_study_group_report/report/1206/ (accessed August 20, 2008).

25. Frederick Kagan, *Choosing Victory in Iraq: A Plan for Success In Iraq*, American Enterprise Institute, December 13, 2006; see also Mark Benjamin, "The Real Iraq Study Group, *Slate*, http://www.salon.com/news/feature/2007/01/06/aei/ (August 21, 2008); Editorial, "A bipartisan path to surrender?" *Washington Times*, December 6, 2006, http://www.washingtontimes.com/news/2006/dec/06/20061206-095730-9143r/.

26. Eli Lake, "Baker Panel Aide Expects Israel Will Be Pressed," *New York Sun*, November 29, 2006, http://www.nysun.com/foreign/baker-panel-aide-expects-israel-will-be-pressed/44310/ (accessed August 19, 2008).

27. Zbigniew Brzezinski and Robert M. Gates, co-chairs, *Iran: Time for a New Approach*, Task Force Report, Council on Foreign Relations, Press, July 2004, http://www.cfr.org/publication/7194/; see Caroline Glick, "Iran's American Protector," *Jerusalem Post*, August 18, 2008, http://www.jpost.com/servlet/Satellite?cid=1218710396905&pagename=JPost%2FJPArticle%2FShowFull (accessed August 18, 2008).

28. On the rise of Shi'ite power and its relation to Iran's stand toward Israel, see Vali Nasr, *The Shia Revival: How Conflicts within Islam Will Shape the Future* (New York: W. W. Norton, 2007).

29. Takeyh, *Hidden Iran*, 195 ff.

30. "Warnings on Iran: The Chairman of the Joint Chiefs of Staff on the nuclear threat from Tehran," *Wall Street Journal* [Editorial], April 6, 2009, http://online.wsj.com/article/SB123897499619091093.html#mod=djemEditorialPage.

31. Whitney Raas and Austin Long, "Ossirak Redux? Assessing Israeli Capabilities to Destroy Iranian Nuclear Facilities," *International Security*, 31, 4 (Spring 2007): 7–33, http://www.mitpressjournals.org/doi/abs/10.1162/isec.2007.31.4.7. For this citation, I am indebted to Daniel Pipes, "Israeli Jets vs. Iranian Nukes," *New York Sun*, June 12, 2007. http://www.nysun.com/article/ 56386.

32. Pipes "Israeli Jets."

33. For a brief description of the F-16I Sufa (Storm) jet, see Global Security.org, http://www.globalsecurity.org/military/world/israel/f-16i.htm; for a description of the F-15I, see Boeing News Release 97-213, "The First F15I for the Israeli Air Force," http://www.geocities.com/capecanaveral/hangar/2848/f15i.htm.

34. Yaakov Katz, "We'll Neutralize the S-300 if they're sold to Iran," *Jerusalem Post*, 8 August 2008. http://www.jpost.com/servlet/Satellite?cid= 1218104239541&pagename=JPArticle%2FShowFull (accessed August 19, 2008).

35. "Russian S-300 anti-air weapon already delivered to Iran," DEBKA*file* Special Report, 24 December 2008. http://www.debka.com/headline.php?hid=5778 and "US: Russia's S-300 missile sale to Iran marks Israel's decision point," DEBKA*file* Special Report, December 28, 2008, http://www.debka.com/headline.php?hid=5789.

36. Dave Majunder, "Israel's Red Line: The S-300 Missile System," *Avuation.com*, August 7, 2008, http://www.aviation.com/technology/080807-iran-and-s-300-missile.html (accessed August 18, 2008).

37. "Geopolitical Diary: The Next Round of the Russian-Iranian Game," *Stratfor*, http://www.stratfor.com/geopolitical_diary/geopolitical_ diary_next_round_russian_iranian_game (accessed August 19, 2008).

38. "Russia May Not Ship S-300 Missiles to Iran Hoping to Improve Ties with USA," *Pravda.RU,* February 17, 2009, http://english.pravda.ru/world/asia/17-02-2009/107115-russia_s300_iran-0.

39. Yaakov Katz, "We'll Neutralize," *Jerusalem Post.*

40. Reuven Pedatzur, "Here's how Israel would destroy Iran's nuclear program," *Haaretz,* May 21, 2009, http://www.haaretz.com/hasen/spages/1085619.html (accessed June 8, 2009). For this citation, I am grateful to Jerome Gordon, "The Necessity of Thinking Outside of the Box—The Israeli Iran Nuclear Attack Scenarios," *The Iconoclast,* May 15, 2009, http://www.newenglishreview.org/blog_display.cfm/blog_id/20948#CurDomainURL#/blog.cfm (accessed June 8, 2009).

41. "IDF trains for simultaneous Hezbollah, Iran, Syria missile strikes," *Haaretz,* June 8, 2008, http://www.haaretz.com/hasen/spages/1008808.html.

42. Firouz Sedarat, "Ahmadinejad says 'Israel would not dare attack Iran,'" *Reuters UK,* January 18, 2008, http://today.reuters.co.uk/news/articlenews.aspx?type=topNews&storyid=2008-0118T101800Z_01_L17614653_RTRUKOC_0_UK-ISRAEL-IRAN-AHMADINEJAD.xml.

43. Anthony Cordesman, "Iran, Israel, and Nuclear War," Center for Strategic and International Studies, November 19, 2007, http://www.csis.org/index.php?option=com_csis_pubs&task=view&id=4172. For citing Cordesman, I am indebted to the *Daniel Pipes' Weblog,* "The Unthinkable Consequences of an Iran-Nuclear Exchange," November 21, 2007, http://www.danielpipes.org/blog/780.

44. Anthony Cordesman and Abdullah Toukan, "Study on a Possible Israeli Strike on Iran's Nuclear Development Facilities," Center for Strategic and International Studies, March 14, 2009, http://www.csis.org/media/csis/pubs/090316_israelistrikeiran.pdf. (accessed June 8, 2009).

45. Cordesman, "Iran, Israel," 31.

46. Cordesman, "Iran, Israel," 5. For a brief, layman's description of the different kinds of nuclear bombs, see Craig Freudenrich and John Fuller, "How Nuclear Bombs Work," *How Stuff Works,* http://science.howstuffworks.com/nuclear-bomb.htm.

47. Cordesman, "Iran, Israel," 6.

48. Cordesman and Toukan, "Possible Israeli Strike," 4.

49. Cordesman, "Iran, Israel," 48.

50. Andrew F. Krepinevich, *7 Deadly Scenarios: A Military Futurist Explores War in the 21st Century,* (New York: Bantam Books, 2009), 125–168.

51. Krepinevich, *7 Deadly,* 127.

52. Krepinevich, *7 Deadly,* 127.

53. Krepinevich, *7 Deadly,* 161.

54. Anthony Shadid, "With Iran Ascendant, U.S. Is Seen as at Fault," *Washington Post,* January 30, 2007, http://www.washingtonpost.com/wp-dyn/content/article/2007/01/29/AR2007012902090.html, cited by Krepinevich, *7 Deadly,* 166.

55. Peter Beaumont and Conal Urquhart, "Israel Deploys Nuclear Arms in Submarines," *The Observer* (UK), October 12, 2003, http://www.guardian.co.uk/world /2003/oct/12/israel1. For an account of Israel's submarine capacity from

a source traditionally less than friendly to Israel, see Thomas R. Stauffer, "Israel Expands its Nuclear Threat Thanks to German 'Donation' of Dolphin Subs," *Washington Report on Middle Eastern Affairs*, December 2003, 12–13, http://www .wrmea.com/archives/December_2003/0312012.html.

56. Cordesman, "Iran, Israel," 43.

57. Aqeel Hussein and Colin Freeman, "Rogue TV Tells Sunnis 'to Eat Shias for Lunch,'" *Daily Telegraph* (UK), November 12, 2006, http://www.telegraph.co.uk /news/main.jhtml?xml=/news/2006/12/10/wirq10.xml.

58. Benny Morris, "Der zweite Holocaust wird nicht so sein wie der erste," *Die Welt* (Hamburg), January 6, 2007, http://www.welt.de/data/2007/01/06/ 1165992.html; English translation, Benny Morris, "The Second Holocaust," *New York Sun*, January 22, 2007, file:///C:/Users/RLR/Documents/Iran/ Benny%20Morris-The%20Second%20Holocaust.htm.

59. Morris, "Der zweite Holocaust."

60. See Seymour M. Hersh, *The Samson Option: Israel's Nuclear Arsenal and American Foreign Policy* (New York: Random House, 1991) 129–142. On the development of Israel's bomb, see Avner Cohen, *Israel and the Bomb* (New York: Columbia University Press, 1998) and Michael Karpin, *The Bomb in the Basement: How Israel Went Nuclear and What That Means for the World* (New York: Simon and Schuster, 2006).

61. Josephus's source for the events at Masada were two women who hid themselves with five children at the time of the mass suicide. Josephus, *The Jewish War, Books IV–VII*, trans. H. St. J. Thackeray (Cambridge: Harvard University Press, 1968), VII, 583–617.

62. Judges 16: 30.

63. Jerome Gordon, "The necessity of thinking outside the box—The Israeli Iran nuclear attack scenarios," *Israpundit*, May 15, 2009, http://www.israpundit. com/2008/?p=13385 (accessed June 9, 2009).

64. Gordon, "The necessity of thinking outside the box." See also "Exclusive: Israel's air maneuver did not simulate possible Iran strike strategy," *DEBKAfile*, June 28, 2008, http://www.debka.com/headline.php?hid=5367 (accessed June 9, 2009).

65. For a report on the capabilities of the Dolphin submarines, see "Weapons of Mass Destruction (WMD): Dolphin," *GlobalSecurity.org*, undated, http://www. globalsecurity.org/wmd/world/israel/dolphin.htm (accessed June 9, 2009). I am indebted to Mr. Gordon for this reference.

66. The United States is also vulnerable to an EMP attack, see "Report of the Commission to Assess the Threat to the United States from Electromagnetic Pulse Attack: Critical National Infrastructures," April 2008, http://www.empcommission.org/docs/A2473-EMP_Commission-7MB.pdf (accessed June 9, 2009).

67. Takeyh, *Hidden Iran*, 194.

68. "Iran Attacks Iraqi Nuclear Reactor," McNair Paper Number 41, Radical Responses to Radical Regimes: Evaluating Preemptive Counter-Proliferation, May 1995, Institute for National Strategic Studies, National Defense University, http://www.ndu.edu/inss/mcnair/mcnair41/41irq.html.

69. For a brief discussion of the Iran-Contra Affair, see Julie Wolf, "The Iran-Contra Affair," The American Experience: PBS, http://www.pbs.org/wgbh/ amex/reagan/ peopleevents/pande08.html.

70. Samuel Huntington, *The Clash of Civilizations and the Remaking of World Order* (New York: Simon & Schuster, 1996).

71. Takeyh, *Hidden Iran*, 210.

72. CNN, "Transcript of Interview with Iranian President Mohammad Khatami," January 7, 1998, http://www.cnn.com/WORLD/9801/07/iran/interview. html.

73. For a sampling of some dissenting opinion, see the symposium on the decision by the State Department to give him a visa, see "Visa Not Denied: On Mohammad Khatami's upcoming visit to the United States," A National Review Online, August 30, 2006, http://article.nationalreview.com/?q=YzhmNTQ0NDQ3MmIxZDlmZWVlNmViMzE0YjkzMTNiYmM=#more.

74. Ray Takeyh, "A Profile in Defiance," *Foreign Affairs,* Spring 2006, http://www.cfr.org/publication/10324/.

75. Takeyh, "A Profile," 196.

76. The full text of the 2007 NIE is available at http://www.worldpoliticsreview.com/blog/blog.aspx?id=1404# and "National Intelligence Estimate: Iran: Nuclear Intentions and Capabilities," Global Security, http://www.globalsecurity.org/intell/library/reports/2007/nie_iran-nuclear_20071203.htm.

77. "Iran Curveball," *Wall Street Journal,* December 8, 2007, A-10, available online at http://online.wsj.com/article/SB119707331779617850.html?mod=google-news_wsj.

78. Naturally occurring uranium consists of two isotopes, Uranium (U-235) (.72 percent) and U-238 (99.2 percent). Such uranium cannot be used directly to fuel a nuclear weapon. U-235 and Plutonium (U-239) are capable of undergoing nuclear fission. In the case of uranium, in order to produce fuel for either civilian nuclear reactors or nuclear weapons, U-235 must be separated from ordinary uranium and enriched. This cannot be done by chemical process since both isotopes are chemically identical. (The term isotope is generally used to distinguish nuclear species of the same chemical element, that is, those having the same number of protons but different numbers of neutrons, such as iodine 127 and iodine 131). Gaseous diffusion and centrifuge enrichment are the principal uranium enrichment technologies, but these processes are energy intensive and technologically extremely difficult. A common feature of all large-scale uranium enrichment is that a number of identical stages must be employed that yield small amounts of successively higher concentrations of U-235. Each stage concentrates the product of the previous stage before being sent to the next stage for further processing. BBC NEWS, September 1, 2006, has a brief but lucid account of the process of uranium enrichment, "Q&A: Uranium enrichment," http://news.bbc.co.uk/2/hi/middle_east/5278806.stm.

The only difference between uranium enriched for civilian and for military purposes is the degree of enrichment. Civilian uranium requires enrichment of the original uranium to about four times the original U-235 or about 2.9 percent (4 percent enrichment); weapons-grade uranium (HEU) requires enrichment to greater than 90 percent. Once the enrichment process is mastered, there is nothing to prevent any collectivity that claims its enrichment is for civilian purposes from continuing until it acquires a sufficient quantity of U-235 for weapons-grade production. I am indebted to Dr. Frederic Leder of Fairfield, Connecticut for assisting me in understanding this topic.

79. Ali Akbar Dareini, "Report: Iran Now Has 6,000 Centrifuges for Uranium," *ABC News International*, July 26, 2008. http://abcnews.go.com/print?id=5454857.

80. Peter Finn, "Russia Ships First Lot of Nuclear Fuel to Iran: Kremlin, U.S. Officials Say Step Removes Need for Tehran to Pursue Enrichment," *Washington Post*, December 18, 2007, A12, http://www.washingtonpost.com/wpdyn/content/article/2007/12/17/AR2007121700220.html.

81. "National Intelligence Estimate: Iran: Nuclear Intentions and Capabilities," November 2007, www.dni.gov/press_releases/20071203_release.pdf.

82. Marc Champion and Jay Solomon, "Group Says Iran Resumed Weapon Program," *Wall Street Journal*, December 11, 2007, A4, http://online.wsj.com/article/ SB119734172703720416.html.

83. Tim Shipman, Philip Sherwell, and Carolynne Wheeler, "Iran 'hoodwinked' CIA over nuclear plans," *Daily Telegraph* (UK), December 12, 2007, file:///C:/Users/RLR/Documents/Iran/Daily%20TelegrahCIA%20Hoodwinked%20ovr%20Iran.htm.

84. "French defense minister says Iran still pursuing nuclear arms," *Agence France Presse*, January 31, 2008, http://afp.google.com/article/ALeqM5g1Zpuhg 0QMACoTxnPW29AZP0XiLw.

85. Elaine Sciolino, "Monitoring Agency Praises US Report but Keeps Wary Eye on Iran," *New York Times*, December 5, 2007, http://www.nytimes.com/2007/12/05/world/middleeast/05iran.html?pagewanted=print.

86. Bret Stephens, "The NIE Fantasy," *Wall Street Journal*, December 11, 2007, A26, http://online.wsj.com/article/SB119734115058520384. html?mod=opinion_columns_featured_lsc.

87. For the initial failure of intelligence in the Cuban Missile Crisis, see Sherman Kent, "A Crucial Estimate Relived," *Studies in Intelligence*, 36, 5 (1992): 111–119, https://www.cia.gov/library/center-for-the-study-of-intelligence/csi-publications/books-and-monographs/sherman-kent-and-the-board-of-national-estimates-collected-essays/9crucial.html; see also Tim Weiner, *Legacy of Ashes: A History of the CIA* (New York: Doubleday, 2007), 194–209; for a succinct overview of the crisis, see "The Cuban Missile Crisis," BBC.co.uk., http://www.bbc.co.uk/dna/h2g2/A563852.

88. For example, at the Senate hearings on Robert Gates's nomination as director of Central Intelligence in 1991 and as secretary of defense in 2006, some former CIA colleagues testified that Gates had unduly slanted and politicized the findings of National Intelligence Estimates. See "For Mr. Gates: Chapter and Verse," *New York Times*, October 3, 1991, http://query.nytimes.com/gst/full page.html?res =9D0CE7D91F3DF930A35753C1A967958260; "The Gates Hearings: Excerpts from the C.I.A. Documents Released in Gates Hearings," *New York Times*, October 2, 1991, http://query.nytimes.com/gst/fullpage.html?res=9D0CE7DD 173FF931A35753C1A967958260; Jennifer Glaudemans, "Has Gates Learned His Lesson? Robert Gates' Nomination as Defense Secretary Will Give Him a Chance to Prove He Knows Better than to Politicize Intelligence," *Los Angeles Times*, November 21, 2006, http://www.latimes.com/news/opinion/la-oeglaudemans-21nov21,0,5803026.story?coll=la-opinion-rightrail.

89. Fred Kaplan, "Nuclear Meltdown: We're Not Going to Bomb Iran," *Slate*, December 3, 2007, http://www.slate.com/id/2179084/ (accessed August 21, 2008).

90. "Thomas Fingar," Office of the Director of National Intelligence," http://www.dni.gov/aboutODNI/bios/fingar_bio.htm.

91. This view was expressed by Maj. Gen. Aharon Ze'evi-Farkash, former Israel Defense Force (IDF) intelligence chief. See "Iran Now Free to Achieve Its Military Nuclear Ambitions: An Israeli Perspective on the U.S. National Intelligence Estimate," *Jewish Center for Public Affairs*, 7, 28 (accessed January 9, 2008), http://www.jcpa.org/JCPA/Templates/ShowPage.asp?DBID=1&LNGID=1&TMID=111&FID=254&PID=0&IID=2009.

92. For a brief, informed analysis of Iranian strategy, see Caroline Glick, "Iran's Game of Grand Strategy," *Jerusalem Post*, February 26, 2008, http://www.jpost.com/servlet/Satellite?cid=1203847464442&pagename=JPost%2FJPArticle%2FShowFull.

93. For an essay expressing similar thoughts, see Emanuel A. Winston, "Peeling the Intelligence Onion Back Another Layer," http://www.jewishindy.com/modules.php?name=News&file=article&sid=7515.

94. David Wyman, *The Abandonment of the Jews: America and the Holocaust 1941–1945* (New York: Pantheon Books, 1984), 105.

95. On the intensification of European anti-Semitism from the pogroms that began in Tsarist Russia in 1881 to the end of World War II, see Richard L. Rubenstein and John K. Roth, *Approaches to Auschwitz: The Holocaust and Its Legacy* (Louisville: Westminster John Knox, 2003), 71–212.

96. On the complex story of Arabist influence on American policy in the Middle East, see Robert D.Kaplan, *The Arabists: The Romance of an American Elite* (New York: Free Press, 1995).

97. For a brief account of the attempt of senior statesmen to dissuade President Truman from recognizing Israel in 1948, See Richard Holbrooke, "Washington's Battle Over Israel's Birth," *Washington Post*, May 7, 2008, http://www.washingtonpost.com/wp-dyn/content/article/2008/05/06/AR2008050602447.html.

98. "Report to the Secretary on the Acquiescence of this Government in the Murder of the Jews," initialed by Randolph Paul for the Foreign Funds Control Unit of the Treasury Department, January 13, 1944, PBS, America and the Holocaust, Primary Sources, http://www.pbs.org/wgbh/amex/holocaust/filmmore/reference/primary/somereport.html; see also Wyman, *The Abandonment of the Jews*, and Richard Breitman, *Official Secrets: What the Nazis Planned, What the British and the Americans Knew* (New York: Farrar, Straus and Giroux, 1998).

99. "Report to the Secretary on the Acquiescence of this Government in the Murder of the Jews," initialed by Randolph Paul for the Foreign Funds Control Unit of the Treasury Department, January 13, 1944, http://www.pbs.org/wgbh/amex/holocaust/filmmore/reference/primary/somereport.html.

100. Louis Lochner, ed., *The Goebbels Diaries 1942–43* (Garden City, NY: Doubleday, 1948), 241.

101. Breitman, *Official Secrets*, 207–211; Wyman, *Abandonment of the Jews*, 288–311; Michael Beschloss, *The Conquerors: Roosevelt, Truman and the Destruction of Hitler's Germany* (New York: Simon and Schuster, 2002), 56–69.

102. Tim Weiner, "Aide Accuses U.S. on Balkan Policy," *New York Times*, February 4, 1994.

103. Richard Johnson, "The Pin-Stripe Approach to Genocide" (manuscript, U.S. Department of State, January 1, 1994), 1.

104. Johnson, "The Pin-Stripe," 9.

105. David Albright and Jacqueline Shire, "IAEA Report on Iran: Nuclear Weapons breakout capability achieved: Centrifuge numbers and low enriched uranium output steady; no progress on safeguards issues," Institute for Science and International Security, February 19, 2009; International Atomic Energy Agency: Board of Governors, "Implementation of the NPT Safeguards, Agreement and relevant provisions of Security Council resolutions 1737 (2006), 1747 (2007), 1803 (2008) and 1835 (2008) in the Islamic Republic of Iran," February 19, 2009.

106. For insight into the many-layered cover-up plot, see Sergio Kiernan, *A Cover-Up Exposed: The 1994 AMI Bombing Case Hits the Wall* (New York: American Jewish Committee, 2004), 6. The text is available in HTML at http://www.ajc.org/site/apps/nl/content3.asp?c=ijITI2PHKoG&b=846739&ct=1043987.

107. Kiernan, *A Cover-Up*, 15–16.

108. "Argentina removes bomb case judge," *BBC News*, December 3, 2003, http://news.bbc.co.uk/2/hi/americas/3289359.stm.

109. Kiernan, *A Cover-Up*, 9.

110. Kiernan, *A Cover-Up*, 6.

111. Kiernan, *A Cover-Up*, 6.

112. Alireza Jafarzadeh, *The Iranian Threat: President Ahmadinejad and the Coming Nuclear Crisis* (New York: Palgrave Macmillan, 2007), 73–76.

113. Melman and Javedanfar, *The Nuclear Sphinx of Teheran*, 119–120.

114. Melman and Javedanfar, *The Nuclear Sphinx of Teheran*, 213–214.

115. David Horovitz, "Editor's Notes: Exposing Iran's ruthlessness," *Jerusalem Post*, December 20, 2007; Melman and Javedanfar, *The Nuclear Sphinx of Teheran*, 214.

116. Dan Senor, "The Long Arm of Iran: The top mullahs have been complicit in terror attacks," *Wall Street Journal*, September 29, 2007, http://opinionjournal.com/extra/?id=110010671.

117. "The Constitution of the Islamic Republic of Iran: Section 8, Article 109," http://www.iranonline.com/iran/iran-info/Government/constitution-8.html.

118. Takeyh, *Hidden Iran*, 25.

119. Larry Rohter, "Argentina Reviews a Clumsy Case by Its Spies," *New York Times*, July 13, 2003, http://query.nytimes.com/gst/fullpage, html?res=9D06E1D B1F3DF930A25754C0A9659C8B63&sec=&spon=&pagewanted=print.

120. Larry Rohter, "Iran Blew Up Jewish Center in Argentina, Defector Says," *New York Times*, July 22, 2002, http://www.nytimes.com/2002/07/22/world/iran-blew-up-jewish-center-in-argentina-defector-says.html.

121. Rohter, "Iran Blew Up."

122. Rohter, "Iran Blew Up."

123. Carlos Gabetta, "Are Menem's Days Numbered?" *Le Monde diplomatique*, (English edition), December 1997, http://mondediplo.com/ 1997/12/argentina.

124. David Horovitz, "Editor's Notes: Exposing Iran's ruthlessness."

125. He met his first wife, Zulema Fatima Yoma, in Damascus where his parents had taken him for an arranged marriage with the daughter of a suitable Syrian Muslim immigrant family that had apparently come to Syria for matchmaking. Unlike

Carlos, Zulema Yoma never converted nor did their son, Carlos Menem Jr., who died in a suspicious helicopter crash. Yoma later asserted in court that "the president's entourage" was responsible for the helicopter crash, which, she claimed, was a Mafia operation. Carlos Jr.'s funeral was the first Muslim funeral to be televised in Argentina. It was viewed by millions in Argentina. See Pedro Brieger and Enrique Herszkowich, "The Muslim Community of Argentina," *The Muslim World*, 92, 1–2 (Spring 2002), http://vnweb.hwwilsonweb.com.proxy.lib.fsu.edu/hww/results/external_link_maincontentframe.jhtml?_DARGS=/hww/results/results_common.jhtml.30 (accessed June 9, 2009). Although I have explored a number of sources on Menem's background, I have found this essay the most reliable.

126. Brieger and Herszkowich, "The Muslim Community."

127. Rohter, "Iran Blew Up Jewish Center In Argentina, Defector Says."

128. "Argentina Charges Iran, Hezbollah in 1994 Jewish Center Bombing," *Agence France Presse*, October 26, 2006, reprinted by *Scholars for Peace in the Middle East*, http://www.spme.net/cgi-bin/articles.cgi?ID=1346.

129. "Buenos Aires bomber 'identified,'" *BBC NEWS*, November 10, 2005, http://news.bbc.co.uk/2/hi/americas/4423612.stm.

130. Mayra Pertossi, "Argentine Judge Wants 9 Held in '94 Bomb," *Washington Post*, November 10, 2006, http://www.washingtonpost.com/wp-dyn/content/article/2006/11/10/AR2006111000223.html.

131. Eliana Raszewski, "Kirchner Says Iran Unhelpful in Bombing Probe," September 25, 2007, http://www.iht.com/articles/ap/2007/11/07/africa/AFGEN-Interpol-Iran.php.

132. "Argentina Asks Iran to Help in 1994 Bombing Probe, *Reuters*," September 22, 2007, http://www.reuters.com/article/worldNews/idUSN2222454320070922.

133. "Interpol Votes against Iran in Argentina terror Case," *International Herald Tribune*, November 6, 2007, http://www.iht.com/articles/ap/2007/11/07/africa/AF-GEN-Interpol-Iran.php.

134. For a concise exploration of the Mykonos operation and the subsequent judicial and diplomatic outcomes, see *Murder at Mykonos: Anatomy of a Political Assassination* (New Haven: Iran Human Rights Documentation Center, March 2007).

135. *Murder at Mykonos*, 17–18.

136. Banisadr served as president of Iran from January 25, 1980, to June 20, 1981.

137. *Murder at Mykonos*, 20–21.

138. William Drozniak, "Former Official Disclosed Iran's Complicity in Murders," *Washington Post*, A 01, April 12, 1997.

139. *Murder at Mykonos*, 22.

140. "German court implicates Iran leaders in '92 killings," *CNN.com*, April 10, 1997, http://www.cnn.com/WORLD/9704/10/germany.iran/.

141. Alan Cowell, "Berlin Court Says Top Iran Leaders Ordered Killings," *New York Times*, April 11, 1997, http://query.nytimes.com/gst/fullpage.html?res=9E00E6D9103CF932A25757C0A961958260&sec=&spon=&pagewanted=print.

142. *Murder at Mykonos*, 8.

143. Kenneth Timmerman, *Countdown to Crisis*, 183–189; See also Louis J. Freeh, "Remember Khobar Towers: NINETEEN American heroes still await justice,"

Wall Street Journal, May 20, 2003, http://www.opinionjournal.com/ editorial/ feature.html?id=110003518; and Freeh, "Khoba Towers: The Clinton administration left many stones unturned," *Wall Street Journal*, June 25, 2006, http://opinion journal.com/extra/?id=110008563.

144. Freeh, "Remember Khobar Towers."

145. "History Makers Series: Former Secretary of Defense William J. Perry," http://www.cfr.org/publication/13564/history_makers_series.html.

146. Dan Eggan, "9/11 Panel Links Al Qaeda Iran," *Washington Post*, June 26, 2004, A12, http://www.washingtonpost.com/wp-dyn/articles/A6581-2004 Jun25.html.

147. Dana Priest and Douglas Farah, "Iranian Force Has Long Ties to Al Qaeda," *Washington Post*, October 14, 2003, http://www.iranianvoice.org/ article1209.html.

148. Personal communication from Kenneth Timmerman, January 6, 2007.

149. Iran's involvement was determined as a finding in law dated 22 December 2006 by Judge Royce Lamberth. The 209-page finding is available on the Internet at http://online.wsj.com/public/resources/documents/law_ktower-opinion.pdf.

150. "Monday, October 24, 1983 Bombings in Beirut," *New York Times*, October 24, 1983, http://select.nytimes.com/search/restricted/article?res= F70C15FF385 F0C778EDDA90994DB484D81.

151. Thomas L. Friedman, "Suspicion in Beirut is Now Focused on a Shiite Splinter Group," *New York Times*, October 27, 1983, http://select.nytimes.com/ search/restricted/article?res=FA0E16F7385F0C748EDDA90994DB484D81.

152. Hala Jaber, *Hezbollah: Born with a Vengeance* (New York: Columbia University Press, 1997), 38. For a brief summary of Imad Mugniyeh's record, see Timmerman, *Countdown to Crisis*, 29–34.

153. "Iran Responsible for 1983 Marine Barracks Bombing Judge Rules," *CNN.com*, May 30, 2003, http://www.cnn.com/2003/LAW/05/30/iran.barracks .bombing/.

154. "Iran Responsible for 1983 Marine Barracks Bombing Judge Rules."

155. Glenn Kessler, "Iran Must Pay $2.6 Billion for '83 Attack," *Washington Post*, September 8, 2007, A7, http://www.washingtonpost.com/wpdyn/content/ article/2007/09/07/AR2007090702494.html.

156. Martin Kramer, "Hizbullah in Lebanon," *The Oxford Encyclopedia of the Modern Islamic World*, vol. 2 (New York and Oxford: Oxford University Press, 1995), 130–33.

157. John Weisman, "Gold Gone to Waste," *Military.com*, June 4, 2003, http:// www.military.com/NewContent/0,13190,Weisman_060403,00.html.

158. John Miller, Interview with Osama bin Laden, *ABC-News*, May 28, 1998, http://www.robert-fisk.com/usama_interview_john_millerabc.htm.

159. "Is Iran Suicidal or Deterrable?" *Economist.com*, November 14, 2007, http://www.economist.com/blogs/democracyinamerica/2007/11/is_iran_ suicidal_or_deterrable.cfm.

160. Matthias Küntzel, "From Khomeini to Ahmadinejad," *Policy Review* (The Hoover Institute), 140 (December 2006), http://www.matthiaskuentzel.de/ contents/from-khomeini-to-ahmadinejad.

161. Küntzel, "From Khomeini."

162. Mahmoud Ahmadinejad, "Very Soon, This Stain of Disgrace [Israel] Will Be Purged From the Center of the Islamic World—and This is Attainable," *MEMRI:* Special Dispatch—No. 1013, October 28, 2005, http://memri.org/bin/articles.cgi?Page=archives&Area=sd&ID=SP101305 (accessed June 10, 2009).

163. This statement is cited by Norman Podhoretz in his book *World War IV: The Long Struggle Against Islamofascism* and in his article "The Case for Bombing Iran," *Commentary*, June 2007. Podhoretz clams that his source for Khomeini's statement was Amir Taheri, *Nest of Spies: America's Journey to Disaster in Iran* (London: Hutchinson, 1988), 269. However, the authenticity of the statement has been challenged in "Is Iran Suicidal or Deterrable?" *The Economist*, online edition http://www.economist.com/blogs/democracyinamerica/2007/11/is_iran_suicidal_or_deterrable.cfm. *The Economist* cites at length Professor Shaul Bakhash of George Mason University who asserts that no identifiable Farsi source can be found for Khomeini's alleged statement. Podhoretz responded by citing a letter from Amir Taheri who identified a Farsi source and observed that in a time of revolutionary upheaval, it is not at all unusual for sources to be tampered with, censored, or edited to suit changing political moods. See "Suicidal Iran: A Reply from Norman Podhoretz and Amir Taheri," *Economist.com*, November 20, 2007, http://www.economist.com/blogs/democracyinamerica/2007/11/a_reply_from_norman_podhoretz.cfm.

164. Küntzel,"From Khomeini."

165. Christiane Hoffmann, "Vom elften Jahrhundert zum 11. September. Märtyrertum und Opferkultur sollen Iran als Staat festigen," *Frankfurter Allgemeine Zeitung*, May 4, 2002. I am indebted to Küntzel for this citation.

166. Suicide attacks against Israelis by groups like the Marxist Popular Front for the Liberation of Palestine took place in the 1970s.

167. Küntzel, "From Khomeini." Künztel cites Dawud Gholamasad and Arian Sepideh, *Iran: Von der Kriegsbegeisterung zur Kriegsmüdigkeit* (Hannover: Internationalismus Verlag, 1988), 15.

168. See Anton La Guardia, "'Divine Mission' Driving Iran's New Leader," *Daily Telegraph*, http://www.telegraph.co.uk/news/main.jhtml?xml=/news/2006/01/14/wiran14.xml&sSheet=/news/2006/01/14/ixworld.html; Scott Peterson, "Waiting for Rapture in Iran," *Christian Science Monitor*, December 21, 2005, http://www.csmonitor.com/2005/1221/p01s04-wome.html.

169. *Kayhan* (Iran), (Persian language daily newspaper), November 29, 2005. Reported by Wahied Wahdat-Hagh, "Basij—The Revolutionary People's Militia of Iran," *MEMRI:* Inquiry and Analysis Series, No. 262, February 1, 2006, http://memri.org/bin/articles.cgi?Page=archives&Area=ia&ID=IA26206.

170. Wahdat-Hagh, "Basij—The Revolutionary People's Militia of Iran."

CHAPTER SIX

1. Jim Platt, "Crossing the Line: Anger vs. Rage," *Working@Dartmouth*, http://74.125.95.104/search?q=cache:PviYnlwDmTAJ:www.dartmouth.edu/~hrs/pdfs/anger.pdf+%22crossing+the+line:+anger+vs.+rage%22&hl=en&ct=clnk&cd=1&gl=us (accessed September 8, 2008).

2. For the analysis of shame and guilt, I am indebted to Michael Lewis, "The Role of the Self in Shame," *Social Research,* 70, 4 (Winter 2003): 1181–1189.

3. W. Walter Menninger, "Uncontained rage: A psychoanalytic perspective on violence," *Bulletin of the Menninger Clinic,* 71, 2 (Spring 2007): 120.

4. Jim Platt, "Crossing."

5. Michael Lewis, "The Role of the Self," 1188.

6. Michael Lewis, "The Role of the Self," 1188–1189.

7. Bernard Lewis, "The Roots of Muslim Rage: Why so many Muslims deeply resent the West and why their bitterness will not be easily mollified," *The Atlantic,* September 1990.

8. Bernard Lewis, "The Roots."

9. Bernard Lewis, "The Roots."

10. Bat Ye'or, "Dhimmitude Past and Present : An Invented or Real History?" C.V. Starr Foundation Lectureship, Brown University, October 10, 2002, http:// www.dhimmitude.org/archive/by_lecture_10oct2002.htm; see also Bat Ye'or, *Islam and Dhimmitude: Where Civilizations Collide,* trans. Miriam Kochan and David Littman (Madison, NJ: Fairleigh Dickinson University Press, 2002).

11. A list of Taliban restrictions and mistreatment of women supplied by the Afghan organization Revolutionary Associations of the Women of Afghanistan can be found at http://www.rawa.org/rules.htm. On gender discrimination by the Taliban, see Ahmed Raschid, *Taliban: Militant Islam, Oil and Fundamentalism in Central Asia* (New Haven: Yale University Press, 2001), 105–116; see also "Humanity Denied: Systematic Violations of Women's Rights in Afghanistan," *Human Rights Watch,* 13, 5 (October 2001), http://www.hrw .org/reports/2001/afghan3/.

12. "Fifteen girls die as zealots 'drive them into blaze,'" *Daily Telegraph* (UK), March 15, 2002, http://www.telegraph.co.uk/news/worldnews/middleeast/ saudiarabia/1387874/15-girls-die-as-zealots-%27drive-them-into-blaze%27.html; see also "Saudi police 'stopped' fire rescue," *BBC News,* March 15, 2002, http:// news.bbc.co.uk/2/hi/middle_east/1874471.stm.

13. "Violence against Women and 'Honor' Crimes," *Human Rights News,* April 6, 2001, http://hrw.org/english/docs/2001/04/06/global268.htm (accessed August 31, 2008); see also James Emery, "'Reputation is Everything: Honor Killings Among the Palestinians," *The World and I Online,* May 2003, http://www.worldandi.com/ newhome/public/2003/may/clpub.asp.

14. See James Emery, "Reputation is Everything."

15. Damien McElroy, "Saudi woman killed for chatting on Facebook," *Telegraph. co.uk,* April 1, 2008, http://www.telegraph.co.uk/news/worldnews/1583420/ Saudi-woman-killed-for-chatting-on-Facebook.html (accessed September 1, 2008).

16. "Jordan: Special Report on Honour Killings," Reuters Foundation Alert Net, Apr 18, 2005, http://www.alertnet.org/thenews/newsdesk/IRIN/6f6d5166f 24330a0e8edcb79796ca5cc.htm (accessed September 1, 2008).

17. Ahmed Raschid, *Taliban,* 111.

18. Robert G. L. Waite, *The Psychopathic God: Adolf Hitler* (New York: New American Library, 1977), 241.

19. Adolf Hitler, *Mein Kampf,* trans. Ralph Mannheim (Boston: Houghton, Mifflin, 1943), 161.

20. Hitler, *Mein Kampf*, 161.
21. Ian Kershaw, *Hitler: 1889–1936 Hubris* (New York: W. W. Norton, 1999), 90.
22. Kershaw, *Hitler*, 92. See also Waite, *The Psychopathic God*, 243.
23. Kershaw, *Hitler*, 95.
24. Hitler, *Mein Kampf*, 202; Kershaw, *Hitler*, 97.
25. Hitler, *Mein Kampf*, 204–206; Waite, *The Psychopathic God*, 244.
26. Hitler, *Mein Kampf*, 205.
27. Wolfgang Schivelbusch, *The Culture of Defeat: On National Trauma, Mourning, and Recovery* (New York: Henry Holt, 2003), 190.
28. Schivelbusch, *Culture of Defeat*, 197.
29. Michael Geyer, "Insurrectionary Warfare: The German Debate about a Levée en Masse in October 1918," *Journal of Modern History*, 73, 3 (September, 2001): 464, 467–468, http://www.jstor.org/stable/3079705 (accessed March 6, 2009).
30. Geyer, "Insurrectionary Warfare," 470. These included Max von Gallwitz and Bruno von Mudra.
31. Wilson stipulated that the Central Powers would be required "immediately to withdraw their forces everywhere from invaded territories." He further insisted on "absolutely satisfactory safeguards and guarantees" for the maintenance "of the present military supremacy of the armies of the United States and its allies in the field." And Wilson explicitly demanded a new government in Germany because "the nations of the world do not and cannot trust the word of those who have hitherto been the masters of German policy." The text of Wilson's replies is to be found in Oliver Marble Gale, *Americanism: Woodrow Wilson's Speeches on the War* (Chicago: Baldwin Syndicate, 1918), 141–144. This book was digitized and made available by Google from the Harvard University Library.
32. Geyer, "Insurrectionary Warfare," 475–502.
33. Wilhelm Deist, ed., *Militär und Innenpolitik im Weltkrieg, 1914–1918* vol. 2 (Dusseldorf: Droste, 1970), 1338–1340; I am indebted to Geyer, "Insurrectionary Warfare," 506, for this citation.
34. Friedrich Payer, *Von Bethmann Hollweg bis Ebert: Erinnerungen und Bilder* (Frankfurt am Main: Frankfurter Societäts-Druckerei, 1923), 142–143; I am indebted to Geyer, "Insurrectionary Warfare," for this citation.
35. Deist, *Militär und Innenpolitik*, 1338–1340.
36. Geyer, "Insurrectionary Warfare."
37. Peter Pulzer, *Jews and the German State: The Political History of a Minority, 1848–1933* (Detroit: Wayne State University Press, 2003), 224.
38. Jacob Rosenthal, *"Die Ehre des jüdischen Soldaten." Die Judenzählung im Ersten Weltkrieg und ihre Folgen* (Frankfurt/Main: Campus Verlag, 2007), 63–89; see also Deutsches Historisches Museum, "Die Judenzählung von 1916," http://www.dhm.de/lemo/html/wk1/innenpolitik/judenzaehlung/index.html (September 30, 2008).
39. Richard Bessel, *Germany after the First World War* (Oxford: Oxford University Press, 1995), 5–6.
40. "The Treaty of Versailles June 28, 1919," Part VIII, Article 231, Avalon Project of the Yale Law School, http://www.yale.edu/lawweb/avalon/imt/partviii.htm (accessed October 4, 2008).

41. Wolfgang Mommsen, "Max Weber and the Peace Treaty of Versailles," in Manfred E. Boemeke, Gerald E. Feldman, and Elisabeth Glaser, eds., *The Treaty of Versailles: A Reassessment after 75 Years*, (Cambridge: Cambridge University Press, 1998), 535.

42. On the Niebelungen tradition, Siegfried and Hagen, see Geyer, "Insurrectionary," 506, 517–520; for a discussion of the role of Judas in transforming the Jews into the perennial betrayer of the Christian world, see Richard L. Rubenstein, *After Auschwitz*, 2nd ed. (Baltimore: Johns Hopkins University Press, 1992), 50–51.

43. They included Gustav Landauer, Eugen Leviné, Ernst Toller, and Towia Axelrod. On the red revolution in Munich see Allan Mitchell, *Revolution in Bavaria, 1918–1919* (Princeton: Princeton University Press, 1965); Ruth Fischer, *Stalin and German Communism* (Cambridge: Harvard University Press, 1948); Charles B. Maurer, *Call to Revolution: The Mystical Anarchism of Gustav Landauer* (Detroit: Wayne State University Press, 1971); Rosa Leviné-Meyer, *Leviné the Spartacist* (London: Gordon and Cremonesi, 1978); Richard Grunberger, *Red Rising in Bavaria* (New York: St. Martin's Press, 1973).

44. Wolfram Wette, *The Wehrmacht: History, Myth, Reality*, trans. Deborah Lucas Schneider (Cambridge, MA: Harvard University Press, 2006), 45–46.

45. John Weiss, *The Ideology of Death: Why the Holocaust Happened in Germany*, (Chicago: Ivan R. Dee, 1996), 211–212.

46. Erich Ludendorff, *Kriegführung und Politik*, 3rd ed. (Berlin: Mittler & Sohn, 1925), 141, 322, 339. For this citation I am indebted to Wette, *The Wehrmacht*, 41.

47. Adolf Hitler, "My Political Testament," United States, Office of United States Chief of Counsel for Prosecution of Axis Criminality, *Nazi Conspiracy and Aggression* (Washington: Government Printing Office, 1946–1948), vol. VI, 259–263, Doc. No. 3569-PS, http://www.ibiblio.org/pha/policy/1945/450429a.html.

48. On Lepanto, see Michael Novak, "Remembering Lepanto: A Battle not Forgotten," *National Review Online*, http://article.nationalreview.com/?q=YW VhYWJmMDJlNzQwZWFhYWViM2FmNjE3MDY3MjZmZWQ=#more (18 Nov. 2008); on the Siege of Vienna and the Treaty of Karlowitz, see Bernard Lewis, *The Middle East: A Brief History of the Last 2,000 Years* (New York: Scribner, 1995), 276–277.

49. See Benny Morris, *1948: The First Arab-Israeli War* (New Haven: Yale University Press, 2008), 419.

50. See the English translation, "The Time Has Come to Say These Things," *New York Review of Books*, 59, 9 (December 4, 2008), http://www.nybooks.com/articles/22112.

51. Gilles Kepel, *Muslim Extremism in Egypt: The Prophet and Pharaoh*, trans. (Berkeley: University of California Press, 2003), 70–71.

52. MEMRI's home page is http://www.memri.org/.

53. The Covenant of the Islamic Resistance Movement, August 18, 1988, The Avalon Project of the Yale Law School, http://avalon.law.yale.edu/20th_century/ hamas.asp.

54. For an analysis of Hamas as a multifaceted organization, see Matthew Levitt, *HAMAS: Politics, Charity, and Terrorism in the Service of Jihad* (New Haven: Yale University Press, 2006).

55. On the significance of this Hadith for contemporary anti-Semitism, see Andrew Bostom, "Why Islam's Jew-Hating Hadith Matter," *Front Page Magazine,* October 3, 2008, http://www.frontpagemag.com/Articles/Read.aspx? GUID=5C31EBDF-5E89-4572-91AB-EFCF84711E0C. On the theory of the Nazi roots of Islamic anti-Semitism, see Matthias Kuntzel, "Islamic Antisemitism and Its Nazi Roots," April 2003, http://www.matthiaskuentzel.de/contents/islamic-antisemitism-and-its-nazi-roots. For an exchange on this issue between Bostom and Kuntzel, see "Debating the Islamist-Nazi Connection," *Front Page Magazine,* January 2, 2008, http://frontpagemagazine .com/Articles/Read. aspx?GUID=1DC2117D-CFAD-47DF-8042-E51CBAC3DD9E.

56. Constantinople Correspondent of the *London Times* (Philip Graves), "London Times Publishes an Exposure Showing How They [The Protocols] are a Paraphrase of a French Book Attacking Governmental Abuses Under Napoleon III., Published 1865," *New York Times,* September 4, 1921, http://query.nytimes .com/gst/abstract.html?res=9F05E1DE1431EF33A25757C0A96F9C946095D6CF& scp=1&sq=Protocols&st=p.

57. The *Protocols* had originally been prepared by the Russian police and given to Tsar Nicholas II to influence policy. Although personally anti-Semitic, the Tsar detected the fraud and refused to use it. See Leon Poliakov, Article "Elders of Zion, Protocols of the Learned," in *Encyclopaedia Judaica,* CD-ROM ed. (Jerusalem: Judaica Multimedia, 1997).

58. The text of Philip Graves's dispatch to the *Times* was reprinted by the *New York Times,* September 4, 1921. See note 74. The complete text of the original *Dialogue aux Enfers* has been made available on the Internet by Google Books at http://books.google.com/books?id=8B8JAAAAQAAJ&dq=Dialogue+aux+Enfe rs+entre+Machiavel+et+Montesquieu,+ou+la+politique+au+xixe+si%C3%A8cle &printsec=frontcover&source=bl&ots=0_2PiRlT8c&sig=JeScUVFjGaPRNSQ2mG -ineTdBe4&hl=en&ei=WlyMSeuLLtCCtwe_1-WUCw&sa=X&oi=book_result&re snum=3&ct=result.

59. Graves, *Times.*

60. This is the apt title of an important study of the *Protocols,* Norman Cohn, *Warrant for Genocide: The Myth of the Jewish World Conspiracy and the Protocols of the Elders of Zion* (London: Serif, 2005). The belief that the Holocaust was not only justified but was regarded as an urgent moral necessity is discussed at length by Peter Haas, *The Nazi Ethic* (Philadelphia: Fortress Press, 1988). Fortress Press is the publishing house of the American Lutheran Church.

61. Daniel Pipes, *Conspiracy: How the Paranoid Style Flourishes and Where It Comes From* (New York: Free Press, 1999), 85.

62. Louis P. Lochner, ed. and trans., *The Goebbels Diaries 1942–1943* (Garden City, NY: Doubleday and Co., 1948), 377. The date of the entry is May 13, 1943. German text in Elke Fröhlich, *Die Tagebücher von Joseph Goebbels,* vol. 2 (München: K.G. Saur, 1993), 287.

63. Daniel J. Wakin, "Anti-Semitic 'Elders of Zion' Gets New Life on Egypt TV," *New York Times,* October 26, 2002, http://query.nytimes.com/gst/fullpage. html?res=9F00E1DE1F3CF935A15753C1A9649C8B63 (accessed December 9, 2008).

64. Wakin, "Anti-Semitic."

65. Dore Gold, "Is Israel Using 'Disproportionate' Force in Gaza?" *Jerusalem Post*, December 30, 2008, http://www.jpost.com/servlet/Satellite?cid=123045653 5626&pagename=JPArticle%2FShowFull.

66. On Hamas's use of the basement of Gaza's Shifa hospital, see Amos Harel, "Sources: Hamas leaders hiding in basement of Israel-built hospital in Gaza," *Haaretz*, January 12, 2009, http://www.haaretz.com/hasen/spages/1054569. html; for Hamas's policy of using of civilians and civilian institutions as human shields, see Steven Erlanger, "A Gaza War Full of Traps and Trickery," *New York Times*, January 11, 2009, http://www.nytimes.com/2009/01/11/world/middleeast/11hamas.html?_r=1&hp.

67. Sandro Magister, "In Gaza, the Vatican Raises the White Flag," *www.chiesa*, January 4, 2008, http://chiesa.espresso.repubblica.it/articolo/213171? eng=y.

68. This attitude has often been expressed but seldom as crudely as it was by the late Daniel Bernard, former French ambassador to the Court of St. James, at a London dinner party in December 2001. The diplomat said, "All the current troubles in the world are because of that shitty little country Israel." He added, "Why should the world be in danger of World War III because of those people?" See Tom Gross, "Prejudice and Abuse," *National Review Online*, January 10, 2002, http://www. nationalreview.com/comment/comment-gross011002 .shtml.

69. For a brief overview on Rwanda, see "Rwanda: How the Genocide Happened," *BBC News*, December 18, 2008, http://news.bbc.co.uk/2/hi/africa/ 1288230.stm, (accessed January 14, 2009). For the figures on Darfur, see "U.N.: 100,000 more dead in Darfur than reported," *CNN.com*, April 22, 2008, http://www.cnn.com/2008/WORLD/africa/04/22/darfur.holmes/index.html?eref=rss_topstories.

70. *Reluctant Witness*, 8(ff).

71. *Reluctant Witness*, 8(ff), emphasis added.

72. *Reluctant Witnesses*, 3.

73. St. Augustine, *City of God*, trans. Henry Bettenson (London: Penguin Books, 1972), Book XVIII, Ch. 45, 828. For this citation, I am indebted to James Carroll, *Constantine's Sword: The Church and the Jews* (Boston: Houghton-Mifflin, 2001), 216–217.

74. John Riley-Smith, *The Crusades: A Short History* (New Haven: Yale University Press, 1987) 16.

75. Herzl sought a top-down solution to the Jewish problem seeking, for example, the support of Kaiser Wilhelm II and Sultan Abdul Hamid II as well as such Jewish notables as Baron Maurice de Hirsch. Moreover, he offered no realistic assessment of the possible response of the Islamic world to the establishment of a Jewish state in Palestine.

76. *Civiltà Cattolica*, May 1, 1897, cited by Sergio Minerbi, *The Vatican and Zionism: Conflict in the Holy Land, 1895–1925* (New York: Oxford University Press, 1990), 96.

77. Theodore Herzl, *The Diaries of Theodore Herzl*, trans. and ed. Marvin Lowenthal (New York: Grosset and Dunlap, 1962), 428.

78. "To Mark 'Holocaust Holiday,' Egyptian Cleric Amin Al-Ansari Revises History, And Comments On Footage of Prisoners Being Tortured in Dachau, Mauthausen, and Belsen, Saying: 'This Is What We Hope Will Happen But, Allah

Willing, at the Hand of the Muslims.'" MEMRI, Special Dispatch No. 2215, January 27, 2009. Video clips with subtitles are available at the website, http://www .memri.org/bin/latestnews.cgi?ID=SD221509. On International Holocaust Memorial Day, see "General Assembly Designates International; Holocaust Remembrance Day," UN News Centre, November 1, 2005, http://www.un.org/apps/ news/story.asp? NewsID=16431&Cr=holocaust&Cr1.

79. Jenny Booth, "Muslim Outrage as Yusuf al-Qaradawi refused UK visa," *TimesOnLine,* February 7, 2008, http://www.timesonline.co.uk/tol/news/uk/article 3325439.ece.

80. For a biographical essay on al-Qaradawi, see Ann Bélen Soage, "Shaykh Yusuf Al-Qaradawi: Portrait of a Leading Islamic Cleric," *Middle East Review of International Affairs,* 12 (March 1,,2008).

81. It is interesting to note that al-Qaradawi has been cited by Georgetown University professor John Esposito as among the eminent scholars who are engaging in the "reformist interpretation of Islam and its relationship to democracy, pluralism and human rights." John Esposito, "Practice and Theory," (A response to the symposium on "Islam and the Challenge of Democracy), *Boston Review: A Political and Literary Forum,* April/May 2003, http://www.bostonreview.net/BR28.2/ esposito.html.

82. See "List of newspapers that reprinted Jyllands-Posten's Muhammad cartoons," *Wikipedia,* http://en.wikipedia.org/wiki/List_of_newspapers_that_ reprinted_Jyllands-Posten%27s_Muhammad_cartoons (accessed January 18, 2009).

83. Religion of Peace Demonstration, London, Google Image Search, http:// images.google.com/images?ndsp=18&um=1&hl=en&q=religion+of+peace+Dem onstration+London&start=36&sa=N (accessed January 18, 2009).

84. This photograph can be found in Nissan Ratzlav-Katz, "Genocidal Chants at Anti-Israel Rallies Worldwide," *Arutz Sheva: IsraelNationalNews.com,* 6 Jan. 2009, http://www.israelnationalnews.com/News/News.aspx/129252.

85. YouTube, "Chilling Islamic Demonstration of Cartoons, London," February 3, 2006, http://www.youtube.com/watch?v=B_kyNIevsIs.

86. YouTube, "Muslims Attack London Police (January 3, 2009)," http:// video.aol.com/video-detail/muslims-attack-london-police-jan-3-2009/24614116 21/?icid=VIDURVNWS04; see also "Police Battle—Gaza Protest (London, January 3, 2009)," http://www.youtube.com/watch?v=ql5l3_iwFXg&feature=related, and YouTube, London, January 11, 2009, YouTube, "Starbucks cafe smashed by protesters (opposite Israeli Embassy)," http://video.aol.com/video-detail/ starbucks-cafe-smashed-by-protesters-in-london-10th-jan-2009-national-demo-in-front-of-the-israeli-embassy/2305843011595498684/?icid=VIDURVNWS01.

87. In this chant, Muhammad, the Prophet and military commander, serves as Islam's sanctified role model. In 629 Muhammad and his followers launched an attack against the Jews of Khaybar in the Arabian peninsula. According to Robert Spencer, "When modern-day jihadists invoke Khaybar, they are . . . recalling an aggressive, surprise raid by Muhammad which resulted in the final eradication of the once considerable Jewish presence in Arabia. To the jihadists, Khaybar means the destruction of the Jews and the seizure of their property by the Muslims." It is what they have in mind for Israel. Robert Spencer, "Khaybar, Khaybar," *Jihad Watch,* August 9, 2006.

88. "War Protests or Pro-Hamas Hate Rallies?" an essay with video clips, *The Investigative Project on Terrorism*, January 14, 2009, http://www.investigative project.org/972/gaza-war-protests-or-pro-hamas-hate-rallies.

89. YouTube, "090103 pro-Hamas Hizbollah expressions during anti-Israel demonstrations," January 3, 2009, http://www.youtube.com/watch?v=PLlHPPO25nM.

90. YouTube, "Pro-Hamas Demonstration - Fort Lauderdale FL," December 30, 2009, http://www.youtube.com/watch?v=j3Xl68kP4wo.

91. YouTube, "Pro-Arabisk Demonstration," Copenhagen, January 10, 2009, http://www.youtube.com/watch?v=AeUzAk1nXy4.

92. "Appels au meurtre des Juifs au centre-ville de Montréal," YouTube, January 4, 2009, http://www.youtube.com/watch?v=Ly4SjTGIL9Y&feature=channel; and "Huit minutes de haine à Montréal," YouTube, January 11, 2009, http://www.youtube. com/watch?v=-99WSxvt_uU&eurl=http://pointdebasculecanada.ca/.

93. Nina Shea, "Worldwide Hate Speech Laws," *The Weekly Standard*, 14, 10 (November 24, 2008), http://www.weeklystandard.com/Content/ Public/ Articles/000/000/015/822stktc.asp; and Glenn Greenwald, "The Noxious Fruits of Hate Speech Laws," *Salon*, January 13, 2008, http://www.salon.com /opinion/ greenwald/2008/01/13/hate_speech_laws/.

94. For an overview of Muslim use of "hate speech" legislation to constrain legitimate discussion of Islam, see "Free Speech in an age of jihad," *The New Criterion: A special pamphlet*, Summer 2008.

95. I discussed the behavior of the police in an e-mail communication with an English colleague who wrote: "The whole demonstration was totally unruly, menacing and disorderly, and if the Police had stopped it they would have been accused of breaking up a 'peaceful' protest . . . and the YouTube footage would only have showed the police reaction to the violence and 'non-violent' protesters being 'attacked' by 'out of control cops!'" E-mail communication to author, January 28, 2009.

96. World Gazetteer, "World's Largest Cities and Towns," http://world-gazetteer.com/wg.php?x=&men=gcis&lng=en&des=wg&srt=npan&col=abcdefghino q&msz=1500&pt=c&va=&srt=pnan (accessed December 29, 2008).

97. Spengler, "The Failed Muslim States to Come," *Asia Times*, December 16, 2008, http://www.atimes.com/atimes/Middle_East/JL16Ak02.html (accessed December 29, 2008). A similar estimate was offered by Ehud Barak, Israel's defense minister. See "Captured terrorist says Israelis specifically targeted in Mumbai, six victims identified," DEBKAfile, December 5, 2008, http://www.debka. com/headline.php ?hid=5742 (accessed December 29, 2008).

98. See the discussion by French filmmaker Pierre Rehov of suicide bomber motivation on MSNBC's "Connected" program, July 15, 2005, "The Psychology Behind Islamic Suicide Bombings," http://www.snopes.com/rumors/soapbox/rehov.asp. For a discussion of the contemporary debate on virgins as a reward for martyrdom in contemporary Islam, see "'72 Black Eyed Virgins': A Muslim Debate on the Rewards of Martyrs," MEMRI, Inquiries and Analysis, 74 (October 31, 2001), http://www. memri.org/bin/articles.cgi?Area=ia&ID=IA7401#_edn27.

99. Matt Wade, "Captured terrorist reveals plot to kill up to 5,000," *The Age* (Australia), December 1, 2008, http://www.theage.com.au/world/captured-terrorist-reveals-plot-to-kill-up-to-5000-20081130-6nrv.html.

100. Wade, "Captured Terrorist."

101. Jeremy Kahn, "Jews of Mumbai, a Tiny and Eclectic Group, Suddenly Reconsider Their Serene Existence," *New York Times,* December 2, 2008, http://www.nytimes.com/2008/12/03/world/asia/03jews.html?fta=y.

102. "Mumbai locals helped us, terrorist tells cops," *The Times of India,* November 30, 2008, http://timesofindia.indiatimes.com/articleshow/msid-3774106,prt-page-1.cms.

103. "Mumbai locals helped us, terrorists tells cops."

104. Damien McElroy, "Mumbai Attacks: Jews tortured before being executed during hostage crisis," *Daily Telegraph* (UK), February 12, 2008, http://www.telegraph.co.uk/news/worldnews/asia/india/3539171/Mumbai-attacks-Jews-tortured-before-executed-during-hostage-crisis.html.

105. On the Albigensian Crusade see, for example, Zoé Oldenbourg, *Massacre at Montségur: A History of the Albigensian Crusade,* trans. Peter Green (New York: Pantheon Books, 1961); see also Joseph R. Strayer, with an epilogue by Carol Lansing, *The Albigensian Crusades* (Ann Arbor: University of Michigan Press, 1992).

106. Sebastian Rotella and Achrene Sicakyuz, "Parisians Stare at the Evil Within," *Los Angeles Times,* February 26, 2006, http://articles.latimes.com /2006/feb/26/world/fg-projects26.

107. See Nidra Poller, "The Murder of Ilan Halimi," *Wall Street Journal,* February 26, 2006, http://www.opinionjournal.com/extra/?id=110008006.

108. Abdullah Iqbal, "Pearl was probing spy agencies' role," Gulfnews.com (United Arab Emirates), March 25, 2002, http://archive.gulfnews.com/articles/02/03/25/45233.html.

109. For an interpretation of what transpired immediately before and during the shooting of the video, see Bernard-Henri Lévy, *Who Killed Daniel Pearl?* trans. James X. Mitchell (Hoboken, NJ: Melville House, 2003), 34–43.

110. "Government urges CBS, Web site host to refrain from airing Pearl murder video," *The News Media and the Law,* Summer 2002, http://www.rcfp.org/newsitems/index.php?i=5962.

111. *The 9/11 Commission Report: Final Report of the National Commission on Terrorists Attacks Upon the United States* (Washington: U.S. Government Printing House, 2004), 145.

112. Verbatim Transcript of Combatant Status Review Tribunal Hearing for ISN 10024 (Unclassified), www.defenselink.mil/news/transcript_ISN10024.pdf (accessed January 3, 2009).

113. A. Guillame, trans., *The Life of Muhammad: A Translation of Ibn Ishaq's Sirrat Rasul Allah* (Karachi: Oxford University Press, 2004), 369. For an explanation of the context of this saying, see danielpipes.org, March 13, 2008, http://www.danielpipes.org/comments/122533.

114. Lawrence Wright, *The Looming Tower: Al-Qaeda and the Road to 9/11* (New York: Alfred A. Knopf, 2006), 252–258: Douglas Jehl, "70 Die in Temple Attack," *New York Times,* November 18, 1997, and "At Ancient Site Along the Nile, Modern Horror," *New York Times,* November 19, 1997.

115. Jason Burke, "You have to kill in the name of Allah until you are killed," *The Observer* (UK), January 27, 2002, http://observer.guardian.co.uk/islam/story/0,1442,640288,00.html; and "Terror video used to lure UK Muslims," *The Observer,* January 27, 2002, http://observer.guardian.co.uk/islam/story/0,,640079,00.html.

116. Jessica Rocha, "Suspect says he meant to kill," *The News & Observer* (Chapel Hill, NC), March 7, 2006, http://www.newsobserver.com/102/story/415421. html; see also Jesse James De Conto, "Taheri-Azar Admits He Wanted to Kill," *The News & Observer*, August 13, 2008, http://www.newsobserver.com/news/crime_safety/taheriazar/story/1175584.html.

117. "Police: Suspect considered UNC attack for two years," *Fayetteville Online*, http://www.fayettxevillenc.com/local/article_ap?id=81878; see Daniel Pipes, "The Quiet-Spoken Muslims Who 'Turn to Terror," *New York Sun*, March 14, 2006, http://www.danielpipes.org/article/3450.

118. Rocha, "Suspect says."

119. Brenda Goodman, "Defendant Offers Details of Jeep Attack at University," *New York Times*, March 18, 2006, http://www.nytimes.com/2006/03/08/national/08carolina.html?_r=1&oref=slogin.

120. Daniel Pipes, "The Quiet-Spoken Muslims Who Turn to Terror."

121. Robert Spencer, "Salt Lake Jihad?" *Front Page Magazine*, February 15, 2007, http://frontpagemagazine.com/Articles/Read.aspx?GUID=BC27E3E0-B300-4E9C-B9BE-8002A99385E7 (accessed November 16, 2008).

122. Over 100 were killed in Nigeria alone. See Lydia Polgreen, "Nigeria Counts 100 Deaths Over Danish Caricatures," *New York Times*, February 24, 2006, http://www.nytimes.com/2006/02/24/international/africa/24nigeria.html (accessed January 5, 2009).

Index

About the Author

Richard L. Rubenstein has devoted the greater part of his professional career to research, writing, and teaching Holocaust and genocide studies. A theologian and historian of religion, he has turned to what he understands to be the greatest threat to Western civilization since National Socialism, the rise of radical Islam. His essays on radical Islam have appeared in English, French, Spanish, and Italian since 1991. Dr. Rubenstein has served as President of the University of Bridgeport where he is currently President Emeritus and Distinguished Professor of Religion. He is also Lawton Distinguished Professor of Religion Emeritus at Florida State University. Among his other books are *After Auschwitz*, *The Cunning of History*, and *Approaches to Auschwitz* coauthored with John K. Roth.